Doing Business in 2006

Creating Jobs

A copublication of the World Bank and the International Finance Corporation

A copublication of the World Bank and the International Finance Corporation.

Additional copies of *Doing Business in 2006: Creating Jobs, Doing Business in 2005: Removing Obstacles to Growth,* and *Doing Business in 2004: Understanding Regulation* may be purchased at http://www.worldbank.org/publications

To preserve endangered forests and natural resources, *Doing Business in 2006* is printed on 100% post-consumer recycled fiber paper, processed chlorine free.

ISBN 0-8213-5749-2
ISSN 1729-2638
E-ISBN: 0-8213-6434-0
DOI: 10.1596/978-0-8213-5749-1

Library of Congress Cataloging-in-Publication data has been applied for.

Contents

Doing Business in 2006: Creating Jobs is the third in a series of annual reports investigating the regulations that enhance business activity and those that constrain it. New quantitative indicators on business regulations and their enforcement can be compared across 155 countries—from Afghanistan to Zimbabwe—and over time. *Doing Business in 2004: Understanding Regulation* presented indicators in 5 topics: starting a business, hiring and firing workers, enforcing contracts, getting credit and closing a business. *Doing Business in 2005: Removing Obstacles to Growth* updated these measures and added another two sets: registering property and protecting investors. *Doing Business in 2006* again updates all previous measures and adds three more sets: dealing with licenses, paying taxes and trading across borders, to create a total of 10 areas measured. The indicators are used to analyze economic outcomes and identify what reforms have worked, where, and why.

Creating jobs: an overview

Who reformed most?
Where is doing business easy?
Less costly does not mean less protection
More reform is needed in Africa
Success requires new jobs in the formal economy

If you were opening a new business in Lao PDR, the start-up procedures would take 198 days. If you were opening one in Syria, you would have to put up $61,000 in minimum capital—51 times average annual income. If you were building a warehouse in Bosnia and Herzegovina, the fees for utility hook-up and compliance with building regulations would amount to 87 times average income. And if you ran a business in Guatemala, it would take you 1,459 days to resolve a simple dispute in the courts. If you were paying all business taxes in Sierra Leone, they would take 164% of your company's gross profit.[1]

Starting a business is a leap of faith even in the best of circumstances. Governments should encourage the daring. And many do. In 2004, 99 countries—two-thirds of the *Doing Business* sample—introduced 185 reforms to make it easier to do business. They simplified some aspect of business regulations, strengthened property rights, reduced exporting and importing costs, eased tax burdens and increased access to credit.

Such reforms allow firms to grow faster and create more jobs. An increasing number of those jobs will be in the formal economy because the benefits of being formal (such as easier access to credit and better utility services) often outweigh the costs (such as taxes). And more formal jobs will mean that more workers are protected by pensions, safety regulations and health benefits.

Women, who now make up three-quarters of workers in the informal sector, will be big beneficiaries. So will young and inexperienced workers looking for their first job.

Jobs are a priority for countries emerging from conflict, to absorb former soldiers into the workforce and quickly enable families to rebuild their lives. Without jobs there is a high risk that these countries will return to conflict. And jobs in the formal economy are a priority for countries in Africa—which have the most obstacles to doing business and are reforming more slowly than anywhere else.

Who reformed most?

In 2004 Serbia and Montenegro led in making the kinds of reforms that can spur growth in firms and jobs, improving in 8 of the 10 areas studied by *Doing Business* (table 1.1). The capital requirement for starting a new business was cut from 5,000 euros to 500. The time to start a new business was reduced from 51 days to 15. A new labor law made it easier to hire workers by allowing firms to offer term contracts rather than having to hire under indefinite contracts even when addressing temporary needs. The time to resolve commercial disputes fell from 1,028 days to 635, thanks to a new code of civil procedure. Payroll and sales tax were replaced by a value added tax, which is easier to collect. The number of new registered (formal) firms in 2004 jumped by 42% over the previous year.

Georgia was the runner-up reformer. A new licensing law cut from 909 to 159 the number of licensed activities. A one-stop shop was created for license applications, so that now businesses can submit all documents there, with no verification by other agencies required. A simplified tax code eliminated 12 of 21 taxes. And the time to register property fell by 75%, and the cost by 70%.

Regionally, the most reform took place in Eastern Europe and Central Asia, where every country took at least one step to make things easier for business (figure 1.1). Many of these reforms were driven by integration with the European Union. Three Eastern European countries—Slovakia, Romania and Latvia—were among the top 12 reformers in 2004 (see table 1.1), and Slovakia was the leading reformer in 2003. All 3 have made it easier for new businesses to open. These efforts appear to be paying off: in 2004 the number of new start-ups jumped by 8% in Latvia, 13% in Slovakia and 22% in Romania. The most common reforms in the region, occurring in half the countries, involved simplifying tax administration and reducing tax burdens. Earlier reforms in Estonia, Russia and Slovakia led the way.

Some of the boldest reforms, driving the biggest improvements in the *Doing Business* indicators, were:

- Serbia and Montenegro's simplification of business start-up.
- Egypt's streamlining of customs procedures and trade documents.
- Brazil's improvements to bankruptcy law.

Serbia and Montenegro moved start-up registrations from its courts to a new administrative registry. Entrepreneurs can register online, and a "silence is consent" rule ensures rapid approval. In addition, a new unified electronic database links the commercial courts, statistics bureau, customs office, national bank and

FIGURE 1.1
Every country in Eastern Europe and Central Asia reformed

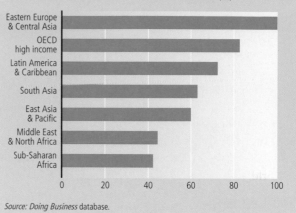

Countries that made at least one reform in 2004 (%)

Source: *Doing Business* database.

municipalities. With these reforms, a company can start operating in 15 days rather than 51 (figure 1.2).

Egypt established a single window for trade documentation and merged 26 approvals into 5. A time limit of 2 days for passing through customs now applies. Improvements at customs were part of a broader reform to cut the number of tariff bands from 27 to 6 and simplify inspection procedures at the border.

Brazil's new bankruptcy law gives insolvent companies the option of remaining open while undergoing restructuring. Creditors have more power to direct reorganization proceedings by establishing creditors' committees that vote on restructuring plans. Secured creditors now get preference over tax claims when assets are sold.

TABLE 1.1
The top reformers in 2004

Country	Starting a business	Dealing with licenses	Hiring and firing	Registering property	Getting credit	Protecting investors	Paying taxes	Trading across borders	Enforcing contracts	Closing a business
Serbia and Montenegro	✓	✓	✓	✓	✓		✓		✓	✓
Georgia	✓	✓	✓	✓			✓			
Vietnam	✓			✓		✓			✓	✓
Slovakia	✓		✓	✓	✓					
Germany	✓		✓					✓	✓	
Egypt	✓			✓	✓		✓			
Finland		✓	✓				✓			✓
Romania	✓				✓		✓		✓	
Latvia	✓			✓			✓		✓	
Pakistan	✓			✓		✓		✓		
Rwanda					✓			✓	✓	
Netherlands		✓		✓			✓			

Note: Countries are ranked on the number of reforms. When countries have the same number of reforms, they are ranked on the impact of the reforms on the *Doing Business* indicators. The larger the improvement in ranking on each set of indicators, the higher the country ranks as a reformer.

Source: *Doing Business* database.

The new law halved the average time for going through bankruptcy from 10 years to 5 and is expected to raise the recovery rate from 0% of company assets to 7.5%.

But not all changes in *Doing Business* indicators were for the better. In 2004, 20 countries—18 of them poor—made it harder to do business. Among them:
• Madagascar raised its minimum capital requirement for starting a business to $6,500—22 times annual income per capita.
• Chad raised transfer taxes and notary fees for registering property. Taxes and fees to buy land or buildings equal 21% of their value—among the highest levels in the world.
• Mauritania raised its corporate income tax rate from 20% to 25%—the only country to increase this tax in 2004.

FIGURE 1.2
Making entry easier in Serbia and Montenegro

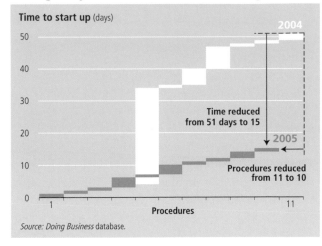

Source: Doing Business database.

Where is doing business easy?

New Zealand has the most business-friendly regulation in the world, as measured by the *Doing Business* indicators (table 1.2). Singapore is the runner-up. The United States is third. Five other East Asian countries—Hong Kong (China), Japan, Thailand, Malaysia and Korea—are among the top 30. So are the Baltic countries—Lithuania, Estonia and Latvia. Their ranking is a remarkable achievement, as only a decade has passed since they first began reforms.

But the rankings on the ease of doing business also show that many reformers still have a long way to go. Although Eastern Europe was the top reforming region, some of its countries still rank poorly on the ease of doing business. For example, Serbia and Montenegro's rank is 92, Croatia's is 118 and Ukraine's 124. Egypt, another top reformer in 2004, ranks 141. And India, though making big gains on collateral recovery and ease of registering property, ranks 116—25 places behind China.

Rankings on the ease of doing business do not tell the whole story. The indicator is limited in scope. It does not account for a country's proximity to large markets, quality of infrastructure services (other than services related to trading across borders), the security of property from theft and looting, macroeconomic conditions or the underlying strength of institutions. Thus while Jamaica ranks close (at 43) on the ease of doing business to France (at 44), this does not mean that businesses are better off operating in Kingston rather than in Paris. Crime and macroeconomic imbalances—2 issues not directly studied in *Doing Business*—make

Jamaica a less attractive destination for investment.

But a high ranking on the ease of doing business does mean that the government has created a regulatory environment conducive to the operation of business. Often, improvements on the *Doing Business* indicators proxy for broader reforms to laws and institutions, which affect more than the administrative procedures and the time and cost to comply with business regulation.

TABLE 1.2
Top 30 economies on the ease of doing business

1	New Zealand	16	Estonia
2	Singapore	17	Switzerland
3	United States	18	Belgium
4	Canada	19	Germany
5	Norway	20	Thailand
6	Australia	21	Malaysia
7	Hong Kong, China	22	Puerto Rico
8	Denmark	23	Mauritius
9	United Kingdom	24	Netherlands
10	Japan	25	Chile
11	Ireland	26	Latvia
12	Iceland	27	Korea
13	Finland	28	South Africa
14	Sweden	29	Israel
15	Lithuania	30	Spain

Note: The rankings for all economies are benchmarked to January 2005 and reported in the Country tables. The ease of doing business averages country rankings across the 10 topics covered in *Doing Business in 2006*. This year's rankings are not comparable to last year's as three new sets of indicators—on dealing with licenses, paying taxes and trading across borders—have been included. See the Data notes for details.

Source: Doing Business database.

Less costly does not mean less protection

Having a high ranking on the ease of doing business does not mean that a country has no regulation. Few would argue that it is every business for itself in New Zealand, that workers are abused in Canada or that creditors seize debtors' assets without a fair process in the Netherlands. And to protect the rights of creditors and investors, as well as establish or upgrade credit registries, more regulation rather than less is needed to make the top 30 list.

All the top ranking countries regulate businesses, but they do so in less costly and burdensome ways. Consider the 5 Nordic countries, all of which are on the top 30 list: Norway (5), Denmark (8), Iceland (12), Finland (13) and Sweden (14). These countries do not regulate too little. Instead, they have simple regulations that allow businesses to be productive, and focus intervention where it counts—protecting property rights and providing social services.

The Nordic countries have moderate to high business taxes—52% of gross profit in Finland and Iceland, 53% in Sweden and 60% in Norway. Yet just 8% of economic activity occurs in unregistered (informal sector) businesses. The reason is that businesses receive excellent public services for what they pay. For example, Denmark has the world's best infrastructure.[2] Norway ranks highest on the human development index produced by the United Nations Development Programme, with Sweden right behind it.[3] In these countries, as well as the rest of the top 30, reformers do not have to choose between making it easy to do business and providing social protection. They have found a way to do both.

More reform is needed in Africa

If reformers of business regulation in Africa are seeking an example, they should look nearby—to Rwanda. In 2001 new company and labor laws made it easier to start businesses and hire workers. The next year the government began land titling reform. And in 2004 Rwanda was among the top 12 reformers (see table 1.1). Customs procedures were streamlined and the credit registry improved. Judicial procedures were also simplified, expediting contract enforcement. The country's president has explained the importance of court reform: "As the saying goes, justice delayed is justice denied. Our courts are clogged with an ever-increasing backlog of cases, some of which date back 10 years or more. The rich, powerful and well connected get preferential treatment . . . One of the bottlenecks that our program of national reconstruction faces is a malfunctioning legal system."[4] Since initiating reform, Rwanda has had economic growth averaging 3.6% a year—among the highest levels in Africa.

There are other Sub-Saharan success stories. In 2004 Nigeria introduced 3 reforms, involving business entry, labor practices and credit information. Mauritius, with a rank of 23 among the easiest places to do business, made 2 reforms. South Africa ranks 28 on the ease of doing business—and Namibia, 33. These countries can inspire others in the region, just as Japan's success motivated reformers elsewhere in East Asia and Chile's success has energized its Latin American neighbors. Some African governments are responding, with ambitious reforms planned in Burkina Faso, Lesotho and Malawi, among others.

Reform is sorely needed. Entrepreneurs face more regulatory obstacles in Africa than in any other region. Yet in 2004 reform was slower there than in other regions (figure 1.3). The 16 West African countries managed just 2 reforms: Cameroon imposed a 7-day limit on customs clearance, and Côte d'Ivoire enabled employers to register workers with the social security fund in 1 day, down from 2 weeks. Across the region, for every 3 countries that improved regulation, 1 made it more burdensome.

FIGURE 1.3
Africa had the lowest reform intensity in 2004

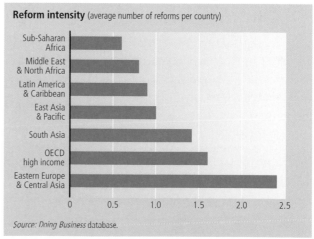

Reform intensity (average number of reforms per country)

Source: Doing Business database.

Success requires new jobs in the formal economy

"First, I would like to have work of any kind," says an 18-year-old Ecuadoran in *Voices of the Poor,* a World Bank survey capturing the perspectives of poor people around the world. People know how to escape poverty (figure 1.4). What they need is to find a decent job. Studies confirm this—the vast majority of people who escape from poverty do so by starting their own business or finding work in an existing one.[5]

Better performance on the ease of doing business is associated with more jobs (figure 1.5). New Zealand, the global leader on the ease of doing business, has 4.7% unemployment. In Greece, the OECD country with the worst ranking (80) on *Doing Business* indicators, unemployment is 10.9%.

Earlier studies confirm this pattern. Quarterly job creation in Portugal, one of the most heavily regulated labor markets, is 59% of that in the United States on a per capita basis. A Portuguese business is 40% less likely than a U.S. one to create jobs during an economic upturn.[6] Such jobless recoveries are common to heavily regulated markets—and mean that some people remain without work for long periods.[7]

Enormous opportunities exist for creating jobs. If Croatia adopted the business environment of Denmark, all else being equal, analysis suggests that unemployment could fall by up to 4 percentage points (see figure 1.5). If Argentina adopted Danish-style business regulation and property rights protection, analysis suggests that unemployment could fall by up to 3.3 percentage points.[8]

But where regulations are costly and burdensome, businesses often operate in the informal economy—and remain small, creating few jobs. Consider an example

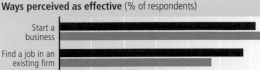

FIGURE 1.4
Starting a business is the main way out of poverty

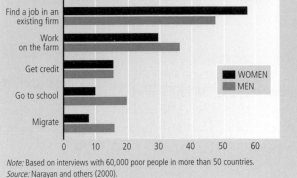

Note: Based on interviews with 60,000 poor people in more than 50 countries.
Source: Narayan and others (2000).

from Burkina Faso. There, Oumarou runs a food supply business. He would like to move into the formal economy so that he can serve larger customers, who demand value added tax receipts. But registering a business requires minimum capital equal to nearly 5 times annual income per capita. Fees alone cost 1.5 times income per capita. To get a bank loan Oumarou would have to put up a large amount of collateral. But he has never registered his property, because doing so would require fees equal to 16% of its value. In the face of such obstacles, Oumarou keeps his business informal—and small. He is not alone: in a country of more than 12 million people, only 50,000 work in the formal sector.

Reform can change this. Improving a country's *Doing Business* indicators to the level of the top quartile is associated with a 9 percentage point fall in the share of GDP accounted for by informal activity (figure 1.6). In

FIGURE 1.5
Greater ease of doing business is associated with fewer unemployed

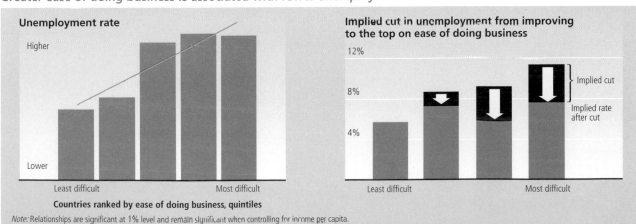

Note: Relationships are significant at 1% level and remain significant when controlling for income per capita.
Source: *Doing Business* database, ILO (2005).

FIGURE 1.6
Greater ease of doing business is associated with less informality

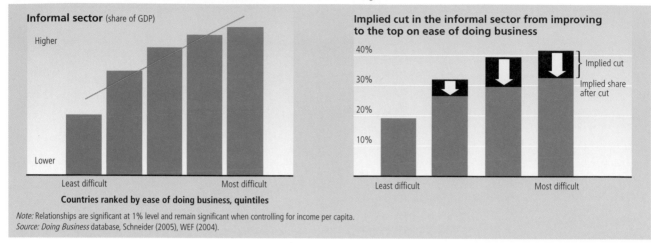

Note: Relationships are significant at 1% level and remain significant when controlling for income per capita.
Source: *Doing Business* database, Schneider (2005), WEF (2004).

other words, reform expands the reach of regulation by bringing businesses and employees into the formal sector.

Female and young workers would benefit the most from these changes. Both groups account for a large share of the unemployed (figure 1.7), and burdensome regulations significantly affect their job opportunities. In Iran, for example, an employer cannot write a term contract unless the job is seasonal. And women are not allowed to work more than 8 hours a day. Not coincidentally, only 28% of women in the labor force are formally employed.

Governments in conflict-affected countries are es-

FIGURE 1.7
Youth unemployment highest in the Middle East

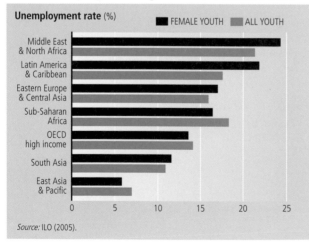

Source: ILO (2005).

pecially hard-pressed to create jobs. Continued peace depends on demobilizing rebel armies and finding livelihoods for thousands of refugees and former combatants. This year *Doing Business* studies 5 conflict-affected countries: Afghanistan, Eritrea, Iraq, Sudan and Timor-Leste. Among these, Afghanistan was the top reformer in 2004. The number of entry procedures for new businesses was cut from 28 to 1, and the time to complete the process from 90 days to 7. Transport infrastructure on major Afghan trading routes was improved. Property records are being compiled and digitized—providing the base for a new property registry (even though the records cover only a quarter of the country). There are also plans to establish a credit registry, owned by the central bank and private commercial banks. Property and credit registries will make it easier for creditors to provide loans.

Successful regulatory reforms abound, with payoffs for job creation. Since 2002 Slovakia's reforms have helped cut the number of unemployed by 43,000.[9] In Colombia reforms of employment and business start-up regulations have created 300,000 jobs in the formal economy.[10] Another success story comes from Peru, where in the past decade the government has issued property titles to 1.3 million urban households. Secure property rights have enabled parents to find jobs rather than staying home to protect their property. Similarly, children can now attend school. As a result, the incidence of child labor has fallen by nearly 30%.[11]

Notes

1. Defined as sales less material and labor cost.
2. WEF (2004).
3. UNDP (2004).
4. Kagame (2002, p. 8).
5. See also Fields and others (2002).
6. Blanchard and Portugal (1998).
7. Holmes (1998).
8. Analysis based on cross-country regression controlling for the standard variables used in the labor literature.
9. Slovak Statistical Office (2005).
10. Echeverry and Maria (2004).
11. Field (2002).

Starting a business

Who is reforming?

What to reform?

Why reform?

Afghanistan may lack reliable electricity and paved roads, but there is one problem that entrepreneurs no longer face: it is now easier to start a new business. Reforms in 2004 cut the number of necessary procedures from 28 to 1, and the time to complete the process from 90 days to 7. This makes Afghanistan the top reformer on business entry in 2004.

Because reforms to make business start-up cheaper and faster are often simple, they have attracted a lot of attention.[1] In 2004 Eastern Europe eased entry the most—Latvia, Romania, Serbia and Montenegro and (for the second year in a row) Slovakia were all among the top 10 reformers. Among the other top reformers, Germany set the registration fee to a nominal amount, reducing costs by 19%. El Salvador slashed the time required from 115 days to 40. Cambodia cut registration fees and requirements and reduced the minimum required capital. Jamaica saved 22 days thanks to a new company law and improved social security and tax registration. And Egypt established a single access point with standardized application forms.

But much remains to be done. Reform in Africa has hardly begun, yet 6 of the 10 countries where it is most difficult to start a business are African (table 2.1). In the Middle East and North Africa high capital requirements make new entry unlikely. Antiquated rules abound: 74 countries require new businesses to publish a registration notice in the newspapers. Doing so costs $424 in the Republic of Congo and $314 in Greece. The alleged benefit is the ability of prospective customers to check the identity of a business. But if a business wanted to verify the information on a prospective partner, an easier way is to consult the public register.

There is no reason to delay reform. Few people would argue that having burdensome business start-up is a good thing. The cost of reform to ease business entry is minor. Often it is done by the stroke of a minister's pen. Even entirely new business registries cost only about $1 million in small countries and $2 million in larger ones.[2] The benefits are enormous. So are the costs of waiting.

TABLE 2.1
Where is starting a business easy—and where not?

Easiest	Most difficult
Canada	Mauritania
Australia	Saudi Arabia
United States	Togo
New Zealand	Haiti
Singapore	Eritrea
Hong Kong, China	Yemen
Puerto Rico	West Bank and Gaza
Romania	Congo, Dem. Rep.
United Kingdom	Chad
Jamaica	Angola

Note: Rankings on the ease of business start-up are the average of the country rankings on the procedures, time, cost and paid-up minimum capital for starting a business. See the Data notes for details.

Source: Doing Business database.

Who is reforming?

Thirty-one countries eased business entry in 2004. Nine of these—Bolivia, Côte d'Ivoire, Hungary, Lithuania, Romania, Russia, Slovakia, Spain and Vietnam—reformed for the second year in a row. On average the top 10 reformers cut the cost by 25%, the minimum capital requirement by a third and the time by half (figure 2.1).

The most popular reform in 2004 was to create a single access point for entrepreneurs. Seven countries did this. Other reforms were also popular. Kazakhstan, Romania, Serbia and Montenegro and Slovakia made company registration an administrative (not judicial) process. Cambodia, Germany, Honduras, Ireland and Latvia cut the cost of starting a business. Ecuador, El Salvador, Germany, Romania, Serbia and Montenegro and Slovakia made the process quicker. Cambodia, Serbia and Montenegro and Tunisia lowered the minimum capital requirement.

Serbia and Montenegro, the second-ranked reformer, transferred registration from the court to a new administrative registry. Entrepreneurs can register online, and a "silence is consent" rule ensures approval in 5 days. If the entrepreneur hasn't heard from the registry in this time, the business can start operation. The country also set up a unified electronic database, linking the courts, the statistics bureau, the customs office, the national bank and the municipalities. And it cut the minimum capital requirement from 5,000 euro to 500. A company can now start operating in 15 days rather than 51.

Slovakia imposed time limits on issuing trade licenses. And it simplified tax registration by introducing a unified tax number for income and value added taxes. Starting a business now takes 25 days, nearly 80 days fewer

than in 2003 (figure 2.2). In Romania registration takes only 11 days. Managers sign a form taking responsibility for the company's compliance with regulations rather than obtaining business permits during registration.

Reforms across the European Union were inspired by competition, with entrepreneurs in an EU member country able to incorporate their company in any other one. Fifteen thousand German businesses have saved on notary and other expenses by registering in London, where the required capital is only £1. Compare that with the minimum required capital of 25,000 euro in Germany. The German government has already proposed legislation to cut the capital requirement to 10,000 euro. The Netherlands plans to scrap it altogether. Reforms have also taken place in Bulgaria, the Czech Republic, Denmark, Estonia, Greece, Hungary, Ireland, Norway and Spain.

Reform in Latin America and the Caribbean is gathering speed. In El Salvador business start-up now takes 75 days fewer than in 2003. Ecuador cut the time by a quarter. Honduras cut registration fees in half, although the total cost of start-up fell by only 12% because notary fees account for the bulk of expenses. A more daring reform is necessary. Jamaica introduced a new company law and streamlined social security and tax registration. Its reforms cut the time by 22 days. Bolivia cut 2 weeks off its lengthy process. Mexico and Paraguay are reforming as well. In Brazil the pressure for easing entry is so great that several thousand entrepreneurs marched to the president's office in June 2005 demanding change. Argentina bucked the trend by imposing a requirement for notary approval of the registration notice.

In the Middle East and North Africa, Tunisia re-

FIGURE 2.1
Top 10 reformers in business start-up

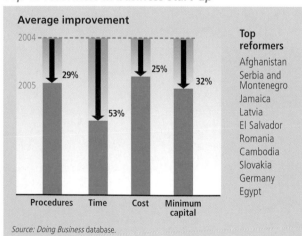

Source: *Doing Business* database.

FIGURE 2.2
Speeding business start-up in Slovakia

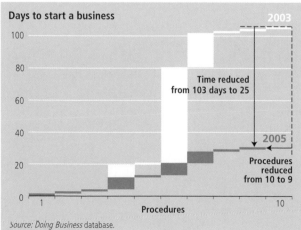

Source: *Doing Business* database.

duced the minimum capital requirement to a tenth of what it had been. Egypt centralized start-up in a single building, where company charters, now submitted electronically, are preapproved by the registry on the spot. Registration is done in a day—but registration fees increased by 80%. Saudi Arabia has started ambitious reforms. Approvals by different ministries are now centralized to speed registration. Time has already fallen by a week, with more improvements expected by the end of 2005. Yemen made it more difficult for new businesses, by doubling the required capital to more than $15,000. With annual incomes averaging $570, there are few takers.

Africa largely didn't reform. Only Côte d'Ivoire made entry easier. Social security registration is now issued on the spot, and the time for business start-up has been cut by a fifth. The Democratic Republic of Congo created a single access point. But hardly anyone knows about it, and the registration center is empty. Other countries went backwards. Kenya added a separate procedure for paying stamp duty. Madagascar increased the minimum capital requirement to $6,474, 22 times the average annual income (table 2.2). This reform is easily the worst of the year.

For the second year in a row the start-up gap between rich and poor countries widened. Since 2003 rich countries have made business start-up 33% faster on average, cutting the time from 29 days to 19 (figure 2.3). They have cut the average cost by 26%, from 9% of income per capita to 7%. Meanwhile, poor countries have reduced the time required by only 10%, from 62 days to 56. The cost remains a staggering 113% of income per capita, and the minimum paid-up capital 299% of income per capita—10 times the level in OECD countries.

FIGURE 2.3
Rich countries are getting even better

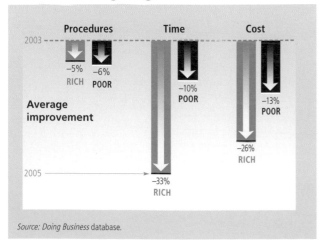

Source: *Doing Business* database.

TABLE 2.2

Who regulates business start-up the least—and who the most?

Procedures (number)

Fewest		Most	
Afghanistan	1	Argentina	15
Australia	2	Bolivia	15
Canada	2	Greece	15
New Zealand	2	Guatemala	15
Denmark	3	Ukraine	15
Finland	3	Belarus	16
Sweden	3	Brazil	17
Belgium	4	Paraguay	17
Ireland	4	Uganda	17
Norway	4	Chad	19

Time (days)

Least		Most	
Australia	2	Azerbaijan	115
Canada	3	Venezuela	116
Denmark	5	Angola	146
Iceland	5	Indonesia	151
United States	5	Brazil	152
Singapore	6	Mozambique	153
Afghanistan	7	Congo, Dem. Rep.	155
Puerto Rico	7	São Tomé and Príncipe	192
France	8	Lao PDR	198
Jamaica	9	Haiti	203

Cost (% of income per capita)

Least		Most	
Denmark	0.0	West Bank and Gaza	275
New Zealand	0.2	Cambodia	276
United States	0.5	Rwanda	280
Sweden	0.7	Congo, Rep.	288
United Kingdom	0.7	Chad	360
Canada	0.9	Niger	465
Puerto Rico	1.0	Congo, Dem. Rep.	503
Singapore	1.1	Angola	642
Finland	1.2	Sierra Leone	835
France	1.2	Zimbabwe	1,442

Minimum capital requirement (% of income per capita, US$)

None (0%)	Most	%	US$
46, including:	Mauritania	878	3,686
Australia	Timor-Leste	909	5,000
Botswana	China	947	12,212
Canada	Jordan	1,012	21,649
France	Saudi Arabia	1,237	129,009
Nepal	West Bank and Gaza	1,410	18,041
Thailand	Ethiopia	1,532	1,685
Uganda	Madagascar	2,158	6,474
United States	Yemen	2,703	15,408
Vietnam	Syria	5,112	60,832

Source: *Doing Business* database.

What to reform?

In the 10 countries ranked highest on the ease of starting a business, the process has 6 features in common. Courts are not used. Online registration in a countrywide database is available (except in Romania). The only cost is a fixed registration fee, regardless of company size. There is no obligation to publish a notice in a journal. Standardized registration forms are used. And the capital requirement is nominal or zero.

Doing Business in 2005 discussed these features. The first—keeping registration out of the courts—is worth repeating, as it does the most to simplify business entry. Company registration is an administrative process and does not need the attention of judges. Instead, judges can be freed to focus on commercial disputes. Take the recent example of Italy, which until 1998 had the most cumbersome regulation of business entry of any European economy, with the process taking 4 months. When Italy took registration out of the courts, it reduced the time required to only 13 days. Three of the top 10 reformers in 2004—Romania, Serbia and Montenegro and Slovakia—made registration an administrative process. The benefits are large: entrepreneurs in countries where registration takes place outside the courts spend 14 fewer days on starting a business.

Here new evidence is provided on 3 other ways to ease business entry:

- Cut the newspaper publication requirement.
- Introduce standardized forms.
- Eliminate annual renewal of licenses.

Cut the newspaper publication requirement

In 1719 the South Sea Company took over most of England's national debt—then saw its stock price quadruple in a matter of days. The folly gathered speed. Many other entrepreneurs issued stocks. Some had viable business ideas; others didn't. One promised to build a wheel for perpetual motion. In months the market had collapsed, and many people lost their savings. The Bubble Act of 1720 was issued, mandating an official notice in the newspapers for company start-up. And so it began.

Today, nearly 300 years later, half the world still requires businesses to announce their formation in a newspaper or the official gazette. This made sense when newspapers were the only way for prospective customers

FIGURE 2.4
Publishing newspaper notice—archaic and costly

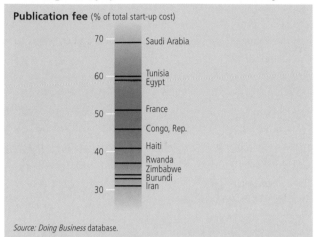

Publication fee (% of total start-up cost)

70	Saudi Arabia
60	Tunisia Egypt
50	France
	Congo, Rep.
40	Haiti
	Rwanda Zimbabwe Burundi
30	Iran

Source: Doing Business database.

or trading partners to get the information. No longer. It is much easier to search the company registry online or call the registrar, which is what happens in practice. Providing such access involves little cost—the information is already compiled.

In Tunisia publishing a notice in the official gazette and 2 daily newspapers costs $157, 60% of the total cost to set up a new business. In 9 other countries publication fees amount to more than a quarter of the total cost (figure 2.4). In São Tomé and Príncipe an entrepreneur cannot complete registration until a notice is published in the official gazette. That could take 3 months. Companies in El Salvador need to publish the establishment notice 3 times in the official journal and a national newspaper, each time for 3-day intervals. In Zimbabwe an application for a trade and business license has to be advertised in a local newspaper twice, delaying entry by 5 weeks.

In 2004 Serbia and Montenegro abolished the requirement to publish a notice in the official gazette. Instead, companies announce their formation on the registry's website. Reform is under way in Germany to end the requirement of publishing a registration notice in the local newspaper and make the publication of the federal gazette electronic. Such reform is easiest in East Asia, where Internet technology is already widely used in company registration. Even the poorer countries in the region are adopting it. In 2004 the Philippines introduced online registration, and Vietnam established electronic name verification, cutting time by 1 week.

Introduce standardized forms

In Kazakhstan 80% of new business applications get rejected for flawed or insufficient paperwork. In El Salvador more than 70% get rejected. In Senegal, 65%. The solution is to introduce standardized forms. With these, entrepreneurs do not get confused about which forms to complete and where to submit them. Countries that have introduced standardized forms have significantly lower rejection rates: 8% in the United Kingdom, 11% in Malaysia and 14% in Costa Rica. These can cover all business forms: sole proprietorship, partnership, limited liability or corporation. The applicant ticks the appropriate box for business form and proceeds by completing the relevant sections. Sample company bylaws can be provided for convenience.

In 2004 the Slovak commercial register issued just such standardized forms, making them available on its website. If documents are found to be defective, companies have 15 days to correct the errors and refile their application without paying additional fees. Only about a quarter of applications are returned for correction, and those are approved within 2 weeks. Before, rejected applications took up to 6 months to resolve in a civil court procedure. Others are taking note: the Czech Republic has amended its civil procedure code to allow standardized forms. In 2006 the United Kingdom too will introduce a standardized registration form.

Countries that introduce standardized forms save their entrepreneurs time. In Jamaica one document—the articles of incorporation—is now required to form a company. It takes 22 fewer days to start a business. In Serbia and Montenegro a company is incorporated by registering the founding deed. The founders may further describe their partnership in a separate contract if they wish, but the contract need not be registered. Thirty-six days are saved.

Eliminate annual renewal of licenses

Fifty-six countries require businesses to obtain licenses as part of start-up. In half—nearly all in Africa and Latin America—these business licenses must be renewed annually. The main purpose in both regions seems to be to shake down the business for money. The beneficiaries differ. In Africa it is usually the ministry of industry. In Latin America it is the municipality.

In Africa inspections often precede the renewal. In Eritrea, Ghana, Malawi, Tanzania, Uganda and Zimbabwe the inspector visits the premises of the business to verify that it has not changed the nature of its activity. "I always worry, as the inspector does not have to justify the reason for rejection," says Naomi, a baker in Lesotho. Businesses often resort to bribes to obtain approval. In Malawi the Ministry of Trade and Industry first verifies whether the location and business use of premises are consistent with the city code. Next, a notice of the license renewal application is posted in the licensing authority's offices for 21 days. Anyone can contest the renewal.

This is not to say that businesses should not be inspected or that licenses should not be withdrawn if businesses have violated sanitary or other codes. Indeed, the next chapter, on dealing with licenses, recommends more focus on risk-based inspections. But license renewal should not be an annual rite, and only violators should pay fines.

Why reform?

If it is easy to set up a business, more businesses are set up. Entrepreneurs registered nearly 1,500 more firms in Serbia and Montenegro in the first half of 2005 than in the first half of 2004—a 42% jump (figure 2.5). This is not an aberration. Following reform, new entry jumped by 28% in Vietnam, 22% in Romania and 16% in Belgium.

There are other benefits. One is the associated increase in investment. Analysis in one study suggests that if Algeria brought its entry regulation to the level in Turkey, it could boost business investment by up to 30%.[3] Other studies show that another benefit is new jobs.[4] In Afghanistan the entry of new companies in 2004 brought 120,000 formal sector jobs.

FIGURE 2.5
More entry after reform

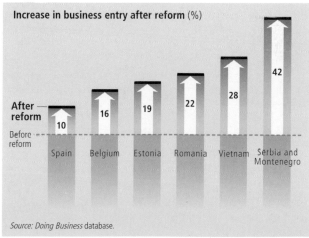

Increase in business entry after reform (%)

Source: Doing Business database.

Cumbersome entry procedures push entrepreneurs into the informal economy, where businesses pay no taxes and many of the benefits that regulation is supposed to provide are missing. Workers lack health insurance and pension benefits. Products are not subject to quality standards. Businesses cannot obtain bank credit or use courts to resolve disputes. Women are disproportionately hurt, since they make up 75% of informal employees. Corruption is rampant, as bureaucrats have many opportunities to extract bribes.[5] These effects were reported in depth in *Doing Business in 2004*.

Enticing enterprises into the formal economy through easier start-up procedures has 2 economic benefits. First, formally registered enterprises, because they have less need to hide from government inspectors and the police, grow to more efficient sizes. On average formal enterprises produce 40% more than informal enterprises in the same sectors, as reported in *Doing Business in 2005*. Second, formal enterprises pay taxes, increasing the tax base for government revenue. As more companies move into the formal economy, governments can lower the corporate tax burden. This gives every business more incentive to produce.

Notes

1. Witness the discussion in the European Union (EU 2004).
2. World Bank (2003).
3. Alesina and others (2003).
4. Fonseca, Lopez-Garcia and Pissarides (2001) and Ebell and Haefke (2003).
5. Djankov and others (2002), Svensson (2003) and Dreher, Kotsogiannis and McCorriston (2004).

Dealing with licenses

Who is reforming?

What to reform?

Why reform?

"If a builder builds a house and does not construct it properly, and if the house falls in and kills its owner, that builder shall be put to death." So says the Code of Hammurabi, written around 1800 BC. This law made construction an unpopular business and housing in ancient Babylon expensive. Indeed, the cost of building then was nearly as high as in Sydney today.[1]

The treatment of builders has softened considerably since Hammurabi's time. A tradeoff remains between protecting the lives of people (including tenants, construction workers and passersby) and containing the cost of building. Most reforms of building codes are driven by concerns about safety. For example, the Great London Fire of 1666, which destroyed two-thirds of the city, led to stricter construction rules 2 years later. Similarly, the San Francisco earthquake of 1906 triggered new building legislation in California and 16 other U.S. states.

Stricter codes result in fewer deaths—except when regulation is so burdensome that construction moves to the informal economy. In *The Mystery of Capital,* Hernando de Soto estimates that illegal buildings in cities of developing countries, constructed without required permits and inspections, have a value of $6.7 trillion.[2] In the wake of the earthquake that hit Algiers in May 2003, the *Daily Star* reported that "many buildings crumbled like sandcastles, disclosing major violations of building codes. Few buildings followed required construction practices." In Turkey, another earthquake zone, 40% of new construction is estimated to be illegal. In the Philippines, 57%. In Egypt, 90%.[3]

In some countries it is expensive to comply with building rules. A recent cross-country survey conducted for this report compared the procedures, time and cost required for a typical medium-size company to construct a 2-story warehouse with an area of 1,300 square meters (14,000 square feet). The warehouse would comply with all zoning and building regulations. It would also have electricity, water and sewerage connections and a regular telephone line. Because warehouses do not house people, there are fewer safety concerns than with construction of offices and homes. At worst, a company's goods could be destroyed by fire, collapse or flooding. What would it take to build such a warehouse legally?

TABLE 3.1

Where is building a warehouse easy—and where not?

Easiest	Most difficult
New Zealand	Bosnia and Herzegovina
Japan	Guatemala
Denmark	Russia
Singapore	Iran
Thailand	Guinea
Estonia	Egypt
Norway	Zimbabwe
Australia	Croatia
Sweden	Burkina Faso
Ireland	Tanzania

Note: Rankings on the ease of dealing with licenses are the average of the country rankings on the procedures, time and cost of building a warehouse. See the Data notes for details.

Source: Doing Business database.

In New Zealand a builder would have to complete 7 procedures requiring 65 days and $6,800—a third of the average annual income—to comply with all regulations. That excludes the time and cost of building. Inspections are contracted to private companies. The efficiency of regulatory and inspection services makes New Zealand the world's easiest place to build a warehouse (table 3.1). In Denmark it takes 7 procedures, 70 days and $31,800, or three-quarters of the average annual income, making Denmark the third easiest place to build a warehouse.

It is not only rich countries that achieve the right balance between safety and costs. Mauritius is among the easiest countries in which to build a warehouse (figure 3.1). And it has the same low rate of construction accidents as Hong Kong (China).

Construction licenses are just one type of business license. Here they are used as the starting point for the discussion of licensing because construction is among the largest sectors in every economy. In OECD countries it accounts for nearly 10% of national income. Moreover, the rationale for such licensing is straightforward: well-built homes and offices save lives. Elsewhere, the rationale for licensing is not always clear. Why do hairdressers in Zambia need a license? Or laundromat owners in Botswana? Couriers in Tanzania? Licensing reform addresses these questions.

FIGURE 3.1
Building a warehouse in Mauritius—easy

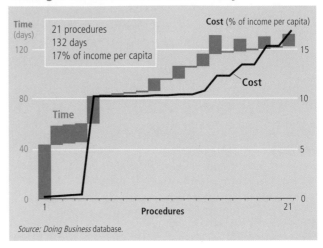

21 procedures
132 days
17% of income per capita

Source: *Doing Business* database.

Striking the right balance between ease of doing business and consumer safety requires continuous reform. In Australia new licensing regulations contain provisions that cause them to automatically expire after a certain period unless renewed by parliament. Sweden takes a "guillotine" approach to licensing reform, where hundreds of obsolete licenses are canceled after the government periodically requires regulators to register essential ones.

Who is reforming?

Poland was the most active reformer of business licensing in 2004, with the Freedom of Economic Activity Act repealing more than 600 licensing and permit requirements at the national and municipal levels (table 3.2). This reform had 2 goals: reducing the number of licensing regulations and requiring that any new ones be approved by parliament. For parliament to consider new licensing legislation, a cost-benefit analysis must be submitted. The new law also limits to 4 weeks the time that small businesses have to spend dealing with inspections, licensing requirements and permit renewals. This target will be achieved by placing time limits on the services of authorizing agencies.

Poland's example spurred reforms in Bulgaria and Georgia. In Bulgaria the new Law on Administrative Regulation replaced 1,500 previous pieces of legislation. It defines principles for introducing new licensing regimes and requires that they be accompanied by assessments of compliance costs. As in Poland, the law also sets time limits on processing of licensing requests. There is one weakness in Bulgaria's law: it does not provide a

TABLE 3.2
Main licensing reforms in 2004

Reform	Country
Cut the number of licensing regimes	Bulgaria, Georgia, Poland
Simplified licensing and inspections	Argentina, Canada, Netherlands
Introduced private inspections	Finland
Established time limits on issuing licenses	Bulgaria, Poland, Serbia and Montenegro
Adopted new building codes	Croatia, Vietnam

Source: *Doing Business* database.

"silence is consent" rule in most business licensing. This oversight has already caused problems with addressing delays in the issuance of licenses.

Georgia's Law on Issuance of Licenses and Permits reduces from 909 to 159 the types of activities subject to licensing. For example, the Ministry of Agriculture can issue only 2 types of licenses: for processing fish and producing baby food. Any activity not mentioned in the law does not need a license.

Canadian construction companies used to complain that building requirements grew every time they met with municipal officials. It worked like this: Once a business received a site plan approval and a building permit, it hired a builder. The builder would then go to the municipality and receive a list of technical requirements. Once these were incorporated in the building plan, the builder would visit the municipality again—only to receive another list. And so on. There was no limit on how many changes could be required.

That is no longer the case. Regulations issued in 2004 limit municipalities to a single list of requirements. Repeat visits are not necessary. It now takes less than 3 months to fulfill the requirements for building a warehouse in Toronto, putting Canada among the fastest places to complete the process (table 3.3).

Finland introduced private inspections in 2004. Several types of inspections—such as for foundations, steelwork and electrical work—can be performed by builders as long as their employees have the required qualifications. If an electrical system malfunctions, the employee who inspected it bears personal responsibility, and his license will be revoked. Previously the building authority was responsible for inspections and had a staff of trained professionals. Because construction is seasonal, inspectors were stretched thin during the summer and fall but idle in the winter. That approach proved costly. Now inspection costs are borne by builders. But because their employees can both install and inspect, there is less idle time. And no days are lost in scheduling appointments and waiting for inspectors.

A word of caution. Finland's reform will not work in developing countries where revocation of professional licenses is not considered a significant penalty. And it will surely fail in countries where the courts are inefficient and corrupt. There, attempts to recover damages due to the negligence of private inspectors may face long delays and uncertainty about what judges will rule. In such countries reformers would do best to focus on strengthening the government inspectorate.

Several other countries also improved construction licensing in 2004. The Netherlands made its rules on building materials more flexible by exempting several basic types, such as mud and soil, from testing. In addition, building permits now differ based on the size of the proposed construction, with small projects receiving less scrutiny. This reform alone saved the government $3 million in annual supervision costs.[4] Argentina unified the granting of fire safety certificates and the final inspecting of buildings. Serbia and Montenegro imposed a time limit for issuing building permits. It now takes

fewer than 20 days to receive one.

Croatia and Vietnam adopted new building laws. Croatia's reform simplified procedures. Yet even after the reform, it takes 28 procedures, 278 days and 12 times the average income to comply with all the regulations for building a warehouse in Zagreb. Vietnam passed its first law on construction licensing, a compilation of existing decrees issued by the Ministry of Construction. Several duplicate procedures were abolished, making it possible

TABLE 3.3

Who regulates licensing the least—and who the most?

Procedures (number)

Fewest		Most	
Denmark	7	Guinea	29
New Zealand	7	China	30
Sweden	8	Egypt	30
Thailand	9	Czech Republic	31
France	10	Kazakhstan	32
Ireland	10	Taiwan, China	32
Germany	11	Turkey	32
Japan	11	Botswana	42
Kenya	11	Burkina Faso	46
Singapore	11	Sierra Leone	48

Time (days)

Least		Most	
Finland	56	Madagascar	356
Korea	60	China	363
New Zealand	65	Cameroon	444
Denmark	70	Brazil	460
United States	70	Nigeria	465
Canada	87	Bosnia and Herzegovina	476
Japan	87	Zimbabwe	481
Mongolia	96	Russia	528
Norway	97	Côte d'Ivoire	569
United Kingdom	115	Iran	668

Cost (% of income per capita)

Least		Most	
Australia	12.3	São Tomé and Príncipe	1,737
Czech Republic	16.1	Ethiopia	1,747
Mauritius	16.7	Serbia and Montenegro	2,195
Iceland	16.8	Niger	2,920
United States	16.9	Tanzania	4,110
Thailand	17.3	Mali	4,903
Lithuania	17.5	Burkina Faso	5,007
Slovakia	18.0	Congo, Dem. Rep.	6,516
Japan	19.7	Bosnia and Herzegovina	8,735
Belarus	22.7	Burundi	10,741

Source: Doing Business database.

to complete all requirements in 5 months rather than nearly a year, as before the reform.

Overall, though, little such reform occurred in poor countries, despite their having the highest regulatory costs (figure 3.2). While it costs less than the average annual income to comply with building regulation in rich countries, it costs nearly 10 times the average income in poor countries. And 50 times in Burkina Faso, 65 times in the Democratic Republic of Congo, 87 times in Bosnia and Herzegovina and 107 times in Burundi (see table 3.3). That compares with 12% or less of income in Australia. When relative income is taken into account, licenses and permits for building a warehouse are 600 times as expensive in Burundi as in Mauritius.

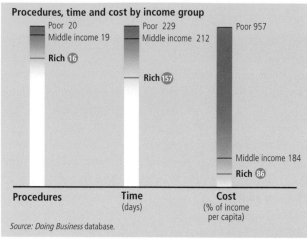

FIGURE 3.2
Rich countries make building easy

Procedures, time and cost by income group

Poor 20
Middle income 19
Rich 16

Poor 229
Middle income 212
Rich 157

Poor 957
Middle income 184
Rich 86

Procedures

Time
(days)

Cost
(% of income
per capita)

Source: Doing Business database.

What to reform?

The rationale for licensing business activity is to protect public safety and health. There is good reason to require licenses for businesses that produce food or medicine, or that use hazardous materials—as in the chemical industry—or build homes. Even then, reforms can make it easier for businesses to obtain licenses. This year, suggestions for reform target licenses and inspections in the construction sector. Five such reforms have been successful:

- Give builders a step-by-step procedure chart.
- Consolidate project clearances at the municipality.
- Introduce risk-based inspections.
- Update zoning maps every 10 years.
- Don't mandate use of specific materials.

Give builders a step-by-step chart

In 2001 it took Latvian businesses 2 years to obtain all the licenses and inspections required to build a warehouse.[5] "With so many offices to visit, some several times, it was very confusing and much time was lost. I often got contradictory directions on what procedure to do next, driving back and forth around Riga like mad," remembers Ugis, a builder. The government took note and prepared a flowchart showing which offices to visit when and with what documents, and listing the offices' addresses, working hours and contact numbers. This simple reform cut 2 months off the process and saved a lot of money on taxi fares.

Consolidate project clearances

In the Czech Republic builders must visit the fire department, health authority, road management agency, environmental agency and electricity provider twice each. These visits are required to receive technical specifications for construction work and to get sign-off that building plans meet these specifications. Only the fire department inspects construction sites. Negotiating the bureaucracy takes so much time that even the new national stadium in Prague began construction without a building permit.

Italian builders used to face similar problems, so in 2003 the government adopted a consolidated construction law. It centralizes all project clearances into a single office at the municipality. Previously companies had to make separate visits to the fire department, worker safety department, water department, sanitation department, health department, project design department and tax department. That process took an average of 8 months. Now it takes 4.5 months.

Introduce risk-based inspections

In Iceland inspectors visit sites after each stage of construction is completed. The rationale is that once the next stage begins, faulty work may be masked and safety jeopardized. Foundations built? Inspector comes. Steelwork completed? Inspector comes. Drainage system built? Inspector comes. Plumbing installed? Inspector comes. This approach is used in all Nordic countries as well as in Australia, Canada, Ghana, Kenya, South Africa, Uganda, the United Kingdom and Zambia.

Not in Sierra Leone. There, municipal inspectors visit construction sites every week. Benin, Botswana, Burkina Faso, Egypt, Guinea and Niger have similar systems. The potential for informal payments is higher in such systems. "He walks around the site, finds a fault and looks expectantly. I pay. The next time it is something else," says Ignace, a contractor in Sierra Leone.

Update zoning maps periodically

In the Serbian city of Belgrade zoning maps date from 1986. Many areas of the city are still deemed agricultural land and so unsuitable for offices or warehouses. To build in such areas, businesses must obtain zoning exemptions that the municipality decides case by case—at a cost of $1,025 apiece (figure 3.3). New construction projects require a location permit or zoning exemption in 45 other countries as well. Such countries might consider following the example of Bangkok, which updated its zoning map in 2002. When applying for a building permit, a business need only specify the address of its proposed site. No cost is involved. Reform is under way in Serbia and Montenegro too. Zoning will be updated by early 2006.

Don't mandate use of specific materials

Some building codes specify what materials can be used in construction. Such materials are tested for their safety and their technical parameters mandated in the code. This approach works when codes are up-to-date. But

FIGURE 3.3
Building a warehouse in Serbia and Montenegro

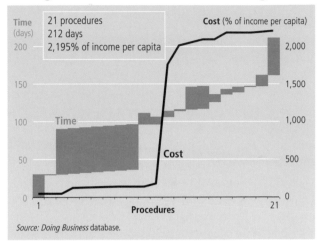

Source: *Doing Business* database.

they rarely are in transition economies. "The [1967] code asks for a roofing material which is no longer produced—it previously came from the Soviet Union— and the fire department does not approve new materials. You either bribe or use fake receipts with the name of the approved material," says Benko, a hotel owner in Bulgaria. Many roofs are built illegally.

Why reform?

There are four reasons to reform licensing regimes. First, countries with simpler procedures and less costly regimes have larger construction sectors. Second, they have cheaper offices and warehouses for all businesses. Third, reducing the cost and hassle of obtaining licenses keeps more businesses in the formal economy, which may improve safety. Finally, governments can save money with fewer and simpler licenses and inspections.

With fewer burdens on construction, the sector expands (figure 3.4). In the United Kingdom the construction sector accounts for 6.2% of national income. In Australia, 7.4%. But in Nigeria and Togo construction generates less than 1% of income. This is not because there is less construction in Lagos or Lomé, but because many buildings are constructed illegally.

FIGURE 3.4
More procedures—a smaller construction sector in Africa

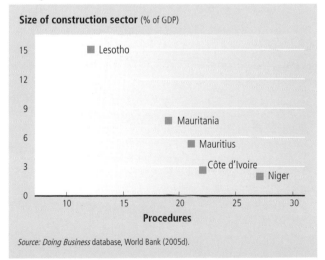

Source: *Doing Business* database, World Bank (2005d).

The effect of burdensome regulation is illustrated by a study of building permits in France.[6] In 1974 the Ministry of Industry adopted legislation to protect small shopkeepers against competition from chain stores. Zoning permits were issued at the discretion of municipal councils. Few such permits were given. Had this regulation not been introduced, employment in the formal retail sector could be up to 10% higher today.

The cost of renting or owning business premises falls when regulation is easily complied with. At $1,500 a square meter, building a business site is 8 times as expensive in Switzerland as in Sierra Leone. Yet Switzerland's average income is 300 times Sierra Leone's, and it requires 33 fewer procedures for construction projects. Building office space in Zagreb is as expensive as in Brussels, at $820 a square meter. It needn't be.

Data from the International Labour Organization show that licensing does not always create safer construction sites.[7] This finding is consistent with *Doing Business in 2004*, which showed that more regulation of the food sector in developing countries did not result in fewer food poisonings.[8] Faced with high regulatory burdens, entrepreneurs move their activity to the informal economy, where they operate with less concern for safety.

Simplifying licensing regimes also saves the government money. In the Netherlands a program for cutting red tape under the aegis of the Ministry of Finance has saved more than $2 billion a year. By 2007 savings are expected to reach $4.5 billion—or a quarter of what the government spent administering licensing regimes and other business controls 5 years earlier. Administrative procedures have been simplified for corporate taxation, social security, environmental regulation and statistical and licensing requirements. An independent agency, Advisory Committee on the Testing of Administrative Burdens, is responsible for studying the costs and benefits of new regulation to ensure it is cost effective.

Notes

1. The Code of Hammurabi states that builders should be paid 2 silver shekels per sar (about 12 square feet) or 1.79 shekels a square meter. A silver shekel also bought 20 liters of wine. In June 2005 the average price of a bottle of wine (0.75 liters) in Sydney was $12. This makes the price of building in Babylon $613 a square meter in current dollars. The going price in Sydney is $675.

2. De Soto (2000, table 2.1, p. 36).

3. De Soto (2000, p. 33).

4. Netherlands, Ministry of Finance (2005).

5. FIAS (2002).

6. Bertrand and Kramarz (2002).

7. The correlation between the number of worker accidents and the number of procedures or the cost of complying with building regulation for 67 countries with available data is positive and statistically insignificant.

8. World Bank (2003); see also Djankov and others (2002).

Hiring and firing workers

Who is reforming?
What to reform?
Why reform?

Yasmine, a recent graduate from Burkina Faso's University of Ouagadougou, is looking for a job. She finished at the top of her class and has good communication skills and excellent references from her professors. Yasmine is invited to interview with a large manufacturing company. The interview goes well. But an older male candidate gets the job. After several months of fruitlessly searching for a job, Yasmine gives up and joins a relative's business. The business operates informally: in a country of more than 12 million, only 50,000 are employed in the formal private sector.

Yasmine's plight can be explained by rigid employment regulation. In Burkina Faso employers cannot write term contracts unless the job is seasonal or requires special skills. Women can work no more than 8 hours a day and until last year weekend work was not allowed. With rigid regulation, common in developing countries, employers choose conservatively. Some workers benefit—mostly men with years of experience on the job. But young, female and low-skilled workers often lose out, denied job opportunities (figure 4.1).

Inflexible labor markets stifle new job creation and push workers into the informal sector. Three-quarters of informal workers are women. They receive no health benefits, no support for their children, no sick leave and no pensions. If abused by their employer, they have no recourse to the courts, because the employment relationship is not documented. Far from protecting the vulnerable, rigid employment regulations exclude them from the market.

Reforms in employment and social security regulation aimed at increasing labor market flexibility have

FIGURE 4.1
Women and youth lose out from rigid employment laws

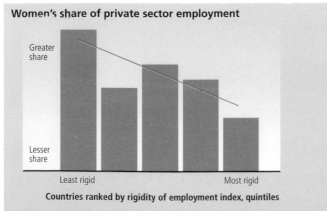
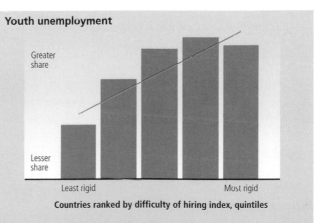

Note: The relationships shown are significant at the 5% level when controlling for income per capita.
Source: Doing Business database, World Bank (2004a), WEF (2004).

FIGURE 4.2
Who pays the highest social security taxes?

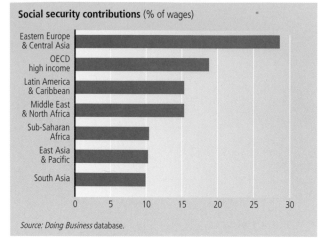

Source: *Doing Business* database.

TABLE 4.1
Where is hiring and firing easy—and where not?

Easiest	Most difficult
Hong Kong, China	Portugal
New Zealand	Congo, Rep.
United States	Mali
Singapore	Greece
Uganda	Romania
Switzerland	Spain
Namibia	Sierra Leone
Australia	Togo
United Kingdom	Niger
Denmark	Burkina Faso

Note: Rankings on the ease of hiring and firing are the average of the country rankings on the difficulty of hiring, rigidity of hours, difficulty of firing, cost of hiring and the cost of firing indices. See the Data notes for details.

Source: *Doing Business* database.

come hard. In Germany the 2004 changes to unemployment benefits were 11 years in the making. The Dutch government reached agreement on labor reforms with labor unions and business organizations in 1982 only after 9 years of failed talks. In Peru the government's attempt to reduce severance payments by 50% in 1996 caused an uproar. The government made a hasty withdrawal. And severance payments were increased.

Opponents of reform argue that because developing countries lack social safety nets, they need more rigid rules on hiring and firing. But social security taxes are nearly universal. Only 9 countries don't levy such taxes: Afghanistan, Bhutan, Cambodia, Lesotho, Malawi, Namibia, New Zealand, Timor-Leste and Tonga. Bosnia and Herzegovina has the world's highest—for every $100 a worker earns, her employer pays $41 in social security taxes. On average, rigid employment regulation is not associated with lower taxes to cover for the risks of unemployment and sickness and for old-age pensions.[1]

The countries of Eastern Europe and Central Asia have the highest social security taxes (figure 4.2). West African countries also pay high taxes—19% of wages in Burkina Faso and Togo, 18% in Benin and Senegal. These rates exceed those in Denmark (1%), Iceland (12%) and Norway (14%). Of course, both African and Nordic countries have other taxes, as reported in chapter 8 on paying taxes. But even when all these are added up, a business in Benin or Togo still has to pay more taxes overall than a business in Denmark or Iceland.

In 2004, 2 reforms met less resistance and have increased labor market flexibility. First, making work hours more flexible, as in Serbia and Montenegro. And second, using apprentice contracts as a way to increase employment among first-time workers. Burkina Faso introduced such contracts in 2004. Still, Sub-Saharan Africa accounts for a large share of the countries with the most rigid labor regulations (table 4.1).

Who is reforming?

Eastern European and Central Asian economies led the way in reforming labor markets in 2004. Armenia, Georgia and Serbia and Montenegro reformed employment regulation. And in July 2005 FYR Macedonia adopted a new labor law. The reforms have 2 features in common. First, they make work hours more flexible, by allowing longer overtime and permitting businesses in cyclical industries to shift work hours between slow and peak seasons. Second, they reduce the administrative burdens on dismissals of redundant workers.

The new labor code in Serbia and Montenegro allows employers to redistribute work hours across seasons or from periods of slow demand to peak periods. This reform put the country on the top 10 list for the most flexible regulation of work hours (table 4.2). In Poland work hours must balance out within 6 months. In Hungary, within a year. Such reforms make overtime hours more predictable for employees while reducing the costs of unpredictable or cyclical demand for businesses. In 2004 Georgia reduced the notice period for redundancy dismissals from 8 weeks to 4 and suspended

TABLE 4.2
Who regulates employment the least—and who the most?

Difficulty of hiring

Least	Most
Australia	Iran
Georgia	Burkina Faso
Hong Kong, China	Mozambique
Israel	Central African Republic
Malaysia	Congo, Rep.
Mauritius	Sierra Leone
Namibia	Congo, Dem. Rep.
Russia	Mauritania
Switzerland	Morocco
United States	Niger

Rigidity of hours

Least	Most
Canada	Chad
Hong Kong, China	Congo, Rep.
Jamaica	Egypt
Lebanon	Mongolia
New Zealand	Niger
Serbia and Montenegro	Brazil
Singapore	Burkina Faso
Tunisia	Congo, Dem. Rep.
United States	Moldova
Chile	Guinea

Difficulty of firing

Least	Most
Costa Rica	Angola
Hong Kong, China	Cameroon
Iceland	Egypt
Japan	Lao PDR
Kuwait	Sri Lanka
Oman	Togo
Saudi Arabia	Ukraine
Singapore	India
Thailand	Nepal
Uruguay	Tunisia

Rigidity of employment

Least	Most
Hong Kong, China	Iraq
Singapore	Chad
United States	Mauritania
New Zealand	Central African Republic
Malaysia	Togo
Zambia	Congo, Rep.
Jamaica	Sierra Leone
Saudi Arabia	Burkina Faso
Uganda	Congo, Dem. Rep.
United Kingdom	Niger

Note: See the Data notes for details on the indices on which the rankings are based.
Source: Doing Business database.

severance payments. This was after the president dismissed 15,000 traffic police, notorious for shaking down motorists for bribes.

Germany was the top reformer in 2004. New businesses can now issue 4-year term contracts for employees. Businesses with fewer than 10 employees are exempt from onerous administrative rules on dismissals. And the maximum time for receiving unemployment pay was cut to 18 months under a new program that unified the unemployment benefits and unemployment insurance programs. Before, a worker could draw unemployment benefits for up to 32 months, getting 60% of his salary—then switch to unemployment insurance, getting half his salary, until he found a suitable job.

The reforms in Germany also make it easier for people looking for new jobs. Employment bureaus are now open on evenings and weekends. And long-term unemployed can take temporary jobs, paid by the government, to brush up their skills.

No country in Latin America undertook labor reform in 2004. Reforms are being discussed in Brazil, Mexico and Paraguay, but so far to no avail.

Several countries have ongoing reforms. Australia intends to exempt small businesses from certain administrative requirements on dismissals. Earlier reforms already cut the costs of redundancy firings, by reducing both severance pay and the notice period. Fiji is making the contracting of new workers more flexible, for example, by allowing more types of temporary contracts. South Africa plans to reduce the "hiring hassle factor" by waiving minimum wage rules for first-time employees, making it easier for small businesses to dismiss redundant workers and allowing more flexibility on work hours.

Others made employment regulation tougher. In 2004 Kazakhstan limited overtime to 4 hours a week. Sri Lanka increased the maximum severance payments for workers with 20 years of service from 36 months of wages to 48, making it the most expensive place in the world to dismiss workers after Sierra Leone (table 4.3). Morocco limited overtime hours to 100 a year and raised the costs of firing a redundant worker with 20 years of

TABLE 4.3

New Zealand and the United States impose the lowest costs on dismissals

Cost to dismiss a redundant worker (weeks of salary)

Lowest		Highest	
New Zealand	0	São Tomé and Príncipe	108
United States	0	Turkey	112
Afghanistan	4	Ecuador	131
Australia	4	Mozambique	141
Georgia	4	Indonesia	145
Iraq	4	Egypt	162
Nigeria	4	Brazil	165
Singapore	4	Sri Lanka	176
Kazakhstan	8	Zambia	176
Switzerland	12	Sierra Leone	188

Source: Doing Business database.

service from 15.3 months of wages to 19.3 months. In both Sri Lanka and Morocco the rationale for increasing severance payments was to insure workers against the risk of becoming unemployed. In countries that lack efficient unemployment insurance or have none at all, severance payments are the only mechanism for doing so. But by imposing such high costs on businesses, Sri Lanka and Morocco create an even bigger risk for workers: never getting a job in the first place.

What to reform?

Employment regulations are designed to protect workers from arbitrary, unfair or discriminatory actions by their employers. These regulations—covering issues from mandatory minimum wage, to premiums for overtime work, to grounds for dismissal, to severance pay—have been introduced to remedy apparent market failures. The failures range from the inability to diversify the risk of unemployment to discrimination on the basis of gender, race or age. Social security regulation insures against the risk of unemployment or sickness and, through pensions, against the risk of poverty in old age.

There are some tradeoffs. Rich countries can afford larger social security systems, while poor countries may need to rely more on employment regulation. As countries develop, they can move to more flexible employment regulation and more generous social security. This balance is observed in East Asia and in east and southern Africa, but not elsewhere in the developing world. The imbalance is greatest in Latin America, where countries like Argentina and Brazil have rigid employment regulations and also require businesses to pay higher social security taxes than richer countries like Denmark and the Netherlands.

Rigid employment regulations often end up protecting some existing jobs at the expense of workers in general. For example, high severance payments are usually adopted in the name of reducing the risk of unemployment—but the beneficiaries are people who already have jobs. Meanwhile, the high cost forces employers to

cut back on new hiring. The result is that few jobs are created. Far from diversifying risks, such policies reduce the odds of finding a job.

Four reforms to employment and social security regulation can reduce the burden on businesses and expand opportunities for workers:

- Raise the retirement age in countries with an aging population.
- Make the retirement ages for men and women equal.
- Move from severance pay to unemployment insurance.
- Introduce apprentice contracts.

Raise the retirement age in countries with an aging population

In 1889 Chancellor Otto von Bismarck introduced the world's first state pension in Germany. Because the retirement age of 65 was so much greater than the life expectancy of 46, only 1 in 16 Germans drew a pension.

Today Germans live to the age of 79 on average, but the mandatory age for retirement hasn't changed. The cost of maintaining pension benefits has increased many times over. Businesses in Germany pay 9.75% of each worker's salary into a retirement fund. Those in other countries pay even more: 21.6% in Finland, 23.4% in Spain, 23.8% in Italy. With aging populations, these and other rich and middle-income countries face a choice: raise taxes to cover the higher costs of their aging population or raise the retirement age? In 2004 Finland raised the retirement age to 68 years. Israel, to 67.

Finland now has the world's highest retirement age. Iceland and Norway are close behind, at 67. Other OECD countries have a retirement age of 65, a regulation that has been in place since after World War II. Yet life expectancy has risen by a decade and now stands at 80. Requiring more years at work will reduce the burden on social security and make it easier for governments to reduce taxes on business.[2]

Make the retirement ages for men and women equal

Greek men have 10 years of retired life on average, Greek women 23. Part of this difference is due to the mandated retirement age: 65 for men and 58 for women. Perhaps this is aimed at benefiting women. If so, it fails—because early retirement reduces pension pay.[3]

Around the world women now live 4 years longer than men on average, and in OECD countries 6 years longer. The difference is largest in Eastern Europe and Central Asia. Women in Belarus and Russia live 12 years longer than men, and those in Lithuania and Ukraine 11 years longer. Yet in 4 of 5 countries in the region the mandatory retirement age for women is lower than that for men (figure 4.3). In Russia, for example, it is 55 years for women and 60 for men. The result: businesses pay high pension contributions—32% of the salary in Ukraine—and lose many of their productive workers early. And women see their career opportunities and pay suffer. An obvious solution is to make the retirement ages equal. In 2004 Slovakia passed legislation to do just that.

Concerned about the unequal treatment of men and women, the European Commission in 1997 obliged its members to adopt identical retirement ages.[4] Nearly all Western European countries have since done so. Others should do the same—especially their eastern neighbors, where the retirement age gap is largest.

Move from severance pay to unemployment insurance

Rather than requiring high severance payments, which hit a troubled business at the worst possible time—during economic downturns—middle-income countries can introduce unemployment insurance. This shifts the focus of regulation from protecting jobs to protecting workers, by helping them deal with the transition to a new job. The Chilean reform of 2002 introduced savings accounts in place of severance payments: the employee pays 0.6% of gross wages and the employer 2.4%, with two-thirds going to an individual account and a third to a common fund. Severance pay is cut from 30 days to 24 for each year worked. Unemployed Chilean workers receive benefits for 5 months, no matter how long they have been insured. The payments are progressively reduced each month, to encourage job searching.

Introduce apprentice contracts

Apprentice contracts are often an easy reform, because of governments' concern for high unemployment among youths. The beneficiaries are easy to target, and businesses have an incentive to keep the workers once they have invested in their training.[5] The contracts work like this: a business hires first-time employees and trains them for 2 years while paying a share of the mandatory wage, typically 75% or 80%. In richer countries the government covers the difference. After the apprentice period the workers get regular jobs. Nearly every OECD country has such contracts. Burkina Faso introduced them in 2004.

FIGURE 4.3
Equality in retirement age—lowest in Eastern Europe

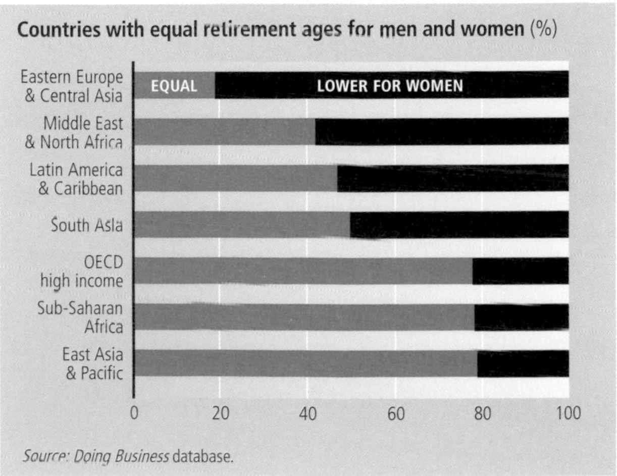

Countries with equal retirement ages for men and women (%)

	EQUAL	LOWER FOR WOMEN
Eastern Europe & Central Asia		
Middle East & North Africa		
Latin America & Caribbean		
South Asia		
OECD high income		
Sub-Saharan Africa		
East Asia & Pacific		

0   20   40   60   80   100

Source: Doing Business database.

Why reform?

The International Labour Organization has established a set of fundamental principles and rights at work, including the freedom of association, the right to collective bargaining, the elimination of forced labor, the abolition of child labor and the elimination of discrimination in hiring and work practices.[6] Beyond adopting and enforcing these regulations, governments struggle to strike the right balance between labor market flexibility and job stability. Most developing countries err on the side of excessive rigidity, to the detriment of businesses and workers alike.

Flexible employment regulation increases productivity. Analysis suggests that if Paraguay adopted the employment regulations of Chile—moving from the 20th to the 80th percentile on the rigidity of employment index—it might increase its annual productivity growth by up to 1 percentage point. That would represent a doubling of the rate.[7]

But if employment regulation is rigid, businesses seek other means of staying competitive. They hire informal workers, pay them under the table and avoid providing social benefits, as *Doing Business in 2005* reported. And when parents fail to find decent employment, children often end up working too.

Reforms of employment regulation reduce business costs by increasing firms' ability to adjust to new technologies, macroeconomic shocks and inflows of immigrant labor.[8] The result is a higher employment rate. In OECD countries with flexible laws, it is 2–2.5 percentage points higher.[9]

Flexible employment regulation also increases the benefits of trade liberalization.[10] As the economy opens, competition from now-cheaper imports drives jobs away from less productive sectors and into more productive ones, expanding the economy. But this happens only if workers can move. Where barriers to hiring and firing are high, labor stays in unproductive sectors. The result is less job creation and a loss of competitiveness, as in much of Latin America in the past decade. These are not the kinds of effects legislators had in mind.

Notes

1. In particular, there is no correlation between social security taxes and the rigidity of employment index.
2. World Bank (2005b).
3. Meadows (2003).
4. European Council (1997).
5. A number of countries have conducted studies on the effectiveness of such reform in attracting young employees and providing them on-the-job training. All have found positive results. See, for example, Neumark and Wascher (2004).
6. ILO (various years). Economic studies show that the presence of such fundamental rights improves productivity.
7. Caballero and others (2005).
8. Angrist and Kugler (2003).
9. Blanchard and Philippon (2004) and Pierre and Scarpetta (forthcoming).
10. Bolaky and Freund (2004).

Registering property

Who is reforming?

What to reform?

Why reform?

"It is slow and bureaucratic to the point of being dysfunctional. The procedures are unclear, can only be learned with experience and can only be guessed at by reading the law. They are not uniform but rather vary from municipality to municipality. The cost is beyond 95% of the citizens." So says João about registering property in Mozambique. No surprise then, that only 10% of properties in Maputo are formally registered. And 20% of those are in dispute.

Things may improve. Last year the government cut the cost to register property in half. No such luck in most other poor countries. It takes 363 days to register property in Bangladesh, but only 1 in Norway and 2 in Sweden. The procedure costs around 21% of the property value in Chad, the Republic of Congo and Zimbabwe, but only 0.1% in Slovakia and New Zealand, the top performer on the ease of registering property (table 5.1). In the Netherlands an entrepreneur can register property online, where she can also check ownership records back to 1832. But in Nigeria an entrepreneur has to complete 21 pen-and-paper procedures, including obtaining the state governor's consent. The process lasts 274 days and requires official fees amounting to more than 27% of the property value. There are few takers.

Making property registration simple, fast and cheap lets entrepreneurs focus on their business. And it strengthens property rights by encouraging formal title.[1] Without that title entrepreneurs invest less and find it harder to get credit.[2] If registering property is cumbersome, ownership quickly slips back to informal. Take the example of Armenia. A $10 million land reform program was at risk of failure because few chose to register property and subsequent transactions. The government streamlined procedures, cutting fees by 50% and the time required to 6 days. Registrations jumped.[3]

TABLE 5.1
Where is registering property easy—and where not?

Easiest	Most difficult
New Zealand	Tanzania
Lithuania	France
Saudi Arabia	Angola
Slovakia	Madagascar
Norway	Côte d'Ivoire
Sweden	Burkina Faso
Armenia	Uzbekistan
United Arab Emirates	Afghanistan
Iceland	Bangladesh
United States	Nigeria

Note: Rankings on the ease of registering property are the average of the country rankings on the procedures, time and cost to register property. See the Data notes for details.

Source: Doing Business database.

Who is reforming?

Sixteen countries made it easier to register property in 2004. Most made the process cheaper. A third made it simpler and cut delays. On average the top 10 reformers reduced the number of procedures by 12%, the time required by 16% and the cost by 43% (figure 5.1).

Countries in Eastern Europe and Central Asia led the way in reforming property registration. Georgia—the top reformer in 2004—made the most progress. The newly created Agency of Public Registry offers expedited registration and combines other procedures to allow entrepreneurs to obtain a registry extract, certificate of property boundaries and proof of no other claims all at the same time. Before, that took visits to 3 agencies. The time required fell from 39 days to 9, and the procedures from 8 to 6 (figure 5.2). Georgia also cut fees and eliminated the transfer tax, reducing the costs of registration by 75%.

Latvia launched an expedited option for obtaining information from the State Land Service. The entrepreneur pays an extra $5.20, but gets results 5 times as fast. Slovakia abolished its 3% transfer tax, eliminating the double taxation with income tax and entering the top 10 list for ease of registering property. The cost fell to only 0.1% of the property value, and 2 steps—the official property valuation and payment of the transfer tax—were cut.

Poland and Serbia and Montenegro are seeing the benefits of comprehensive reform. By starting to computerize land records, Poland freed up 7 more days of an entrepreneur's time for business. Further improvements are expected as more records go online. Croatia is starting similar reforms. Serbia and Montenegro shortened

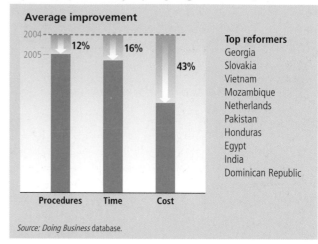

FIGURE 5.1
Top 10 reformers in property registration in 2004

Source: Doing Business database.

the registration process by 40% by unifying its registration system—linking the physical boundary maps of the cadastre with the legal records of the land registry. Titles are also more accurate now. The new procedures cover 65% of the country, and delays are expected to drop further as the coverage is completed.

OECD countries already had the most efficient property registration and they improved even more in 2004. Switzerland eliminated its 1% transfer tax, entering the top 10 ranking on least costly property registration (table 5.2). Now registering costs only 0.4% of the property value. The Netherlands simplified property registration to just 2 procedures and 2 days by introducing online title search, execution and registration—and moved up into the top 10 list for both procedures and time. Australia also launched online services, cutting the time from 7 days to 5—but raised costs by 50%.

FIGURE 5.2
Making property registration easier in Georgia

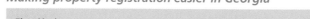

Source: Doing Business database.

In Latin America, Honduras and the Dominican Republic adopted new property laws. The new Honduran law takes registration out of the courts and places it under a new agency that reports to the executive branch. Honduras also cut the cost of registration by a fifth by reducing the transfer tax and registration fee and eliminating the stamp duty. The Dominican Republic's law sets time limits on registration and guarantees that the property is not transferred during the time that the registrar takes to transfer the title. A separate reform in 2004 reduced taxes from 4% of the property value to 3%. Elsewhere in the region, Ecuador abolished the registration tax and tax payments to the defense board and water company, cutting 2 procedures and reducing the cost by 13%. Other countries have also started efforts to streamline registration. Argentina is digitizing records and regularizing informal titles. And in Mexico a new property registration law in Baja California may bring future improvements in efficiency.

The Middle East saw 2 reforms. In Saudi Arabia a new law was adopted, establishing the country's first property registry. Until the law takes effect in late 2005, registration will continue to take place before a notary at no cost—an efficient but less secure titling system. Egypt cut the property registration fee by a third, from 4.5% of the property value to 3%.

Reforms in South Asia and Africa also targeted costs. The Indian state of Maharashtra halved the stamp duty from 10% of the property value to 5%. Pakistan reduced its duty from 3% to 2%. In Africa only Mozambique made improvements. But progress was significant, with the transfer tax cut from 10% of the property value to 2.4%, the largest cost reduction by any country.

Not all news was good. For every 4 countries that made registering property easier, another made it harder. Kenya imposed an official valuation of property before transfer. That added a step and sharply increased delays—from 39 days to 73. The biggest backslide took place in Bhutan, which added a new procedure at the court and lengthened existing ones, extending the time to register property by 28 days. Other countries increased fees. Cambodia raised its cadastral transfer fee from 20,000 riels to 350,000, increasing the total cost by 12%. Guatemala increased costs by 20%. Chad increased notary fees, transfer taxes and registration taxes, raising the total cost from an already steep 17% of the property value to 21%.

TABLE 5.2

Who regulates property registration the least—and who the most?

Procedures (number)

Fewest		Most	
Norway	1	Ukraine	10
Sweden	1	Afghanistan	11
Nepal	2	Bangladesh	11
Netherlands	2	Greece	12
New Zealand	2	Tanzania	12
Thailand	2	Uzbekistan	12
United Kingdom	2	Brazil	15
Finland	3	Ethiopia	15
Iceland	3	Algeria	16
Singapore	3	Nigeria	21

Time (days)

Least		Most	
Norway	1	Nigeria	274
Nepal	2	Bosnia and Herzegovina	331
Netherlands	2	Angola	334
New Zealand	2	Bangladesh	363
Sweden	2	Côte d'Ivoire	369
Thailand	2	Rwanda	371
Lithuania	3	Ghana	382
Iceland	4	Slovenia	391
Saudi Arabia	4	Haiti	683
Australia	5	Croatia	956

Cost (% of property value)

Least		Most	
Saudi Arabia	0.0	Central African Republic	17.3
Slovakia	0.1	Senegal	18.0
New Zealand	0.1	Burundi	18.9
Belarus	0.1	Cameroon	19.0
Switzerland	0.4	Mali	20.0
Azerbaijan	0.4	Chad	21.3
Russia	0.4	Congo, Rep.	22.1
United States	0.5	Zimbabwe	22.6
Estonia	0.5	Nigeria	27.1
Armenia	0.5	Syria	30.4

Source: Doing Business database.

What to reform?

To ease property registration, *Doing Business in 2005* recommended simplifying and combining procedures, linking and then unifying the agencies involved and providing easier access to the registries. It warned against viewing technology as a panacea, especially in poor countries. The analysis here shows that those reforms work. Here are 3 more ways to ease property registration:

- Make registration an administrative process.
- Simplify taxes and fees.
- Make the involvement of notaries optional.

Make registration an administrative process

Property registration is an administrative matter, not a judicial one. Involving the courts in the process costs the entrepreneur on average 70% more time (figure 5.3). Croatia, Bosnia and Herzegovina and Slovenia have some of the longest court delays, extending the registration process by months or even years. Poland's 2004 reforms to digitize land records helped. But they missed the main bottleneck—a 6-month court delay.

Judges who deal with property registration have less time for their main business—resolving commercial disputes. Poland and Syria involve judges. They also rank among the bottom countries on the time to enforce commercial contracts. In Croatia and Slovenia property transactions in the courts account for half the case backlog. One solution: let court clerks, not judges, handle the registration, as in Norway and Sweden.

Taking registration entirely out of the courts means that it can be more easily unified or linked with the cadastre. That makes it easier to detect overlapping and duplicate titles, saving time in due diligence and improving the security of property rights. Entrepreneurs in countries where the cadastre and registry are in the same agency spend on average 40 fewer days to register property. Unifying the cadastre and registry is the second most needed reform cited by *Doing Business* respondents (after computerization). Among countries that involve courts in registration, only 15% have a unified cadastre and registry. Among countries without courts in the process, more than half have a unified registry and cadastre. El Salvador took registration out of the courts and unified the registry with the cadastre in 1999, cutting several months off the time to register property. Honduras is following its lead in 2005, and so is Serbia and Montenegro. Sweden plans to do the same.

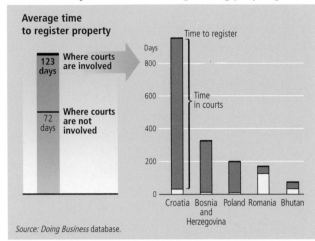

FIGURE 5.3
Courts—a major bottleneck in registering property

Source: *Doing Business* database.

Simplify taxes and fees

To register a property transfer, a Filipino entrepreneur has to visit 3 agencies—to pay a registration fee, then a transfer tax, then a stamp duty. On top of that he pays for the deed to be notarized. And after that he pays capital gains tax and value added tax. Another 41 countries require 3 different types of transaction taxes. More than 20 of those require notarization, value added tax or capital gains tax as well.

In countries that demand a range of fees and taxes for property registration, the cost is significantly higher, even relative to country income levels. These countries also have more procedures, since each fee is usually paid at a different agency. The higher cost encourages informal transactions and underreporting of property values. And the complex process breeds opportunities for corruption. The solution is to consolidate fees. Thirty-one countries, from Mongolia to Denmark, combine the fees into a single payment, usually at the property registry.

Beyond simplifying payments, reformers can cut them. That doesn't mean reducing revenues. Take India. There, transfer costs of around 13% of the property value were discouraging formal real estate transactions. Evasion was rife. Some buyers did not record their transactions. Others used cumbersome and often less secure ways to legally avoid taxes, such as replacing deeds with cooperative housing, long-term leases, agreements without possession and transfers under court decrees. And a $17 billion business in fraudulent stamps was thriving, to the benefit of some police officials.[4] In July 2004 the state of Maharashtra cut stamp duties from 10% to 5%—and boasted a 20% increase in overall stamp duty revenues, about 80% of which come from property transfers

FIGURE 5.4
Cutting duties increases tax revenue in India

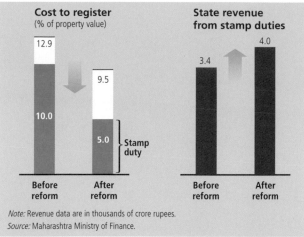

Note: Revenue data are in thousands of crore rupees.
Source: Maharashtra Ministry of Finance.

Make the involvement of notaries optional

The Honduran efforts to streamline registration costs looked promising. Transfer taxes and registration fees were halved, and stamp duties abolished altogether. But costs fell only from 8.8% of the property value to 5.8%—still among the highest in Latin America. The reason is that notaries account for the bulk of the costs and their fees remained the same.

Notaries have useful purposes. In some countries they manage the property registry. In most others they prepare the sale-purchase agreement, certify the identity of parties and assure the legality of documents. But this function is often irrelevant in countries where registry officials perform the same tasks. And it significantly increases costs. In countries where notaries are responsible for the entire registration process, costs average 33% higher than in countries that do not require notaries. With such high fees, there is little incentive to change. In Peru overcoming the objections of notaries to property rights reform took considerable effort.[5]

Other countries make it mandatory for a notary or lawyer to prepare the sale-purchase agreement, including Greece, Guatemala and Nigeria. Costs are 26% higher. A better way is to standardize documents. In Thailand, which has among the most efficient property registration, contracts are prepared at the land registry as a part of registration. In Norway registration forms can be obtained on the Internet or in bookstores.

Three of 4 countries manage property registration without compulsory use of notaries. Property rights are no less secure, and efficiency is greater. Some property owners still use notaries, but they do so by choice.

(figure 5.4). Now more properties are registered formally and the registry holds better information on property values and on who owns what. That supports the collection of capital gains and property taxes.

Others have discovered the same. Mozambique cut its transfer tax by 75% without affecting revenues much—and increased registrations. Slovakia abolished its transfer tax as a part of broader tax reform, and saw only slight declines in overall revenue. Pakistan saw both registrations and revenues rise slightly over the previous year after cutting its fee. Chad learned the lesson the hard way. In 2004 it hiked registration taxes from 10% of the property value to 15% in an effort to increase revenues. That effort failed. Both revenues and registrations dropped dramatically—so much so that the government announced that it would put the rates back to 10%.

Why reform?

Efficient property registration strengthens property rights. Some would argue that more regulation and a formalized property registration process ensure due diligence, enhancing property rights. But complexity breeds uncertainty, increases transactions costs and offers opportunities for fraud. And more bureaucracy produces more mistakes about who owns what. *Doing Business* respondents rate security of title higher when the number of steps and the time and cost to register property are lower. This remains true even when country income levels are controlled for.

Greater title security stimulates property and credit markets. Enterprise surveys show that access to land

and finance are greater with efficient property registration (figure 5.5). More efficient property registration is also associated with more private credit as a share of GDP, more private investment, less corruption and less informality.[6]

Country experience shows the benefits of formalizing title and keeping it that way. Thailand's land reform has issued more than 8.5 million property titles and created one of the most efficient registration systems in the world. Land values and investment almost doubled, and access to credit increased threefold for people with formal titles.[7] Peru's experience was just as striking. More than 1.3 million titles were issued from the late 1990s, and two-thirds of those issued to individuals

FIGURE 5.5
Simple property registration—more access to land and credit

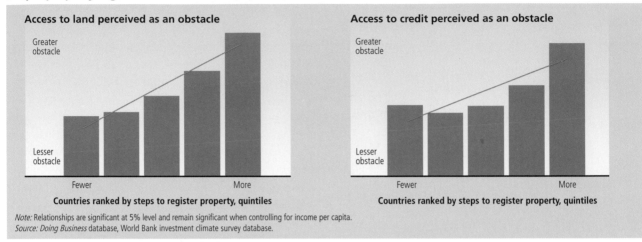

Note: Relationships are significant at 5% level and remain significant when controlling for income per capita.
Source: *Doing Business* database, World Bank investment climate survey database.

went to women. The time required to formalize property fell from 6 years to 45 days. Registrations of subsequent transactions increased from 58,000 in 1999 to 137,000 in 2003. More than 20,000 mortgages were registered on the new titles. Titled property was improved twice as often as untitled property.[8] And one study found that more people who had received formal title were employed outside the home, reducing the reliance on child labor for income.[9]

Property accounts for between half and three-quarters of wealth in most economies.[10] In poor countries a large share of it is unregistered. Formalizing title is essential there. And making property registries efficient will ensure that a formal title is more valuable—for getting credit, for investing and for generating growth.

Notes

1. *Doing Business* focuses on registering property. Other important determinants of property rights include types of property tenure, property market controls and coverage and organization of the cadastre. Some of these were discussed in *Doing Business in 2005*. Although *Doing Business* focuses on entrepreneurs, many of the results hold for individual title also.

2. See Deininger (2003).

3. Burns (2005).

4. Alm, Annez and Modi (2004).

5. Burns (2005).

6. World Bank (2004a).

7. Feder (2002).

8. Burns (2005) and World Bank (2004a).

9. Field (2002).

10. Ibbotson, Siegel and Love (1985).

Getting credit

Who is reforming?

What to reform?

Why reform?

Chinese businesses hold more than $2 trillion in dead capital—assets that cannot be used as collateral because of restrictions in laws.[1] This is enough to build another Great Wall. Lihong is one of the many entrepreneurs affected: "When I went to get a loan, the loan officer questioned my business plan and passed me to 3 other bankers for interviews on my finances and family wealth. Another bank employee visited the company premises to inspect the business and view my accounts—but none of them could be used to secure the loan. I had to ask my sister to coguarantee it. Why is all this necessary? In Malaysia my cousin gets loans in a day."

Improvements are on the way in China. A draft property law would expand the scope of assets that can be used as collateral. And plans for a credit bureau are being formed. Another 33 countries went further and made it easier to get credit in 2004. Poor countries reformed the most. Many reformers set up or improved credit information systems. A few made it easier to take and enforce collateral (or security). India—the top reformer—did both, establishing a new consumer credit bureau and implementing a much faster proceeding for enforcing collateral agreements. Banks can now check the credit history of more than 12 million borrowers and in some cases, enforce collateral in 6 months rather than 10 years. They report higher loan approval rates and fewer nonperforming loans as a result.

Lenders look at the borrower's credit history and collateral when extending loans. Where credit registries and effective collateral laws are lacking—as they are in most poor countries—banks make fewer loans. Credit to the private sector averages 16% of GDP in the 10 economies ranking at the bottom on how well collateral laws and credit registries facilitate credit markets (table 6.1). In the top 10, credit tops 120% of GDP.

TABLE 6.1
Where is getting credit easy—and where not?

Easiest	Most difficult
United Kingdom	Algeria
Hong Kong, China	Congo, Dem. Rep.
Australia	Egypt
Botswana	Eritrea
Germany	Guinea
Malaysia	Timor-Leste
New Zealand	Togo
Singapore	Lao PDR
Ireland	Afghanistan
United States	Cambodia

Note: Rankings on the ease of getting credit are based on the sum of the strength of legal rights index and the depth of credit information index. See the Data notes for details.

Source: Doing Business database.

Who is reforming?

In 2004, 25 countries improved the way credit information is shared. Eight new private credit bureaus kicked off operations—in India, Indonesia, the Kyrgyz Republic, Lithuania, Nigeria, Romania, Saudi Arabia and Slovakia. New public registries started up in Armenia and Azerbaijan. Several of the new registries are still getting off the ground and have only sparse coverage of borrowers (table 6.2).

Other reforms to sharing credit information took 5 directions:

- *Passing new regulations.* In 2004 the most popular reform was to eliminate obstacles to sharing credit information through a special law or regulation—as in India, Israel, Kazakhstan, Nicaragua and Russia— or through amendment of the banking act—as in Azerbaijan, Kenya, FYR Macedonia and Mauritius. The revised New Zealand code launched a consumer complaints procedure and strict controls on accuracy of data. The Italian code stressed reliability and timeliness of credit reports, but cut the time that historical data can be stored. Greece and Uruguay introduced new data protection laws designed to safeguard borrowers' privacy and the integrity of data.

- *Expanding the scope of information.* In Bangladesh the public registry incorporated consumer credit card data into its database. The Egyptian registry set up a list of borrowers defaulting on small credit card and car loans. Honduras now requires all banks to report both positive and negative information.[2] In Lebanon, FYR Macedonia, Romania and Rwanda more comprehensive credit reports are now distributed.

- *Including more loans.* Egypt's public registry cut the minimum loan size above which it collects data from $6,900 to $5,200. Lebanon's registry lowered its cutoff from $6,600 to $6,000, adding 10,000 more borrowers to the registry. And the public registries in Bulgaria, Iran, Romania and Vietnam scrapped their minimum loan cutoff altogether. In Vietnam coverage of borrowers increased by a third. In Bulgaria it expanded ninefold—although these developments stalled the initiative for a private bureau.

- *Providing data online.* The Bulgarian public registry launched an online system, cutting the time to re-

TABLE 6.2
Who has the most credit information—and who the least?
Borrowers covered as % of adults

Most		Least	
Australia	100	Kyrgyz Republic	0.20
Canada	100	Mauritania	0.19
Iceland	100	Chad	0.19
Ireland	100	Nepal	0.14
Norway	100	Kenya	0.14
Sweden	100	Rwanda	0.12
United States	100	Indonesia	0.09
New Zealand	96	Serbia and Montenegro	0.08
Argentina	95	Yemen	0.08
Germany	88	Guinea	0.02

Note: The rankings reflected in the table include only countries with public or private credit registries (111 in total). Another 44 countries have no registry and therefore no coverage.

Source: Doing Business database.

trieve data from 3 days to just seconds. The Rwandan central bank computerized the database in its public registry, although data are still collected and distributed manually.

- *Enhancing data quality.* In Mongolia a penalty of up to $900 may now be imposed on banks every time they fail to update credit histories. Nepal imposed penalties on banks and their staff for withholding credit information. Coverage of borrowers increased by 13%. More than half of countries impose penalties for distributing erroneous data. But it is possible to go too far. When Thailand made directors of credit bureaus personally liable for errors in 2003, the Thai bureaus closed for 5 months until the requirement was relaxed. Countries can keep penalties moderate and focus on improving quality through data protection laws—for example, by allowing borrowers the right to access their data and to demand corrections.

Ten countries made it easier to create and enforce collateral agreements in 2004: Bosnia and Herzegovina, Brazil, Croatia, Finland, India, Japan, Romania, Serbia and Montenegro, Sweden and Ukraine. Reforms in Bosnia and Herzegovina, Serbia and Montenegro and Ukraine covered all aspects of secured transactions law: creation, priority, registration and enforcement of collateral. The new pledge law in Bosnia and Herzegovina allows general descriptions of assets, permitting a much wider scope of assets to be used as collateral, including inventory and accounts receivable. It streamlined en-

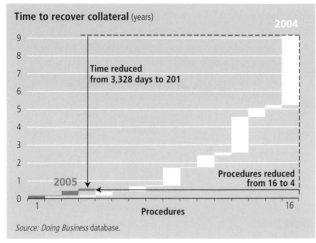

FIGURE 6.1
Big improvements in India

Time to recover collateral (years)

Time reduced from 3,328 days to 201

2004

2005

Procedures reduced from 16 to 4

Procedures

Source: Doing Business database.

TABLE 6.3
Who has the most legal rights for borrowers and lenders—and who the least?
Strength of legal rights index (0–10)

Most		Least	
Hong Kong, China	10	China	2
Singapore	10	Haiti	2
United Kingdom	10	Lao PDR	2
Albania	9	Peru	2
Australia	9	Yemen	2
Botswana	9	Egypt	1
New Zealand	9	Rwanda	1
Germany	8	Turkey	1
Malaysia	8	Afghanistan	0
Netherlands	8	Cambodia	0

Note: See the Data notes for details on the index.
Source: Doing Business database.

forcement and clarified rules on who had the priority claim to collateral. And creditors can now check whether there are other claims to collateral in an electronic unified registry of collateral notices.

Ukraine also expanded the scope of assets that can be used as collateral, and gave secured creditors first priority to their collateral and its proceeds. In addition, it gave creditors the ability to enforce collateral privately, bypassing the lengthy court procedures required before. And a new centralized collateral registry started operating in August 2004. Already the benefits are obvious: more than 15,000 notices of collateral agreements were registered in the first 4 months of operation.

Other countries had success with partial reforms. India made enforcing security significantly easier. The time to enforce fell from up to 10 years to 6 months in some cases because of a new summary proceeding requiring minimal court involvement (figure 6.1). Croatia cut several months from enforcement by making it harder for debtors to delay the enforcement process. Movable collateral can now be seized and sold not just by the courts but also by authorized private firms. And Japan broadened the scope of permissible collateral to include future accounts receivable. Previously only receivables on current transactions could be used as security.

Other reformers eased the recovery of collateral from bankrupt firms. In Brazil the claims of secured creditors now have priority over taxes in bankruptcy. In Portugal creditors were given more powers to participate in a bankrupt firm's reorganization. In Romania secured creditors can now seek exceptions to an automatic stay—

or ban—on collecting their collateral in bankruptcy. And in Sweden creditors are able to take more flexible types of collateral with a new floating charge covering 55% of a debtor's assets and with priority for the creditor.

Not all reforms are working yet. Two years ago in Serbia and Montenegro, an entrepreneur could not use movable property as collateral without giving the creditor possession of the asset. Hardly practical. Now that a new law on pledges came into effect in January 2004, that entrepreneur can use almost all movable property as collateral without giving up possession. If she defaults, the creditor can by law collect the collateral without going through the courts. But collateral agreements are valid only after registration, and the registry is not yet running.

There is much to do. Laws in Lao PDR do not allow businesses to pledge movable assets without surrendering possession of the assets, ranking the country among the bottom 10 on legal rights for borrowers and lenders (table 6.3). Women in Lesotho cannot pledge assets without their husband's consent. Nicaragua requires a specific description of assets in collateral agreements. That makes it impossible to use changing pools of assets such as inventory or accounts receivable as collateral. Entrepreneurs there need more than twice the value of the loan in collateral.

In China more than 10 separate government agencies register security interests. None are linked across geographic regions, and all are paper based. Each registry requires a substantive review of the collateral agreement, yet other countries have shown that only a notice of the agreement is needed.

What to reform?

Businesses have greater access to credit in countries where credit registries distribute both positive and negative information; include data from trade creditors, retailers and utilities; and collect and make information available electronically. Access to loans is also expanded in countries where collateral laws allow all assets to be used as collateral, provide for a unified registry of security interests and permit out-of-court enforcement of collateral agreements. All these features are consistent with reforms discussed in earlier editions of *Doing Business.*

Four other reforms expand access to credit:
- Eliminate legal obstacles to sharing credit information.
- Focus public registries on supervision.
- Give secured creditors clear priority to collateral.
- Introduce summary enforcement proceedings.

Eliminate legal obstacles to sharing information

Secrecy provisions in banking laws and data protection or privacy laws sometimes prohibit sharing credit information. In Uzbekistan a credit bureau registered in 2000 is still unable to operate because it lacks the legal authority to share data. In Slovakia the bureau's launch was delayed because laws restricted collection of historical data. In some countries, such as Bosnia and Herzegovina and Germany, bureaus can circumvent restrictions if would-be borrowers give consent. But in others, including Georgia and Kazakhstan, borrower consent is insufficient.

Laws on credit information can provide clear authority to collect and distribute data. In 2004, 15 countries introduced regulations to eliminate obstacles to data sharing (other reforms were administrative). In rich countries the trend is for new data protection laws to safeguard borrowers' privacy and create incentives for registries to maintain high-quality data (figure 6.2). In the Czech Republic laws were amended to permit sharing between financial and nonfinancial institutions. Laws in Croatia, Iceland, India and Slovakia still prohibit this. In another 40% of countries bureaus do not share data with nonfinancial institutions. In these countries businesses have significantly less access to credit.

Governments can also compel lenders to submit consumer data to bureaus, as Israel, Kazakhstan and Russia have done through new laws. Colombia, Hong Kong (China), Mexico and 7 other economies create automatic demand for bureaus by requiring financial institutions to consult with bureaus before extending credit.

Focus public registries on supervision

Public registries can substitute for private bureaus in poor countries. There, and in other highly concentrated lending markets, it may be difficult to start a private credit bureau because the demand for credit information may be too low to make the bureau profitable. Establishing a public registry offers the advantage of rapid setup because it relies on central bank regulation rather than new laws. Enforcement by bank supervisors can counter lenders' unwillingness to participate. Starting a public registry is cheap: the one in Mozambique cost less than $1 million. And public registries usually get the job done—a recent study shows that in poor countries they increase the flow of credit to businesses.[3]

FIGURE 6.2

Growing regulation of private credit bureaus

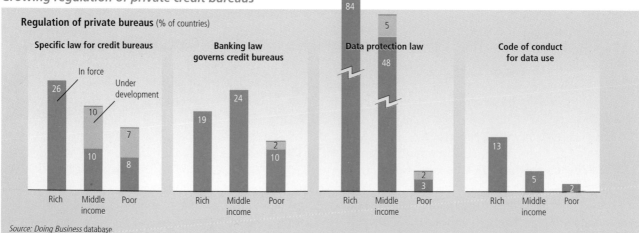

Source: *Doing Business* database

But public registries are less effective than private bureaus in most countries (figure 6.3). Private bureaus are better set up to serve lenders, covering 5 times as many borrowers and scoring 73% higher on the depth of credit information index. Fewer than 10% of public registries report offering such services as credit scoring or borrower monitoring—compared with 90% of private bureaus. But in some countries private bureaus are struggling because public registries are performing some of the same functions—as in Armenia, Bolivia, Bulgaria, Indonesia and Malaysia. In Belgium the private bureau closed down in 2003 after the public registry expanded its operations.

Public registries can leave room for private bureaus by focusing on loan information that matters for systemic risk—typically large loans for corporations—as those in Austria, Germany and Saudi Arabia do. The Colombian central bank went further and closed its public registry, keeping the data only for the purpose of supervising banks. In countries where public registries focus on bank supervision, private bureaus score higher on the depth of credit information index and cover more borrowers.

Another solution is to join forces. The bureaus in India, Sri Lanka and Thailand were established as public-private partnerships. Chile outsourced operation of the registry to a private bureau. The bureaus in Romania, Saudi Arabia and Singapore are private but were set up with support from the central banks. Some public registries collect information from banks and share it with private bureaus, including those in Argentina, Bolivia and the Dominican Republic. And in March 2005 the Nepalese public registry was reincorporated as a limited liability company, 90% owned by financial institutions and 10% by the central bank.

Give secured creditors clear priority to collateral

Securing a loan with collateral reduces lending risk and gives entrepreneurs better terms of credit. But these benefits are eroded if the secured creditor loses priority to other claimants—taxes, workers, judgment creditors, buyers of collateral or others. This can happen in bankruptcy or outside it. More credit is available when secured creditors have absolute priority (figure 6.4).

Reforming secured transactions and bankruptcy laws is not always enough to assure priority. Other laws may interfere. The Malawi Companies Act places secured creditor claims first, but the labor laws put worker claims ahead. In China the security law gives priority to the secured creditor, while the tax law allows it to be taken away in favor of unpaid taxes. Reformers need to ensure that such conflicts are addressed when revising laws.

Priority rules work best with a unified collateral registry, so that prospective lenders can easily establish whether there is a prior claim on an asset. And even if other claimants are given priority—a second best for credit markets—laws can require that such claims be registered in the collateral registry. Ukraine's reform made registration mandatory for all claimants, even the state. If tax liens are not registered, they lose priority. That way banks can account for the risk, and choose whether or not to lend.

Introduce summary enforcement proceedings

With summary proceedings, collateral enforcement is resolved quickly when it winds up in court. Only 2 pieces of evidence need to be presented to a court in a summary proceeding: a valid security agreement and proof of default. Fifty-six countries have summary proceedings. Those that do require 50% less time to enforce collateral

FIGURE 6.3
Private bureaus serve lenders better

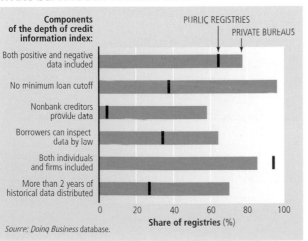

Source: Doing Business database.

FIGURE 6.4
More credit when secured creditors have priority

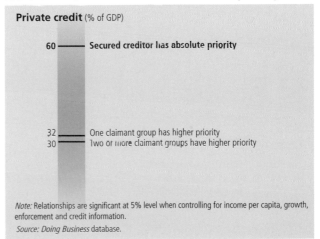

Note: Relationships are significant at 5% level when controlling for income per capita, growth, enforcement and credit information.
Source: Doing Business database.

than countries that rely on other judicial measures.

When creditors can seize and sell collateral without resorting to the courts, enforcement can be even faster. But summary proceedings are also important as a backstop to out-of-court enforcement.

Albania introduced a summary proceeding in 1999. With a registered collateral agreement in place, a creditor may seek an enforcement order from the court when a borrower defaults, after giving the debtor 5 days' notice. The order is issued within a few days. An execution officer may then seize the collateral and deliver it to the creditor. Enforcement takes less than a month. Bulgaria, India and Romania have introduced similar proceedings. Such reforms are especially successful when they limit grounds for appeal and allow enforcement to proceed pending appeal.

Why reform?

Businesses get better access to loans and better terms of credit when creditors and borrowers have stronger legal rights and good credit information is available.[4] Take Romania. In 1999 it expanded the scope of collateral, clarified priority rules and expedited enforcement. It also set up an online collateral registry. Since then more than 200,000 notices of security interests have been registered. The number of borrowers has increased threefold, and the volume of credit by 50%. And interest rates have fallen.[5] After Slovakia adopted laws permitting the pledging of movable assets, more than 70% of new business credit was secured by such collateral—and private credit jumped by 10% in a year.

Benefits flow beyond access to credit. Countries with more legal rights for borrowers and lenders and more credit information have fewer nonperforming loans and lower financial system risk (figure 6.5). With better-functioning credit markets, investment and growth increase.[6] Small firms and women, who face the biggest hurdles in accessing credit, are the ones who gain most when collateral laws and credit information support lending decisions.[7]

Some governments attempt to protect borrowers by weakening creditors' ability to take and enforce security. Laws in Benin and Syria cap the interest rates that lenders can charge. Côte d'Ivoire and Italy make a bankrupt debtor immune from debt collection for the entire insolvency proceeding—by which time the bankruptcy estate is whittled to nothing. This is folly. The best way to help borrowers is to improve credit information and make it easier to take and enforce collateral.

FIGURE 6.5
Legal rights and credit information reduce risk

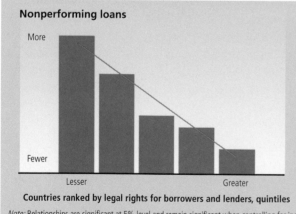

Nonperforming loans

Countries ranked by legal rights for borrowers and lenders, quintiles

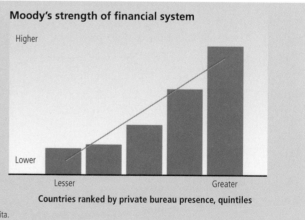

Moody's strength of financial system

Countries ranked by private bureau presence, quintiles

Note: Relationships are significant at 5% level and remain significant when controlling for income per capita.
Source: Doing Business database, IMF (2005a).

Notes

1. Based on national statistics.
2. Positive information covers loans outstanding and payment behavior on accounts in good standing; negative information covers defaults and arrears.
3. Djankov, McLiesh and Shleifer (2005).
4. Davydenko and Franks (2005), Qian and Strahan (2005), Djankov, McLiesh and Shleifer (2005) and Avery, Calem and Canner (2004).
5. Chaves, de la Peña and Fleisig (2004).
6. Acemoglu (2001) and King and Levine (1993).
7. World Bank (2004a) and Love and Mylenko (2003).

Protecting investors

Who is reforming?

What to reform?

Why reform?

Executives at Elf Aquitaine, France's largest oil company, took bribes in exchange for awarding business deals. Along with the extra cash, they got 7 years in jail and a 2 million euro fine for abuse of power.[1] Russian oil firm Gazprom purchased materials for new pipelines through intermediaries owned by company officers. The high prices charged for the materials raised eyebrows, but not court battles.[2]

Big cases like these make headlines, but looting by corporate insiders occurs every day on a smaller scale. And it often goes undetected. Protecting investors against self-dealing—the use of corporate assets for personal gain— is necessary for equity markets to develop. It is just one corporate governance issue, but it is the most important one. Other issues in investor protection—for example, writing management contracts that provide incentives for optimal investment decisions— are not discussed in the chapter.

To document investor protections against self-dealing, *Doing Business* measures how countries would regulate a standardized case.[3] The case facts are simple. Mr. James, who owns 60% of the stock in a public company and sits on its board, proposes that the company purchase 50 used trucks from a private company of which he owns 90%. The price is higher than the going price. Mr. James benefits from the transaction, since for each dollar that his private company receives, 40 cents come from income belonging to the minority investors in the public company. This is not fraud—such transactions are perfectly legal if proper disclosures are made and approvals obtained. Several questions arise. Who approves the transaction? What information must be

disclosed? What company documents can investors access? What do minority shareholders have to prove to stop the transaction or to receive compensation from Mr. James? An index of investor protection is constructed based on these and other answers.

New Zealand protects investors against self-dealing the most (table 7.1). Singapore is next. Regulation is so extensive in Singapore that one lawyer describes practicing law there as "tip toeing through the tulips." The countries that best protect against self-dealing have several things in common. They require immediate disclosure of the transaction and Mr. James's conflict of interest. They require prior approval of the transaction by other shareholders. They enable shareholders to hold the company's directors liable and to have the trans-

TABLE 7.1

Where are investors protected—and where not?

Most protected	Least protected
New Zealand	Costa Rica
Singapore	Croatia
Canada	Albania
Hong Kong, China	Ethiopia
Malaysia	Iran
Israel	Ukraine
United States	Venezuela
South Africa	Vietnam
United Kingdom	Tanzania
Mauritius	Afghanistan

Note: Rankings are on the strength of investor protection index. See the Data notes for details.
Source: Doing Business database.

action voided if its terms are unfair. And they permit shareholders who take the company directors to court to access all relevant documents.

Several developing countries protect investors well. Mauritius and South Africa are among the top 10 on the strength of investor protections, and Pakistan is not far behind. But on average poor countries regulate self-dealing less than rich countries, especially in requiring disclosure. Albania, Guatemala, Tunisia and 7 other countries require no public disclosure on "related-party" transactions like the one involving Mr. James. They also permit the top manager to approve the transaction rather than requiring that the "disinterested shareholders" —those who do not stand to gain personally—approve the deal.

Some poor countries try to compensate for the lack of shareholder access to information and the courts by relying on government inspectors (figure 7.1). "Shareholders find this cheaper, more efficient and more effective than bringing the suit themselves, both because they don't have to pay for it and because inspectors can require more information from the defendant," a Tunisian lawyer explained. This is a second-best choice when private action is unlikely to bring results. But government regulators may have different incentives than the minority investors—for example, in deciding which cases to investigate.

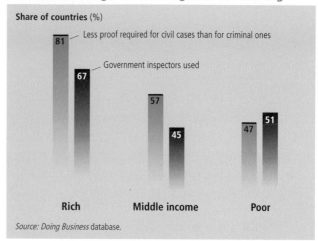

FIGURE 7.1
Rich countries regulate more against self-dealing

Source: Doing Business database.

The payoff from protecting investors is large. Where expropriation of minority investors is curbed, equity investment is higher and ownership concentration lower.[4] Investors gain portfolio diversification. Entrepreneurs gain access to cash. Without investor protections, equity markets fail to develop and banks become the only source of finance. Yet weak collateral or property registration systems block many businesses in poor countries from obtaining even bank loans. The result: businesses do not reach efficient size for lack of financing, and economic growth is held back.

Who is reforming?

Fifteen economies reformed investor protections in 2004 (table 7.2). Thailand was the top reformer. It now requires that in listed companies, directors *and* shareholders without personal interest in the deal must approve any related-party transaction. Such transactions are defined broadly—for example, by including family members and other entities controlled by a director—cutting off many loopholes.

Spain introduced directors' duty of loyalty into its corporate law for public firms. Directors must now put the best interests of the company above any personal gains they might receive through the company's operations. Spain also requires a semiannual "corporate governance report." Listed companies must report any related-party transactions and document their compliance with the new corporate governance guidelines.

Turkey now requires companies to post an "investor relations" page on their website. The page must reveal directors' ownership and information on privileged

shares as well as board minutes and transactions made by directors. Vietnam asked managers and directors to publish their ownership stakes in the company for the first time, including the ownership interests of spouses and children.

Jamaica defined standards of care for directors in its new Companies Act. For example, directors with accounting training will have to review the company's financial statements with the eye of an accountant, not merely "with the judgment and care of a reasonable person," as before.

Pakistan introduced tough penalties for violating self-dealing regulations. In July 2004 the National Accountability Ordinance mandated criminal liability for managers and directors who "fraudulently misappropriate any property entrusted" to them. Conviction comes with unlimited fines and up to 14 years in jail. But experience in other countries—including those with the toughest liability for directors (table 7.3)—suggests that judges are seldom willing to put businesspeople behind bars.

TABLE 7.2
Increased disclosure was the most popular reform in 2004

Reform	Economy
Increased disclosure requirements	Israel, Italy, Pakistan, Spain Thailand, Turkey, Vietnam
Regulated related-party transactions	Jamaica, Thailand
Defined directors' duties	Jamaica, Namibia, Spain
Increased penalties for self-dealing	Malaysia, Pakistan
Strengthened auditing requirements	Costa Rica, Indonesia, Thailand
Introduced governance codes	Hong Kong (China), Iceland, Turkey
Allowed class-action suits	Korea

Source: Doing Business database.

TABLE 7.3
Who regulates the liability of directors the most—and who the least?

Most	Least
New Zealand	Nepal
Singapore	Moldova
Malaysia	Zimbabwe
Canada	São Tomé and Príncipe
United States	Lebanon
Cambodia	Vietnam
Israel	Senegal
Hong Kong, China	Mexico
South Africa	Dominican Republic
Mauritius	Afghanistan

Note: Rankings are on the extent of director liability index. See the Data notes for details.
Source: Doing Business database.

Iceland and Turkey adopted corporate governance codes for public companies. While compliance is voluntary, companies straying from the recommendations must explain in public reports why they did not follow them.

Malaysia and Thailand introduced incentives for better investor protection. Kuala Lumpur's stock exchange now offers an annual award for the company with the best corporate governance, as measured by compliance with the "best practices of corporate governance" outlined in the listing rules. Companies compete for the award and the publicity that comes with it. Thailand went a step further. The Thai Securities and Exchange Commission offers tax breaks to companies abiding by the stock exchange's 15 principles of good investor protection.

What to reform?

The corporate lawyers participating in the *Doing Business* survey were asked to rank the major obstacles to protecting investors. While not a representative sample, they advise many domestic and foreign investors on where to put their money, and they deal with weaknesses in the law every day. Lack of information on related-party transactions ranked high. So did an impossibly high standard of proof to show wrongdoing of directors (table 7.4).

TABLE 7.4
Major obstacles to protecting investors

Obstacle	Share of countries (%)
Lack of information on related-party transactions	53
Investors must prove their case to the level of certainty in criminal cases	39
Directors keep profits from self-dealing even after being convicted of breach of duty	37
Liability for directors only if they act fraudulently or in bad faith	13
No access to company's or defendant's documents	8

Source: Doing Business database.

Four reforms improve the protection of investors against self-dealing:

- Notify investors of directors' interests in deals.
- Require approval by disinterested directors or investors for related-party transactions.
- Eliminate loopholes in rules for shareholder approval.
- Where courts are strong, help investors bring lawsuits.

Notify investors of directors' interests in deals

The easiest reform everywhere is increasing disclosure. It is also the most needed, especially in South Asia and Latin America (figure 7.2). Investors need to know what stakes directors have in proposed deals so they can stop those deals through a vote if shareholder interests would be hurt—or sue for damages. This is less expensive than it sounds. The Internet makes the distribution of financial and ownership information cheap. Flexible proxy rules—for example, allowing voting by fax or email—reduce the expense to companies of administering shareholder votes.

FIGURE 7.2
East Asia requires the most disclosure

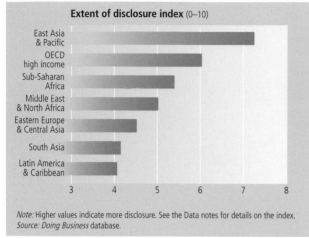

Note: Higher values indicate more disclosure. See the Data notes for details on the index.
Source: Doing Business database.

FIGURE 7.3
Who votes on related-party transactions?

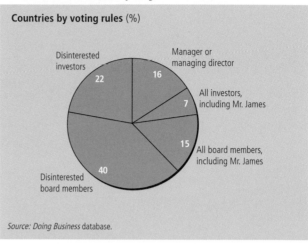

Source: Doing Business database.

Malaysia, with among the most stringent disclosure rules, requires extensive disclosure on a related-party transaction before it is put to a vote of the company's disinterested shareholders (table 7.5). Violators face 7 years in jail and a substantial fine. In contrast, Bolivia, Croatia and Ethiopia don't require directors to disclose their interests in a transaction to the rest of the board—even when they vote on that transaction.

Require approval by disinterested parties

In Australia and another 2 dozen countries related-party transactions automatically trigger review and a vote by shareholders without a personal stake in the deal (figure 7.3). This is often not the case. Finland, Mexico and 15 other countries require special approval procedures for transactions above a certain size. But they do not have similar treatment of related-party transactions. And

TABLE 7.5
Who requires the most disclosure of related-party transactions—and who the least?

Most	Least
New Zealand	Philippines
Singapore	Honduras
Malaysia	Greece
Hong Kong, China	Ethiopia
United Kingdom	Ukraine
Zambia	Belarus
Thailand	Azerbaijan
France	Tunisia
China	Albania
Ireland	Afghanistan

Note: Rankings are on the extent of disclosure index. See the Data notes for details.
Source: Doing Business database.

some countries, such as Germany, regulate transactions with a director but not those with an entity controlled by a director. This invites abuse.

Eliminate loopholes in rules for shareholder approval

In Lebanon disinterested investors must approve every transaction between a company and its directors. That sounds sufficient, but in practice shareholders grant approvals at the annual meeting for all related-party transactions arising during the coming year. This practice meets the statutory requirements, but shareholders do not review each transaction individually.

Another common loophole is granting exceptions for transactions conducted "in the ordinary course of business." Reforms in Senegal and several other West African countries required approval by disinterested shareholders for related-party transactions, but excluded transactions conducted as part of the "day-to-day" activities of a company. "The details on day-to-day activities are rather vague in the law. Any transaction can fit the bill," states a lawyer in Cameroon.

Where courts are strong, help investors bring suits

The United States, long the top destination of international capital, protects investors through broad court review of directors' actions.[5] During trial all company documents related to the case are open for inspection. In court, plaintiffs can directly question all witnesses, including the defendant, without prior judicial review of the questions posed. Directors must show that the transaction was fair to the company—both in price and in dealing. This makes the United States one of the easiest places to bring shareholder suits (table 7.6).

Good investor protections are the ones a country

TABLE 7.6
Who makes it easiest to bring shareholder suits—and who most difficult?

Easiest	Most difficult
New Zealand	United Arab Emirates
Kenya	Albania
Singapore	Venezuela
Canada	Vietnam
Israel	Afghanistan
United States	Syria
Ireland	Morocco
Mauritius	Algeria
Colombia	Iran
Nepal	Tanzania

Note: Rankings are on the ease of shareholder suits index. See the Data notes for details.
Source: Doing Business database.

FIGURE 7.4
Efficient courts help protect minority shareholders

Note: Relationship is significant at the 1% level when controlling for income per capita.
Source: Doing Business database, WEF (2004).

can enforce. Even the best rules are useless if enforcement is weak.[6] Some transition economies have adopted strong company or securities laws. But in the Kyrgyz Republic and Moldova, for example, no cases of minority investor abuse have ever been resolved in the courts. And neither country has managed to maintain an active stock market. Nepal also has strong protections on the books (see table 7.6), but these are rarely invoked and equity markets are nascent.

As in any other commercial dispute, the speed, cost and fairness of judgment determine whether small investors will resort to the courts. Potential expropriators know this as well and calculate the risk of being caught and punished. In countries like New Zealand and Singapore, where courts perform well, less abuse of investors is seen (figure 7.4).

Why reform?

Poor investor protection means less equity investment.[7] If the rights of investors are not protected, majority ownership in a business is the only way to eliminate the risk of expropriation of their investment. But few entrepreneurs would agree to have their business controlled by someone else. Those who do have less incentive to work hard, because the payoffs from success go to someone else. Meanwhile, investors must devote more oversight to fewer investments. The result: entrepreneurship is suppressed, and fewer profitable projects are undertaken.

A recent study of private equity transactions finds

FIGURE 7.5
Better investor protection —higher market capitalization and more listed firms

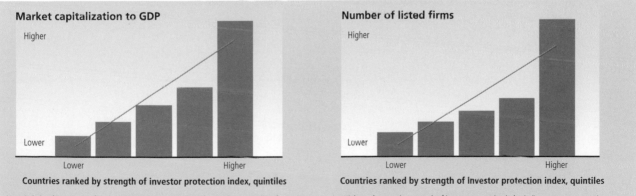

Note: Relationships are significant at 5% level and remain significant when controlling for income per capita. Higher values on the strength of investor protection index indicate greater protection. See the Data notes for details.
Source: Doing Business database, World Bank (2005d).

this exact pattern. In countries with higher risk of expropriation, investment as a share of GDP is half that in countries with good investor protections. Two deals take place for every 3 in countries that protect investors. And investors acquire majority stakes, limiting their opportunity for diversification.[8]

All this is reflected in the size of stock markets. When small investors see a high risk of expropriation, they do not invest. The market stays underdeveloped (figure 7.5). And fewer firms bother to list. So protecting investors can bring sizable gains. If Hungary were to adopt the more stringent disclosure regulations of Thailand, analysis suggests that stock market capitalization might increase by up to 50%, and the value of trades by up to 35%.[9]

Notes

1. Associated Press Newswires, "France Oil Scandal: Appeals Court Sentences Former Elf Official to Seven Years in Prison," March 31, 2005.

2. *The Economist*, "Laughing Gas," June 4, 2005.

3. The case is developed in Djankov, La Porta and Shleifer (2005), and the survey conducted in partnership with Lex Mundi, a global association of leading independent law firms. All academic citations should refer to this paper.

4. Djankov, La Porta and Shleifer (2005). See also La Porta and others (1997) and Shleifer and Wolfenzon (2002).

5. See La Porta, López-de-Silanes and Shleifer (forthcoming).

6. Berglof and Claessens (2004).

7. See Black (2001).

8. Lerner and Schoar (2005).

9. Calculations based on La Porta, López-de-Silanes and Shleifer (forthcoming).

Paying taxes

Who is reforming?

What to reform?

Why reform?

Tax collection has long been a despised activity. In biblical times the Pharisees scorned the disciples by asking, "Why does your teacher eat with tax collectors and sinners?"[1] Things had not improved by the French Revolution—tax collectors were convicted of treason and sent to the guillotine.

Yet taxes are essential. Without them there would be no money to build schools, hospitals, courts, roads, airports or other public infrastructure that helps businesses and society to be more productive and better off.

Still, there are good ways and bad ways to collect taxes. Imagine a medium-size business—TaxpayerCo—that produces and sells consumer goods. In Hong Kong (China) the business pays 1 income tax and 1 fuel tax totaling 14% of gross profit (sales less materials and labor costs; figure 8.1). It takes 1 annual electronic filing and 80 hours to comply with tax requirements. Meanwhile, in Belarus TaxpayerCo is subject to 11 taxes, including an income tax, value added tax (VAT), transport duty, land tax, property tax, ecological tax, fuel tax and a turnover tax where taxes are paid on inputs and again on outputs. Despite many deductions and exemptions, required payments add up to 122% of gross profit—leaving the business with 2 choices: stop operating or start evading. The business would make 113 tax payments to 3 agencies, all by paper, and spend 1,188 hours doing so. Tax refunds would take 2 years to process. This complexity and delay make Belarus's tax system among the world's most burdensome (box 8.1).

FIGURE 8.1

Few tax payments in Hong Kong (China), many in Belarus

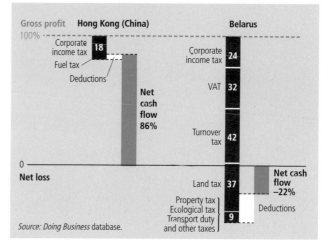

Source: Doing Business database.

Arguments for business tax reform usually emphasize rates, especially corporate income tax rates. That is misleading on 3 counts. First, corporate income taxes are only a small share of the total business tax burden—less than 25% on average. For example, Hungary's nominal corporate income tax is only 16% of net profit, but the total business tax bill is 57% of gross profit because of VAT, property tax, land tax, local business tax, community tax, vehicle tax and 9 others, after taking into account deductions and exemptions. In several Eastern European countries simplification has not had the desired impact on perceived business obstacles, in part because it focused on income tax only.[2]

BOX 8.1

Who makes paying taxes easy—and who does not?

Total tax payable (% of gross profit)

Lowest		Highest	
Saudi Arabia	1	Uzbekistan	76
Oman	5	Mauritania	76
Iraq	6	Uruguay	80
Kuwait	8	Argentina	98
United Arab Emirates	9	Belarus	122
Malaysia	12	Yemen	129
Hong Kong, China	14	Congo, Dem. Rep.	135
Iran	15	Brazil	148
Puerto Rico	18	Sierra Leone	164
Singapore	20	Burundi	173

Payments (number per year)

Fewest		Most	
Hong Kong, China	1	Côte d'Ivoire	71
Afghanistan	2	Jamaica	72
Norway	3	Bosnia and Herzegovina	73
Sweden	5	Benin	75
Mauritius	7	Ukraine	84
Portugal	7	Dominican Republic	85
Spain	7	Congo, Rep.	94
Chile	8	Kyrgyz Republic	95
Ireland	8	Belarus	113
New Zealand	8	Uzbekistan	118

Time to comply (hours per year)

Least		Most	
United Arab Emirates	12	Czech Republic	930
Singapore	30	São Tomé and Príncipe	1,008
Iraq	48	Vietnam	1,050
Namibia	50	Bolivia	1,080
Ethiopia	52	Armenia	1,120
Oman	52	Nigeria	1,120
Thailand	52	Belarus	1,188
Spain	56	Cameroon	1,300
Switzerland	63	Ukraine	2,185
New Zealand	70	Brazil	2,600

Ease of paying taxes

Easiest	Most difficult
Hong Kong, China	Uruguay
United Arab Emirates	Bolivia
Oman	Venezuela
Saudi Arabia	Armenia
Kuwait	Colombia
Iraq	Algeria
Afghanistan	Ukraine
Singapore	Congo, Rep.
Switzerland	Mauritania
Malaysia	Belarus

Note: Gross profit is sales less materials and labor costs. Rankings on the ease of paying taxes are the averages of the country rankings on the tax payable, number of payments and time to comply with tax regulations. See the Data notes for details.

Source: Doing Business database.

Doing Business asked accountants in 155 countries to review the financial statements and a list of transactions of a standardized firm called TaxpayerCo.[3] The business started with the same financial position in every country. Respondents were asked the total tax that the business must pay and the process for doing so. All taxes—from corporate income tax to VAT to advertising or environmental tax—and all applicable deductions and exemptions are taken into account to calculate the total burden.[4]

Take Uruguay as an example. The country's VAT is 23% of value added (sales less materials costs). When labor costs are considered, this is equivalent to 41% of gross profit (sales less materials and labor costs). After taking into account deductions and exemptions, the corporate income tax is 30% of net profit—equivalent to 11% of gross profit. On top of that the business pays a social contribution tax of 27% of gross profit, a capital tax of 1% and 8 other taxes totaling 1%. Thus tax payments total 80% of gross profit, leaving TaxpayerCo with only 20% to pay all other expenses, maintain equipment, invest in new products and distribute to shareholders.

Uruguay is among the 10 countries with the highest business taxes. In 6 of these, business taxes add up to more than gross profit. TaxpayerCo would not operate in the formal sector in those countries. And in many other countries incentives to evade are strong. In Albania evading 20% of the tax bill increases the business's gross profit by 50%. In Kenya, by 43%. And in Bolivia, by 35%.

Administrative requirements are also a burden in many countries. *Doing Business* measures the number of payments TaxpayerCo would have to make to tax authorities, as well as the time required to prepare and file tax payments. It takes 84 payments and 2,185 hours a year in Ukraine, but only 11 payments and 104 hours in Estonia.

Rankings on the ease of paying taxes are the average of the country rankings on total taxes, number of payments and time required to comply. Middle Eastern and East Asian countries make paying taxes the easiest. Latin American countries impose the heaviest burdens, mainly because of compliance costs. Africa follows, largely because of high taxes. OECD countries impose the smallest administrative burdens and charge moderate tax bills.

FIGURE 8.2
Rich countries have lower and simpler business taxes

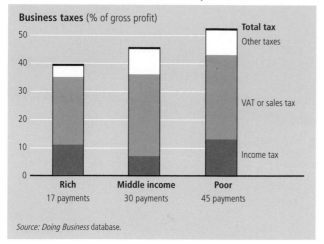

Business taxes (% of gross profit)

Total tax
Other taxes

VAT or sales tax

Income tax

| Rich | Middle income | Poor |
| 17 payments | 30 payments | 45 payments |

Source: Doing Business database.

FIGURE 8.3
High taxes create strong incentives to evade

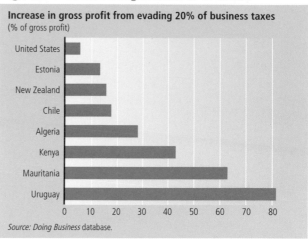

Increase in gross profit from evading 20% of business taxes
(% of gross profit)

United States
Estonia
New Zealand
Chile
Algeria
Kenya
Mauritania
Uruguay

Source: Doing Business database.

Second, the complexity of tax compliance matters too. Norway collects 60% of companies' gross profit using 3 taxes filed electronically. In contrast, it takes 14 taxes and 62 interactions with the tax authorities to collect 46% of gross profit in the Philippines. Firms in 90% of surveyed countries rank tax administration among the top 5 obstacles to doing business. In several—including Bangladesh, Cambodia, the Kyrgyz Republic, Russia and Uzbekistan—working with the tax bureaucracy is considered a bigger problem than tax rates.[5]

Finally, businesses care about what they get for their taxes. Finland has higher business taxes, at 52% of gross profit, than Mexico, at 31%. But firms there have fewer complaints about the tax burden. That businesses rate Finland among the top 10 countries on quality of

infrastructure and social services could have something to do with it.

Rich countries tend to have lower business taxes and make them less complex (figure 8.2). Simple, moderate taxes and fast, cheap administration mean less hassle for business—as well as higher revenues. In contrast, poor countries tend to use business as a collection point, charging higher business taxes. Such burdensome taxes create incentives for evasion. In the United States business taxes add up to 21% of gross profit. So if a company started with $100 in gross profit, evading 20% of its tax bill would raise gross profit after tax from $79 to $83—equivalent to increasing gross profit by 5%. But in Mauritania profit would jump 63% (figure 8.3).

Who is reforming?

In 2004, 28 countries made major changes to their tax systems. Following a long-term trend, most countries cut corporate tax rates. Several focused on increasing compliance and the tax base, thereby boosting revenues while cutting or maintaining rates.

In 1994 Estonia radically reformed its tax law, levying a 26% flat tax on corporate and personal income. Its success sparked a rush by other Eastern European countries to do the same. In 2004 Romania and Georgia became the latest. Romania introduced a 16% flat tax and cut payroll taxes—though at 49.5%, they are still high. Georgia's new tax code levies a 20% income tax on businesses and a 12% flat tax (down from 20%) on personal income. In addition, social taxes were cut from 33% to 20% and the number of taxes from 21 to 9, and

invoices and receipts were simplified.

Serbia and Montenegro followed another trend, joining the 90% of countries with a VAT. The advantages are clear: a VAT avoids cascading taxes, where taxes are paid on taxes. And a VAT is partially self-enforcing—because companies receive tax credits for a VAT paid on their purchases, they will want to trade with other companies registered for the VAT.

Corporate income tax cuts swept through other Eastern European countries, sealing the region's rank as the top tax reformer (table 8.1). Western European countries also joined the trend, partly in response to competition from new EU members. Although such cuts were the most common reform, they have a relatively small impact: globally, income taxes account for only about a quarter of business taxes (figure 8.4).

TABLE 8.1
Most 2004 tax reforms in Eastern Europe—and to corporate income tax rates

Region	All reforms (number)	Reforms including cuts in corporate income tax rate (%)
Eastern Europe & Central Asia	12	Albania 25 to 23
		Bulgaria 19.5 to 15
		Czech Republic 28 to 26
		Estonia 26 to 24
		Latvia 19 to 15
		Moldova 20 to 18
		Poland 27 to 19
		Uzbekistan 18 to 15
OECD high income	6	Austria 34 to 25
		Denmark 30 to 28
		Finland 29 to 26
		Greece 35 to 32
		Netherlands 34.5 to 31.5
Sub-Saharan Africa	3	Ghana 32.5 to 28
		Senegal 35 to 33
Latin America & Caribbean	2	Mexico 33 to 30
South Asia	1	Afghanistan 25 to 20
East Asia & Pacific	0	
Middle East & North Africa	0	

Source: Doing Business database.

FIGURE 8.4
Total business taxes are lowest in East Asia

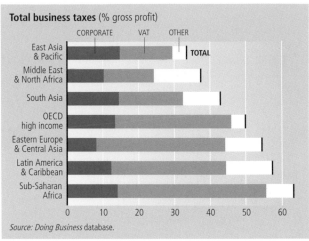

Source: Doing Business database.

Other countries focused on reforming tax administration. Spain introduced rules streamlining audits and appeals and increasing penalties. Lithuania did the same, and provided for electronic filing. Tax administrators there must now prove the basis for any tax recalculation.

Businesses in Africa face the highest taxes (see figure 8.4). In 2004, 3 countries in the region—Ghana, Tanzania and Senegal—revamped their tax codes and eased tax burdens. Ghana cut corporate tax rates and launched a unit to ease tax administration for large businesses. But it raised the VAT by 2.5 percentage points.

Three-quarters of businesses in Tanzania complain that taxes and their administration are a severe obstacle.[6] But things have gotten easier. A new income tax law broadened the tax base, closing loopholes and introducing taxpayer self-assessments. Improvements were also made in Senegal. Small businesses can now pay 1 tax that has a lower rate and consolidates 4 previous taxes. In addition, several exemptions were abolished to widen the tax base. And the company income tax rate fell from 35% to 33%. Mauritania took the opposite path, raising corporate taxes from 20% to 25%—making it the only country to increase this tax in 2004–05.

In Latin America, Mexico reduced its corporate income tax—from 33% to 30%—and announced further cuts for the next 2 years. El Salvador reformed its VAT and income tax laws as well as the tax code, with an aim to increase the tax base. It also levied a 1% monthly VAT advance. Tax rates rose in the Dominican Republic, with the VAT hiked from 12% to 16%. Several other countries in the region introduced minor reforms. Honduras modified penalties in an effort to improve compliance—easing sanctions for late payments and making tax evasion a criminal rather than civil offense. Argentina extended its financial transactions tax, and Bolivia introduced one.

Aid accounts for more than half of government revenue in Afghanistan. But with a new tax law, this may begin to change. Taxpayer identification numbers were issued in preparation for the law, and the corporate income tax was cut from 25% to 20%. Elsewhere in South Asia, Nepal raised its VAT from 10% to 13%, while India and Pakistan continued implementing reforms launched before 2004.

The regions with the lowest tax rates—East Asia and the Pacific and the Middle East and North Africa—reformed the least in 2004. Samoa increased its VAT from 10% to 12.5%. Saudi Arabia reformed its corporate tax law, but that change affects only foreign firms. Like many of its neighbors, the government relies on oil revenue to fund spending. As a result businesses in the region pay some of the lowest tax rates in the world. Morocco introduced some administrative reforms, with a new finance law imposing a 10% penalty on late payments.

What to reform?

Tax reforms inspire political debate and can be hotly contested. But both business and government benefit when taxes are simple and fair and set incentives for growth. Here are 4 ways to start:

- Consolidate the number of taxes.
- Cut back special exemptions and privileges.
- Simplify filing requirements.
- Broaden the tax base by keeping rates moderate in developing countries.

Consolidate the number of taxes

"Our system is characterized by a flood of taxes that overload business with administration. The primary taxes are income tax, value added tax, import duty, export tax, excise duty and special excise, provincial turnover tax and property tax. There are taxes at different levels of government. There is also the social responsibility levy, debits tax, share transaction levy, economic service charge, financial transactions tax and various stamp duties. And there is a whole host of industry-specific taxes. It is way too complicated." So says Anil, an accountant in Sri Lanka.

Having more types of taxes requires more interaction between businesses and tax agencies. Businesses complain that a higher number of taxes increases hassle (figure 8.5). The problem is greatest in poor countries, which rely more on "other taxes" rather than income tax and VAT. In Tanzania, for example, local authorities impose 50 business taxes and fees.[7] But the number of taxes is a burden in some rich countries too. In New York City income taxes are levied at the municipal, state and fed-

eral levels.[8] Each is calculated on a different tax base, so businesses must keep 3 sets of books. Such an approach costs governments more in collection costs as well.

Reformers can look to Georgia, which in 2004 cut the number of taxes from 21 to 9. Businesses have praised the new, simpler system.[9] In 2001 Russia consolidated several business taxes, cutting the number of taxes from 20 to 15.[10] And Iran recently merged 3 taxes into 1 to ease payment.

Some taxes can be dropped altogether. Reforms should target minor excises and stamp duties—which cost money to administer but do not raise much revenue—or particularly distorting taxes. An example is a turnover tax, which is levied on a firm's inputs and again on its outputs, so tax is paid on tax. The main alternative to a turnover tax, a VAT, levies tax only on the difference between inputs and outputs (the value added), avoiding double taxation. Another alternative, a sales tax, does the same by taxing only outputs, as in the United States. Mozambique abolished its turnover tax in 1999, replacing it with a VAT. Georgia eliminated its turnover tax, which was levied on top of a VAT, as a part of its 2004 reform. But another 22 countries maintain a turnover tax, including Argentina, Belarus and Tunisia. Almost all have a VAT or sales tax as well.

Cut back special exemptions and privileges

Tax systems have been forged through competing political pressures, lobbying and attempts to stimulate specific industries or activities. In most countries these processes have resulted in a proliferation of exemptions, deductions, privileges and other rules, not to mention increasingly complex tax codes. In the Czech Republic tax regulation more than quadrupled over the past 10 years, from 10,000 pages to 44,000. In Australia it went from 3,600 pages to 9,600.

Special exemptions erode the tax base. Businesses left in the system end up paying more. The system becomes less transparent and more costly to run. It distorts resource allocation. And incentive schemes create possibilities for rent seeking and arbitrage as businesses seek to minimize their tax with legal ways of manipulating income.[11]

Estonia's 1994 reform replaced its concession-laden system with a single flat tax offering no exemptions. "We could not afford to maintain a more complex system," said a representative of the Ministry of Finance. The country's tax base broadened, and revenues have not suffered. In 2003 Slovakia streamlined its convoluted

FIGURE 8.5
More taxes and payments—more hassle

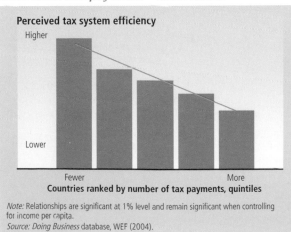

Note: Relationships are significant at 1% level and remain significant when controlling for income per capita.
Source: Doing Business database, WEF (2004).

incentive schemes into a single flat tax, with similar results.[12] Colombia, El Salvador, Indonesia, Jamaica and Mexico have eliminated distortions by cutting ineffective incentive schemes—and increased revenues in the process.[13]

Simplify filing requirements

A popular way to make paying taxes easier is by introducing electronic filing. Businesses can enter financial information online and file it with one click—and no calculations. Errors can be identified instantly, and returns processed quickly. Singapore led the way. In the early 1990s its tax department was plagued by a mounting backlog of unprocessed tax returns and the lowest public satisfaction rating of all public services. In response a new department, the Internal Revenue Authority of Singapore, was created. In 1998 the department launched an e-filing system. Filing taxes is now entirely paperless (except for a verification receipt) and takes just a day—and 90% of corporate taxpayers express satisfaction with tax administration.[14]

Another 45 countries have made e-filing possible, and the list is growing. In 2004 Armenia and Lithuania introduced online filing. Lebanon began automating its payroll tax. Businesses in Slovakia can now email tax returns, with no signature or paper evidence. And South Africa is implementing an e-filing system. Such reforms pay off. In countries with online filing it takes less time to comply with tax regulations: 15 days compared with 25.

Simplifying paper filing is another way to make things easier. Doing so works everywhere but is especially important in poor countries, which may not have the demand or capacity to support e-filing. In many countries return and payment forms are cluttered with information requirements that are never processed. In the 1990s the monthly Polish VAT form required 105 entries—including 37 just for identification—and 38 calculations.[15] At one point entrepreneurs had to get a stamped VAT certificate for every business lunch. Things have improved, but it still takes 2 pages for each monthly filing and 3 days a year to complete VAT filing requirements. In Switzerland it takes 1 page per quarter and 1 day a year to deal with VAT paperwork. Brazil still has a long way to go: 6 forms are needed just to pay income tax. To complete just 1 of those forms, taxpayers must first read 300 pages of instructions. For the VAT at least 3 forms are needed.

Eliminating excessive paperwork cuts the time that businesses spend complying with tax laws. To increase compliance, the United Kingdom shortened its VAT return to 1 page. In 2004 Pakistan did the same for its income tax return, significantly shortening the time required to file.

Broaden the tax base by keeping rates moderate in developing countries

Poor countries try to levy the highest amount of tax on businesses (see figure 8.2). Some claim that these high taxes are needed to fund public services and correct fiscal deficits. This argument would be more compelling if there were evidence to support it. Obviously, generating government revenue is essential. But higher rates typically do not achieve that goal in poor countries (figure 8.6). Instead they push businesses into the informal economy. As a result the tax base shrinks and less revenue is collected.[16]

A better way to meet revenue targets is to encourage tax compliance by keeping rates moderate. Russia's large tax cuts in 2001 did exactly that. Corporate tax rates fell from 35% to 24%, and a simplified tax scheme lowered rates for small business. Yet tax revenue increased—by an annual average of 14% over the next 3 years. One study showed that the new revenue was due to increased compliance.[17]

The 2004 reformers have shown similar results. Ghana exceeded its midyear revenue targets despite significant cuts in corporate tax rates. Albania's corporate tax revenue rose 21% after the rate was cut, while in Moldova it jumped 28% and in Latvia, 37%. And in Romania budget revenues grew 8% in real terms in the first quarter of 2005 relative to the same period in

FIGURE 8.6

Taxes and revenue—unrelated in poor countries

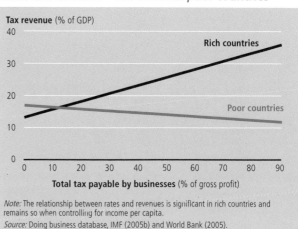

Note: The relationship between rates and revenues is significant in rich countries and remains so when controlling for income per capita.
Source: Doing business database, IMF (2005b) and World Bank (2005).

2004, despite the new flat tax. Economic growth in these countries is a factor in the increased revenues. But compliance is also up.

Lower rates work best when their administration is simple. And they are undermined by exemptions that shrink the tax base. Tax revenue has fallen in Uzbekistan, where the enthusiasm for income tax cuts was not matched by efforts to improve tax administration and expand the tax base.

Why reform?

Businesses prefer lower tax rates that are simply applied. Or, if rates are high, businesses want something in return for tax payments. All too often that is not the case, especially in developing countries. Often either a large informal sector or inefficient public spending is the problem—not insufficient tax rates. Across countries, higher taxes payable are not associated with better social outcomes, even controlling for country income levels. They do not increase government spending on health and education, raise literacy or life expectancy or lower child mortality. Nor are they associated with better infrastructure and other public services.[18]

Moreover, burdensome taxes generate undesirable outcomes. For example, they breed corruption. Businesses in the bottom 30 countries on ease of paying taxes are twice as likely as those in the top 30 to report that informal payments are a problem. Every point of contact between a bureaucrat and an entrepreneur is another chance for a bribe. And confusion on voluminous, often contradictory rules creates room for discretion. Faced with this, many entrepreneurs avoid the system altogether, operating in the informal economy (figure 8.7). There they pay no taxes, shrinking the revenue available for essential public services.

It is not just businesses that gain from reform. Streamlining taxes also brings savings for government. A complicated tax system costs a lot of money to run—funds that could be better spent on education, health care and infrastructure. In Denmark 1 kroner spent on tax administration generates 113 kroner of tax revenue. In Hungary 1 forint produces only 77. In Mexico 1 peso produces only 33.

Tax reform also creates more vibrant businesses. A smaller tax burden encourages firms to invest (figure 8.7). One recent study found that a 10% cut in indirect taxes, such as the VAT, may imply a rise in investment of up to 7%.[19] "Businesses are happy with the change and responding by investing more," says Kenneth, an accountant, about corporate tax reform in Ghana. Moreover, such investment yields higher returns when taxes are streamlined. A study in India estimates that tax reform can increase productivity by up to 60%.[20]

Overall growth is also higher with lower taxes and better collection.[21] And with tax incentives aligned to encourage work, more firms and more jobs are created. A cut of 1 percentage point in corporate tax rates is associated with up to a 3.7% increase in the number of firms and up to 1.1% higher employment.[22]

FIGURE 8.7

Burdensome taxes are associated with more informality, less investment

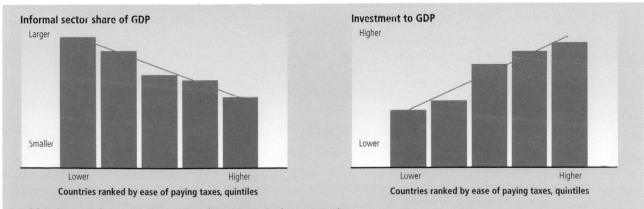

Note: Relationships are significant at 1% level and remain significant when controlling for income per capita.
Source: Doing Business database, Schneider (2005), World Bank (2005d).

Notes

1. Matthew 9: 11.

2. Engelschalk (2004).

3. The survey was conducted in partnership with Pricewater-houseCoopers, using a methodology developed in an ongoing research project by Mihir Desai, Caralee McLiesh, Rita Ramalho and Andrei Shleifer.

4. A common method for assessing tax rates is the marginal effective tax rate (METR) method, which estimates the tax payable resulting from investing one more unit of capital, or hiring one more worker, or producing one more unit of output. See the Data notes for a description of the main differences between the METR and *Doing Business* methods.

5. World Bank Investment Climate Survey database, available at http://rru.worldbank.org.

6. World Bank (2004b).

7. Fjeldstad and Rakner (2003).

8. Not all cities in the United States have a municipal business tax. In addition, in several states the tax base is the same for federal and state income taxes.

9. Georgia Business Council interview.

10. FIAS (2004).

11. See, for example, Tanzi and Zee (2000).

12. Moore (2005).

13. World Bank (1991).

14. Bird and Oldman (2000) and Tan, Pan and Lim (2005).

15. Bird (2003).

16. A similar result holds between fiscal regulation and economic growth. See Loayza, Oviedo and Serven (2004).

17. Ivanova, Keen and Klemm (2005).

18. Based on analysis of *Doing Business* indicators with health, education and infrastructure indicators in the World Bank's World Development Indicators (2005d) and Global Competitiveness Report 2004–05 (WEF 2004). The results hold controlling for income per capita.

19. Desai, Foley and Hines (2004).

20. World Bank (2004b).

21. Engen and Skinner (1996), Lee and Gordon (2004) and Slemrod (1995).

22. Goolsbee (2002).

Trading across borders

Who is reforming?

What to reform?

Why reform?

Fabien, a shop owner in Bujumbura, sells bicycles. No one makes bicycles in Burundi, so he imports from China. Fabien has a choice of ports: Mombasa in Kenya or Dar es Salaam in Tanzania. Terminal handling and storage fees are a third lower in Dar es Salaam and there is a rail line to Lake Tanganyika. The choice is made. After 50 days of prearrival approvals, 8 days of port handling, 15 days of going through customs and a month-long train ride, the shipment is on Burundi's border. Here it goes through 12 days of customs, gets loaded on a barge and passes through customs at Bujumbura port. In all, it takes 124 days, 19 documents and 55 signatures to get the bicycles from Dar es Salaam to Fabien's shop (figure 9.1).

Moussa, a shirt maker in Damascus, exports to Italy. For each shipment he needs a license and a certificate of origin from the Ministry of Trade. Every box of shirts is inspected before being loaded into a container. Customs is cleared twice, in Damascus and at the Syrian port of Latakia. It takes 49 days, 12 documents and 19 signatures from the moment the shirts leave Moussa's factory to the time they are on the ship to Naples.

Contrast this with the single signature a German or Swedish exporter needs to ship goods abroad. Or the 5 days and 3 documents necessary to import or export in Denmark, the country friendliest to traders (table 9.1). Fabien and Moussa should be so lucky.

The benefits of trade are well documented. So are some of the barriers to trade.[1] Tariffs, quotas and distance from large markets greatly increase the cost of goods, sometimes enough to prevent trading completely. But global and regional agreements have lessened these

FIGURE 9.1
Importing into Burundi—painful

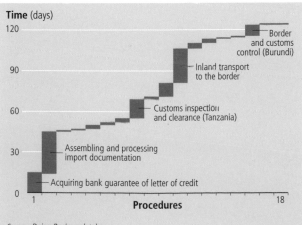

Source: Doing Business database.

TABLE 9.1
Where is trading easy—and where not?

Easiest	Most difficult
Denmark	Syria
Sweden	Mali
Germany	Eritrea
Finland	Kyrgyz Republic
Netherlands	Zambia
Singapore	Uzbekistan
Norway	Rwanda
Austria	Burundi
Belgium	Niger
Spain	Iraq

Note: Rankings on the ease of trading index are the average of the country rankings on the days, documents and signatures to import and export. See the Data notes for details.

Source: Doing Business database.

trade barriers.[2] And with faster ships and bigger planes, the world is shrinking.

Yet Africa's share of global trade is smaller today than 25 years ago. So is the Middle East's, excluding oil exports. One reason is that entrepreneurs in these regions face numerous regulatory hurdles to exporting. In the case of manufactured goods, customs and transport together represent the single greatest cost of trading in developing countries—even higher than the cost of tariffs on their exports imposed by rich countries. Trade agreements, except those with the European Union and between Central American countries and the United States, do not address these high costs. As a consequence, much of the reform fails to remove the largest barriers to trade. This is why *Doing Business* studies the procedures and time of going through customs and using trade infrastructure such as roads, ports and warehousing (box 9.1).

BOX 9.1

What are the *Doing Business* trade indicators?

Doing Business compiles the procedural requirements for exporting and importing a standardized cargo of goods. A procedure is counted from the time the business starts preparing the necessary documents to the time the cargo is in the client's warehouse. Every official procedure is counted—from the contractual agreement between the 2 parties to the delivery of goods—along with the time necessary for completion. All documents and signatures required for clearance of the goods across the border are also recorded. For example, the importing process is divided into 4 stages: prearrival documentation necessary for the cargo to be loaded on the ship or train, procedures necessary during the vessel's arrival at the port and the associated terminal handling, going through customs and cargo inspections, and inland transport for the cargo's delivery to the warehouse (box table 9.1).

On average, the 2 stages that require "hard infrastructure"—ports and inland transport—account for only a quarter of the time. The preparation of prearrival documents accounts for more than half the time (box figure 9.1). The time when the cargo is at sea is not counted. Once the trader has completed the prearrival documents, the counting of time stops; it starts again when the ship is docked. If the destination is a landlocked country, the time for inland transport includes transit time.

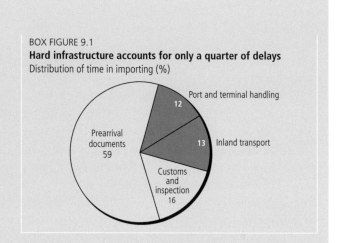

BOX FIGURE 9.1

Hard infrastructure accounts for only a quarter of delays
Distribution of time in importing (%)

Information on the documents and signatures required and the time to complete each procedure is provided by local freight forwarders, shipping lines, customs brokers and port officials, using several assumptions: The traded product travels in a dry-cargo, 20-foot, full container load. It is not a hazardous product, does not require refrigeration and meets international phyto sanitary and environmental safety standards. The survey respondents consider several product categories: textile yarn, fabrics, apparel and clothing accessories, coffee, tea, cocoa and spices.

BOX TABLE 9.1
Days to complete each stage of importing

Region	Prearrival documents	Port and terminal handling	Customs and inspections	Inland transport to warehouse	Total time
OECD high income	8	2	2	2	14
East Asia & Pacific	18	3	4	3	28
Latin America & Caribbean	24	4	5	3	36
Middle East & North Africa	25	5	9	4	43
Eastern Europe & Central Asia	25	4	7	7	43
South Asia	24	6	7	10	47
Sub-Saharan Africa	33	8	10	9	59
World	23	5	6	5	39

Source: Doing Business database

Who is reforming?

In 2004, 25 countries reformed their customs or trade transport (table 9.2). Egypt was the top reformer. It established a single window for trade documentation and merged 26 approvals into 5. A time limit of 2 days for clearing customs now applies. Improvements were part of a broader reform that cut the number of tariff bands from 27 to 6 and simplified inspections. The inspiration was the association agreement with the European Union.

Rwanda came second. Preshipment inspection is no longer required. The customs declaration can be made electronically, although hard copies are still inspected when the cargo is picked up.

Colombia, Guatemala, Peru and 4 other countries set lower time limits for going through customs. Colombia reduced the time limit from 5 days to 2, Guatemala from 4 to 2, and Peru from 6 to 2. If the allowed time expires and the cargo is not cleared, the trader can claim it.

Fiji and Hungary introduced electronic filing of customs documents. The file is submitted before the cargo reaches the border and usually approved within 10 minutes. Now 88% of shipments go through without stopping. For the rest, risk assessment software sends an alert. Documents are checked in detail for 10% of trade, and only 2% of containers are opened and inspected.

Pakistan eliminated the requirement for an import or export license for each shipment. Previously a trader needed to obtain a license each time he brought goods across the border. Now the license is given to the trader, not each cargo, and lasts 2 years. Yemen abolished licensing for imported shipments. Instead, a general import license is now in place. These reforms saved costs and numerous trips to the Ministry of Trade.

TABLE 9.2
Major customs or trade transport reforms in 2004

Reform	Country
Set time limits on customs	Cameroon, Colombia, Egypt, Guatemala, Jamaica, Peru, Russia
Introduced electronic filing	Fiji, Hungary
Abolished trade licenses	Germany, Pakistan, Uganda, Yemen
Introduced risk analysis for inspections	Austria, Mauritius, Timor-Leste
Stopped mandating preshipment inspection	Philippines, Rwanda
Improved road and port infrastructure	Afghanistan, China, Mauritania United Arab Emirates
Automated trade tax payment	Iran, Panama, Spain

Source: *Doing Business* database.

In the United Arab Emirates new berths were added at Jebel Ali port. In 2004 it took 6 days to load cargo. Now, an average of 17 hours. Similar improvements in Shanghai cut loading time by two-thirds. In Mauritania the Nouakchott port now operates around the clock. Previously it was open just 60 hours a week.

More than half the reforms in 2004 took place in poor countries. But on average it still takes 3 times as many days, nearly twice as many documents and 6 times as many signatures to import in a poor country as it does in rich countries (figure 9.2). Obstacles to exporting are just as large. Trade in Africa takes the longest—45 days on average to export and 59 to import. Typical regulations in Africa require 18 signatures to export and 28 to import. Outside the OECD, traders in East Asia have the easiest time (figure 9.3). Latin America ranks next. Many of the recent reforms there are inspired by regional trade agreements with the United States.

FIGURE 9.2
More hurdles for importers in poor countries

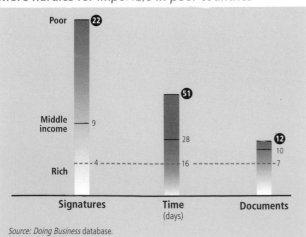

Source: *Doing Business* database.

FIGURE 9.3
Less bureaucracy in East Asia

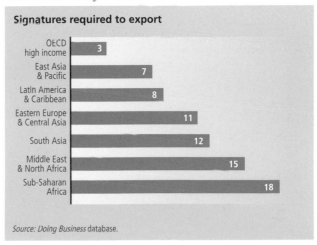

Source: *Doing Business* database.

What to reform?

In reducing the regulatory and transport costs of trading, the 3 most effective reforms in 2004 were these:

- Make document filing electronic.
- Use a risk assessment policy for inspections.
- Go regional with reform of customs and transport rules.

Another popular reform was to contract out preshipment inspection and customs management. But beware: contracting out has often failed to deliver better services, may not reduce smuggling and has sometimes been blamed for increased corruption.

TABLE 9.3

Who makes exporting easy—and who makes it difficult?

Days

Fewest		Most	
Denmark	5	Burundi	67
Germany	6	Mali	67
Lithuania	6	Azerbaijan	69
Senegal	6	Eritrea	69
Singapore	6	Burkina Faso	71
Sweden	6	Sudan	82
Belgium	7	Chad	87
Finland	7	Kazakhstan	93
Netherlands	7	Iraq	105
Norway	7	Central African Republic	116

Documents

Fewest		Most	
Denmark	3	Iran	11
Austria	4	Mongolia	11
Finland	4	Nigeria	11
Germany	4	Ecuador	12
Norway	4	Lao PDR	12
Spain	4	Syria	12
Sweden	4	Uganda	13
Australia	5	Kazakhstan	14
Lithuania	5	Rwanda	14
Singapore	5	Zambia	16

Signatures

Fewest		Most	
Germany	1	Ethiopia	33
Sweden	1	Mali	33
Australia	2	Georgia	35
Austria	2	Sudan	35
Canada	2	Central African Republic	38
Denmark	2	Nigeria	39
Estonia	2	Azerbaijan	40
Israel	2	Congo, Rep.	42
New Zealand	2	Congo, Dem. Rep.	45
Singapore	2	Iraq	70

Source: Doing Business database.

Make document filing electronic

In 1989 Singapore introduced electronic filing of all documents necessary for trading. TradeNet linked 34 government agencies responsible for customs clearance, export and import permits, import duties, certificates of origin and trade statistics. The trader fills in a single form and sends it to TradeNet. TradeNet reads the application and forwards each section to the relevant agency, which has a limited time to respond. Within 2 years the time for cargo clearance was cut from 4 days to 30 minutes. The number of shipments processed rose threefold, to 32,000 a day. And the cost to businesses of handling trade documents fell by a third.[3] The reform made Singapore one of the easiest places for exporters and enhanced its position as a global trading center (table 9.3).

Many countries have followed suit. Mauritius invited TradeNet's inventors to set up shop in Port Louis. By 1996 the number of documents for exporting fell from 36 to 5. The time to clear customs, from 7 days to 2. From Mauritius the modified TradeNet technology was exported to Ghana. Before its introduction at Kotoka airport and Tema port in 2003, an exporter went through 23 different procedures in 2 weeks. An importer had to submit 13 copies of the shipping manifest to customs. Now 18% of goods at the airport clear in 2 hours, and 75% clear the same day.[4] But at the port improvements have yet to materialize.

Two dozen other countries have implemented electronic filing for trade documents—most in Europe and some in East Asia and Latin America. In Africa, Uganda has made the most progress. In North Africa, Tunisia introduced electronic documents in 2000.[5] Three

FIGURE 9.4

Electronic filing can combine steps and save time

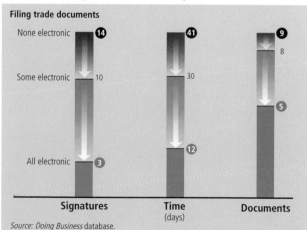

Source: Doing Business database.

documents are processed electronically: the certificate for external trade, the customs declaration and technical control sheets. The payment of customs and port duties is also electronic and takes one hour. Before the reform it took a full day.

In another 50 countries there have been partial advances. In Botswana, Brazil and Russia customs declarations are submitted through the Internet, but other documents are required in hard copy—hardly practical. Delays are reduced but not by much (figure 9.4).

Use a risk assessment policy for inspections

In Africa and South Asia almost 70% of imported cargo containers are opened and inspected when clearing customs (figure 9.5). Every container is opened in Burkina Faso, Kenya, Malawi and Mali. The same is true in Nepal, Pakistan and Sri Lanka. In the Middle East more than 60% are opened and inspected. Contrast this with OECD countries, where 5% of imports undergo inspection.

The difference is explained by the risk assessment policy used in OECD countries. It works like this. When a customs officer receives the cargo documents, she runs them through the computer. A software program calculates the probability that the shipment should be inspected. The probability is based on the profiles of the business and the freight forwarders and on the nature of the goods and their destination. In some countries the containers are scanned for weight and the shapes of objects inside. If nothing suspicious arises, the container gets a green light and sails through customs. Above a certain risk threshold a yellow light comes on and the documentation is thoroughly checked. The container remains sealed. At a still-higher threshold a red light

blinks and the container is opened for inspection. This system has allowed Mexico to limit inspections to 10% of shipments, Thailand to 15%, and Latvia to 20%. It has also increased the detection of smuggled goods.

Risk analysis can reduce delays. Ten years ago shipments took nearly 20 days to clear customs in Peru.[6] By 2000 the introduction of risk analysis meant that green channel goods were cleared in 90 minutes, and even those in the red channel were cleared overnight. By law, only 15% of cargo can go through the red channel.

But risk analysis is only as useful as the data on which it is based. Even the most sophisticated risk analysis software will not help if there is no information

FIGURE 9.5
Many inspections in South Asia

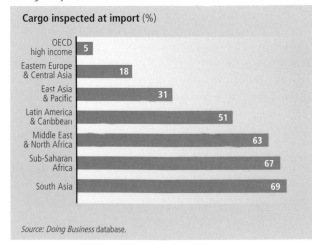

Cargo inspected at import (%)

OECD high income	5
Eastern Europe & Central Asia	18
East Asia & Pacific	31
Latin America & Caribbean	51
Middle East & North Africa	63
Sub-Saharan Africa	67
South Asia	69

Source: Doing Business database.

TABLE 9.4
Who makes importing easy—and who makes it difficult?

Days

Fewest		Most	
Denmark	5	Niger	89
Germany	6	Rwanda	92
Sweden	6	Afghanistan	97
Finland	7	Chad	111
Norway	7	Sudan	111
Netherlands	8	Central African Republic	122
Singapore	8	Burundi	124
Austria	9	Kyrgyz Republic	127
Belgium	9	Iraq	135
United States	9	Uzbekistan	139

Documents

Fewest		Most	
Denmark	3	Azerbaijan	18
Finland	3	Kazakhstan	18
Sweden	3	Kyrgyz Republic	18
Germany	4	Syria	18
Ireland	4	Uzbekistan	18
Netherlands	4	Burundi	19
Norway	4	Iraq	19
United Kingdom	4	Niger	19
Austria	5	Rwanda	19
United States	5	Zambia	19

Signatures

Fewest		Most	
Canada	1	Congo, Rep.	51
Denmark	1	Niger	52
Finland	1	Azerbaijan	55
Germany	1	Burundi	55
Netherlands	1	Afghanistan	57
Sweden	1	Mali	60
Belgium	2	Nigeria	71
Iceland	2	Central African Republic	75
New Zealand	2	Iraq	75
Singapore	2	Congo, Dem. Rep.	80

Source: Doing Business database.

from which to develop the necessary profiles of traders, freight forwarders and the like. Reforms to introduce risk assessment—for example, the one started in 2004 in Timor-Leste—require patience.

Go regional with reform of customs and transport

Being landlocked is viewed as a curse. Yet in Europe being a trader in a landlocked country is not that different from being one elsewhere. It takes 1 day to get imports to Berlin from the port of Hamburg, and just 2 extra days to get them to Bratislava in landlocked Slovakia. European integration gets the credit. Once on land, the cargo moves effortlessly across borders. There are no further checks.

African entrepreneurs like Fabien face delays of 65 days if importing to landlocked countries, but only 38 days to countries with a port. Yet there is no reason why landlocked Burkina Faso, Mali and Niger and the other countries of West Africa cannot replicate some of Europe's reforms and move off the list of the most difficult countries for importing (table 9.4). In southern Africa, Botswana, Namibia, Lesotho and South Africa share customs forms. This reduces paperwork and cost. The next step for them is to remove border checks altogether and introduce harmonized transport rules.

Beware of contracting out preshipment inspection and customs management

When the reputation of the customs office is damaged, because of long delays or corruption, reformers may contract out the service to a private company. This re-

form was successful in Bulgaria, where it started in 2002. By the following year annual customs revenue rose by 18%, or nearly $500 million.[7] The number of fines for smuggling increased threefold, to 12,000 a year.

It rarely works so smoothly. In Mozambique customs were contracted out in 1996. Few of the goals set in the management agreement had been met by 1999. One bright spot: the seizure of smuggled shipments tripled from 559 in 1997 to 1,709 in 1999.[8] But delays remained the same. Customs revenue increased somewhat, but mostly because of greater trade volume. The management agreement was extended in the hope of better results. In other countries contracting is blamed for increased corruption: several high-profile cases have made the news in recent years.[9]

In many developing countries the contracting out of preshipment inspection has been a disappointment. Angola, Benin, the Republic of Congo, Côte d'Ivoire and Togo, among others, all have concession agreements for the management of cargo inspections. Two complaints are heard most often. First, to increase revenue, private inspection companies push for new regulation to make preshipment inspection mandatory for all cargo. This increases trade costs. Second, inspection companies introduce their own forms to fill out, on top of the documents already required by customs. If a trader sends goods to a country where preshipment inspection is contracted out to a company different from the one in his country, he has to fill out nearly 3 times as many forms. That's the case for an entrepreneur in Angola sending goods to Togo, for example.

Why reform?

For manufactured exports, the cost of trade transactions in developing countries—which includes the cost of dealing with customs and the cost of inland transport—exceeds the cost imposed by tariffs in the European Union and the United States. Red tape is estimated to cost more than 10% of the value of exports in developing countries.[10] Trade costs represent 14% of the value of exports in Georgia and 18% in Nigeria. And inefficient customs and trade transport mean that businesses must hold larger inventories at their warehouse, adding 4–6% to production costs.[11] "Just in time" manufacturing is just a dream.

The countries that have efficient customs and trade transport—fewer documents and signatures, less time

necessary to comply with procedures—export and import more (figure 9.6). They also make it cheaper for exporters to operate. Studies suggest that each additional day in transport delays costs 0.5% of the cargo value for goods transported by ship or rail. In other words, if transporting a cargo now takes 20 days and reform can reduce transport time to 10 days, it may save the exporter 5% of the cargo's value.[12] Even poor countries can make rapid progress, as the burden imposed by complicated procedures exceeds that imposed by poor transport infrastructure.

Filing more documents is associated with more corruption in customs (see figure 9.6). Faced with long delays and frequent demands for bribes, many traders avoid customs altogether. Instead, they smuggle goods across the border. Smuggling defeats the very reason to

FIGURE 9.6
More red tape in trading—less trade, larger bribes

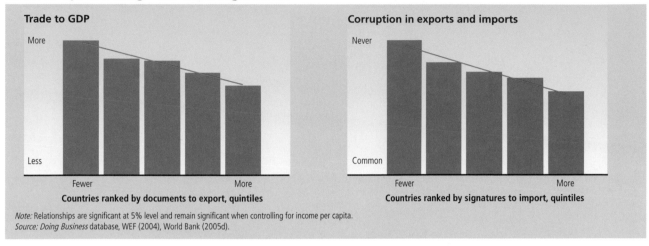

Note: Relationships are significant at 5% level and remain significant when controlling for income per capita.
Source: Doing Business database, WEF (2004), World Bank (2005d).

have border control of trade: to ensure high quality of goods and levy taxes.

That brings us back to Fabien, the shop owner in Burundi. High transport and customs costs may not be his biggest headache. Demand is low—a new bicycle is a luxury for most people in Burundi, where annual incomes average $90. And the police periodically come to his shop to receive "presents." But if the government wants to make it easier to run businesses, reducing trade costs is a good place to start.

Notes

1. Bhagwati (2004).

2. Freund (2000).

3. De Wulf (2004).

4. De Wulf (2004).

5. Alavi (2004).

6. Goorman (2004).

7. Velchev (2005). Some of this increase is due to a favorable exchange rate with the dollar during this period.

8. Mwangi (2004).

9. For example, a consultant for Société Générale de Surveillance (SGS), a Swiss company, is alleged to have channeled $9 million to a former prime minister of Pakistan, to persuade the government to retain SGS. See Miller and Balgobin (2002).

10. UNCTAD (2004).

11. See Hausman, Subramanian and Lee (2005) and Subramanian and Anderson (2005).

12. Hummels (2001).

Enforcing contracts

Who is reforming?

What to reform?

Why reform?

Tiago, who runs a textiles business in Timor-Leste, summarizes his experience with the courts: "I never use them. None of the businesses that I deal with use them either. What's the point? Whoever pays the larger bribe wins the case. Even then, collecting your debt would be a miracle." A miracle indeed— it takes 69 procedures and 990 days to resolve a commercial dispute in the country's courts. To collect a debt of $1,000, a business would have to pay $1,800 in court and attorney fees, making Timor-Leste the most difficult place to enforce a contract (table 10.1).

The inefficiency of the courts in Timor-Leste may be extreme, but there is room for improvement everywhere. The most common complaint involves delays in the courts and in executing judgments once a judge has ruled (figure 10.1). The second most common complaint is protracted appeals. The third is incompetent court clerks, bailiffs and other judicial officials. And corruption is considered a problem in 43 countries.

In 2004, 16 countries reformed procedures for contract enforcement. Serbia and Montenegro cut nearly 400 days off the time it takes to go through court. Kazakhstan, Latvia, Slovenia and Vietnam also reduced delays.

The most popular reform was to streamline appeals and impose time limits on their filing. Five countries—Brazil, Burundi, the Czech Republic, Romania and Rwanda—introduced rules to ensure that debtors do not abuse the process. The time and cost savings allowed more businesses to use the courts. Uganda saw a 62% increase in commercial cases filed after similar reforms in 2002. "We have more faith in the courts now, more trust," says Musoke, a local businessman. "The president is now mentioning us in his speeches," adds a judge in Kampala.

TABLE 10.1
Where is enforcing contracts easy—and where not?

Easiest	Most difficult
Norway	Benin
Denmark	Kyrgyz Republic
Japan	Congo, Rep.
New Zealand	Syria
Iceland	Chad
Tunisia	Sudan
Lithuania	Cameroon
Greece	Central African Republic
Switzerland	Congo, Dem. Rep.
United States	Timor-Leste

Note: Rankings on the ease of enforcing contracts are the average of the country rankings on the procedures, time and cost to collect a debt through the courts. See the Data notes for details.
Source: Doing Business database.

FIGURE 10.1
What is the biggest obstacle to enforcing a contract?

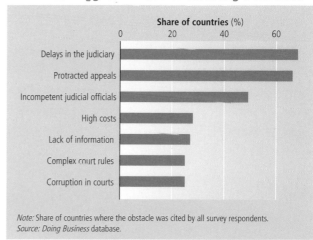

Note: Share of countries where the obstacle was cited by all survey respondents.
Source: Doing Business database.

Who is reforming?

Serbia and Montenegro, the country with the third longest delay in 2003, went from 1,028 days to 635 days. Two new laws—on civil procedure and enforcement of judgments—were passed. These contain strict time limits. For example, a debtor has only 3 days to file an appeal after the judge rules. The judge then has 3 days to decide its merit. Previously this back-and-forth could take 10 months.

Africa has the least efficient courts. But 2 countries made significant reforms in 2004. Burundi introduced a new summary procedure for debt recovery, requiring fewer steps and written statements. In addition, the deadline for filing an appeal was cut from 60 days to 30. And enforcement can now be done by private bailiffs, not just by court officials. Similar reforms in Colombia in 2003 and in Slovakia in 2002 have enjoyed tremendous success.

Rwanda created specialized chambers in trial courts for litigation related to business, financial and tax matters. Moreover, 1 professional judge now presides over such cases, assisted by 2 lay judges. Previously a 3-judge jury was required. "I was suspicious of the changes at first, but now I am a believer. Cases that sat in the courts for years are now resolved in months," says Andre, a trader. Still, big problems remain: some chambers have yet to become operational for lack of trained lay judges.

The top 10 reformers cut the average time to resolve

FIGURE 10.2
Reforms cut time in court for entrepreneurs

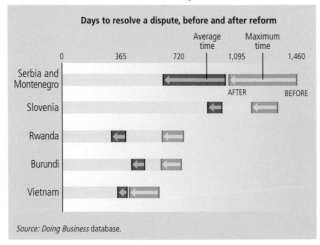

Source: *Doing Business* database.

TABLE 10.2
Major court reforms in 2004

Reform	Country
Streamlined appeals	Belarus, Brazil, Burundi, Czech Republic, Romania, Rwanda, Serbia and Montenegro
Shortened time for enforcement	Germany, Kazakhstan, Latvia, Poland, Rwanda
Set time limits on judgments	Philippines, Rwanda, Serbia and Montenegro, Vietnam
Introduced summary proceedings	Burundi, Latvia
Established case management	Slovenia

Source: *Doing Business* database.

a dispute by 12%, with Serbia and Montenegro reducing delays by 38% and Rwanda by 22% (figure 10.2). Reforms also lowered costs—for example, in Rwanda attorney fees fell by 15%. The most popular court reform in 2004—introduced in 7 countries—dealt with delays in appeals (table 10.2). Burundi, Romania and Rwanda introduced a rehearing with the judge who presided over the original case and has already reviewed the evidence. This is in lieu of a first appeal and saves considerable time. Previously appellate judges reviewed the evidence from scratch. Now they review the process, not the evidence. Brazil and Serbia and Montenegro set time limits on the filing of appeals. These reforms may seem like an attack on due process, and there is clearly a balance to be struck between the rights of debtors and creditors. Yet the trend in streamlining appeals suggests that excessive delays deny justice more than a well-intentioned but prone-to-abuse appeals process.

The second most common reform—introduced in 6 countries—shortened time for the enforcement of judgments. Establishing case management systems in the courts continues to be the main reform in transition economies. In Armenia reforms have become so popular that the country's most-watched television drama features the deputy minister of justice in an improvised court. Viewers are now asking for legal advice and assistance as they recognize that the courts can now resolve disputes effectively.

What to reform?

Courts should be fast, fair and affordable. Long delays, as experienced in Italy and Guatemala (table 10.3), force businesses to look for other means of resolving disputes. If going to court is expensive, as in Timor-Leste and the Democratic Republic of Congo, fewer business transactions occur—and those that do involve only a small group of people linked by kinship, ethnicity or previous dealings. Less wealth is created.

Three reforms are most urgent:
- Reduce delays in deciding cases.
- Cut the number of appeals to the supreme court.
- Make enforcement competitive.

Reduce delays in deciding cases

Four types of reform reduce the time it takes to enforce a contract. One is introducing summary proceedings or simplified trial procedures. Another is simplifying procedures for collecting and hearing evidence. A third is changing case management practices. The final one is using lower courts to decide simple commercial cases.

In a summary proceeding the creditor need only present the judge with evidence of the transaction and nonpayment. Debt cases no longer go through preliminary investigation before court clerks. In Burundi this reform cut nearly 3 months off the time to recover debt. In Latvia the creditor can enforce payment immediately after the hearing. Not all reforms bring the desired results. For example, in Poland a simplified trial procedure exists for small claims up to $3,000. But few people use it. Restricted access—with claims arising from unpaid utility bills ineligible—and court fees that equal those for the regular procedure explain the lack of enthusiasm.

In 94 countries only written evidence is admitted for a judge's consideration. When judges hear cases, they read and approve the record of any new evidence. This takes days, sometimes weeks, to transcribe. In 2004 Brazil allowed oral evidence in its courts. In Germany a judge need no longer hear witnesses or experts if they have already testified on the same matter before another judge. This is possible even without the consent of the parties to the case. And if judges decide they have enough evidence, they can interrupt hearings and issue judgments. In Finland hearings are now optional. Judges can decide on cases based solely on the evidence submitted.

Case management is illustrated by Slovenia's reforms, which involved 2 changes. First, judges are re-

TABLE 10.3

Where is enforcing contracts the most efficient—and where the least?

Procedures (number)

Fewest		Most	
Australia	11	Kuwait	52
Greece	14	Lao PDR	53
Iceland	14	United Arab Emirates	53
Norway	14	Egypt	55
Tunisia	14	Cameroon	58
United Kingdom	14	Sierra Leone	58
Denmark	15	Iraq	65
Uganda	15	São Tomé and Príncipe	67
Hong Kong, China	16	Sudan	67
Ireland	16	Timor-Leste	69

Time (days)

Least		Most	
Tunisia	27	Lebanon	721
Netherlands	48	Nigeria	730
New Zealand	50	Congo, Dem. Rep.	909
Japan	60	Slovenia	913
Singapore	69	Sudan	915
France	75	Poland	980
Korea	75	Timor-Leste	990
Denmark	83	Angola	1,011
Norway	87	Italy	1,390
Belgium	112	Guatemala	1,459

Cost (% of overdue debt)

Least		Most	
Norway	4.2	São Tomé and Príncipe	69.5
New Zealand	4.8	Central African Republic	72.2
Switzerland	5.2	Burkina Faso	95.4
Denmark	5.3	Papua New Guinea	110.3
Korea	5.4	Bhutan	113.8
Sweden	5.9	Cambodia	121.3
Belgium	6.2	Indonesia	126.5
Finland	6.5	Malawi	136.5
United States	7.5	Timor-Leste	183.1
Taiwan, China	7.7	Congo, Dem. Rep.	256.8

Source: Doing Business database.

sponsible for following cases from start to finish rather than sending the parties from one court administrator to another. Second, a preliminary hearing clarifies the nature of the dispute so that parties come to the main hearing prepared. In its first year case management has cut Slovenia's average time to resolve disputes by 90 days.

Attorney fees tend to be lower in countries with case management: the average cost of resolving a dispute about a debt is 15% of the debt's value in countries with case management and 29% in countries without, even after controlling for income per capita. This is because cases move faster. Georgia is implementing case management in 15 pilot courts. In these courts the number of cases pending for more than a year dropped 23% by June 2005 compared with a year earlier. In contrast, the number of such cases fell by 5% in other courts.

Vietnam expedited contract enforcement by 2 months by moving cases to lower jurisdictions. This was accomplished by abolishing a provision mandating that provincial courts hear cases involving more than 50 million dong ($3,200). Such cases now go to district courts. A similar reform in Lao PDR in 2003 allowed debt collection cases worth less than $2,500 to be handled in district courts.

Cut the number of appeals to the supreme court

Appeals are necessary for fair justice and are allowed in every country. But they needn't automatically go all the way to the supreme court. Such abuse is exemplified in Brazil, where debtors use the tactic to stall enforcement: 88% of judgments in commercial cases are appealed. As a result Brazil's supreme court handles more than 115,000 cases a year. In comparison, the U.S. supreme court takes about 200 cases, as it deals mainly with constitutional issues. Federal circuit courts and state courts of appeal are the main venue for appeals on commercial cases. These intermediate courts are the most important source of due process for litigants. Access to them is generally easy since the grounds for appeal to the supreme court are limited.

The old system in the Czech Republic worked like this: when a debtor appealed the decision of the first-instance court, the case was sent to an appeals court, which often overruled the decision and sent the case for retrial to the original court. Now the appeals court has expanded authority to issue a final and binding judgement. Fewer cases go to the supreme court. As a result the process is 4 months shorter.

Not everyone has gotten such reforms right. The 2004 civil procedure code in Burkina Faso establishes a stay on the execution of appealed judgments under several conditions. If granted, the stay could last 2 years while the case is sent to the supreme court. This more than doubles the average time to enforce a contract: rather than 446 days, such a case would take more than 1,200. A possible fix is to introduce an appeal bond—money put aside by the debtor until the appeal is considered. Such bonds are used to guarantee that judgments will be satisfied after appeals. The money should be allowed to accumulate interest, as its value may deteriorate quickly in countries with high inflation.

Make enforcement competitive

The best way to speed the recovery of overdue debt is by allowing competition in enforcing judgments. Colombia did this in 2003 by scrapping the monopoly of the courts to enforce judges' rulings. Private companies quickly moved into the business. The result: time was cut by nearly 2 months.

Hungary and Slovakia have introduced private enforcement in the past 5 years. In the Netherlands a 2001 reform removed territorial monopolies of private enforcement companies. Now they compete for business nationally. Kazakhstan has done the same, as has Burundi. In Kazakhstan it takes 20 days fewer to recover overdue debt. The effects in Burundi are still unclear, as the new industry is just being created.

Why reform?

There are several strong arguments for court reform. First, easier contract enforcement is associated with higher bank lending (figure 10.3). Consider Italy. A study of 27 judicial districts found that the average commercial case lasts 53 months, or nearly 4.5 years.[1] This is just over the 1,390 days documented using the *Doing Business* methodology. The delays cause large case backlogs. In efficient judicial districts like Venice, there are 22 cases pending per 1,000 inhabitants. Lending to the private sector is equivalent to 40% of the region's annual income. In Calabria, where the backlog is 50 cases per 1,000 inhabitants, lending is just 10% of the region's income. The price of loans is affected as well. Banks in Italian regions with the shortest court delays extended loans at 4 percentage points less interest than in regions with the longest delays.

Second, efficient courts increase entry by new firms and hiring by established ones. In Central and Eastern Europe cumbersome court procedures are associated with an 8% reduction in the number of new businesses. They also limit company growth: businesses, that are otherwise similar hire 18% fewer workers in countries with slow contract enforcement.[2]

Third, reform reduces demands on the government budget. For example, Croatia, Poland, Serbia and Montenegro and Slovenia have the most judges and court administrative staff (on a per capita basis) in Europe. These countries also have the most complex court procedures and longest court delays in the region. Simplified con-

FIGURE 10.3
Better courts—more credit

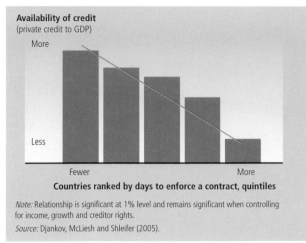

Note: Relationship is significant at 1% level and remains significant when controlling for income, growth and creditor rights.
Source: Djankov, McLiesh and Shleifer (2005).

FIGURE 10.4
Large staff numbers in some European courts

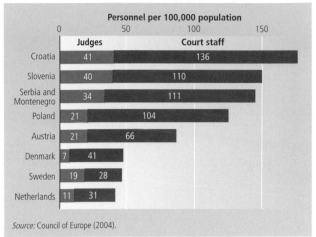

Source: Council of Europe (2004).

tract enforcement would temper requests for larger court budgets. Dutch and Danish courts, for example, have only a quarter of the judges and administrators used in Croatia on a per capita basis (figure 10.4).

If Bulgaria were to adopt the Estonian process for enforcing contracts, which would imply revising the civil procedure code, a third of its judiciary budget could be reallocated to better uses.[3] An easier judicial process would also bring more cases to the courts, as an estimated

FIGURE 10.5
Fewer procedures—less bribery

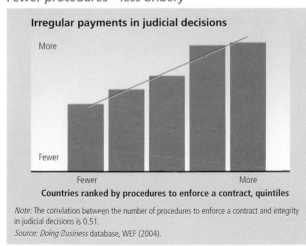

Note: The correlation between the number of procedures to enforce a contract and integrity in judicial decisions is 0.51.
Source: Doing Business database, WEF (2004).

$4 billion in overdue credit is currently handled outside the judicial system. Analysis suggests that in just 5 years such reform might create about 70,000 jobs, since more money would be available for new business activity.

Fourth, the integrity of the judiciary is higher in countries with faster resolution of cases and fewer procedures (figure 10.5). And businesses use courts more if they see value in their dispute resolution services.

Legal experts often argue that stricter procedural requirements lead to more fairness. They do not, at least in developing countries. Procedural complexity makes it difficult for typical businesses to understand the process. As a result they avoid courts in favor of simpler, often informal, alternatives.[4] And countries with more procedures to enforce a contract, such as Egypt, are not the ones where businesses consider the process fairer. Quite the opposite: a World Bank survey of more than 10,000 enterprises in 82 countries shows that fewer procedures are associated with more fairness and impartiality in the legal system.[5] This makes for happier clients and a more credible justice system.

Notes

1. Jappelli, Pagano and Bianco (2005).
2   Desai, Gompers and Lerner (2004).
3. Dimitrov and Stanchev (2005).
4. See recent evidence on Poland in World Bank (2005c).
5. Batra, Kaufmann and Stone (2003).

Closing a business

Who is reforming?

What to reform?

Why reform?

"To my friends, everything. To my enemies, the law," says a Brazilian proverb. The case of Engesa shows why. In 1985 the Brazilian manufacturer hit financial difficulties. When its fortunes continued to fall and workers became redundant, there was no cash for severance. Engesa filed for reorganization in 1990. A complicated liquidation trial was launched, with the judge besieged by disputes and appeals. It took more than 2 years just to compile a list of claimants. Fifteen years after the bankruptcy filing, less than half the debts have been resolved.

No more. Brazil passed a new bankruptcy law in 2004. A reorganization procedure gives troubled companies a better chance to stay alive. Creditors have more power to influence the proceedings. Secured creditors enjoy preference over tax claims, and labor claims are limited. The expected time to go through bankruptcy was halved, from 10 years to 5. If Brazil's new law works as a similar law in Spain did, it could inject 204 billion reals into the economy in 6 years.[1] If this money were put to productive uses, more than 400,000 jobs could be saved.[2]

Brazil joins 88 other countries with major reforms to bankruptcy law since World War II. More than half the reforms happened in the past 10 years, and most in rich countries. The reforms have typically worked. Recovery rates for bankruptcy claimants—creditors, workers and government—are significantly higher for the reformers, even controlling for country income levels (figure 11.1). The reason: reformed bankruptcy regimes allow viable businesses to weather a short-term liquidity crisis, and insolvent businesses are rapidly liquidated.

Every country needs effective procedures for closing a failed business or saving a viable one that is experienc-

ing temporary problems. But bankruptcy is not the only solution. In poor countries bankruptcy is rarely used. Rich countries averaged around 10,000 bankruptcy filings between 1999 and 2003. Poor countries, fewer than 50. Cameroon, Georgia and Lao PDR have each seen fewer than 10.

These countries are not short of failed enterprises. But it is naive to expect that complex bankruptcy proceedings will rejuvenate businesses. Even in rich countries rates of successful reorganization, where the business comes out of bankruptcy without changing ownership or management, are low—12% in the United States, 3% in France and 2% in the United Kingdom.[3] Reformers in poor countries would do better to focus on improving foreclosure of secured debt outside of bankruptcy, thus reducing reliance on the courts.

FIGURE 11.1

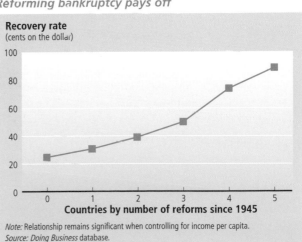

Note: Relationship remains significant when controlling for income per capita.
Source: Doing Business database.

Who is reforming?

Bankruptcy laws were revamped in 9 countries during 2004. Seven of them—Brazil, Finland, Indonesia, Japan, Portugal, Serbia and Montenegro and Vietnam—passed new bankruptcy acts. But Madagascar and Thailand reduced efficiency with amendments making bankruptcy more complex.

In Portugal a new insolvency code sped proceedings and enlarged creditors' powers. The law provides for a single insolvency proceeding. The judge, administrator and creditors jointly examine the company's prospects and decide whether to pursue liquidation or reorganization. In the old system liquidation and reorganization were pursued through separate channels. The new system expands the range of conditions that trigger proceedings, making it easier to file for bankruptcy. The changes cut 6 months off the time to go through insolvency. Recovery rates, calculated using the *Doing Business* methodology, jumped from 69 cents on the dollar to 75 (figure 11.2).

In Serbia and Montenegro recovery rates are expected to jump by 45%—to 29 cents on the dollar— thanks to a new law adopted in August 2004. Under the old laws few private companies went through bankruptcy proceedings, because that could take up to 12 years. The new law sets strict time limits: parties have 5 days to raise objections to the resolution, appeals must be made within 8 days after the ruling, and the court has 30 days to issue a decision on an appeal. The changes will cut the time to an estimated 1.5 years.

East Asia saw the most reform. Indonesia and Vietnam clarified and improved their bankruptcy laws. Indonesia's new law gives more precise definitions and codifies case law. Creditors now have expanded powers to file and vote on reorganization plans. *Doing Business* respondents estimate that the time to resolve bankruptcy has fallen by 6 months, increasing recovery from 10 cents on the dollar to 13.

Vietnam's 1993 bankruptcy law had been rarely used in the past dozen years. Only 45 businesses were declared bankrupt, and many of those were state owned. The 2004 law makes it easier to file for bankruptcy. Only one condition is required: that a business be unable to pay a due debt on request. Before, the business also had to suffer losses for 2 years and attempt reorganization. Another change: secured creditors' claims rank ahead of those of the tax office. The reforms are expected to cut 6 months off the process. And recovery rates have

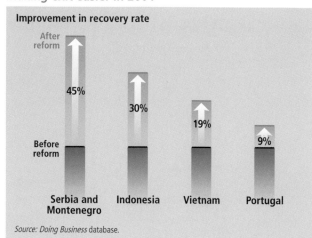

FIGURE 11.2
Making exit easier in 2004

Improvement in recovery rate

Source: *Doing Business* database.

increased from 16 cents on the dollar to 19.

Japan's reforms sped bankruptcy by allowing more companies to file in the better-equipped Tokyo and Osaka courts and permitting the liquidator to sell assets free of other claims. Before, consent of all creditors was required to sell assets, delaying the process. Finland improved efficiency by abolishing a 3-stage appointment of the administrator. But costs rose slightly because powers were transferred from the court to the (more expensive) administrator. Both countries changed the priority order of claimants. Japan now favors the bankruptcy trustee, taxes and employees. Finland favors secured creditors.

Some reforms were for the worse. A common tactic for delaying the bankruptcy process is to appeal: Thailand made it easier for debtors to use and abuse the appeals process. It abolished a 1999 provision that limited interlocutory appeals—appeals of decisions during the trial—as well as appeals on reorganization. On the bright side the reforms reduced asset collection fees, cutting costs by 2%. Madagascar—the only African reformer—also went backward, introducing complex reorganization provisions in a country that has had only a handful of bankruptcies. Delays increased.

Another dozen countries made minor changes. FYR Macedonia streamlined asset auction procedures and will introduce a new bankruptcy law in 2006. Burkina Faso increased the number of judges and cut the backlog of bankruptcy cases. In Bosnia and Herzegovina only 8 months of salary now take priority over secured creditors. Before the reform all salaries owed had priority. Chile, Italy and Slovakia adopted changes that will come into effect in late 2005.

What to reform?

Bankruptcy is hopelessly inefficient in most countries. Claims are eroded by long delays, by high costs and by laws that either kill viable businesses or keep unviable ones alive. On average, only 32 cents of every dollar owed creditors, workers, tax agencies and other claimants are available for distribution. South Asian countries have the worst recovery rate, averaging 17 cents, followed by African countries with 27 cents. Only in the OECD and some middle-income economies can creditors recover half or more of overdue debt (table 11.1).

Poor countries can most easily boost recovery rates by improving foreclosure processes. For middle-income countries, speeding liquidation should be the priority. Other helpful reforms: providing specialized expertise, limiting appeals, reducing court powers and paying administrators for maximizing the estate value. These were discussed in earlier editions of *Doing Business*. Reforms can also:

- Encourage continuous operation of viable businesses.
- Set up creditors' committees.
- Give entrepreneurs a chance for a fresh start.

Encourage continuous operation of viable businesses

Efficient bankruptcy laws break up unviable firms and save viable ones. In the hope of keeping viable firms alive, more than 60 countries have adopted reorganization laws in the past 25 years. But adopting reorganization is not the same thing as helping distressed businesses restructure their finances and operations.

Albania's reorganization procedure has not preserved a single viable business. And countries in which *Doing Business* respondents indicate that a firm will go through reorganization proceedings are no more likely to save viable firms (figure 11.3). Procedures such as Algeria's, Ecuador's and, until 2004, Vietnam's—which require attempts at reorganization before liquidation—seldom keep a viable firm in operation.

TABLE 11.1
Where is bankruptcy the most efficient—and where the least?

Time (years)

Least		Most	
Ireland	0.4	Philippines	5.7
Japan	0.6	Belarus	5.8
Canada	0.8	Turkey	5.9
Singapore	0.8	Angola	6.2
Taiwan, China	0.8	Oman	7.0
Belgium	0.9	Mauritania	8.0
Finland	0.9	Czech Republic	9.2
Norway	0.9	Brazil	10.0
Spain	1.0	Chad	10.0
United Kingdom	1.0	India	10.0

Cost (% of estate)

Least		Most	
Colombia	1.0	Albania	38
Kuwait	1.0	Dominican Republic	38
Netherlands	1.0	Philippines	38
Norway	1.0	Venezuela	38
Singapore	1.0	Guyana	42
Belgium	3.5	Sierra Leone	42
Canada	3.5	Ukraine	42
Finland	3.5	Chad	63
Japan	3.5	Central African Republic	76
Taiwan, China	3.5	Lao PDR	76

Recovery rate (cents on the dollar)

Highest		Lowest	
Japan	92.6	Haiti	2.9
Singapore	91.3	Niger	2.6
Norway	91.1	Zimbabwe	2.1
Canada	90.1	Congo, Dem. Rep.	1.6
Taiwan, China	89.4	Angola	0.6
Finland	89.0	Brazil	0.5
Ireland	88.0	Timor-Leste	0.0
Netherlands	86.7	Lao PDR	0.0
Belgium	86.6	Central African Republic	0.0
United Kingdom	85.3	Chad	0.0

Source: Doing Business database.

FIGURE 11.3
Reorganization does not mean viable businesses get saved

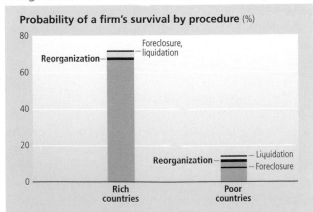

Probability of a firm's survival by procedure (%)

Note: Different procedures make no significant difference in survival rates.
Source: Doing Business database.

FIGURE 11.4
Higher recovery with creditor involvement

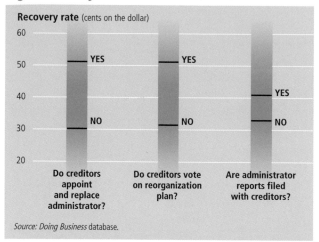

Source: *Doing Business* database.

FIGURE 11.5
How to discourage entrepreneurs: penalize the honest ones

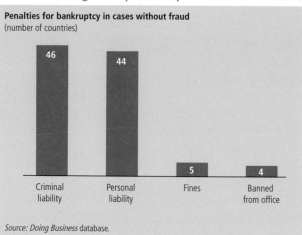

Source: *Doing Business* database.

Foreclosures and liquidations, by contrast, can keep businesses in operation. Foreclosure often leads to the sale of the entire firm to new owners, who keep it running as a going concern. And even in liquidation the firm can keep operating, as in Botswana, Denmark, Poland and Sweden. Creditors win, because saving viable firms yields higher recovery. Workers win too, because they keep their jobs.

There are better ways than reorganization to save viable firms. First, don't require interruption of business operations. Twenty-five countries require firms to discontinue operations once the bankruptcy petition is approved. Second, keep the bankruptcy process moving. By the time companies are in their third year of bankruptcy, the chance of surviving is slim. Short processes help maximize the value of the estate. Long ones often lead to the stripping of enterprise assets.

Brazil's new law encourages going-concern sales at the beginning of liquidation and allows buyers to take assets free of tax and labor liabilities. Previously asset sales could start only after liquidation proceedings ended, and they were subject to existing claims. Other reforms also help. One is allowing the administrator to rescind or compel performance on contracts. Another: letting the business obtain fresh loans that have priority for the lender—which could increase the chance of survival from 22% to 38%. And yet another: allowing management to dismiss employees during the bankruptcy process to help keep the company going. Many jobs will be saved if a viable business can continue operating. The benefits are large. Countries that keep viable firms alive have recovery averaging 59 cents on the dollar. Those that don't, 21 cents.

Set up creditors' committees

Finland's reforms gave creditors the right to set up a creditors' committee that advises the administrator. This is obligatory for large estates. Six of the other 8 reformers expanded the powers of creditors. Doing so is associated with higher recovery rates (figure 11.4). The reason is that such reforms align the incentives of creditors with reorganizing viable firms and closing down unviable ones. When creditors participate in decisions, proceedings tend to maximize recovery. And when creditors have the right to choose which bankruptcy procedure to follow—reorganization or liquidation—they opt for reorganization only when the chances of successful recovery are high.

Other countries are recognizing the benefits of involving creditors. Chile's reforms in May 2005 authorized creditors—rather than the courts—to appoint the trustee. Slovakia's upcoming bankruptcy law does the same. Indonesia's reform gives secured creditors the right to vote in reorganization. And Brazil's also brings secured creditors into the voting on reorganization proceedings.

Give entrepreneurs a chance for a fresh start

In Greece bankrupt entrepreneurs lose their trading license. A Lithuanian entrepreneur may face criminal penalties even in the absence of fraud. Such measures are common. In two-thirds of countries managers of bankrupt firms can be punished for negligence even if there is no fraud (figure 11.5). In 39% of countries managers can be barred from taking corporate positions. The ban lasts an average of 4 years. In Chad and Lebanon it lasts 10.

Such measures discourage the use of bankruptcy. And they dampen entrepreneurship: studies in the United States show that entrepreneurs try several business ideas before succeeding. Punishing fraud is justified, but bankruptcy is different. An entrepreneur can have bad luck or make mistakes. Bankrupt debtors face stigma anyway. Why compound it with legal penalties?

Reforming such penalty provisions in bankruptcy laws has been popular. Madagascar's new law separates management sanction from liquidation. Previously they were one and the same, whether or not there was fraud. Thailand's 2004 reform distinguishes fraudulent bankrupts from those in good faith. In Poland before 2003, bankrupt entrepreneurs were automatically banned from getting a fresh start for 5 years. Now it could be for 3–10 years, but only if the court decides the case involves fraud. The United Kingdom's Enterprise Act of 2002 removed automatic penalties on bankrupt debtors.

Why reform?

Bottlenecks in bankruptcy cut the amount that claimants can recover.[4] In countries where bankruptcy is used, this is a strong deterrent to investment. Access to credit shrinks. And nonperforming loans and financial risk rise because creditors cannot recover overdue loans (figure 11.6). Even in poor countries, where bankruptcy is rarely used, efficient laws can serve as a threat and encourage debtors to negotiate and restructure outside of bankruptcy. In Egypt an estimated 95% of bankruptcy filings are made to speed informal workouts and enforcement.[5]

Easier exit means easier entry. Bankruptcy laws can also encourage entrepreneurs. One study shows that reforms to encourage a fresh start have raised rates of entrepreneurship by 8–9%.[6] The freedom to fail, and to do so through an efficient process, puts people and capital to its most effective use. The result is more productive businesses, and more jobs.

FIGURE 11.6

Higher recovery—fewer defaults, fewer credit constraints

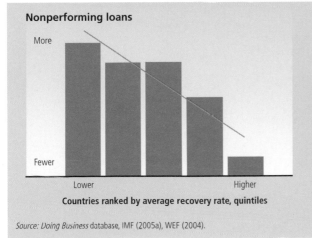

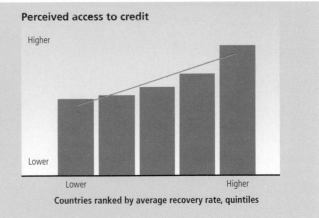

Source: *Doing Business* database, IMF (2005a), WEF (2004).

Notes

1. *Gazeta Mercantil* (Brazil), "New Bankruptcy Law Could Inject R$204 bn," June 2, 2005.

2. Azar and Lu (2004).

3. Couwenberg (2001).

4. World Bank (2004a) and Franks and Loranth (2005).

5. Data from *Doing Business* local partners.

6. Armour and Cumming (2005).

References

Acemoglu, Daron. 2001. "Credit Market Imperfections and Persistent Unemployment." *European Economic Review* 45 (4–6): 665–79.

Alavi, Hamid. 2004. "Good Practice in Trade Facilitation: Lessons from Tunisia." PREM Economic Policy Note 89. World Bank, Washington, D.C.

Alesina, Alberto, Silvia Ardagna, Giuseppe Nicoletti and Fabio Schiantarelli. 2003. *Regulation and Investment.* NBER Working Paper 9560. Cambridge, Mass.: National Bureau of Economic Research.

Alm, James, Patricia Annez and Arbind Modi. 2004. "Stamp Duties in Indian States: A Case for Reform." Policy Research Working Paper 3413. World Bank, Washington, D.C.

Angrist, Joshua, and Adriana Kugler. 2003. "Protective or Counter-Productive? Labor Market Institutions and the Effect of Immigration on EU Natives." *Economic Journal* 113 (488): 302–31.

Armour, John, and Douglas Cumming. 2005. "Bankruptcy Law and Entrepreneurship." University of Cambridge Centre for Business Research Working Paper 300.

Avery, Robert, Paul Calem and Glenn Canner. 2004. "Credit Report Accuracy and Access to Credit." *Federal Reserve Board Bulletin* (summer): 297–322.

Azar, Ziad Raymond, and Marcelo Lu. 2004. "Comparing the Old and New Brazilian Bankruptcy Law." Inter-American Trade Report 12(3).

Batra, Geeta, Daniel Kaufmann and Andrew Stone. 2003. *Investment Climate around the World: Voices of the Firms from the World Business Environment Survey.* Washington, D.C.: World Bank.

Berglof, Erik, and Stijn Claessens. 2004. "Enforcement and Corporate Governance." Policy Research Working Paper 3409. World Bank, Washington, D.C.

Bertrand, Marianne, and Francis Kramarz. 2002. "Does Entry Regulation Hinder Job Creation? Evidence from the French Retail Industry." *Quarterly Journal of Economics* 117 (4): 1369–413.

Bhagwati, Jagdish. 2004. *In Defense of Globalization.* Oxford: Oxford University Press.

Bird, Richard. 2003. "Administrative Dimensions of Tax Reform." Draft module prepared for course on Practical Issues of Tax Policy in Developing Countries, World Bank, Washington, D.C., April 28–May 1.

Bird, Richard, and Oliver Oldman. 2000. "Improving Taxpayer Service and Facilitating Compliance in Singapore." PREM Note 48. World Bank, Poverty Reduction and Economic Management Network, Washington, D.C. http://www1 .worldbank.org/prem/PREMNotes/premnote 48.pdf.

Black, Bernard. 2001. "The Legal and Institutional Preconditions for Strong Securities Markets." *UCLA Law Review* 48 (3): 781–855.

Blanchard, Olivier, and Thomas Philippon. 2004. "The Quality of Labor Regulations and Unemployment." Massachusetts Institute of Technology, Department of Economics, Cambridge, Mass.

Blanchard, Olivier, and Pedro Portugal. 1998. *What Hides Behind an Unemployment Rate: Comparing Portuguese and U.S. Unemployment.* NBER Working Paper 6636. Cambridge, Mass.: National Bureau of Economic Research.

Bolaky, Bineswaree, and Caroline Freund. 2004. "Trade, Regulations, and Growth." Policy Research Working Paper 3255. World Bank, Washington, D.C.

Botero, Juan, Simeon Djankov, Rafael La Porta, Florencio López-de-Silanes and Andrei Shleifer. 2004. "The Regulation of Labor." *Quarterly Journal of Economics* 119 (4): 1339–82.

Burns, Tony. 2005. "Registering Property: Country Case Studies of Reform in Armenia, Ghana, New Zealand, Peru, Thailand." Working paper. World Bank Group, Private Sector Development Vice Presidency, Monitoring, Analysis and Policy Unit, Washington, D.C.

Caballero, Ricardo, Kevin Cowan, Eduardo Engel and Alejandro Micco. 2005. "Effective Labor Regulation and Microeconomic Flexibility." MIT Department of Economics

Working Paper 04-30. Massachusetts Institute of Technology, Cambridge, Mass.

Chaves, Rodrigo, Nuria de la Peña and Heywood Fleisig. 2004. "Secured Transactions Reform: Early Results from Romania." CEAL Issues Brief. Center for the Economic Analysis of Law, Washington, D.C.

Council of Europe. 2004. "European Judicial Systems 2002." European Commission for the Efficiency of Justice, Strasbourg.

Couwenberg, Oscar. 2001. "Survival Rates in Bankruptcy Systems: Overlooking the Evidence." *European Journal of Law and Economics* 12 (3): 253–73.

Davydenko, Sergei, and Julian Franks. 2005. "Do Bankruptcy Codes Matter? A Study of Defaults in France, Germany and the UK." Finance Working Paper 89. European Corporate Governance Institute, Brussels.

de Soto, Hernando. 2000. *The Mystery of Capital.* New York: Basic Books.

De Wulf, Luc. 2004. "Ghana." In Luc De Wulf and José B. Sokol, eds., *Customs Modernization Initiatives: Case Studies.* Washington, D.C.: World Bank.

Deininger, Klaus. 2003. *Land Policies for Growth and Poverty Reduction.* World Bank Policy Research Report. New York: Oxford University Press.

Desai, Mihir A., C. Fritz Foley and James R. Hines Jr. 2004. "Foreign Direct Investment in a World of Multiple Taxes." *Journal of Public Economics* 88: 2727–44.

Desai, Mihir, Paul Gompers and Josh Lerner. 2004. "Institutions, Capital Constraints and Entrepreneurial Firm Dynamics: Evidence from Europe." Harvard Business School, Cambridge, Mass.

Dimitrov, Martin, and Krasen Stanchev. 2005. "Privatizing Enforcement." *Economic Policy Brief* 8 (213): 3–8.

Djankov, Simeon, Rafael La Porta and Andrei Shleifer. 2005. "The Law and Economics of Self-Dealing." Harvard University, Department of Economics, Cambridge, Mass.

Djankov, Simeon, Caralee McLiesh and Rita Ramalho. 2004. "Regulation and Growth." Working paper. World Bank Group, Private Sector Development Vice Presidency, Monitoring, Analysis and Policy Unit, Washington, D.C.

Djankov, Simeon, Caralee McLiesh and Andrei Shleifer. 2005. *Private Credit in 129 Countries.* NBER Working Paper 11078. Cambridge, Mass.: National Bureau of Economic Research.

Djankov, Simeon, Rafael La Porta, Florencio López-de-Silanes and Andrei Shleifer. 2002. "The Regulation of Entry." *Quarterly Journal of Economics* 117 (1): 1–37.

———. 2003. "Courts," Quarterly Journal of Economics, 118 (2): 453–517.

Dreher, Axel, Christos Kotsogiannis and Steve McCorriston. 2004. "Corruption around the World: Evidence from a Structural Model." University of Exeter, Department of Economics.

———. 2005. "How Do Institutions Affect Corruption and the Shadow Economy?" University of Exeter, Department of Economics.

Dulleck, Uwe, Paul Frijters and Rudolf Winter-Ebmer. 2003. "Reducing Start-Up Costs for New Firms: The Double

Dividend on the Labor Market." IZA Discussion Paper 923. Institute for the Study of Labor, Bonn.

Ebell, Monique, and Christian Haefke. 2003. "Product Market Deregulation and Labor Market Outcomes." IZA Discussion Paper 957. Institute for the Study of Labor, Bonn.

Engelschalk, Michael. 2004. "Creating a Favorable Tax Environment for Small Business." In James Alm, Jorge Martinez-Vazquez and Sally Wallace, eds., *Taxing the Hard to Tax: Lessons from Theory and Practice.* Boston: Elsevier.

Engen, Eric, and Jonathan Skinner. 1996. "Taxation and Economic Growth." *National Tax Journal* 49 (4): 617–42.

EU (European Union). 2004. *Facing the Challenge: The Lisbon Strategy for Growth and Employment.* Brussels.

European Council. 1997. Council Directive 96/97/EC. *Official Journal of the European Community* 46, 17.2.1997.

Feder, Gershon. 2002. "The Intricacies of Land Markets: Why the World Bank Succeeds in Economic Reform through Land Registration and Tenure Security." Paper presented at the Conference of the International Federation of Surveyors, Washington, D.C., April 19–26.

FIAS (Foreign Investment Advisory Service). 2002. *Administrative Barriers to Investment in Latvia.* Washington, D.C.: World Bank.

———. 2004. *Administrative Barriers to Investment in the Russian Federation.* Washington, D.C.: World Bank.

Field, Erica. 2002. "Entitled to Work: Urban Property Rights and Labor Supply in Peru." Princeton Law & Public Affairs Working Paper 02-1. Princeton University, Princeton, N.J.

———. 2004. "Property Rights, Community Public Goods, and Household Time Allocation in Urban Squatter Communities." *William and Mary Law Review* 45 (3): 837–87.

Fields, Gary, Paul L. Cichello, Marta Menendez and David Newhouse. 2002. "Household Income Dynamics: A Four-Country Study." *Journal of Development Studies* 40(2).

Fjeldstad, Odd-Helge, and Lise Rakner. 2003. *Taxation and Tax Reforms in Developing Countries: Illustrations from Sub-Saharan Africa.* CMI Report R 2003: 6. Bergen, Norway: Chr. Michelsen Institute.

Fonseca, Raquel, Paloma Lopez-Garcia and Christopher Pissarides. 2001. "Entrepreneurship, Start-Up Costs and Employment." *European Economic Review* 45 (4–6): 692–705.

Franks, Julian, and Gyongyi Loranth. 2005. "A Study of Inefficient Going Concerns in Bankruptcy." CEPR Discussion Paper 5035. Centre for Economic Policy Research, London.

Freund, Caroline. 2000. "Multilateralism and the Endogenous Formation of Preferential Trade Agreements." *Journal of International Economics* 52 (2): 359–76.

Goolsbee, Austan. 2002. *The Impact and Inefficiency of the Corporate Income Tax: Evidence from State Organizational Form Data.* NBER Working Paper 9141. Cambridge, Mass.: National Bureau of Economic Research.

Goorman, Adrien. 2004. "Peru." In Luc De Wulf and José B. Sokol, eds., *Customs Modernization Initiatives: Case Studies.* Washington, D.C.: World Bank.

Gropp, Reint, J. Karl Scholz and Michelle White. 1997. "Personal Bankruptcy and Credit Supply and Demand." *Quarterly Journal of Economics* 112: 217–52.

Hausman, Warren, Uma Subramanian and Hau Lee. 2005. "The Role of Logistics and Supply Chain Indicators on Trade Competitiveness." World Bank, Investment Climate Department, Washington, D.C.

Heckman, James, and Carmen Pagés, eds. 2004. *Law and Employment: Lessons from Latin America and the Caribbean*. Chicago: University of Chicago Press for National Bureau of Economic Research.

Holmes, Thomas. 1998. "The Effect of State Policies on the Location of Manufacturing: Evidence from State Borders." *Journal of Political Economy* 106 (4): 667–705.

Hummels, David. 2001. "Toward a Geography of Trade Costs." Purdue University, Department of Economics, West Lafayette, Ind.

Ibbotson, Roger, Laurence Siegel and Kathryn Love. 1985. "World Wealth: Market Values and Returns." *Journal of Portfolio Management* 12 (1): 4–23.

ILO (International Labour Organization). (1998, 2000, 2001, 2002, 2003). *ILO Declaration on Fundamental Principles and Rights at Work*. Geneva.

———. 2004. *Household Labour Force Survey in Turkey*. Geneva.

ILO (International Labour Organization). 2005. Laborsta database at http://laborsta.ilo.org. Visited July 2005.

IMF (International Monetary Fund). 2005a. *International Financial Statistics*. Washington, D.C.

———. 2005b. *Government Finance Statistics*. International Monetary Fund, Washington, D.C.

Iradian, Garbis. 2005. "Inequality, Poverty and Growth: Cross-Country Evidence." IMF Working Paper WP/05/28. International Monetary Fund, Washington, D.C.

Ivanova, Anna, Michael Keen and Alexander Klemm. 2005. "The Russian Flat Tax Reform." IMF Working Paper WP/05/16. International Monetary Fund, Washington, D.C.

Jappelli, Tullio, Marco Pagano and Magda Bianco. 2005. "Courts and Banks: Effects of Judicial Enforcement on Credit Markets." *Journal of Money, Credit and Banking* 37 (2): 223–44.

Kagame, Paul. 2002. Remarks by the President of the Republic of Rwanda at the occasion marking the fifth anniversary of the Rwandan bar association, Kigali, November 9.

King, Robert, and Ross Levine. 1993. "Finance and Growth: Schumpeter Might Be Right." *Quarterly Journal of Economics* 108 (3): 717–37.

La Porta, Rafael, Florencio López-de-Silanes and Andrei Shleifer. Forthcoming. "What Works in Securities Laws?" *Journal of Finance*.

La Porta, Rafael, Florencio López-de-Silanes, Andrei Shleifer and Robert Vishny. 1997. "Legal Determinants of External Finance." *Journal of Finance* 52 (3): 1131–50.

———. 1998. "Law and Finance." *Journal of Political Economy*, 106 (6): 1113–55.

Lee, Young, and Roger Gordon. 2004. "Tax Structure and Economic Growth." University of California at San Diego, Department of Economics. http://www.econ.ucsd.edu/%7Erogordon/papers.html.

Lerner, Josh, and Antoinette Schoar. 2005. "Does Legal Enforcement Affect Financial Transactions? The Contractual Channel in Private Equity." *Quarterly Journal of Economics* 120 (1): 223–46.

Loayza, Norman, Ana Maria Oviedo and Luis Serven. 2004. "Regulation and Macroeconomic Performance." Policy Research Working Paper 3469. World Bank, Washington, D.C.

Love, Inessa, and Nataliya Mylenko. 2003. "Credit Reporting and Financing Constraints." Policy Research Working Paper 3142. World Bank, Washington, D.C.

Meadows, Pamela. 2003. "Retirement Ages in the UK: A Review of the Literature." Employment Relations Research Series 18. U.K. Department of Treasury and Industry, London.

Micco, Alejandro, and Carmen Pagés. 2004. "Employment Protection and Gross Job Flows: A Difference-in-Difference Approach." Research Department Working Paper 505. Inter-American Development Bank, Washington, D.C.

Miller, William, and Nadia Balgobin. 2002. "Overcoming the Ethics Crisis: Société Générale de Surveillance." *International Business Ethics Institute Magazine* 5 (1): 5–9.

Moore, David. 2005. "Slovakia's 2004 Tax and Welfare Reforms." IMF Working Paper WP/05/133. International Monetary Fund, Washington, D.C.

Mwangi, Anthony. 2004. "Mozambique." In Luc De Wulf and José B. Sokol, eds., *Customs Modernization Initiatives: Case Studies*. Washington, D.C.: World Bank.

Narayan, Deepa, with Raj Patel, Kai Schafft, Anne Rademacher and Sarah Koch-Schulte. 2000. *Voices of the Poor: Can Anyone Hear Us?* New York: Oxford University Press.

Netherlands, Ministry of Finance. 2005. *Reducing Administrative Burdens: Now Full Steam Ahead*. The Hague.

Neumark, David, and William Wascher. 2004. "Minimum Wages, Labor Market Institutions, and Youth Employment: A Cross-National Analysis." *Industrial and Labor Relations Review* 57 (2): 223–48.

Pierre, Gaelle, and Stefano Scarpetta. Forthcoming. "Employment Protection: Do Firms' Perceptions Match with Legislation?" *Economic Letters*.

Qian, Jun, and Philip Strahan. 2005. *How Law and Institutions Shape Financial Contracts: The Case of Bank Loans*. NBER Working Paper 11052. Cambridge, Mass.: National Bureau of Economic Research.

Saavedra, Jaime, and Máximo Torero. 2004. "The Effect of Job Security Regulations on Labor Market Flexibility: Evidence from the Colombian Labor Market Reform." In James Heckman and Carmen Pagés, eds., *Law and Employment: Lessons from Latin America and the Caribbean*. Chicago: University of Chicago Press for National Bureau of Economic Research.

Schneider, Friedrich. 2005. "The Informal Sector in 145 Countries," University of Linz, Department of Economics.

Shleifer, Andrei, and Daniel Wolfenzon. 2002. "Investor Protection and Equity Markets." *Journal of Financial Economics* 66 (1): 3–27.

Slemrod, Joel. 1995. "What Do Cross-Country Studies Teach about Government Involvement, Prosperity, and Economic Growth?" *Brookings Papers on Economic Activity*, no. 2: 373–431.

Slovak Statistical Office. 2005. *Labour Force Survey*. Bratislava.

Subramanian, Uma, and William Anderson. 2005. "Are We There Yet? The Impact of Logistics Time on Trade." World Bank, Investment Climate Department, Washington, D.C.

Svensson, Jakob. 2003. "Who Must Pay Bribes and How Much? Evidence from a Cross-Section of Firms." *Quarterly Journal of Economics* 118 (1): 207–30.

Tan Chee-Wee, Pan Shan-Ling, and Eric T. K. Lim. 2005. "Towards the Restoration of Public Trust in Electronic Governments: A Case Study of the E-Filing System in Singapore." In *Proceedings of the 38th Hawaii International Conference on System Sciences.* http://csdl2.computer.org/comp/proceedings/hicss/2005/2268/05/22680126c.pdf.

Tanzi, Vito, and Howell Zee. 2000. "Tax Policy for Emerging Markets: Developing Countries." IMF Working Paper WP/00/35. International Monetary Fund, Washington, D.C.

UNCTAD (United Nations Conference on Trade and Development). 2004. *Handbook of Statistics 2004.* Geneva.

UNDP (United Nations Development Programme). 2004. *Human Development Report 2004.* New York: Oxford University Press.

Velchev, Milen. 2005. "On the Occasion of Signing a New Contract with Crown Agents." Bulgaria, Ministry of Finance, Press Office, Sofia.

World Bank. 1991. *Lessons of Tax Reform*. Washington, D.C.

———. 2003. *Doing Business in 2004: Understanding Regulation.* Washington, D.C.

———. 2004a. *Doing Business in 2005: Removing Obstacles to Growth.* Washington, D.C.

———. 2004b. *Improving Enterprise Performance and Growth in Tanzania.* Washington, D.C.

———. 2005a. "Aide Memoire: Judicial Reform Project in Armenia." Europe and Central Asia Region, Poverty Reduction and Economic Management, Washington, D.C.

———. 2005b. *Old Age Income Support in the 21st Century.* Washington, D.C.

———. 2005c. "Poland: Legal Barriers to Contract Enforcement." Private Sector Development Vice Presidency, Foreign Investment Advisory Service, Washington, D.C.

———. 2005d. *World Development Indicators 2005.* Washington, D.C.

WEF (World Economic Forum). 2004. *Global Competitiveness Report 2004/2005.* Geneva.

Data notes

Economy characteristics
Starting a business
Dealing with licenses
Hiring and firing workers
Registering property
Getting credit

Protecting investors
Paying taxes
Trading across borders
Enforcing contracts
Closing a business

The indicators presented and analyzed in *Doing Business* measure government regulation and the protection of property rights—and their effect on businesses, especially small and medium-size domestic firms. First, the indicators document the degree of regulation, such as the number of procedures to start a business or register commercial property. Second, they gauge regulatory outcomes, such as the time and cost to enforce a contract, go through bankruptcy or trade across borders. Third, they measure the extent of legal protections of property, for example, the protections of investors against looting by the company directors or the scope of assets that can be used as collateral according to secured transactions laws. Fourth, they measure the flexibility of employment regulation. Finally, a new set of indicators documents the tax burden on businesses. The data for all sets of indicators in *Doing Business in 2006* are for January 2005.

Based on the study of laws and regulations—with input and verification by more than 3,500 government officials, lawyers, business consultants, accountants and other professionals routinely administering or advising on legal and regulatory requirements—the *Doing Business* methodology offers several advantages. It uses factual information about what laws and regulations say and allows for multiple interactions with local respondents to clarify potential misinterpretations of questions. Having representative samples of respondents is not an issue, as the texts of the relevant laws and regulations are collected and answers checked for accuracy. The methodology is inexpensive, so data can be collected in a large sample of economies—155 published in *Doing Business in 2006*. Because the same standard assumptions are applied in the data collection, which is transparent and easily replicable, comparisons and benchmarks are valid across countries. And the data not only highlight the extent of ob-

stacles but also help identify their source, supporting policymakers in designing reform.

The *Doing Business* methodology has 4 limitations that should be considered when interpreting the data. First, in many cases the collected data refer to businesses in the country's most populous city and may not be representative of regulatory practices in other parts of the country. Second, the data often focus on a specific business form—a limited liability company of a specified size—and may not be representative of the regulation on other businesses, for example, sole proprietorships. Third, the measures of time involve an element of judgment by the expert respondents. Therefore, if sources indicate different estimates, the time indicators reported in *Doing Business* represent the median values of several responses given under the assumptions of the case study. Fourth, the methodology assumes that the business has full information on what is required and does not waste time in completing procedures. In practice, completing a procedure may take longer if the business lacks information or is unable to follow up promptly.

Questions on the methodology and challenges to data may be submitted through the "Ask a Question" function on the *Doing Business* website at http://www.doingbusiness.org. Updated indicators, as well as any revisions of or corrections to the printed data, are posted on the website. Since the publication of last year's report, 26 complaints on data have been received. In 4 instances data were corrected as a result of these complaints: the number of procedures and time to start a business in Burkina Faso, the cost of registering property in Senegal, the time to go through bankruptcy in Switzerland and the time and cost to go through bankruptcy in Russia. In 22 other cases past data were corrected during the updating of the indicators for this year's report.

Economy characteristics

Region and income group

Doing Business uses the World Bank regional and income group classifications, available at http://www.worldbank.org/data/countryclass/countryclass.html. Throughout the report the term *rich economies* refers to the high-income group, *middle income economies* to the upper-middle-income group and *poor economies* to the lower-middle-income and low-income groups.

Gross national income (GNI) per capita

Doing Business in 2006 reports 2004 income per capita, as published in the World Bank's *World Development Indicators 2005.* Income is calculated using the Atlas method (current US$). For cost indicators expressed as a percentage of income per capita, 2004 GNI in local currency units, as reported in *World Development Indicators 2005,* is used as the denominator.

Population

Doing Business in 2006 reports midyear 2004 population statistics as published in *World Development Indicators 2005.*

Starting a business

Doing Business records all generic procedures that are officially required for an entrepreneur to start up an industrial or commercial business. These include obtaining all necessary licenses and permits and completing any required notifications, verifications or inscriptions with relevant authorities. After a study of laws, regulations and publicly available information on business entry, a detailed list of procedures, time, cost and paid-in minimum capital requirements is developed. Subsequently, local incorporation lawyers and government officials complete and verify the data on applicable procedures, the time and cost of complying with each procedure under normal circumstances and the paid-in minimum capital. On average 4 law firms participate in each country. Information is also collected on the sequence in which procedures are to be completed and whether procedures may be carried out simultaneously. It is assumed that any required information is readily available and that all government and nongovernment agencies involved in the start-up process function efficiently and without corruption. If answers by local experts differ, inquiries continue until the data are reconciled.

To make the data comparable across countries, several assumptions about the business and the procedures are used.

Assumptions about the business

The business:
- Is a limited liability company. If there is more than one type of limited liability company in the country, the most popular limited liability form among domestic firms is chosen. Information on the most popular form is obtained from incorporation lawyers or the statistical office.
- Operates in the country's most populous city.
- Is 100% domestically owned and has 5 owners, none of whom is a legal entity.
- Has start-up capital of 10 times income per capita at the end of 2004, paid in cash.
- Performs general industrial or commercial activities, such as the production or sale of products or services to the public. It does not perform foreign trade activities and does not handle products subject to a special tax regime, for example, liquor or tobacco. The business is not using heavily polluting production processes.
- Leases the commercial plant and offices and is not a proprietor of real estate.
- Does not qualify for investment incentives or any special benefits.
- Has up to 50 employees 1 month after the commencement of operations, all of them nationals.
- Has a turnover at least 100 times income per capita.
- Has a company deed 10 pages long.

Assumptions about procedures

- A procedure is defined as any interaction of the company founder with external parties (government agencies, lawyers, auditors, notaries). Interactions between company founders or company officers and employees are not considered separate procedures.
- The founders complete all procedures themselves, without middlemen, facilitators, accountants or lawyers, unless the use of such a third party is mandated by law.
- Procedures that are not required by law for starting a business are ignored. For example, obtaining exclusive rights over the company name is not counted in a country where businesses may use a number as identification.
- Shortcuts are counted only if they fulfill 3 criteria: they are legal, they are available to the general public, and avoiding them causes substantial delays.
- Only procedures required of all businesses are covered. Industry-specific procedures are excluded. For example, procedures to comply with environmental regulations are included only when they apply to all businesses.
- Procedures that the company undergoes to connect to electricity, water, gas and waste disposal services are not included unless they entail inspections required before starting operations.

Time

Time is recorded in calendar days. It is assumed that the minimum time required for each procedure is 1 day. Time captures the median duration that incorporation lawyers indicate is necessary to complete a procedure. If a procedure can be accelerated for an additional cost, the fastest procedure is chosen. It is assumed that the entrepreneur does not waste time and commits to completing each remaining procedure without delay. The time that the entrepreneur spends on gathering information is ignored. It is assumed that the entrepreneur is aware of all entry regulations and their sequence from the beginning.

Cost

The text of the company law, the commercial code and specific regulations and fee schedules are used as sources for calculating the cost of start-up. If there are conflicting sources and the laws are not clear, the most authoritative source is used. The constitution supersedes the company law, and the law prevails over regulations and decrees. If conflicting sources are of the same rank, the source indicating the most costly procedure is used, since an entrepreneur never second-guesses a government official. In the absence of fee schedules, a government officer's estimate is taken as an official source.

In the absence of a government officer's estimate, estimates of incorporation lawyers are used. If several incorporation lawyers provide different estimates, the median reported value is applied. In all cases the cost excludes bribes.

Paid-in minimum capital requirement

The paid-in minimum capital requirement reflects the amount that the entrepreneur needs to deposit in a bank before registration starts. This amount is typically specified in the commercial code or the company law. Many countries require paid-in capital but allow businesses to pay only a part of it before registration, with the rest to be paid after the first year of operation. In Mozambique in January 2005, for example, the minimum capital requirement for limited liability companies was 1,500,000 meticais, of which half was payable before registration. In the Philippines the minimum capital requirement was 5,000 pesos, but only a quarter needed to be paid before registration.

This methodology was originally developed in Djankov and others (2002) and is adopted here with minor changes.

Dealing with licenses

Doing Business records all procedures required for a business in the construction industry to build a standardized warehouse. These include obtaining all necessary licenses and permits, completing all required notifications and inspections and submitting the relevant documents (for example, building plans and site maps) to the authorities. *Doing Business* also records procedures for obtaining utility connections, such as electricity, telephone, water and sewerage. The survey divides the process of building a warehouse into distinct procedures and calculates the time and cost of completing each procedure under normal circumstances.

Information is collected from construction lawyers, construction firms and public officials who deal with building regulations. To make the data comparable across countries, several assumptions about the business and the procedures are used.

Assumptions about the construction company (BuildCo)

The business (BuildCo):
- Is a limited liability company.
- Operates in the country's most populous city.
- Is 100% domestically owned and has 5 owners, none of whom is a legal entity.
- Carries out construction projects, such as building a warehouse.
- Has up to 20 builders and other employees, all of them nationals with the technical expertise and professional experience necessary to develop architectural and technical plans for building a warehouse.

Assumptions about the warehouse project

The warehouse:
- Has 2 stories and approximately 14,000 square feet (1,300.6 square meters) of space.
- Is located in the most populous city in the country.
- Is located on land 100% owned by BuildCo, a plot of 8,000 square feet (743.2 square meters) that is accurately registered in the cadastre and land registry.
- Is a new construction (there was no previous construction on the land).
- Has complete architectural and technical plans.
- Will be connected to electricity, water, sewerage and one regular phone line.
- Will be used for storing books.

Assumptions about procedures

- A procedure is any interaction of the company's employees or managers with external parties (government agencies, public inspectors, notaries, land registry and cadastre, technical experts apart from architects and engineers). Interactions between company employees, such as development of the warehouse plans and inspections conducted by employees, are not considered separate procedures.
- Procedures that the company undergoes to connect to electricity, water, sewerage and phone services are included.

Time

Time is recorded in calendar days. It is assumed that the minimum time required for each procedure is 1 day. Time captures the median duration that construction lawyers and construction company managers indicate is necessary to complete a procedure. If a procedure can be accelerated for an additional cost, the fastest procedure is chosen. It is assumed that BuildCo does not waste time and commits to completing each remaining procedure without delay. The time that BuildCo spends on gathering information is ignored. It is assumed that BuildCo is aware of all building requirements and their sequence from the beginning.

Cost

All the fees associated with completing the procedures to legally build a warehouse are included. The cost measure is based on information received from lawyers and construction companies as well as information in local construction regulations.

Hiring and firing workers

Every economy has established a complex system of laws and institutions intended to protect the interests of workers and to guarantee a minimum standard of living for its population. The *OECD Job Study* and the *International Encyclopedia for Labour Law and Industrial Relations* identify 4 areas subject to statutory regulation in all countries: employment, social security, industrial relations and occupational health and safety. *Doing Business* focuses on the regulation of employment, specifically the hiring and firing of workers and the rigidity of working hours. This year data on social security payments by the employer and pension benefits, including the mandatory retirement age, have been added.

The data on hiring and firing workers are based on a detailed survey of employment and social security regulations. The survey is completed by local law firms. The employment laws of most countries are available online in the NATLEX database, published by the International Labour Organization. In all cases both actual laws and secondary sources are used to ensure accuracy. Conflicting answers are further checked against 2 additional sources, including a local legal treatise on employment regulation.

To make the data comparable across countries, several assumptions about the worker and the business are used.

Assumptions about the worker

The worker:
- Is a nonexecutive, full-time male employee who has worked in the same company for 20 years.
- Earns a salary plus benefits equal to the country's average wage during the entire period of his employment.
- Has a wife and 2 children. The family resides in the country's most populous city.
- Is a lawful citizen who belongs to the same race and religion as the majority of the country's population.
- Is not a member of the labor union, unless membership is mandatory.

For this year's report data were also collected for an employee who has worked in the same company for only 3 years. This change influences several indicators, for example, the notice period and severance payment in redundancy dismissals as well as the number of vacation days. In Sri Lanka an employee with 3 years of service receives 2.5 months of wages in severance payment for every year of work, for a total of 7.5 months

of wages. The formula for employees with 20 or more years of service is $38 + (y - 19)$, where y is the years of service. Thus for a worker with 20 years of service, that makes for 39 months of wages paid in severance. In Argentina a worker with 3 years of service is entitled to 15 vacation days. A worker with 20 years receives 25 vacation days. The choice of years of service does not influence country rankings, as benefits to the employee increase linearly with the years of service everywhere.

Assumptions about the business

The business:
- Is a limited liability company.
- Operates in the country's most populous city.
- Is 100% domestically owned.
- Operates in the manufacturing sector.
- Has 201 employees.
- Abides by every law and regulation but does not grant workers more benefits than what is legally mandated.
- Is subject to collective bargaining agreements in countries where collective bargaining covers more than half the manufacturing sector.

The last assumption is especially important in Western Europe, where labor laws are sometimes silent on such issues as minimum wages, notice period and severance pay. These are covered in collective bargaining agreements. In Denmark, for example, the labor law does not mandate a notice period or severance pay for redundancy dismissals. Collective bargaining does. For a worker with 20 years of service, a 26-week notice period and a 3-month severance payment are required. This is what *Doing Business* records, as collective agreements are prevalent in the country. Similarly, in Germany the labor law does not mandate a minimum wage. Industry-level collective bargaining in the metal industry specifies 7.25 euro an hour as the minimum wage. This is what *Doing Business* records, as more than half of German manufacturing is covered by collective agreements.

Rigidity of employment index

The rigidity of employment index is the average of three subindices: a difficulty of hiring index, a rigidity of hours index and a difficulty of firing index. All the subindices have several components. And all take values between 0 and 100, with higher values indicating more rigid regulation.

The difficulty of hiring index measures (i) whether term contracts can be used only for temporary tasks; (ii) the maximum duration of term contracts; and (iii) the ratio of the mandated minimum wage (or apprentice wage, if available) to the average value added per worker. A country is assigned a score of 1 if term contracts can be used only for temporary tasks, and a score of 0 if they can be used for any task. A score of 1 is assigned if the maximum duration of term contracts is 3 years or less; 0.5 if it is between 3 and 5 years; and 0 if term contracts can last more than 5 years. Finally, a score of 1 is assigned if the ratio of the minimum wage to the average value added per worker is higher than 0.75; 0.67 for a ratio between 0.50 and 0.75; 0.33 for a ratio between 0.25 and 0.50; and 0 for a ratio less than 0.25. In Nepal, for example, term contracts are allowed only for temporary tasks (a score of 1), but there is no limit on their duration (a score of 0). The ratio of the mandated minimum wage to the value added per worker is 0.54 (a score of 0.67). Averaging the three subindices and scaling the index to 100 gives Nepal a score of 56.

The rigidity of hours index has 5 components: (i) whether night work is unrestricted; (ii) whether weekend work is allowed; (iii) whether the workweek can consist of 5.5 days; (iv) whether the workday can extend to 12 hours or more (including overtime); and (v) whether the annual paid vacation days are 21 or fewer. For each of these questions, if the answer is no, the country is assigned a score of 1; otherwise a score of 0 is assigned. For example, Lithuania imposes restrictions on night work (a score of 1) and weekend work (a score of 1), allows 5.5 day workweeks (a score of 0), permits the workday—with overtime—to extend to 12 hours (a score of 0) and requires paid vacation of 28 days (a score of 1). Adding the scores and scaling the sum to 100 gives a final index of 60 for Lithuania.

The difficulty of firing index has 8 components: (i) whether redundancy is not considered fair grounds for dismissal; (ii) whether the employer needs to notify the labor union or the labor ministry to fire 1 redundant worker; (iii) whether the employer needs to notify the labor union or the labor ministry for group dismissals; (iv) whether the employer needs approval from the labor union or the labor ministry for firing 1 redundant worker; (v) whether the employer needs approval from the labor union or the labor ministry for group dismissals; (vi) whether the law mandates training or replacement before dismissal; (vii) whether priority rules apply for dismissals; and (viii) whether priority rules apply

for reemployment. For each question, if the answer is yes, a score of 1 is assigned (for questions i and iv, a score of 2); otherwise a score of 0 is given. Questions (i) and (iv), as the most restrictive regulations, have double weight in the construction of the index.

In Nicaragua, for example, redundancy is considered fair grounds for dismissal (a score of 0). An employer has to both notify (a score of 1) and seek approval (a score of 2) from third parties when dismissing a redundant worker, and he has to both notify (a score of 1) and seek approval (a score of 1) when dismissing a group of workers. The law does not mandate retraining or alternative placement before dismissal (a score of 0). There are no priority rules for dismissal (a score of 0) or reemployment (a score of 0). Adding up the scores and scaling to 100 gives a final index of 50 for Nicaragua.

Hiring cost

The hiring cost indicator measures all social security payments (including retirement fund; sickness, maternity and health insurance; workplace injury; family allowance; and other obligatory contributions) and payroll taxes associated with hiring an employee. The cost is expressed as a percentage of the worker's salary. In Algeria, for example, the social security contributions paid by the employer amount to 27.5% of the worker's wages and include 7.5% for the retirement fund; 12.5% for sickness, maternity and health insurance; 1% for workplace safety insurance; 2.5% for unemployment insurance; and 4% for family allowances.

Firing cost

The firing cost indicator measures the cost of advance notice requirements, severance payments and penalties due when dismissing a redundant worker, expressed in weekly wages. In Mozambique, for example, an employer is required to give 12 weeks' notice before a redundancy dismissal, and the severance pay for workers with 20 years of service equals 30 months of wages. Redundancy is considered legitimate grounds for dismissal in the labor law, so no penalty is levied. Altogether, the employer pays the equivalent of 141 weeks of salary to dismiss the worker.

This methodology was originally developed in Botero and others (2004) and is adopted here with minor changes.

Registering property

Doing Business records the full sequence of procedures necessary when a business purchases land and a building to transfer the property title from the seller to the buyer. Every required procedure is included, whether it is the responsibility of the seller or the buyer or required to be completed by a third party on their behalf. Local property lawyers and property registries provide information on required procedures as well as the time and cost to complete each of them.

To make the data comparable across countries, several assumptions about the business, the property and the procedures are used.

Assumptions about the business

The business:
- Is a limited liability company.
- Is located in a periurban area of the country's most populous city.

- Is 100% domestically and privately owned (no foreign or state ownership).
- Has 50 employees, all of whom are nationals.
- Performs general commercial activities.

Assumptions about the property

The property:
- Has a value of 50 times income per capita.
- Is fully owned by another domestic limited liability company.
- Has no mortgages attached and has been under the same ownership for the past 10 years.
- Is adequately measured and filed in the cadastre, registered in the land register and free of title disputes.
- Is located in a periurban commercial zone, and no rezoning is required.
- Consists of land and a building. The land area is 6,000 square feet (557.4 square meters). A warehouse of 10,000 square feet (929 square meters) is located on the land. The warehouse is 10 years old, is in good condition and complies with all safety standards, building codes and other legal requirements.
- Will not be subject to renovations or additional building following the purchase.
- Has no trees, natural water sources, natural reserves or historical monuments of any kind.
- Will not be used for special purposes, and no special permits, such as for residential use, industrial plants, waste storage or certain types of agricultural activities, are required.
- Has no occupants (legal or illegal), and no other party holds a legal interest in it.

Procedures

A procedure is defined as any interaction of the buyer or the seller, their agents (if the agent is required by law) or the property with external parties, including government agencies, inspectors, notaries and lawyers. Interactions between company officers and employees are not considered. All procedures that are legally required for registering property are recorded, even if they may be avoided in exceptional cases. It is assumed that the buyer follows the fastest legal option available. Although the business may use lawyers or other professionals where necessary in the registration process, it is assumed that it does not employ an outside facilitator in the registration process unless required to by law.

Time

Time is recorded in calendar days. It is assumed that the minimum time required for each procedure is 1 day. Time captures the median duration that property lawyers or registry officials indicate is necessary to complete a procedure. It is assumed that the buyer does not waste time and commits to completing each remaining procedure without delay. If a procedure can be accelerated for an additional cost, the fastest procedure is chosen. If procedures may be undertaken simultaneously, it is assumed that they are. It is assumed that the parties involved are aware of all regulations and their sequence from the beginning. Time spent on gathering information is not considered.

Cost

Only official costs are recorded. These include fees, transfer taxes, stamp duties and any other payment to the property registry, notaries, public agencies or lawyers, if required by law. Other taxes, such as capital gains tax or value added tax, are excluded from the cost measure. If cost estimates differ among sources, the median reported value is used. Costs are expressed as a percentage of the property value, assumed to be equivalent to 50 times income per capita.

Getting credit

Doing Business constructs measures on the legal rights of lenders and credit information sharing. The first set of indicators describes how well collateral and bankruptcy laws facilitate lending. The second set measures the coverage, scope, quality and accessibility of credit information available through public and private credit registries.

The data on credit information sharing are built in 2 stages. First, banking supervision authorities and public information sources are surveyed to confirm the presence of public credit registries and private credit information bureaus. Second, when applicable, a detailed survey on the public or private credit registry's structure, law and associated rules collects data in 5 areas:
- Coverage of the market.
- Scope of distributed information.
- Access to data.
- Quality of data.
- Laws on information sharing and quality of data.

Survey responses are verified through several rounds of follow-up communication with respondents as well as by contacting third parties and consulting public sources. The survey data are confirmed through teleconference calls in more than half the countries.

Strength of legal rights index

This index, reflecting the legal rights of borrowers and lenders, measures the degree to which collateral and bankruptcy laws facilitate lending. It is based on data collected through study of collateral and insolvency laws, supported by the responses to the survey on secured transactions laws. The index includes 3 aspects related to legal rights in bankruptcy and 7 aspects found in collateral law. A score of 1 is assigned for each of the following features of the laws:

- Secured creditors are able to seize their collateral when a debtor enters reorganization—there is no "automatic stay" or "asset freeze" imposed by the court.
- Secured creditors, rather than other parties such as government or workers, are paid first out of the proceeds from liquidating a bankrupt firm.
- Management does not stay during reorganization. An administrator is responsible for managing the business during reorganization.
- General, rather than specific, description of assets is permitted in collateral agreements.
- General, rather than specific, description of debt is permitted in collateral agreements.
- Any legal or natural person may grant or take security in the property.
- A unified registry that includes charges over movable property operates.
- Secured creditors have priority outside of bankruptcy.
- Parties may agree on enforcement procedures by contract.
- Creditors may both seize and sell collateral out of court.

The index ranges from 0 to 10, with higher scores indicating that collateral and bankruptcy laws are better designed to expand access to credit.

Depth of credit information index

This index measures rules affecting the scope, accessibility and quality of credit information available through either public or private bureaus. A score of 1 is assigned for each of the following 6 features of the credit information system:

- Both positive and negative credit information (for example, on payment history, number and kinds of accounts, number and frequency of late payments and any collections or bankruptcies) is distributed.
- Data on both firms and individuals are distributed.
- Data from retailers, trade creditors or utilities as well as financial institutions are distributed.
- More than 2 years of historical data are distributed.
- Data on loans above 1% of income per capita are distributed.
- By law, borrowers have the right to access their data.

The index ranges from 0 to 6, with higher values indicating that more credit information is available from either a public registry or a private bureau to facilitate lending decisions. In Uruguay, for example, both a public and a private registry operate. The private bureau distributes only negative information, but the public registry distributes both negative and positive information (a score of 1). Both the public and the private registries distribute data on firms as well as individuals (a score of 1). Although the public registry shares data only among supervised financial institutions, lenders can access information from retailers and utilities through the private bureau (a score of 1). The public registry distributes more than 2 years of historical data (a score of 1). It collects data only on loans of $11,000 or more—3.6 times income per capita—but the private bureau collects information on loans above 100 pesos, less than 1% of income per capita (a score of 1). Borrowers do not have the right to access their data (score of 0). Summing across the indicators gives Uruguay a total score of 5.

Public credit registry coverage

A public credit registry is defined as a database managed by the public sector, usually by the central bank or the superintendent of banks, that collects information on the creditworthiness of borrowers (persons or businesses) in the financial system and makes it available to financial institutions. The coverage indicator reports the number of individuals and firms listed in the public credit registry with current information on repayment history, unpaid debts or credit outstanding. The number is expressed as a percentage of the adult population. If no public registry operates, the coverage value is 0.

Private credit bureau coverage

A private credit bureau is defined as a private firm or nonprofit organization that maintains a database on the creditworthiness of borrowers (persons or businesses) in the financial system and facilitates the exchange of credit information among banks and financial institutions. Credit investigative bureaus and credit reporting firms that do not directly facilitate information exchange between financial institutions are not considered. The coverage indicator reports the number of individuals or firms listed by the private credit bureau with current information on repayment history, unpaid debts or credit outstanding. The number is expressed as a percentage of the adult population. If no private bureau operates, the coverage value is 0.

This methodology, adapted from La Porta and others (1998), is developed in Djankov, McLiesh and Shleifer (2005).

Protecting investors

Doing Business measures the strength of minority shareholder protections against directors' misuse of corporate assets for personal gain. The indicators distinguish 3 dimensions of investor protection: transparency of transactions (extent of disclosure index), liability for self-dealing (extent of director liability index) and shareholders' ability to sue officers and directors for misconduct (ease of shareholder suits index). The data come from a survey of corporate lawyers and are based on company laws, codes of civil procedure and securities regulations.

To make the data comparable across countries, several assumptions about the business and the transaction are used.

Assumptions about the business

The business (Buyer):
- Is a publicly traded corporation listed on the country's most important stock exchange. If there are no publicly traded companies in the country, it is assumed that Buyer is a large private company with multiple shareholders.
- Has a board of directors and a chief executive officer (CEO) who has the legal capacity to act on behalf of Buyer where permitted, even if this is not specifically required by law.
- Has only national shareholders.
- Has invested only in the country and has no subsidiaries or operations abroad.
- Is a food manufacturer.
- Has its own distribution network.

Assumptions about the transaction

- Mr. James is Buyer's controlling shareholder and a member of Buyer's board of directors. He owns 60% of Buyer and elected 2 directors to Buyer's 5-member board of directors.
- Mr. James also owns 90% of Seller, a company that operates a chain of retail hardware stores. Seller recently shut a large number of its stores. As a result, its fleet of trucks is idle.
- Mr. James proposes to Buyer that Buyer purchase Seller's unused fleet of trucks to expand Buyer's distribution of its food products. Buyer agrees. The price is equal to 10% of Buyer's assets.
- The proposed transaction is part of the company's ordinary course of business and is not outside the authority of the company.
- Buyer enters into the transaction. All required approvals were obtained, and all required disclosures made.
- The transaction is unfair to Buyer. Shareholders sue the interested parties and the members of the board of directors.

Extent of disclosure index

The extent of disclosure index measures (i) what corporate body can provide legally sufficient approval for the transaction (a score of 0 is assigned if it is the CEO or the managing director alone; 1 if the board of directors or shareholders must vote but Mr. James is permitted to vote; 2 if the board of directors must vote and Mr. James is not permitted to vote; 3 if shareholders must vote and Mr. James is not permitted to vote); (ii) whether immediate disclosure of the transaction to the public, the shareholders or both is required (a score of 0 is assigned if no disclosure is required; 1 if disclosure on the terms of the transaction is required; 2 if disclosure on both the terms and Mr. James's conflict of interest is required); (iii) whether disclosure in the annual report is required (a score of 0 is assigned if no disclosure on the transaction is required; 1 if disclosure about the terms of the transaction is required; 2 if disclosure on both the terms and Mr. James's conflict of interest is required); (iv) whether disclosure by Mr. James to the board of directors is required (a score of 0 is assigned if no disclosure is required; 1 if disclosure on Mr. James's conflict of interest is required but without any specifics; 2 if full disclosure of all material facts about his interest in the transaction is required); and (v) whether it is required that an external body, for example, an external auditor, review the transaction before it takes place (a score of 0 is assigned if no; 1 if yes).

The index ranges from 0 to 10, with higher values indicating greater disclosure. Poland, for example, requires approval from the board of directors for the transaction and Mr. James is not allowed to vote (a score of 2). Buyer is required to disclose immediately all information affecting the stock price, including the conflict of interest (a score of 2). In its annual report Buyer must also disclose the terms of the transaction and Mr. James's ownership in Buyer and Seller (a score of 2). Before the transaction Mr. James must disclose his conflict of interest to the other directors, but he is not required to provide specific information about it (a score of 1). Poland does not require an external body to review the transaction (a score of 0). Adding these numbers gives Poland a score of 7 on the extent of disclosure index.

Extent of director liability index

The extent of director liability index measures (i) a plaintiff's ability to hold Mr. James liable for damages to the company (a score of 0 is assigned if Mr. James is not liable or is liable only for fraud or bad faith; 1 if Mr. James is liable if he influenced the approval of the transaction or was negligent; 2 if Mr. James is liable if the transaction was unfair or prejudicial to the other shareholders); (ii) a plaintiff's ability to hold the approving body (the CEO or board of directors) liable for damages to the company (a score of 0 is assigned if the approving body is not liable or is liable only in case of fraud or bad faith; 1 if the approving body can be held liable for negligence; 2 if the approving body can be held liable when the transaction is unfair or prejudicial to the other shareholders); (iii) a plaintiff's ability to void the transaction (a score of 0 is assigned if rescission is unavailable or is available only in case of fraud; 1 if rescission is available when the transaction is oppressive or prejudicial to the other shareholders; 2 if rescission is available when the transaction is unfair or entails a conflict of interest); (iv) whether Mr. James pays damages for the harm caused to the company (a score of 0 is assigned if no; 1 if yes); (v) whether Mr. James repays profits made from the transaction (a score of 0 is assigned if no; 1 if yes); (vi) whether fines and imprisonment can be applied against Mr. James (a score of 0 is assigned if no; 1 if yes); (vii) the ability of minority shareholders to sue directly or derivatively for damages that the company suffered as a result of the transaction (a score of 0 is assigned if suits are not available or are available only for shareholders holding more than 10% of the company's share capital; 1 if direct or derivative suits are available for shareholders holding 10% or less of share capital).

The index ranges from 0 to 10, with higher values indicating greater liability of directors. To hold Mr. James liable in Panama, for example, a plaintiff must prove that Mr. James influenced the approving body or acted negligently (a score of 1). To hold the other directors liable, a plaintiff must prove that they acted negligently (a score of 1). The unfair transaction cannot be voided (a score of 0). If Mr. James is found liable, he must pay damages (a score of 1), but he is not required to disgorge his profits (a score of 0). Mr. James cannot be fined or imprisoned (a score of 0). Direct suits are available (a score of 1). Adding these numbers gives Panama a score of 4 on the extent of director liability index.

Ease of shareholder suits index

The ease of shareholder suits index measures (i) the range of documents available to the plaintiff from the defendant and witnesses during trial (a score of 1 is assigned for each of the following types of documents available: information that the defendant has indicated he intends to rely on for his defense; information that directly proves specific facts in the plaintiff's claim; any information relevant to the subject matter of the claim; and any information that may lead to the discovery of relevant information); (ii) whether the plaintiff has the ability to directly examine the defendant and witnesses dur-

ing trial (a score of 0 is assigned if no; 1 if yes, with prior approval of the questions by the judge; 2 if yes, without prior approval); (iii) whether the plaintiff can obtain any documents from the defendant without identifying them specifically (a score of 0 is assigned if no; 1 if yes); (iv) whether shareholders owning 10% or less of the company's share capital can request an inspector (a score of 0 is assigned if no; 1 if yes); (v) whether shareholders owning 10% or less of the company's share capital have the right to inspect the transaction documents before filing suit (a score of 0 is assigned if no; 1 if yes); and (vi) whether the standard of proof for civil suits is lower than that for a criminal case (a score of 0 is assigned if no; 1 if yes).

The index ranges from 0 to 10, with higher values indicating greater powers of shareholders to challenge the transaction. In Chad, for example, shareholders suing directors can access documents that the defendant intends to rely on for his defense and that directly prove facts in the plaintiff's claim (a score of 2). The plaintiff can examine the defendant and witnesses during trial only with prior approval of the questions by the court (a score of 1). The plaintiff must specifically identify the documents he seeks (for example, the Buyer-Seller purchase agreement of July 15, 2003) and cannot just request categories (for example, all documents related to the transaction) (a score of 0). Any shareholder can request that an inspector review suspected mismanagement by the defendant (a score of 1). And any shareholder can inspect the transaction documents before deciding whether to sue (a score of 1). The standard of proof for civil suits is the same as the standard for criminal suits (a score of 0). Adding these numbers gives Chad a score of 5 on the ease of shareholder suits index.

Strength of investor protection index

The strength of investor protection index is the average of the extent of disclosure index, the extent of director liability index and the ease of shareholder suits index. The index ranges from 0 to 10, with higher values indicating better investor protection.

This methodology was originally developed in Djankov, La Porta and Shleifer (2005) and is adopted here with minor changes.

Paying taxes

Doing Business records the tax that a medium-size company must pay or withhold in a given year, as well as measures of the administrative burden in paying taxes. Taxes are measured at all levels of government and include the corporate income tax, the personal income tax withheld by the company, the value added tax or sales tax, property taxes, property transfer taxes, the dividend tax, the capital gains tax, the financial transactions tax, waste collection taxes and vehicle and road taxes.

To measure the tax paid by a standardized business and the complexity of a country's tax law, a case study is prepared with a set of financial statements and assumptions about transactions made over the year. Experts in each country compute the taxes owed for their jurisdiction based on the standardized case facts. Information on the frequency of filing, audits and other costs of compliance is also compiled. The project is developed and implemented in cooperation with PricewaterhouseCoopers.

To make the data comparable across countries, several assumptions about the business and the taxes are used.

Assumptions about the business

The business:

- Is a limited liability, taxable company. If there is more than one type of limited liability company in the country, the most popular limited liability form among domestic firms is chosen. Information on the most popular form is obtained from incorporation lawyers or the statistical office.
- Started operations on January 1, 2003. At that time the company purchased all the assets shown in its balance sheet and hired all its workers.
- Operates in the country's most populous city.
- Is 100% domestically owned and has 5 owners, all of whom are natural persons.
- Has a start-up capital of 102 times income per capita at the end of 2003.
- Performs general industrial or commercial activities. Specifically, it produces ceramic flowerpots and sells them at retail. It does not participate in foreign trade (no import or export) and does not handle products subject to a special tax regime, for example, liquor or tobacco.
- Owns 2 plots of land, 1 building, machinery, office equipment, computers and 1 truck and leases another truck.
- Does not qualify for investment incentives or any special benefits apart from those related to the age or size of the company.
- Has 60 employees—4 managers, 8 assistants and 48 workers. All are nationals, and one of the managers is also an owner.
- Has a turnover of 1,050 times income per capita.
- Makes a loss in the first year of operation.
- Distributes 50% of its profits as dividends to the owners at the end of the second year.
- Sells one of its plots of land at a profit during the second year.
- Is subject to a series of detailed assumptions on expenses and transactions to further standardize the case.

Assumptions about the taxes

- All the taxes paid or withheld in the second year of operation are recorded. A tax is considered distinct if it has a different name or is collected by a different agency. Taxes with the same name and agency, but charged at different rates depending on the business, are counted as the same tax.
- The number of times the company pays or withholds taxes in a year is the number of different taxes multiplied by the frequency of payment (or withholding) for each tax. The frequency of payment includes advance payments (or withholding) as well as regular payments (or withholding).

Tax payments

This indicator measures the total number of taxes paid and withheld, the method of payment or withholding, the frequency of payment or withholding and the number of agencies involved for this standardized case during the second year of operation. It takes into account electronic filing. Where electronic filing is allowed, the tax is counted as paid once a year even if the payment is more frequent.

Time

This indicator measures the time, in hours per year, it takes to prepare, file and pay (or withhold) three major types of taxes: the corporate income tax; the value added tax or sales tax; and labor taxes, including payroll taxes and social security contributions.

Total tax payable

This indicator measures the total amount of taxes payable by the business in the second year of operation except for labor taxes. Labor taxes (such as payroll taxes and social security contributions) are included in the hiring cost indicator (see the section on hiring and firing workers). The total amount of taxes is the sum of all the different taxes payable after accounting for deductions and exemptions. The taxes withheld but not paid by the company are not included. Payable taxes are presented as a share of gross profit (defined as sales minus cost of goods sold and labor costs).

A common method for assessing tax rates is the marginal effective tax rate (METR) method, which estimates the tax payable resulting from investing one more unit of capital, or hiring one more worker, or producing one more unit of output. According to this method each input or output has a separate METR. The *Doing Business* measure differs from the METR in several ways: First, it estimates the total tax that a standardized company has to pay, while the METR is the incremental tax. Second, the Doing Business method aggregates all different tax rates into one. Third, the METR of capital takes into account the life of the asset by computing the present discounted value of the future taxes associated with investing one more unit of capital today, while the Doing Business measure is built on one fiscal year only. Fourth, the METRs can be positive, negative or zero because they measure if an activity (e.g., buy a new piece of machinery) is encouraged, discouraged, or unaffected by the tax system. The Doing Business tax measure is always positive unless the company pays no tax at all. Finally, the METR method normally looks at the effect of depreciation in corporate income tax only. It generally ignores small taxes such as property tax, which are included in the Doing Business measure.

This methodology was developed in "Tax Burdens around the World," an ongoing research project by Mihir Desai, Caralee McLiesh, Rita Ramalho and Andrei Shleifer.

Trading across borders

Doing Business compiles procedural requirements for exporting and importing a standardized cargo of goods. Every official procedure for importing and exporting the goods is recorded—from the contractual agreement between the two parties to the delivery of goods—along with the time necessary for completion. All documents and signatures required for clearance of the goods across the border are also recorded. For importing goods, procedures range from the vessel's arrival at the port of entry to the cargo's delivery at the factory warehouse. For exporting goods, procedures range from the packing of the goods at the factory to their departure from the port of exit.

Local freight forwarders, shipping lines, customs brokers and port officials provide information on required documents and signatures as well as the time to complete each procedure. To make the data comparable across countries, several assumptions about the business and the traded goods are used.

Assumptions about the business

The business:
- Has 100 or more employees.
- Is located in the country's most populous city.
- Is a private, limited liability company, formally registered and operating under commercial laws and regulations of the country. It does not operate within an export processing zone or an industrial estate with special export or import privileges.
- Is domestically owned with no foreign ownership.
- Exports more than 10% of its sales to international markets.

Assumptions about the traded goods

The traded product travels in a dry-cargo, 20-foot, full container load. The product:
- Is not hazardous nor does it include military arms or equipment.
- Does not require refrigeration or any other special environment.

- Does not require any special phytosanitary or environmental safety standards other than accepted international standards.

The following Standard International Trade Classification (SITC) Revision 3 categories are considered by the respondents:
- SITC 65: textile yarn, fabrics, made-up articles.
- SITC 84: articles of apparel and clothing accessories.
- SITC 07: coffee, tea, cocoa, spices and manufactures thereof.

Documents

All documents required to export and import the goods are recorded. It is assumed that the contract and letter of credit have already been agreed upon and signed by both parties. Documents include port filing documents, customs declaration and clearance documents and official documents exchanged between the concerned parties. Documents filed simultaneously or in packages are considered different documents but with the same time frame for completion.

Signatures

A signature is defined as an approval, signature or stamp that clears one or more formal procedures. It need not be a physical signature. Electronic signatures are also counted. A mandatory verification from supervisors is also considered a signature. If a document requires approval from several departments or from several individuals within a department, approvals or signatures from all levels are counted. Signatures of the importer and exporter are excluded.

Time

Time is recorded in calendar days. The time calculation for a procedure starts from the moment it is initiated and runs until it is completed. If a procedure can be accelerated for an additional cost, the fastest legal procedure is chosen. It is assumed that neither the importer nor the exporter wastes time and that each commits to completing each remaining procedure without delay. Procedures that can be completed in parallel are treated as simultaneous for the purpose of measuring time. The waiting time between procedures (for example, during unloading of the cargo) is included in the measure.

Enforcing contracts

Indicators on enforcing contracts measure the efficiency of the judicial (or administrative) system in the collection of overdue debt. The data are built by following the step-by-step evolution of a payment dispute either before local courts or through an administrative process, if such a process is available and preferred by creditors. The data are collected through study of the codes of civil procedures and other

court regulations as well as surveys of local litigation lawyers. At least 2 lawyers participate in each country, and in a quarter of the countries judges also complete the survey. To ensure comparability, survey respondents are provided with significant detail, including the amount of the claim, the location and main characteristics of the litigants, the presence of city regulations, the nature of the remedy requested by the plaintiff, the merit of the plaintiff's and the defendant's claims and the social implications of the judicial outcomes.

Assumptions about the case

To make the case comparable across countries, 10 assumptions are used:
- The debt value equals 200% of the country's income per capita.
- The plaintiff has fully complied with the contract (that is, the plaintiff is 100% right).
- The case represents a lawful transaction between businesses residing in the country's most populous city.
- The bank refuses payment for lack of funds in the debtor's account.
- The plaintiff attempts to recover the debt by filing a lawsuit or going through an administrative process, if such a process is available and preferred by creditors.
- The debtor attempts to delay service of process but it is finally accomplished.
- The debtor opposes the complaint (default judgment is not an option).
- The judge decides every motion for the plaintiff.
- The plaintiff attempts to introduce documentary evidence and to call one witness. The debtor attempts to call one witness. Neither party presents objections.
- The judgment is in favor of the plaintiff.

Procedures

All procedures mandated by law or court regulation that demand interaction between the parties, or between them and the judge (or administrator) or court officer, are recorded.

Time

The time required for dispute resolution is recorded in calendar days, counted from the moment the plaintiff files the lawsuit in court until settlement or payment. This includes both the days when actions take place and the waiting periods between actions. The respondents make separate estimates of the average duration of different stages of dispute resolution: for the completion of service of process (time to notify the defendant), the issuance of judgment (time for the trial or administrative process) and the moment of payment or repossession (time for enforcement).

Cost

The cost indicator measures the official cost of going through court procedures, including court costs and attorney fees where the use of attorneys is mandatory or common, or the costs of an administrative debt recovery procedure, expressed as a percentage of the debt value.

This methodology was originally developed in Djankov and others (2003) and is adopted here with minor changes.

Closing a business

Doing Business studies the time and cost of bankruptcy proceedings involving domestic entities. The data are derived from survey responses by local law firms. Answers are provided by a senior partner at each firm in cooperation with 1 or 2 junior associates.

To make the data comparable across countries, several assumptions about the business and the case are used.

Assumptions about the business

The business:
- Is a limited liability company.
- Operates in the country's most populous city.
- Is 100% domestically owned, with the founder, who is also the chairman of the supervisory board, owning 51% (besides the founder, no other shareholder holds more than 1% of shares).
- Has downtown real estate, where it runs a hotel, as its major asset.
- Has a professional general manager.
- Has had average annual revenue of 1,000 times income per capita over the past 3 years.
- Has 201 employees and 50 suppliers, each of whom is owed money for the last delivery.

- Borrowed from a domestic bank 5 years ago (the loan has 10 years to full repayment) and bought real estate (the hotel building), using it as security for the bank loan.
- Has observed the payment schedule and all other conditions of the loan up to now.
- Has a mortgage, with the value of the mortgage principal being exactly equal to the market value of the hotel.

Assumptions about the case

- In January 2005 the business is experiencing liquidity problems. The company's loss in 2004 brought its net worth to a negative figure. There is no cash to pay the bank interest or principal in full, due on January 2, 2005. Therefore, the business defaults on its loan. Management believes that losses will be incurred in 2006 and 2007 as well.
- The bank holds a floating charge against the hotel in countries where floating charges are possible. If the law does not permit a floating charge but contracts commonly use some other provision to that effect, this provision is specified in the lending contract.
- The business has too many creditors to renegotiate out of court. It has the following options: a procedure aimed at rehabilitation or any procedure that will reorganize the business to permit further operation; a procedure aimed at liquidation; or a procedure aimed at selling the hotel, as

a going concern or piecemeal, either enforced through court (or by a government authority like a debt collection agency) or out of court (receivership).

Time

Time is recorded in calendar years. It captures the average duration to complete a procedure as estimated by bankruptcy lawyers. Information is collected on the sequence of the bankruptcy procedures and on whether any procedures can be carried out simultaneously. Delays due to legal derailment tactics that parties to the bankruptcy may use—in particular, the extension of response periods or appeals—are considered.

Cost

The cost of the bankruptcy proceedings is calculated on the basis of survey responses by practicing insolvency lawyers. If several respondents report different estimates, the median reported value is used. Costs include court costs as well as fees of insolvency practitioners, independent assessors, lawyers, accountants and the like. Bribes are excluded. The cost figures are averages of the estimates on a multiple-choice question, where the respondents choose among the following options: 0–2%, 3–5%, 6–8%, 9–10%, 11–18%, 19–25%, 26–33%, 34–50%, 51–75% and more than 75% of the estate value of the bankrupt business.

Recovery rate

The recovery rate measures the efficiency of foreclosure or bankruptcy procedures. It estimates how many cents on the dollar claimants—creditors, tax authorities and employees—recover from an insolvent firm. The calculation takes into account whether the business is kept as a going concern during the proceedings, as well as court, attorney and other related costs and the discounted value due to the time spent closing down. If the business keeps operating, no value is lost on the initial claim, set at 100 cents on the dollar. If it does not, the initial 100 cents on the dollar are reduced to 70 cents on the dollar. Then the official costs of the insolvency procedure are deducted (1 cent for each percentage of the initial value). Finally, the value lost due to the time that the money remains tied up in insolvency procedures is taken into account, including the loss of value due to depreciation of the hotel furniture. Consistent with international accounting practice, the depreciation rate for office furniture is taken to be 20%. The value of the furniture is assumed to be a quarter of the total value of assets. The recovery rate is the present value of the remaining proceeds, based on end-2004 lending rates from the International Monetary Fund's *International Financial Statistics,* supplemented with data from central banks.

This methodology was developed in "Efficiency in Bankruptcy," an ongoing research project by Simeon Djankov, Oliver Hart, Caralee McLiesh and Andrei Shleifer.

Ease of doing business: an appendix

The ease of doing business index ranks economies from 1 to 155 (table A.1). The index is calculated as the ranking on the simple average of country percentile rankings on each of the 10 topics covered in *Doing Business in 2006*. The ranking on each topic is the simple average of the percentile rankings on its component indicators (table A.2).

One example: The ranking on starting a business is the average of the country percentile rankings on the procedures, days, cost and paid-in minimum capital requirement to register a business. It takes 5 procedures, 5 days and 2.9% of annual income per capita in fees to open a business in Iceland. The minimum capital required amounts to 17% of income per capita. On these 4 indicators, Iceland ranks in the 7th, 1st, 8th and 48th percentiles. So on average, Iceland ranks in the 16th percentile on the ease of starting a business. It ranks in the 15th percentile on trading across borders, 8th percentile on enforcing contracts, 7th percentile on closing a business, 52nd percentile on protecting investors and so on. Higher ranks indicate simpler regulation and stronger protections of property rights. The simple average of Iceland's percentile rankings on all topics is 22%. When all countries are ordered by their average percentile rank, Iceland is in 12th place.

The data for all sets of indicators are for January 2005. Based on the study of laws and regulations—with input and verification by more than 3,500 government officials, lawyers, business consultants, accountants and other professionals routinely administering or advising on legal and regulatory requirements—the *Doing Business* methodology offers several advantages. It uses factual information about what laws and regulations say and allows for multiple interactions with local respondents to clarify potential misinterpretations. It is inexpensive, so data can be collected in a large sample of economies. Because the same standard assumptions are applied in the data collection, which is transparent and easily replicable, comparisons and benchmarks are valid across countries. And the data not only highlight the extent of obstacles but also help identify their source, supporting policymakers in designing reform.

Each indicator set studies a different aspect of the business environment. Country rankings vary across indicator sets. For example, Iceland ranks in the 7th percentile on closing a business, its highest, and in the 52nd percentile on protecting investors, its lowest. This points to priorities for reform: Protecting investors is one place to start in further improving business conditions in Iceland. Across all 155 economies, the average correlation coefficient between the 10 sets of indicators is 0.39, and the coefficients between any 2 sets of indicators range between 0.16 (between hiring and firing workers and trading across borders) and 0.64 (between closing a business and enforcing contracts) (table A.3). The low correlations suggest that countries rarely score universally well or universally badly on the indicators. In other words, there is much room for partial reform.

There remains an unfinished agenda for research on what regulations constitute binding constraints, what package of reforms is most effective and how this is shaped by country context. The *Doing Business* indicators provide a new empirical dataset that may improve understanding of these issues.

The ease of doing business index is limited in scope. It does not account for a country's proximity to large markets, quality of infrastructure services (other than services related to trading across borders), the security of property from theft and looting or macroeconomic conditions or the strength of underlying institutions. Thus while Jamaica ranks similarly (at 43) on the ease of doing business to France (at 44), this clearly does not mean that businesses are better off operating in Kingston rather than in Paris. For example, crime and macroeconomic imbalances—2 issues not directly studied in *Doing Business*—make Jamaica a less attractive destination for investment.

Having a high ranking on the ease of doing business does not mean that a country has no regulation. Few would argue that it is every business for itself in New Zealand, that workers are abused in Canada or that creditors seize debtors' assets without a fair process in the Netherlands. And to protect the rights of creditors and investors, as well as establish or upgrade property and credit registries, more regulation rather than less is needed to have a high ranking.

Nor do higher rankings necessarily mean better regulation. While on average high rankings on the *Doing Business* indicators are associated with better economic and social outcomes, this association need not be linear. For example, expedient court procedures to resolve commercial disputes are welcomed by businesses. But to ensure fair process, some procedural requirements are necessary, and these may cause delays. Likewise there are tradeoffs between job protection and labor market flexibility.

But a high ranking on the ease of doing business does mean that the government has created a regulatory environment conducive to business operations. Often, improvements on the *Doing Business* indicators proxy for broader reforms, which affect more than the procedures, time and cost to comply with business regulation and the ease of access to credit. Such improvements are also associated with an expanded reach of regulation, as simpler and less burdensome rules may entice informal businesses to join the formal sector.

Five groups of countries stand out in the rankings on the ease of doing business (see table A.1). First, the 5 Nordic

TABLE A.1
Ease of doing business ranking

1	New Zealand	40	Botswana	79	Russia	118	Croatia
2	Singapore	41	Czech Republic	80	Greece	119	Brazil
3	United States	42	Portugal	81	Macedonia, FYR	120	Venezuela
4	Canada	43	Jamaica	82	Ghana	121	Syria
5	Norway	44	France	83	Moldova	122	Afghanistan
6	Australia	45	Kiribati	84	Kyrgyz Republic	123	São Tomé and Príncipe
7	Hong Kong, China	46	Armenia	85	Uruguay	124	Ukraine
8	Denmark	47	Kuwait	86	Kazakhstan	125	West Bank and Gaza
9	United Kingdom	48	Marshall Islands	87	Bosnia and Herzegovina	126	Zimbabwe
10	Japan	49	Vanuatu	88	Paraguay	127	Mauritania
11	Ireland	50	Palau	89	Costa Rica	128	Algeria
12	Iceland	51	Oman	90	Yemen	129	Benin
13	Finland	52	Hungary	91	China	130	Cameroon
14	Sweden	53	Solomon Islands	92	Serbia and Montenegro	131	Madagascar
15	Lithuania	54	Poland	93	Turkey	132	Senegal
16	Estonia	55	Nepal	94	Nigeria	133	Cambodia
17	Switzerland	56	Micronesia	95	Lebanon	134	Haiti
18	Belgium	57	Panama	96	Malawi	135	Angola
19	Germany	58	Tunisia	97	Lesotho	136	Sierra Leone
20	Thailand	59	Nicaragua	98	Azerbaijan	137	Eritrea
21	Malaysia	60	Pakistan	99	Vietnam	138	Uzbekistan
22	Puerto Rico	61	Mongolia	100	Georgia	139	Rwanda
23	Mauritius	62	Bulgaria	101	Ethiopia	140	Tanzania
24	Netherlands	63	Slovenia	102	Morocco	141	Egypt
25	Chile	64	Papua New Guinea	103	Dominican Republic	142	Timor-Leste
26	Latvia	65	Bangladesh	104	Bhutan	143	Burundi
27	Korea	66	Colombia	105	Guyana	144	Guinea
28	South Africa	67	Zambia	106	Belarus	145	Côte d'Ivoire
29	Israel	68	Kenya	107	Ecuador	146	Mali
30	Spain	69	United Arab Emirates	108	Iran	147	Lao PDR
31	Maldives	70	Italy	109	Guatemala	148	Congo, Rep.
32	Austria	71	Peru	110	Mozambique	149	Togo
33	Namibia	72	Uganda	111	Bolivia	150	Niger
34	Fiji	73	Mexico	112	Honduras	151	Sudan
35	Taiwan, China	74	Jordan	113	Philippines	152	Chad
36	Tonga	75	Sri Lanka	114	Iraq	153	Central African Republic
37	Slovakia	76	El Salvador	115	Indonesia	154	Burkina Faso
38	Saudi Arabia	77	Argentina	116	India	155	Congo, Dem. Rep.
39	Samoa	78	Romania	117	Albania		

Source: Doing Business database.

countries all rank in the top 15. Second, 3 Southern European countries have the lowest ranks among OECD countries—with France at 44, Italy at 70 and Greece at 80. France ranks among the top 10 on starting a business and has very efficient contract enforcement, but scores low on registering property, getting credit, and labor market flexibility. Italy has average performance on most indicators. Greece has efficient courts and bankruptcy procedures, but lags on other indicators. Third, Saudi Arabia (38), Kuwait (47) and Oman (51) rank high, especially on paying taxes and labor market flexibility. Fourth, 3 of the largest emerging market economies—Brazil (119), India (116) and Indonesia (115)—have below-average ranks. The 3 display a similar pattern: reforms to ease access to credit (for example, by reforming bankruptcy and investor protection) are not accompanied by reforms to simplify regulation for opening a business, hiring workers and paying taxes. Finally, the Pacific islands, which closely follow the business regulations of Australia, New Zealand and the United States, have high scores. For example, Fiji ranks 34, and Samoa 39.

Empirical research is needed to establish the optimal level of business regulation—for example, what the duration of court procedures should be and what the optimal degree of social protection is. The indicators compiled in the *Doing Business* project allow such research to take place. Since the start of the project in November 2001, more than 200 academic papers have used one or more indicators constructed in *Doing Business* and the related background papers by its authors. These citations can be found by typing "Doing Business" and the names of the background papers or their authors (listed in the Data notes) at http://www.scholar.google.com/advanced_scholar_search.

Questions on the methodology and challenges to the data may be submitted through the "Ask a Question" function on the *Doing Business* website at http://www.doingbusiness.org. Updated indicators, as well as any revisions of or corrections to the printed data, are posted on the website. *Doing Business* now publishes more than 5700 data points. Since the publication of last year's report in September 2004, 26 complaints

about data have been received. In 4 instances data were corrected as a result of these complaints: the number of procedures and time to start a business in Burkina Faso, the cost of registering property in Senegal, the time to go through bankruptcy in Switzerland and the time and cost to go through bankruptcy in Russia. The other complaints were resolved without a need for corrections, through explanations of the assumptions underlying the methodology and the date as of which the data are collected. In 22 other cases past data were corrected by the *Doing Business* team during the updating of the indicators for this publication.

TABLE A.2
Which indicators make up the ranking?

Indicator set

Starting a business
- Procedures, time, cost and minimum capital to open a new business

Dealing with licenses
- Procedures, time and cost of business inspections and licensing (construction industry)

Hiring and firing workers
- Difficulty of hiring index, rigidity of hours of index, difficulty of firing index, hiring cost and firing cost

Registering property
- Procedures, time and cost to register commercial real estate

Getting credit
- Strength of legal rights index, depth of credit information index

Protecting investors
- Indices on the extent of disclosure, extent of director liability and ease of shareholder suits

Paying taxes
- Number of taxes paid, hours per year spent preparing tax returns and total tax payable as share of gross profit

Trading across borders
- Number of documents, number of signatures and time necessary to export and import

Enforcing contracts
- Procedures, time and cost to enforce a debt contract

Closing a business
- Time and cost to close down a business, and recovery rate

Source: Doing Business database.

TABLE A.3
Correlation coefficients between sets of *Doing Business* indicators

Indicator set	Ease of starting a business	Ease of hiring and firing	Ease of licensing	Ease of registering property	Ease of getting credit	Strength of investor protection	Ease of paying taxes	Ease of trading	Ease of enforcing contracts
Ease of hiring and firing	0.38								
Ease of licensing	0.49	0.47							
Ease of registering property	0.41	0.27	0.51						
Ease of getting credit	0.48	0.18	0.41	0.41					
Strength of investor protection	0.44	0.39	0.38	0.17	0.43				
Ease of paying taxes	0.35	0.45	0.38	0.34	0.20	0.29			
Ease of trading	0.49	0.15	0.57	0.42	0.56	0.34	0.31		
Ease of enforcing contracts	0.55	0.20	0.43	0.39	0.45	0.28	0.36	0.54	
Ease of closing a business	0.54	0.16	0.42	0.37	0.62	0.36	0.27	0.62	0.64

Source: Doing Business database.

	Starting a Business				Dealing with Licenses		
	JANUARY 2005				JANUARY 2005		
Economy	Procedures (number)	Time (days)	Cost (% of income per capita)	Minimum capital (% of income per capita)	Procedures (number)	Time (days)	Cost (% of income per capita)
Afghanistan	1	7	52.8	0.0	..	..	..
Albania	11	41	31.1	39.9	22	344	227.4
Algeria	14	26	25.3	55.1	25	244	70.5
Angola	14	146	642.8	485.4	15	326	1674.7
Argentina	15	32	13.4	6.6	23	288	47.9
Armenia	10	25	6.1	4.0	20	176	64.9
Australia	2	2	1.9	0.0	16	121	12.3
Austria	9	29	5.7	61.5	14	195	81.6
Azerbaijan	14	115	12.5	0.0	28	212	1326.2
Bangladesh	8	35	81.4	0.0	13	185	291.0
Belarus	16	79	22.9	42.8	18	354	22.7
Belgium	4	34	11.1	13.5	15	184	64.1
Benin	8	32	190.8	323.1	22	335	287.9
Bhutan	11	62	10.7	0.0	26	249	62.5
Bolivia	15	50	154.8	4.1	13	187	268.2
Bosnia and Herzegovina	12	54	40.9	57.4	17	476	8735.4
Botswana	11	108	10.9	0.0	42	160	298.8
Brazil	17	152	10.1	0.0	19	460	184.4
Bulgaria	11	32	9.6	104.2	24	212	325.1
Burkina Faso	12	45	149.9	483.8	46	241	5002.3
Burundi	11	43	200.7	0.0	18	302	10740.5
Cambodia	10	86	276.1	80.7	28	247	606.7
Cameroon	12	37	172.8	216.5	15	444	1094.2
Canada	2	3	0.9	0.0	15	87	123.0
Central African Republic	10	14	211.6	568.1	21	237	308.3
Chad	19	75	360.8	619.1	16	199	1703.1
Chile	9	27	10.3	0.0	12	191	125.2
China	13	48	13.6	946.7	30	363	126.0
Colombia	12	43	25.3	0.0	12	150	697.3
Congo, Dem. Rep.	13	155	503.3	215.9	16	306	6516.3
Congo, Rep.	8	67	288.8	220.1	15	174	1422.2
Costa Rica	11	77	23.8	0.0	19	120	150.3
Côte d'Ivoire	11	45	134.0	225.2	22	569	194.9
Croatia	12	49	13.4	22.7	28	278	1236.7
Czech Republic	10	40	9.5	39.0	31	245	16.1
Denmark	3	5	0.0	47.0	7	70	71.3
Dominican Republic	10	75	30.9	1.2	12	150	255.1
Ecuador	14	69	38.1	9.2	19	149	100.0
Egypt	10	34	104.9	739.8	30	263	1067.1
El Salvador	12	40	118.0	124.4	22	144	204.2
Eritrea	13	91	128.6	535.2	19	187	1254.2
Estonia	6	35	6.2	41.4	12	116	41.4
Ethiopia	7	32	65.1	1532.0	12	133	1746.5
Fiji	8	46	28.4	0.0	29	117	35.3
Finland	3	14	1.2	28.0	17	56	76.2
France	7	8	1.2	0.0	10	185	78.0
Georgia	8	21	13.7	46.8	29	282	144.6
Germany	9	24	4.7	47.6	11	165	82.8
Ghana	12	81	78.6	27.9	16	127	1549.7
Greece	15	38	24.6	121.4	17	176	71.9
Guatemala	15	39	58.4	29.3	22	294	667.8
Guinea	13	49	178.8	405.0	29	278	512.2

	Starting a Business				Dealing with Licenses		
	JANUARY 2005				JANUARY 2005		
Economy	Procedures (number)	Time (days)	Cost (% of income per capita)	Minimum capital (% of income per capita)	Procedures (number)	Time (days)	Cost (% of income per capita)
Guyana	8	46	101.4	0.0	17	202	96.7
Haiti	12	203	153.1	155.0	12	186	1129.6
Honduras	13	62	64.1	34.1	14	199	759.6
Hong Kong, China	5	11	3.4	0.0	22	230	38.5
Hungary	6	38	22.4	79.6	25	213	279.1
Iceland	5	5	2.9	17.1	20	124	16.8
India	11	71	61.7	0.0	20	270	678.5
Indonesia	12	151	101.7	97.8	19	224	364.9
Iran	8	47	6.3	1.7	21	668	818.0
Iraq	11	77	37.4	31.6	14	210	311.5
Ireland	4	24	5.3	0.0	10	181	23.6
Israel	5	34	5.3	0.0	21	219	93.5
Italy	9	13	15.7	10.8	17	284	147.3
Jamaica	6	9	8.3	0.0	13	242	526.1
Japan	11	31	10.7	75.3	11	87	19.7
Jordan	11	36	45.9	1011.6	17	122	506.3
Kazakhstan	7	24	8.6	26.6	32	258	68.3
Kenya	13	54	48.2	0.0	11	170	40.0
Kiribati	6	21	71.0	38.4	..	..	..
Korea	12	22	15.2	308.8	14	60	232.6
Kuwait	13	35	2.2	133.8	26	149	278.9
Kyrgyz Republic	8	21	10.4	0.6	16	152	325.2
Lao PDR	9	198	15.1	23.4	24	208	224.5
Latvia	7	18	4.2	31.8	21	160	43.9
Lebanon	6	46	110.6	68.5	16	275	214.6
Lesotho	9	92	56.1	16.4	12	254	134.2
Lithuania	8	26	3.3	57.3	14	151	17.5
Macedonia, FYR	13	48	11.3	145.2	18	214	67.5
Madagascar	11	38	54.3	2158.0	19	356	447.8
Malawi	10	35	139.6	0.0	23	205	244.7
Malaysia	9	30	20.9	0.0	25	226	82.7
Maldives	6	12	12.4	6.6	9	131	40.3
Mali	13	42	190.7	490.8	17	260	4903.0
Marshall Islands	7	22	27.4	0.0	6	76	36.9
Mauritania	11	82	143.6	877.5	19	152	987.1
Mauritius	6	46	8.8	0.0	21	132	16.7
Mexico	9	58	15.6	13.9	12	222	159.0
Micronesia	7	36	27.7	50.3	6	53	41.4
Moldova	10	30	17.1	22.0	20	122	215.0
Mongolia	8	20	6.2	140.2	18	96	58.8
Morocco	5	11	12.0	700.3	21	217	1302.8
Mozambique	14	153	95.0	12.0	14	212	148.6
Namibia	10	95	18.8	0.0	11	169	892.0
Nepal	7	21	69.9	0.0	12	147	314.7
Netherlands	7	11	13.0	64.6	18	184	142.7
New Zealand	2	12	0.2	0.0	7	65	29.3
Nicaragua	8	42	139.1	0.0	12	192	1243.8
Niger	13	35	465.4	760.8	27	165	2920.3
Nigeria	9	43	73.8	43.3	16	465	355.8
Norway	4	13	2.7	27.0	13	97	53.9
Oman	9	34	4.8	97.3	16	271	1014.0
Pakistan	11	24	18.6	0.0	12	218	1170.7

Economy	Starting a Business JANUARY 2005				Dealing with Licenses JANUARY 2005		
	Procedures (number)	Time (days)	Cost (% of income per capita)	Minimum capital (% of income per capita)	Procedures (number)	Time (days)	Cost (% of income per capita)
Palau	8	33	10.2	7.3	6	67	18.8
Panama	7	19	24.8	0.0	22	128	114.3
Papua New Guinea	8	56	30.2	0.0	20	218	124.7
Paraguay	17	74	147.8	0.0	15	273	544.5
Peru	10	102	38.0	0.0	19	201	366.3
Philippines	11	48	20.3	2.0	23	197	121.0
Poland	10	31	22.2	220.1	25	322	83.1
Portugal	11	54	13.4	39.4	20	327	57.7
Puerto Rico	7	7	1.0	0.0	20	137	103.3
Romania	5	11	5.3	0.0	15	291	187.7
Russia	8	33	5.0	4.4	22	528	353.7
Rwanda	9	21	280.2	0.0	17	252	510.9
Samoa	7	68	18.8	0.0	19	88	107.3
São Tomé and Príncipe	9	192	97.0	0.0	13	259	1737.1
Saudi Arabia	13	64	68.5	1236.9	18	131	82.1
Senegal	9	57	108.7	260.4	18	185	175.9
Serbia and Montenegro	10	15	6.0	9.5	21	212	2195.0
Sierra Leone	9	26	835.4	0.0	48	236	268.9
Singapore	6	6	1.1	0.0	11	129	24.0
Slovakia	9	25	5.1	41.0	13	272	18.0
Slovenia	9	60	10.1	17.0	14	207	128.7
Solomon Islands	5	35	48.4	0.0	..	..	..
South Africa	9	38	8.6	0.0	18	176	38.0
Spain	10	47	16.5	15.7	12	277	77.1
Sri Lanka	8	50	10.4	0.0	18	167	144.0
Sudan	10	38	68.1	0.0	..	..	..
Sweden	3	16	0.7	35.0	8	116	119.6
Switzerland	6	20	8.7	31.3	15	152	59.2
Syria	12	47	34.5	5111.9	20	134	359.8
Taiwan, China	8	48	6.0	216.3	32	235	250.9
Tanzania	13	35	161.3	6.0	26	313	4110.2
Thailand	8	33	6.1	0.0	9	147	17.3
Timor-Leste	10	92	125.4	909.1	24	192	51.0
Togo	13	53	218.3	459.9	14	273	1223.4
Tonga	4	32	11.7	0.0	15	81	198.0
Tunisia	9	14	10.0	29.8	21	154	340.0
Turkey	8	9	27.7	20.9	32	232	368.7
Uganda	17	36	117.8	0.0	19	155	861.8
Ukraine	15	34	10.6	183.0	18	265	229.4
United Arab Emirates	12	54	44.3	416.9	21	125	2.1
United Kingdom	6	18	0.7	0.0	19	115	70.2
United States	5	5	0.5	0.0	19	70	16.9
Uruguay	11	45	43.9	151.7	17	146	95.0
Uzbekistan	9	35	15.5	20.2	..	..	..
Vanuatu	8	39	65.6	0.0	7	82	427.1
Venezuela	13	116	15.7	0.0	13	276	547.2
Vietnam	11	50	50.6	0.0	14	143	64.1
West Bank and Gaza	11	106	275.4	1409.8	18	144	779.2
Yemen	12	63	240.2	2703.2	13	131	274.4
Zambia	6	35	18.1	2.1	16	165	1671.2
Zimbabwe	10	96	1442.5	53.0	21	481	1509.6

Economy	Hiring and Firing Workers						Registering Property		
	JANUARY 2005						JANUARY 2005		
	Difficulty of hiring index (0–100)	Rigidity of hours index (0–100)	Difficulty of firing index (0–100)	Rigidity of employment index (0–100)	Hiring cost (% of salary)	Firing Cost (weeks of salary)	Procedures (number)	Time (days)	Cost (% of property value)
Afghanistan	67	20	30	39	0	4	11	252	9.5
Albania	44	80	20	48	31	64	7	47	3.6
Algeria	44	60	50	51	27	17	16	52	9.0
Angola	33	80	80	64	8	62	7	334	11.1
Argentina	44	60	40	48	30	94	5	44	8.3
Armenia	17	60	70	49	19	17	4	6	0.5
Australia	0	40	10	17	21	4	5	5	7.1
Austria	11	80	40	44	31	55	3	32	4.5
Azerbaijan	33	40	40	38	27	42	7	61	0.4
Bangladesh	11	40	20	24	0	47	11	363	11.0
Belarus	0	40	40	27	39	21	7	231	0.1
Belgium	11	40	10	20	55	16	7	132	12.8
Benin	39	80	40	53	27	35	3	50	15.1
Bhutan	78	60	0	46	0	94	5	72	1.0
Bolivia	61	60	0	40	14	98	7	92	5.0
Bosnia and Herzegovina	56	40	30	42	42	33	7	331	6.0
Botswana	11	40	40	30	0	19	6	69	5.1
Brazil	67	80	20	56	27	165	15	47	4.0
Bulgaria	61	60	10	44	32	30	9	19	2.3
Burkina Faso	83	100	70	84	23	57	8	107	16.2
Burundi	67	80	60	69	7	25	5	94	18.9
Cambodia	67	80	30	59	0	39	7	56	4.7
Cameroon	28	60	80	56	15	40	5	93	19.0
Canada	11	0	30	14	12	28	6	10	1.7
Central African Republic	89	80	60	76	18	37	3	69	17.3
Chad	67	80	70	72	21	21	6	44	21.3
Chile	33	20	20	24	3	51	6	31	1.3
China	11	40	40	30	30	90	3	32	3.1
Colombia	72	60	40	57	28	44	7	23	3.5
Congo, Dem. Rep.	100	100	70	90	9	31	8	106	10.2
Congo, Rep.	89	80	70	80	16	42	6	103	22.1
Costa Rica	56	60	0	39	24	34	6	21	3.6
Côte d'Ivoire	44	80	10	45	15	68	7	369	14.3
Croatia	61	60	50	57	17	38	5	956	5.0
Czech Republic	33	20	20	24	37	22	4	123	3.0
Denmark	11	40	10	20	1	39	6	42	0.6
Dominican Republic	22	80	30	44	14	77	7	107	5.1
Ecuador	44	60	70	58	13	131	10	21	6.7
Egypt	0	80	80	53	26	162	7	193	6.1
El Salvador	44	60	20	41	15	86	5	52	3.6
Eritrea	0	60	20	27	2	69	6	91	9.1
Estonia	33	80	40	51	33	33	4	65	0.5
Ethiopia	33	60	30	41	0	40	15	56	10.4
Fiji	22	40	0	21	8	28	3	48	12.0
Finland	44	60	40	48	22	24	3	14	4.0
France	78	80	40	66	47	32	9	183	6.5
Georgia	0	60	70	43	31	4	6	9	0.6
Germany	44	80	40	55	21	67	4	41	4.1
Ghana	11	40	50	34	13	25	7	382	3.7
Greece	78	80	40	66	30	69	12	23	13.7
Guatemala	61	40	20	40	13	101	5	69	4.7
Guinea	33	80	30	48	27	26	6	104	15.6

Economy	Hiring and Firing Workers JANUARY 2005						Registering Property JANUARY 2005		
	Difficulty of hiring index (0–100)	Rigidity of hours index (0–100)	Difficulty of firing index (0–100)	Rigidity of employment index (0–100)	Hiring cost (% of salary)	Firing Cost (weeks of salary)	Procedures (number)	Time (days)	Cost (% of property value)
Guyana	..	..	..	..	7	..	4	24	2.5
Haiti	11	40	20	24	9	26	5	683	8.1
Honduras	22	40	40	34	10	46	7	36	5.8
Hong Kong, China	0	0	0	0	5	13	5	83	5.0
Hungary	11	80	20	37	34	34	4	78	11.0
Iceland	33	60	0	31	12	13	3	4	2.4
India	56	40	90	62	12	79	6	67	7.9
Indonesia	61	40	70	57	10	145	7	42	11.0
Iran	78	60	10	49	23	90	9	36	5.0
Iraq	78	80	50	69	12	4	5	8	7.7
Ireland	28	40	30	33	11	52	5	38	10.3
Israel	0	80	20	33	6	90	7	144	7.5
Italy	61	80	30	57	33	47	8	27	0.9
Jamaica	11	0	20	10	12	60	5	54	13.5
Japan	17	40	0	19	13	21	6	14	4.1
Jordan	11	40	50	34	11	90	8	22	10.0
Kazakhstan	0	60	10	23	22	8	8	52	1.6
Kenya	33	20	30	28	5	47	8	73	4.1
Kiribati	0	0	50	17	8	46	4	58	0.1
Korea	44	60	30	45	17	90	7	11	6.3
Kuwait	0	60	0	20	11	42	8	75	0.6
Kyrgyz Republic	33	40	40	38	27	21	7	10	5.3
Lao PDR	11	60	80	50	5	36	9	135	4.2
Latvia	67	40	70	59	22	17	9	54	2.1
Lebanon	33	0	40	24	22	17	8	25	5.9
Lesotho	56	60	10	42	0	47	6	101	8.5
Lithuania	33	60	40	44	28	34	3	3	0.8
Macedonia, FYR	61	60	40	54	33	41	6	74	3.6
Madagascar	67	60	50	59	18	41	8	134	11.0
Malawi	22	20	20	21	1	90	6	118	3.4
Malaysia	0	20	10	10	13	65	4	143	2.3
Maldives	0	20	0	7	0	20	..	..	..
Mali	78	60	60	66	24	81	5	44	20.0
Marshall Islands	33	0	0	11	11	0	4	12	1.7
Mauritania	100	60	60	73	17	31	4	49	6.8
Mauritius	0	60	50	37	7	15	5	210	16.5
Mexico	33	60	60	51	24	75	5	74	5.3
Micronesia	33	0	0	11	6	0	3	8	1.1
Moldova	33	100	70	68	30	21	6	48	1.5
Mongolia	11	80	10	34	19	17	5	11	2.3
Morocco	100	40	40	60	18	83	3	82	6.1
Mozambique	83	80	20	61	4	141	8	42	5.2
Namibia	0	60	20	27	0	24	9	28	9.3
Nepal	56	20	90	55	0	90	2	2	6.2
Netherlands	28	60	60	49	16	16	2	2	6.2
New Zealand	11	0	10	7	0	0	2	2	0.1
Nicaragua	11	80	50	47	17	24	7	65	6.5
Niger	100	100	70	90	16	76	5	49	14.0
Nigeria	33	60	20	38	8	4	21	274	27.1
Norway	44	40	30	38	14	12	1	1	2.5
Oman	44	60	0	35	9	13	4	16	3.0
Pakistan	67	40	30	46	12	90	5	49	3.2

Economy	Hiring and Firing Workers						Registering Property		
	JANUARY 2005						JANUARY 2005		
	Difficulty of hiring index (0–100)	Rigidity of hours index (0–100)	Difficulty of firing index (0–100)	Rigidity of employment index (0–100)	Hiring cost (% of salary)	Firing Cost (weeks of salary)	Procedures (number)	Time (days)	Cost (% of property value)
Palau	0	0	0	0	6	0	3	14	0.3
Panama	78	40	70	63	14	47	7	44	2.4
Papua New Guinea	22	20	20	21	8	38	4	72	5.2
Paraguay	56	60	60	59	17	99	7	48	2.0
Peru	44	60	40	48	10	56	5	33	3.2
Philippines	56	40	40	45	9	90	8	33	5.7
Poland	11	60	40	37	26	25	6	197	1.6
Portugal	33	80	60	58	24	98	5	83	7.4
Puerto Rico	56	20	30	35	16	0	8	15	1.6
Romania	67	60	50	59	34	98	8	170	2.0
Russia	0	60	30	30	36	17	6	52	0.4
Rwanda	56	60	60	59	8	54	5	371	9.6
Samoa	11	20	0	10	6	42	5	147	1.9
São Tomé and Príncipe	61	60	60	60	6	108	6	51	12.6
Saudi Arabia	0	40	0	13	11	79	4	4	0.0
Senegal	61	60	70	64	23	38	6	114	18.0
Serbia and Montenegro	44	0	40	28	25	21	6	111	5.3
Sierra Leone	89	80	70	80	10	188	8	58	15.4
Singapore	0	0	0	0	13	4	3	9	2.8
Slovakia	17	60	40	39	35	13	3	17	0.1
Slovenia	61	80	50	64	17	43	6	391	2.0
Solomon Islands	11	20	20	17	8	52	6	86	10.2
South Africa	56	40	60	52	3	38	6	23	11.0
Spain	67	80	50	66	32	56	3	25	7.2
Sri Lanka	0	40	80	40	16	176	8	63	5.1
Sudan	0	60	70	43	19	37	..	..	..
Sweden	28	60	40	43	33	24	1	2	3.0
Switzerland	0	40	10	17	14	12	4	16	0.4
Syria	11	60	50	40	17	79	4	34	30.4
Taiwan, China	78	60	30	56	10	90	3	5	6.2
Tanzania	67	80	60	69	16	38	12	61	12.2
Thailand	33	20	0	18	5	47	2	2	6.3
Timor-Leste	67	20	50	46	0	21	7	71	10.0
Togo	78	80	80	79	25	66	6	212	7.5
Tonga	0	40	0	13	0	0	4	108	10.3
Tunisia	61	0	100	54	19	29	5	57	6.1
Turkey	44	80	40	55	22	112	8	9	3.2
Uganda	0	20	20	13	10	12	8	48	5.1
Ukraine	44	60	80	61	36	17	10	93	3.8
United Arab Emirates	0	80	20	33	13	96	3	9	2.0
United Kingdom	11	20	10	14	9	34	2	21	4.1
United States	0	0	10	3	8	0	4	12	0.5
Uruguay	33	60	0	31	20	26	8	66	7.1
Uzbekistan	33	40	30	34	36	31	12	97	10.5
Vanuatu	39	40	10	30	6	55	2	188	7.0
Venezuela	33	80	0	38	15	46	7	33	2.1
Vietnam	44	40	70	51	17	98	5	67	1.2
West Bank and Gaza	33	60	20	38	13	90	7	58	4.7
Yemen	0	80	30	37	17	17	6	21	3.9
Zambia	0	20	10	10	9	176	6	70	9.6
Zimbabwe	11	40	20	24	6	29	4	30	22.6

Economy	Getting Credit				Protecting Investors			
	JANUARY 2005				JANUARY 2005			
	Strength of legal rights index (0–10)	Depth of credit information index (0–6)	Public registry coverage (% of adults)	Private bureau coverage (% of adults)	Extent of disclosure index (0–10)	Extent of director liability index (0–10)	Ease of shareholder suits index (0–10)	Strength of investor protection index (0–10)
Afghanistan	0	0	0.0	0.0	0	0	2	0.7
Albania	9	0	0.0	0.0	0	6	2	2.7
Algeria	3	0	0.0	0.0	8	4	1	4.3
Angola	3	4	2.9	0.0	5	6	6	5.7
Argentina	3	6	22.1	95.0	7	2	7	5.3
Armenia	4	3	2.6	0.0	..	..	..	..
Australia	9	5	0.0	100.0	8	2	8	6.0
Austria	5	6	1.2	45.4	2	5	4	3.7
Azerbaijan	6	3	0.4	0.0	0	5	7	4.0
Bangladesh	7	2	0.4	0.0	6	7	7	6.7
Belarus	5	3	..	0.0	1	4	7	4.0
Belgium	5	4	55.3	0.0	8	7	7	7.3
Benin	4	1	3.5	0.0	5	8	4	5.7
Bhutan	3	0	0.0	0.0	6	6	4	5.3
Bolivia	3	4	10.3	24.6	1	5	7	4.3
Bosnia and Herzegovina	8	5	0.0	19.3	3	6	5	4.7
Botswana	9	5	0.0	30.8	8	2	3	4.3
Brazil	2	5	9.6	53.6	5	7	4	5.3
Bulgaria	6	3	13.6	0.0	8	1	7	5.3
Burkina Faso	4	1	1.9	0.0	6	5	3	4.7
Burundi	2	3	0.2	0.0	..	..	..	..
Cambodia	0	0	0.0	0.0	5	9	2	5.3
Cameroon	4	2	0.8	0.0	8	3	6	5.7
Canada	7	6	0.0	100.0	8	9	9	8.7
Central African Republic	3	2	1.2	0.0	..	..	..	..
Chad	3	2	0.2	0.0	3	6	5	4.7
Chile	4	6	45.7	22.1	8	4	5	5.7
China	2	3	0.4	0.0	10	1	2	4.3
Colombia	4	4	0.0	31.7	7	1	9	5.7
Congo, Dem. Rep.	3	0	0.0	0.0	3	4	5	4.0
Congo, Rep.	2	2	2.3	0.0	4	5	6	5.0
Costa Rica	4	6	34.8	4.5	2	5	2	3.0
Côte d'Ivoire	2	1	3.0	0.0	6	5	3	4.7
Croatia	4	0	0.0	0.0	2	5	2	3.0
Czech Republic	6	5	2.8	37.9	2	5	8	5.0
Denmark	7	4	0.0	7.7	7	5	7	6.3
Dominican Republic	4	5	19.2	34.6	3	0	9	4.0
Ecuador	3	4	13.6	0.0	1	5	6	4.0
Egypt	1	2	1.2	0.0	5	2	5	4.0
El Salvador	5	5	17.3	78.7	6	2	6	4.7
Eritrea	3	0	0.0	0.0	4	5	5	4.7
Estonia	4	5	0.0	12.5	8	4	6	6.0
Ethiopia	5	0	0.0	0.0	1	4	3	2.7
Fiji	8	4	0.0	28.3	5	5	7	5.7
Finland	6	5	0.0	14.7	6	4	7	5.7
France	3	2	1.8	0.0	10	1	5	5.3
Georgia	7	0	0.0	0.0	4	4	4	4.0
Germany	8	6	0.6	88.2	5	5	6	5.3
Ghana	5	0	0.0	0.0	7	7	4	6.0
Greece	3	4	0.0	17.7	1	4	5	3.3
Guatemala	4	5	0.0	9.9	1	3	7	3.7
Guinea	2	1	0.0	0.0	5	6	3	4.7

Economy	Getting Credit				Protecting Investors			
	JANUARY 2005				JANUARY 2005			
	Strength of legal rights index (0–10)	Depth of credit information index (0–6)	Public registry coverage (% of adults)	Private bureau coverage (% of adults)	Extent of disclosure index (0–10)	Extent of director liability index (0–10)	Ease of shareholder suits index (0–10)	Strength of investor protection index (0–10)
Guyana	3	0	0.0	0.0	5	4	4	4.3
Haiti	2	2	0.3	0.0	4	3	4	3.7
Honduras	5	4	11.2	18.7	1	5	4	3.3
Hong Kong, China	10	5	0.0	64.5	10	8	8	8.7
Hungary	6	5	0.0	4.0	1	5	8	4.7
Iceland	7	5	0.0	100.0	4	5	6	5.0
India	5	2	0.0	1.7	7	4	7	6.0
Indonesia	5	3	0.0	0.1	8	5	3	5.3
Iran	5	3	13.7	0.0	3	5	0	2.7
Iraq	4	0	0.0	0.0	4	5	5	4.7
Ireland	8	5	0.0	100.0	9	5	9	7.7
Israel	8	5	0.0	0.7	8	8	9	8.3
Italy	3	6	6.1	59.9	7	2	5	4.7
Jamaica	6	0	0.0	0.0	3	8	5	5.3
Japan	6	6	0.0	61.2	6	7	7	6.7
Jordan	6	2	0.6	0.0	5	2	4	3.7
Kazakhstan	5	0	0.0	0.0	7	2	6	5.0
Kenya	8	5	0.0	0.1	4	2	10	5.3
Kiribati	6	0	0.0	0.0	6	5	8	6.3
Korea	6	5	0.0	80.7	7	2	5	4.7
Kuwait	5	4	0.0	16.1	5	5	5	5.0
Kyrgyz Republic	8	2	0.0	0.2	8	1	8	5.7
Lao PDR	2	0	0.0	0.0	4	2	4	3.3
Latvia	8	3	1.1	0.0	5	4	8	5.7
Lebanon	4	4	3.5	0.0	8	1	4	4.3
Lesotho	5	0	0.0	0.0	2	2	8	4.0
Lithuania	4	6	2.5	12.1	5	4	7	5.3
Macedonia, FYR	6	3	1.9	0.0	5	7	6	6.0
Madagascar	4	2	0.3	0.0	5	6	6	5.7
Malawi	7	0	0.0	0.0	4	7	5	5.3
Malaysia	8	6	33.7	..	10	9	7	8.7
Maldives	4	0	0.0	0.0	0	8	8	5.3
Mali	3	1	2.3	0.0	6	5	3	4.7
Marshall Islands	6	0	0.0	0.0	2	0	8	3.3
Mauritania	7	1	0.2	0.0	..	..	..	..
Mauritius	7	0	0.0	0.0	6	8	9	7.7
Mexico	2	6	0.0	49.4	6	0	5	3.7
Micronesia	6	0	0.0	0.0	0	0	8	2.7
Moldova	6	0	0.0	0.0	7	1	6	4.7
Mongolia	5	3	4.7	0.0	..	..	..	..
Morocco	2	1	2.0	0.0	6	5	1	4.0
Mozambique	4	4	0.8	0.0	..	..	..	..
Namibia	5	5	0.0	35.2	8	5	7	6.7
Nepal	4	3	0.0	0.1	4	1	9	4.7
Netherlands	8	5	0.0	68.9	4	3	6	4.3
New Zealand	9	5	0.0	95.8	10	9	10	9.7
Nicaragua	4	4	8.1	0.0	4	5	6	5.0
Niger	4	1	0.9	0.0	6	5	3	4.7
Nigeria	7	3	0.0	0.3	6	7	4	5.7
Norway	6	4	0.0	100.0	7	6	7	6.7
Oman	3	0	0.0	0.0	8	6	3	5.7
Pakistan	4	4	0.3	0.9	6	6	7	6.3

Economy	Getting Credit				Protecting Investors			
	JANUARY 2005				JANUARY 2005			
	Strength of legal rights index (0–10)	Depth of credit information index (0–6)	Public registry coverage (% of adults)	Private bureau coverage (% of adults)	Extent of disclosure index (0–10)	Extent of director liability index (0–10)	Ease of shareholder suits index (0–10)	Strength of investor protection index (0–10)
Palau	5	0	0.0	0.0	0	0	8	2.7
Panama	6	6	0.0	40.2	3	4	7	4.7
Papua New Guinea	6	0	0.0	0.0	5	5	8	6.0
Paraguay	3	6	8.7	52.2	6	5	6	5.7
Peru	2	6	30.2	27.8	7	5	7	6.3
Philippines	3	2	0.0	3.7	1	2	7	3.3
Poland	3	4	0.0	38.1	7	4	8	6.3
Portugal	5	4	64.3	9.8	7	5	6	6.0
Puerto Rico	6	5	0.0	63.6	..	..	..	..
Romania	4	4	1.4	1.0	8	5	4	5.7
Russia	3	0	0.0	0.0	7	3	5	5.0
Rwanda	1	2	0.1	0.0	..	..	..	..
Samoa	7	0	0.0	0.0	5	6	8	6.3
São Tomé and Príncipe	..	0	0.0	0.0	6	1	6	4.3
Saudi Arabia	4	5	0.2	10.2	8	4	3	5.0
Senegal	3	1	4.3	0.0	7	1	3	3.7
Serbia and Montenegro	5	1	0.1	0.0	7	6	4	5.7
Sierra Leone	5	0	0.0	0.0	3	6	5	4.7
Singapore	10	4	0.0	38.6	10	9	9	9.3
Slovakia	9	2	0.5	18.1	2	4	6	4.0
Slovenia	6	3	2.7	0.0	3	8	6	5.7
Solomon Islands	6	0	0.0	0.0	5	6	8	6.3
South Africa	5	5	0.0	63.4	8	8	8	8.0
Spain	5	6	42.1	6.5	4	6	4	4.7
Sri Lanka	3	3	0.0	2.2	4	5	7	5.3
Sudan	5	0	0.0	0.0	..	..	..	..
Sweden	6	5	0.0	100.0	2	5	7	4.7
Switzerland	6	5	0.0	23.3	1	5	6	4.0
Syria	5	0	0.0	0.0	5	7	1	4.3
Taiwan, China	4	5	0.0	57.1	8	4	4	5.3
Tanzania	5	0	0.0	0.0	3	3	0	2.0
Thailand	5	4	0.0	18.4	10	2	6	6.0
Timor-Leste	3	0	0.0	0.0	7	1	3	3.7
Togo	2	1	3.5	0.0	4	3	5	4.0
Tonga	5	0	0.0	0.0	3	6	8	5.7
Tunisia	4	2	8.2	0.0	0	4	6	3.3
Turkey	1	5	4.9	27.6	8	3	4	5.0
Uganda	5	0	0.0	0.0	7	5	4	5.3
Ukraine	8	0	0.0	0.0	1	3	4	2.7
United Arab Emirates	4	2	1.5	0.0	4	8	2	4.7
United Kingdom	10	6	0.0	76.2	10	7	7	8.0
United States	7	6	0.0	100.0	7	9	9	8.3
Uruguay	4	5	5.5	80.0	3	4	8	5.0
Uzbekistan	5	0	0.0	0.0	4	6	3	4.3
Vanuatu	6	0	0.0	0.0	5	6	8	6.3
Venezuela	4	4	16.8	0.0	3	2	2	2.3
Vietnam	3	3	1.1	0.0	4	1	2	2.3
West Bank and Gaza	5	0	0.0	0.0	..	..	..	..
Yemen	2	2	0.1	0.0	6	4	3	4.3
Zambia	6	0	0.0	0.0	10	4	8	7.3
Zimbabwe	7	0	0.0	0.0	8	1	4	4.3

	Paying Taxes			Trading across Borders					
	JANUARY 2005			JANUARY 2005					
Economy	Payments (number)	Time (hours per year)	Total tax payable (% of gross profit)	Documents for export (number)	Signatures for export (number)	Time for export (days)	Documents for import (number)	Signatures for import (number)	Time for import (days)
Afghanistan	2	80	21.4	..	..	..	10	57	97
Albania	53	240	71.6	6	13	37	12	17	38
Algeria	63	504	58.5	8	8	29	8	12	51
Angola	30	656	32.5	..	..	..	10	28	64
Argentina	35	580	97.9	6	6	23	7	9	30
Armenia	50	1120	53.8	7	12	34	6	15	37
Australia	12	107	37.0	5	2	12	11	2	16
Austria	20	272	50.8	4	2	8	5	3	9
Azerbaijan	35	756	41.4	7	40	69	18	55	79
Bangladesh	17	640	50.4	7	15	35	16	38	57
Belarus	113	1188	121.8	7	9	33	7	10	37
Belgium	10	160	44.6	5	2	7	6	2	9
Benin	75	270	53.1	8	10	36	11	14	49
Bhutan	30	370	23.3	10	12	39	14	12	42
Bolivia	41	1080	64.0	9	15	43	9	16	49
Bosnia and Herzegovina	73	100	19.7	9	15	32	15	18	43
Botswana	24	140	52.9	6	7	37	9	10	42
Brazil	23	2600	147.9	7	8	39	14	16	43
Bulgaria	27	616	38.6	7	5	26	10	4	24
Burkina Faso	40	270	48.3	9	19	71	13	37	66
Burundi	41	140	173.5	11	29	67	19	55	124
Cambodia	27	97	31.1	8	10	43	12	18	55
Cameroon	51	1300	47.6	10	11	39	14	20	53
Canada	10	119	32.5	6	2	12	7	1	12
Central African Republic	66	504	60.9	9	38	116	10	75	122
Chad	65	122	51.3	7	32	87	14	42	111
Chile	8	432	46.7	6	7	23	8	8	24
China	34	584	46.9	6	7	20	11	8	24
Colombia	54	432	75.1	6	7	34	11	12	48
Congo, Dem. Rep.	34	312	134.7	8	45	50	15	80	67
Congo, Rep.	94	576	66.9	8	42	50	12	51	62
Costa Rica	41	402	54.3	7	8	36	13	8	42
Côte d'Ivoire	71	270	46.9	7	11	21	16	21	48
Croatia	39	232	47.1	9	10	35	15	10	37
Czech Republic	14	930	40.1	5	3	20	8	4	22
Denmark	18	135	63.4	3	2	5	3	1	5
Dominican Republic	85	124	57.2	6	3	17	11	6	17
Ecuador	33	600	33.9	12	4	20	11	7	42
Egypt	39	504	32.1	8	11	27	9	8	29
El Salvador	65	224	32.2	7	10	43	15	11	54
Eritrea	18	216	66.3	11	20	69	17	33	69
Estonia	11	104	39.5	5	2	12	5	5	14
Ethiopia	20	52	43.6	8	33	46	13	45	57
Fiji	22	140	44.4	6	5	22	13	2	22
Finland	19	..	52.1	4	3	7	3	1	7
France	29	72	42.8	7	3	22	13	3	23
Georgia	49	448	49.7	9	35	54	15	42	52
Germany	32	105	50.3	4	1	6	4	1	6
Ghana	35	304	45.3	6	11	47	13	13	55
Greece	32	204	47.9	7	6	29	11	9	34
Guatemala	50	260	53.4	8	6	20	7	5	36
Guinea	55	416	51.2	7	11	43	12	23	56

Economy	Paying Taxes JANUARY 2005			Trading across Borders JANUARY 2005					
	Payments (number)	Time (hours per year)	Total tax payable (% of gross profit)	Documents for export (number)	Signatures for export (number)	Time for export (days)	Documents for import (number)	Signatures for import (number)	Time for import (days)
Guyana	45	288	20.7	8	10	42	11	15	54
Haiti	53	..	31.7	8	20	58	9	35	60
Honduras	48	424	43.2	7	17	34	15	21	46
Hong Kong, China	1	80	14.3	6	4	13	8	3	16
Hungary	24	304	56.8	6	4	23	10	5	24
Iceland	19	175	52.2	7	3	15	6	2	15
India	59	264	43.2	10	22	36	15	27	43
Indonesia	52	560	38.8	7	3	25	10	6	30
Iran	28	..	14.6	11	30	45	11	45	51
Iraq	13	48	5.6	10	70	105	19	75	135
Ireland	8	76	45.3	5	5	14	4	5	15
Israel	33	210	57.5	5	2	10	5	4	13
Italy	20	360	59.8	8	5	28	16	10	38
Jamaica	72	414	49.4	5	7	20	8	7	26
Japan	26	315	34.6	5	3	11	7	3	11
Jordan	10	101	39.8	7	6	28	12	5	28
Kazakhstan	34	156	41.6	14	15	93	18	17	87
Kenya	17	372	68.2	8	15	45	13	20	62
Kiribati	16	..	15.6	6	5	31	11	6	32
Korea	26	290	29.6	5	3	12	8	5	12
Kuwait	14	..	8.2	5	10	30	11	12	39
Kyrgyz Republic	95	204	59.4	..	..	..	18	27	127
Lao PDR	31	180	24.7	12	17	66	16	28	78
Latvia	39	320	38.7	9	6	18	13	7	21
Lebanon	33	208	30.4	6	15	22	12	35	34
Lesotho	19	564	37.7	..	..	..	10	15	50
Lithuania	13	162	41.6	5	5	6	12	4	17
Macedonia, FYR	54	96	40.1	10	8	32	10	11	35
Madagascar	29	400	58.9	7	15	50	9	18	59
Malawi	33	782	56.5	9	12	41	6	20	61
Malaysia	28	..	11.6	6	3	20	12	5	22
Maldives	1	0	5.5	7	4	24	12	4	29
Mali	60	270	44.0	10	33	67	16	60	61
Marshall Islands	20	160	42.6	..	..	..	6	6	14
Mauritania	61	696	75.8	9	13	42	7	25	40
Mauritius	7	158	38.2	5	4	16	7	4	16
Mexico	49	536	31.3	6	4	18	8	11	26
Micronesia	8	128	32.1	..	..	..	14	5	33
Moldova	44	250	44.7	7	12	33	7	13	35
Mongolia	43	..	45.3	11	21	66	10	27	74
Morocco	28	690	54.8	7	13	31	11	17	33
Mozambique	35	230	50.9	6	12	41	16	12	41
Namibia	23	50	43.9	9	7	32	14	7	25
Nepal	23	408	31.8	7	12	44	10	24	38
Netherlands	22	700	53.3	5	3	7	4	1	8
New Zealand	8	70	44.2	5	2	8	9	2	13
Nicaragua	64	240	54.3	6	4	38	7	5	38
Niger	44	270	49.4	..	..	..	19	52	89
Nigeria	36	1120	27.1	11	39	41	13	71	53
Norway	3	87	60.1	4	3	7	4	3	7
Oman	13	52	5.2	9	7	23	13	9	27
Pakistan	32	560	57.4	8	10	33	12	15	39

Economy	Paying Taxes			Trading across Borders					
	JANUARY 2005			JANUARY 2005					
	Payments (number)	Time (hours per year)	Total tax payable (% of gross profit)	Documents for export (number)	Signatures for export (number)	Time for export (days)	Documents for import (number)	Signatures for import (number)	Time for import (days)
Palau	17	128	40.0	7	3	20	9	4	26
Panama	45	424	32.9	8	3	30	12	3	32
Papua New Guinea	43	198	36.7	5	5	30	10	6	32
Paraguay	33	328	37.9	9	7	34	13	11	31
Peru	53	424	50.7	8	10	24	13	13	31
Philippines	62	94	46.4	6	5	19	8	7	22
Poland	43	175	55.6	6	5	19	7	8	26
Portugal	7	328	45.4	6	4	18	7	5	18
Puerto Rico	41	140	17.8	9	3	15	10	3	19
Romania	62	188	51.1	7	6	27	15	10	28
Russia	27	256	40.8	8	8	29	8	10	35
Rwanda	42	168	53.9	14	27	63	19	46	92
Samoa	35	224	35.8	6	4	12	8	6	13
São Tomé and Príncipe	29	1008	27.4	7	8	31	9	12	40
Saudi Arabia	13	70	1.4	5	12	36	9	18	44
Senegal	59	696	45.0	6	8	6	10	12	26
Serbia and Montenegro	41	168	46.3	9	15	32	15	17	44
Sierra Leone	20	399	163.9	7	8	36	7	22	39
Singapore	16	30	19.5	5	2	6	6	2	8
Slovakia	31	344	39.5	9	8	20	8	10	21
Slovenia	29	272	47.3	9	7	20	11	9	24
Solomon Islands	33	80	13.5	..	..	..	7	5	24
South Africa	32	350	43.8	5	7	31	9	9	34
Spain	7	56	48.4	4	3	9	5	3	10
Sri Lanka	42	..	49.4	8	10	25	13	15	27
Sudan	..	..	..	9	35	82	15	50	111
Sweden	5	122	52.6	4	1	6	3	1	6
Switzerland	25	63	22.0	8	5	21	13	5	22
Syria	22	336	20.8	12	19	49	18	47	63
Taiwan, China	15	296	23.6	8	9	14	8	11	14
Tanzania	48	248	51.3	7	10	30	13	16	51
Thailand	44	52	29.2	9	10	23	14	10	25
Timor-Leste	15	640	34.9	6	9	32	11	12	37
Togo	51	270	50.9	8	8	34	11	14	43
Tonga	11	156	32.0	6	4	11	9	5	11
Tunisia	31	112	52.7	5	8	25	8	12	33
Turkey	18	254	51.1	9	10	20	13	20	25
Uganda	31	237	42.9	13	18	58	17	27	73
Ukraine	84	2185	51.0	6	9	34	10	10	46
United Arab Emirates	15	12	8.9	6	3	18	6	3	18
United Kingdom	22	..	52.9	5	5	16	4	5	16
United States	9	325	21.5	6	5	9	5	4	9
Uruguay	54	300	80.2	9	10	22	9	12	25
Uzbekistan	118	152	75.6	..	..	..	18	32	139
Vanuatu	32	120	28.1	9	6	7	14	9	9
Venezuela	68	864	48.9	8	6	34	13	9	42
Vietnam	44	1050	31.5	6	12	35	9	15	36
West Bank and Gaza	49	..	42.0	6	10	27	9	18	42
Yemen	32	248	128.8	6	8	33	9	20	31
Zambia	36	132	38.6	16	25	60	19	28	62
Zimbabwe	59	216	48.6	9	18	52	15	19	66

Economy	Enforcing Contracts JANUARY 2005			Closing a Business JANUARY 2005		
	Procedures (number)	Time (days)	Cost (% of debt)	Time (years)	Cost (% of estate)	Recovery rate (cents on the dollar)
Afghanistan	..	400	24.0	NO PRACTICE	NO PRACTICE	0.0
Albania	39	390	28.6	4.0	38.0	26.9
Algeria	49	407	28.7	3.5	3.5	37.4
Angola	47	1011	11.2	6.2	22.0	0.6
Argentina	33	520	15.0	2.8	14.5	34.9
Armenia	24	185	17.8	1.9	4.0	41.0
Australia	11	157	14.4	1.0	8.0	79.9
Austria	20	374	9.8	1.1	18.0	73.3
Azerbaijan	25	267	19.8	2.7	8.0	33.0
Bangladesh	29	365	21.3	4.0	8.0	24.2
Belarus	28	225	26.7	5.8	22.0	21.6
Belgium	27	112	6.2	0.9	3.5	86.6
Benin	49	570	29.6	3.1	14.5	9.4
Bhutan	20	275	113.8	NO PRACTICE	NO PRACTICE	0.0
Bolivia	47	591	10.6	1.8	14.5	36.9
Bosnia and Herzegovina	36	330	19.6	3.3	9.0	32.0
Botswana	26	154	24.8	2.2	14.5	54.4
Brazil	24	546	15.5	10.0	9.0	0.4
Bulgaria	34	440	14.0	3.3	9.0	33.5
Burkina Faso	41	446	95.4	4.0	9.0	6.3
Burundi	47	433	32.5	4.0	18.0	16.4
Cambodia	31	401	121.3	NO PRACTICE	NO PRACTICE	0.0
Cameroon	58	585	36.4	3.2	14.5	23.5
Canada	17	346	12.0	0.8	3.5	90.1
Central African Republic	45	660	72.2	4.8	76.0	0.0
Chad	52	526	54.9	10.0	63.0	0.0
Chile	28	305	10.4	5.6	14.5	23.1
China	25	241	25.5	2.4	22.0	31.5
Colombia	37	363	18.6	3.0	1.0	55.1
Congo, Dem. Rep.	51	909	256.8	5.2	22.0	1.6
Congo, Rep.	47	560	43.0	3.0	24.0	19.2
Costa Rica	34	550	41.2	3.5	14.5	18.2
Côte d'Ivoire	25	525	47.6	2.2	18.0	14.9
Croatia	22	415	10.0	3.1	14.5	28.4
Czech Republic	21	290	9.1	9.2	14.5	17.8
Denmark	15	83	5.3	3.3	9.0	63.0
Dominican Republic	29	580	35.0	3.5	38.0	5.4
Ecuador	41	388	15.3	4.3	18.0	20.7
Egypt	55	410	18.4	4.2	22.0	16.1
El Salvador	41	275	12.5	4.0	9.0	30.5
Eritrea	27	385	19.9	NO PRACTICE	NO PRACTICE	0.0
Estonia	25	150	10.6	3.0	9.0	39.0
Ethiopia	30	420	14.8	2.4	14.5	36.9
Fiji	26	420	53.8	1.8	38.0	20.6
Finland	27	228	6.5	0.9	3.5	89.0
France	21	75	11.7	1.9	9.0	47.6
Georgia	18	375	31.7	3.3	3.5	20.8
Germany	26	175	10.5	1.2	8.0	53.0
Ghana	23	200	14.4	1.9	22.0	23.7
Greece	14	151	12.7	2.0	9.0	45.9
Guatemala	37	1459	14.5	4.0	14.5	21.2
Guinea	44	306	27.6	3.8	8.0	23.3

AFGHANISTAN

Ease of doing business (rank)	122	South Asia Low income		GNI per capita (US$) Population (m)	250 23.9

Starting a business
Procedures (number)	1
Time (days)	7
Cost (% of income per capita)	52.8
Minimum capital (% of income per capita)	0.0

Dealing with licenses
Procedures (number)	. .
Time (days)	. .
Cost (% of income per capita)	. .

Hiring and firing workers
Difficulty of hiring index (0–100)	67
Rigidity of hours index (0–100)	20
Difficulty of firing index (0–100)	30
Rigidity of employment index (0–100)	39
Hiring cost (% of salary)	0
Firing cost (weeks of salary)	4

Registering property
Procedures (number)	11
Time (days)	252
Cost (% of property value)	9.5

Getting credit
Strength of legal rights index (0–10)	0
Depth of credit information index (0–6)	0
Public registry coverage (% of adults)	0.0
Private bureau coverage (% of adults)	0.0

Protecting investors
Extent of disclosure index (0–10)	0
Extent of director liability index (0–10)	0
Ease of shareholder suits index (0–10)	2
Strength of investor protection index (0–10)	0.7

Paying taxes
Payments (number)	2
Time (hours per year)	80
Total tax payable (% of gross profit)	21.4

Trading across borders
Documents for export (number)	. .
Signatures for export (number)	. .
Time for export (days)	. .
Documents for import (number)	10
Signatures for import (number)	57
Time for import (days)	97

Enforcing contracts
Procedures (number)	. .
Time (days)	400
Cost (% of debt)	24.0

Closing a business
Time (years)	no practice
Cost (% of estate)	no practice
Recovery rate (cents on the dollar)	0.0

ALBANIA

Ease of doing business (rank)	117	Eastern Europe & Central Asia Lower middle income		GNI per capita (US$) Population (m)	2,080 3.2

Starting a business
Procedures (number)	11
Time (days)	41
Cost (% of income per capita)	31.1
Minimum capital (% of income per capita)	39.9

Dealing with licenses
Procedures (number)	22
Time (days)	344
Cost (% of income per capita)	227.4

Hiring and firing workers
Difficulty of hiring index (0–100)	44
Rigidity of hours index (0–100)	80
Difficulty of firing index (0–100)	20
Rigidity of employment index (0–100)	48
Hiring cost (% of salary)	31
Firing cost (weeks of salary)	64

Registering property
Procedures (number)	7
Time (days)	47
Cost (% of property value)	3.6

Getting credit
Strength of legal rights index (0–10)	9
Depth of credit information index (0–6)	0
Public registry coverage (% of adults)	0.0
Private bureau coverage (% of adults)	0.0

Protecting investors
Extent of disclosure index (0–10)	0
Extent of director liability index (0–10)	6
Ease of shareholder suits index (0–10)	2
Strength of investor protection index (0–10)	2.7

Paying taxes
Payments (number)	53
Time (hours per year)	240
Total tax payable (% of gross profit)	71.6

Trading across borders
Documents for export (number)	6
Signatures for export (number)	13
Time for export (days)	37
Documents for import (number)	12
Signatures for import (number)	17
Time for import (days)	38

Enforcing contracts
Procedures (number)	39
Time (days)	390
Cost (% of debt)	28.6

Closing a business
Time (years)	4
Cost (% of estate)	38
Recovery rate (cents on the dollar)	26.9

ALGERIA

Ease of doing business (rank)	128	Middle East & North Africa Lower middle income		GNI per capita (US$) Population (m)	2,280 31.8

Starting a business
Procedures (number)	14
Time (days)	26
Cost (% of income per capita)	25.3
Minimum capital (% of income per capita)	55.1

Dealing with licenses
Procedures (number)	25
Time (days)	244
Cost (% of income per capita)	70.5

Hiring and firing workers
Difficulty of hiring index (0–100)	44
Rigidity of hours index (0–100)	60
Difficulty of firing index (0–100)	50
Rigidity of employment index (0–100)	51
Hiring cost (% of salary)	27
Firing cost (weeks of salary)	17

Registering property
Procedures (number)	16
Time (days)	52
Cost (% of property value)	9.0

Getting credit
Strength of legal rights index (0–10)	3
Depth of credit information index (0–6)	0
Public registry coverage (% of adults)	0.0
Private bureau coverage (% of adults)	0.0

Protecting investors
Extent of disclosure index (0–10)	8
Extent of director liability index (0–10)	4
Ease of shareholder suits index (0–10)	1
Strength of investor protection index (0–10)	4.3

Paying taxes
Payments (number)	63
Time (hours per year)	504
Total tax payable (% of gross profit)	58.5

Trading across borders
Documents for export (number)	8
Signatures for export (number)	8
Time for export (days)	29
Documents for import (number)	8
Signatures for import (number)	12
Time for import (days)	51

Enforcing contracts
Procedures (number)	49
Time (days)	407
Cost (% of debt)	28.7

Closing a business
Time (years)	4
Cost (% of estate)	4
Recovery rate (cents on the dollar)	37.4

ANGOLA

| Ease of doing business (rank) | 135 | Sub-Saharan Africa
Lower middle income | | GNI per capita (US$)
Population (m) | 1,030
13.5 |

Starting a business

		Registering property		**Trading across borders**	
Procedures (number)	14	Procedures (number)	7	Documents for export (number)	. .
Time (days)	146	Time (days)	334	Signatures for export (number)	. .
Cost (% of income per capita)	642.8	Cost (% of property value)	11.1	Time for export (days)	. .
Minimum capital (% of income per capita)	485.4			Documents for import (number)	10
		Getting credit		Signatures for import (number)	28
Dealing with licenses		Strength of legal rights index (0–10)	3	Time for import (days)	64
Procedures (number)	15	Depth of credit information index (0–6)	4		
Time (days)	326	Public registry coverage (% of adults)	2.9	**Enforcing contracts**	
Cost (% of income per capita)	1674.7	Private bureau coverage (% of adults)	0.0	Procedures (number)	47
				Time (days)	1011
Hiring and firing workers		**Protecting investors**		Cost (% of debt)	11.2
Difficulty of hiring index (0–100)	33	Extent of disclosure index (0–10)	5		
Rigidity of hours index (0–100)	80	Extent of director liability index (0–10)	6	**Closing a business**	
Difficulty of firing index (0–100)	80	Ease of shareholder suits index (0–10)	6	Time (years)	6
Rigidity of employment index (0–100)	64	Strength of investor protection index (0–10)	5.7	Cost (% of estate)	22
Hiring cost (% of salary)	8			Recovery rate (cents on the dollar)	0.6
Firing cost (weeks of salary)	62	**Paying taxes**			
		Payments (number)	30		
		Time (hours per year)	656		
		Total tax payable (% of gross profit)	32.5		

ARGENTINA

| Ease of doing business (rank) | 77 | Latin America & Caribbean
Upper middle income | | GNI per capita (US$)
Population (m) | 3,720
36.8 |

Starting a business

		Registering property		**Trading across borders**	
Procedures (number)	15	Procedures (number)	5	Documents for export (number)	6
Time (days)	32	Time (days)	44	Signatures for export (number)	6
Cost (% of income per capita)	13.4	Cost (% of property value)	8.3	Time for export (days)	23
Minimum capital (% of income per capita)	6.6			Documents for import (number)	7
		Getting credit		Signatures for import (number)	9
Dealing with licenses		Strength of legal rights index (0–10)	3	Time for import (days)	30
Procedures (number)	23	Depth of credit information index (0–6)	6		
Time (days)	288	Public registry coverage (% of adults)	22.1	**Enforcing contracts**	
Cost (% of income per capita)	47.9	Private bureau coverage (% of adults)	95.0	Procedures (number)	33
				Time (days)	520
Hiring and firing workers		**Protecting investors**		Cost (% of debt)	15.0
Difficulty of hiring index (0–100)	44	Extent of disclosure index (0–10)	7		
Rigidity of hours index (0–100)	60	Extent of director liability index (0–10)	2	**Closing a business**	
Difficulty of firing index (0–100)	40	Ease of shareholder suits index (0–10)	7	Time (years)	3
Rigidity of employment index (0–100)	48	Strength of investor protection index (0–10)	5.3	Cost (% of estate)	15
Hiring cost (% of salary)	30			Recovery rate (cents on the dollar)	34.9
Firing cost (weeks of salary)	94	**Paying taxes**			
		Payments (number)	35		
		Time (hours per year)	580		
		Total tax payable (% of gross profit)	97.9		

ARMENIA

| Ease of doing business (rank) | 46 | Eastern Europe & Central Asia
Lower middle income | | GNI per capita (US$)
Population (m) | 1,120
3.1 |

Starting a business

		Registering property		**Trading across borders**	
Procedures (number)	10	Procedures (number)	4	Documents for export (number)	7
Time (days)	25	Time (days)	6	Signatures for export (number)	12
Cost (% of income per capita)	6.1	Cost (% of property value)	0.5	Time for export (days)	34
Minimum capital (% of income per capita)	4.0			Documents for import (number)	6
		Getting credit		Signatures for import (number)	15
Dealing with licenses		Strength of legal rights index (0–10)	4	Time for import (days)	37
Procedures (number)	20	Depth of credit information index (0–6)	3		
Time (days)	176	Public registry coverage (% of adults)	2.6	**Enforcing contracts**	
Cost (% of income per capita)	64.9	Private bureau coverage (% of adults)	0.0	Procedures (number)	24
				Time (days)	185
Hiring and firing workers		**Protecting Investors**		Cost (% of debt)	17.8
Difficulty of hiring index (0–100)	17	Extent of disclosure index (0–10)	. .		
Rigidity of hours index (0–100)	60	Extent of director liability index (0–10)	. .	**Closing a business**	
Difficulty of firing index (0–100)	70	Ease of shareholder suits index (0–10)	. .	Time (years)	2
Rigidity of employment index (0–100)	49	Strength of investor protection index (0–10)	. .	Cost (% of estate)	4
Hiring cost (% of salary)	19			Recovery rate (cents on the dollar)	41.0
Firing cost (weeks of salary)	17	**Paying taxes**			
		Payments (number)	50		
		Time (hours per year)	1120		
		Total tax payable (% of gross profit)	53.8		

AUSTRALIA

Ease of doing business (rank)	6	OECD: High Income High income	GNI per capita (US$)	26,900
			Population (m)	19.9

Starting a business		**Registering property**		**Trading across borders**	
Procedures (number)	2	Procedures (number)	5	Documents for export (number)	5
Time (days)	2	Time (days)	5	Signatures for export (number)	2
Cost (% of income per capita)	1.9	Cost (% of property value)	7.1	Time for export (days)	12
Minimum capital (% of income per capita)	0.0			Documents for import (number)	11
		Getting credit		Signatures for import (number)	2
Dealing with licenses		Strength of legal rights index (0–10)	9	Time for import (days)	16
Procedures (number)	16	Depth of credit information index (0–6)	5		
Time (days)	121	Public registry coverage (% of adults)	0.0	**Enforcing contracts**	
Cost (% of income per capita)	12.3	Private bureau coverage (% of adults)	100.0	Procedures (number)	11
				Time (days)	157
Hiring and firing workers		**Protecting investors**		Cost (% of debt)	14.4
Difficulty of hiring index (0–100)	0	Extent of disclosure index (0–10)	8		
Rigidity of hours index (0–100)	40	Extent of director liability index (0–10)	2	**Closing a business**	
Difficulty of firing index (0–100)	10	Ease of shareholder suits index (0–10)	8	Time (years)	1
Rigidity of employment index (0–100)	17	Strength of investor protection index (0–10)	6.0	Cost (% of estate)	8
Hiring cost (% of salary)	21			Recovery rate (cents on the dollar)	79.9
Firing cost (weeks of salary)	4	**Paying taxes**			
		Payments (number)	12		
		Time (hours per year)	107		
		Total tax payable (% of gross profit)	37.0		

AUSTRIA

Ease of doing business (rank)	32	OECD: High Income High income	GNI per capita (US$)	32,300
			Population (m)	8.1

Starting a business		**Registering property**		**Trading across borders**	
Procedures (number)	9	Procedures (number)	3	Documents for export (number)	4
Time (days)	29	Time (days)	32	Signatures for export (number)	2
Cost (% of income per capita)	5.7	Cost (% of property value)	4.5	Time for export (days)	8
Minimum capital (% of income per capita)	61.5			Documents for import (number)	5
		Getting credit		Signatures for import (number)	3
Dealing with licenses		Strength of legal rights index (0–10)	5	Time for import (days)	9
Procedures (number)	14	Depth of credit information index (0–6)	6		
Time (days)	195	Public registry coverage (% of adults)	1.2	**Enforcing contracts**	
Cost (% of income per capita)	81.6	Private bureau coverage (% of adults)	45.4	Procedures (number)	20
				Time (days)	374
Hiring and firing workers		**Protecting investors**		Cost (% of debt)	9.8
Difficulty of hiring index (0–100)	11	Extent of disclosure index (0–10)	2		
Rigidity of hours index (0–100)	80	Extent of director liability index (0–10)	5	**Closing a business**	
Difficulty of firing index (0–100)	40	Ease of shareholder suits index (0–10)	4	Time (years)	1
Rigidity of employment index (0–100)	44	Strength of investor protection index (0–10)	3.7	Cost (% of estate)	18
Hiring cost (% of salary)	31			Recovery rate (cents on the dollar)	73.3
Firing cost (weeks of salary)	55	**Paying taxes**			
		Payments (number)	20		
		Time (hours per year)	272		
		Total tax payable (% of gross profit)	50.8		

AZERBAIJAN

Ease of doing business (rank)	98	Eastern Europe & Central Asia Lower middle income	GNI per capita (US$)	950
			Population (m)	8.2

Starting a business		**Registering property**		**Trading across borders**	
Procedures (number)	14	Procedures (number)	7	Documents for export (number)	7
Time (days)	115	Time (days)	61	Signatures for export (number)	40
Cost (% of income per capita)	12.5	Cost (% of property value)	0.4	Time for export (days)	69
Minimum capital (% of income per capita)	0.0			Documents for import (number)	18
		Getting credit		Signatures for import (number)	55
Dealing with licenses		Strength of legal rights index (0–10)	6	Time for import (days)	79
Procedures (number)	28	Depth of credit information index (0–6)	3		
Time (days)	212	Public registry coverage (% of adults)	0.4	**Enforcing contracts**	
Cost (% of income per capita)	1326.2	Private bureau coverage (% of adults)	0.0	Procedures (number)	25
				Time (days)	267
Hiring and firing workers		**Protecting investors**		Cost (% of debt)	19.8
Difficulty of hiring index (0–100)	33	Extent of disclosure index (0–10)	0		
Rigidity of hours index (0–100)	40	Extent of director liability index (0–10)	5	**Closing a business**	
Difficulty of firing index (0–100)	40	Ease of shareholder suits index (0–10)	7	Time (years)	3
Rigidity of employment index (0–100)	38	Strength of investor protection index (0–10)	4.0	Cost (% of estate)	8
Hiring cost (% of salary)	27			Recovery rate (cents on the dollar)	33.0
Firing cost (weeks of salary)	42	**Paying taxers**			
		Payments (number)	35		
		Time (hours per year)	756		
		Total tax payable (% of gross profit)	41.4		

BANGLADESH

| | | South Asia | GNI per capita (US$) | 440 |
| Ease of doing business (rank) | 65 | Low income | Population (m) | 138.0 |

Starting a business
Procedures (number)	8
Time (days)	35
Cost (% of income per capita)	81.4
Minimum capital (% of income per capita)	0.0

Dealing with licenses
Procedures (number)	13
Time (days)	185
Cost (% of income per capita)	291.0

Hiring and firing workers
Difficulty of hiring index (0–100)	11
Rigidity of hours index (0–100)	40
Difficulty of firing index (0–100)	20
Rigidity of employment index (0–100)	24
Hiring cost (% of salary)	0
Firing cost (weeks of salary)	47

Registering property
Procedures (number)	11
Time (days)	363
Cost (% of property value)	11.0

Getting credit
Strength of legal rights index (0–10)	7
Depth of credit information index (0–6)	2
Public registry coverage (% of adults)	0.4
Private bureau coverage (% of adults)	0.0

Protecting investors
Extent of disclosure index (0–10)	6
Extent of director liability index (0–10)	7
Ease of shareholder suits index (0–10)	7
Strength of investor protection index (0–10)	6.7

Paying taxes
Payments (number)	17
Time (hours per year)	640
Total tax payable (% of gross profit)	50.4

Trading across borders
Documents for export (number)	7
Signatures for export (number)	15
Time for export (days)	35
Documents for import (number)	16
Signatures for import (number)	38
Time for import (days)	57

Enforcing contracts
Procedures (number)	29
Time (days)	365
Cost (% of debt)	21.3

Closing a business
Time (years)	4
Cost (% of estate)	8
Recovery rate (cents on the dollar)	24.2

BELARUS

| | | Eastern Europe & Central Asia | GNI per capita (US$) | 2,120 |
| Ease of doing business (rank) | 106 | Lower middle income | Population (m) | 9.9 |

Starting a business
Procedures (number)	16
Time (days)	79
Cost (% of income per capita)	22.9
Minimum capital (% of income per capita)	42.8

Dealing with licenses
Procedures (number)	18
Time (days)	354
Cost (% of income per capita)	22.7

Hiring and firing workers
Difficulty of hiring index (0–100)	0
Rigidity of hours index (0–100)	40
Difficulty of firing index (0–100)	40
Rigidity of employment index (0–100)	27
Hiring cost (% of salary)	39
Firing cost (weeks of salary)	21

Registering property
Procedures (number)	7
Time (days)	231
Cost (% of property value)	0.1

Getting credit
Strength of legal rights index (0–10)	5
Depth of credit information index (0–6)	3
Public registry coverage (% of adults)	. .
Private bureau coverage (% of adults)	0.0

Protecting investors
Extent of disclosure index (0–10)	1
Extent of director liability index (0–10)	4
Ease of shareholder suits index (0–10)	7
Strength of investor protection index (0–10)	4.0

Paying taxes
Payments (number)	113
Time (hours per year)	1188
Total tax payable (% of gross profit)	121.8

Trading across borders
Documents for export (number)	7
Signatures for export (number)	9
Time for export (days)	33
Documents for import (number)	7
Signatures for import (number)	10
Time for import (days)	37

Enforcing contracts
Procedures (number)	28
Time (days)	225
Cost (% of debt)	26.7

Closing a business
Time (years)	6
Cost (% of estate)	22
Recovery rate (cents on the dollar)	21.6

BELGIUM

| | | OECD: High Income | GNI per capita (US$) | 31,030 |
| Ease of doing business (rank) | 18 | High income | Population (m) | 10.4 |

Starting a business
Procedures (number)	4
Time (days)	34
Cost (% of income per capita)	11.1
Minimum capital (% of income per capita)	13.5

Dealing with licenses
Procedures (number)	15
Time (days)	184
Cost (% of income per capita)	64.1

Hiring and firing workers
Difficulty of hiring index (0–100)	11
Rigidity of hours index (0–100)	40
Difficulty of firing index (0–100)	10
Rigidity of employment index (0–100)	20
Hiring cost (% of salary)	55
Firing cost (weeks of salary)	16

Registering property
Procedures (number)	7
Time (days)	132
Cost (% of property value)	12.8

Getting credit
Strength of legal rights index (0–10)	5
Depth of credit information index (0–6)	4
Public registry coverage (% of adults)	55.3
Private bureau coverage (% of adults)	0.0

Protecting investors
Extent of disclosure index (0–10)	8
Extent of director liability index (0–10)	7
Ease of shareholder suits index (0–10)	7
Strength of investor protection index (0–10)	7.3

Paying taxes
Payments (number)	10
Time (hours per year)	160
Total tax payable (% of gross profit)	44.6

Trading across borders
Documents for export (number)	5
Signatures for export (number)	2
Time for export (days)	7
Documents for import (number)	6
Signatures for import (number)	2
Time for import (days)	9

Enforcing contracts
Procedures (number)	27
Time (days)	112
Cost (% of debt)	6.2

Closing a business
Time (years)	1
Cost (% of estate)	4
Recovery rate (cents on the dollar)	86.6

BENIN

Ease of doing business (rank)	129	Sub-Saharan Africa Low income		GNI per capita (US$) Population (m)		530 6.7

Starting a business
Procedures (number)	8
Time (days)	32
Cost (% of income per capita)	190.8
Minimum capital (% of income per capita)	323.1

Dealing with licenses
Procedures (number)	22
Time (days)	335
Cost (% of income per capita)	287.9

Hiring and firing workers
Difficulty of hiring index (0–100)	39
Rigidity of hours index (0–100)	80
Difficulty of firing index (0–100)	40
Rigidity of employment index (0–100)	53
Hiring cost (% of salary)	27
Firing cost (weeks of salary)	35

Registering property
Procedures (number)	3
Time (days)	50
Cost (% of property value)	15.1

Getting credit
Strength of legal rights index (0–10)	4
Depth of credit information index (0–6)	1
Public registry coverage (% of adults)	3.5
Private bureau coverage (% of adults)	0.0

Protecting investors
Extent of disclosure index (0–10)	5
Extent of director liability index (0–10)	8
Ease of shareholder suits index (0–10)	4
Strength of investor protection index (0–10)	5.7

Paying taxes
Payments (number)	75
Time (hours per year)	270
Total tax payable (% of gross profit)	53.1

Trading across borders
Documents for export (number)	8
Signatures for export (number)	10
Time for export (days)	36
Documents for import (number)	11
Signatures for import (number)	14
Time for import (days)	49

Enforcing contracts
Procedures (number)	49
Time (days)	570
Cost (% of debt)	29.6

Closing a business
Time (years)	3
Cost (% of estate)	15
Recovery rate (cents on the dollar)	9.4

BHUTAN

Ease of doing business (rank)	104	South Asia Low income		GNI per capita (US$) Population (m)		760 0.9

Starting a business
Procedures (number)	11
Time (days)	62
Cost (% of income per capita)	10.7
Minimum capital (% of income per capita)	0.0

Dealing with licenses
Procedures (number)	26
Time (days)	249
Cost (% of income per capita)	62.5

Hiring and firing workers
Difficulty of hiring index (0–100)	78
Rigidity of hours index (0–100)	60
Difficulty of firing index (0–100)	0
Rigidity of employment index (0–100)	46
Hiring cost (% of salary)	0
Firing cost (weeks of salary)	94

Registering property
Procedures (number)	5
Time (days)	72
Cost (% of property value)	1.0

Getting credit
Strength of legal rights index (0–10)	3
Depth of credit information index (0–6)	0
Public registry coverage (% of adults)	0.0
Private bureau coverage (% of adults)	0.0

Protecting investors
Extent of disclosure index (0–10)	6
Extent of director liability index (0–10)	6
Ease of shareholder suits index (0–10)	4
Strength of investor protection index (0–10)	5.3

Paying taxes
Payments (number)	30
Time (hours per year)	370
Total tax payable (% of gross profit)	23.3

Trading across borders
Documents for export (number)	10
Signatures for export (number)	12
Time for export (days)	39
Documents for import (number)	14
Signatures for import (number)	12
Time for import (days)	42

Enforcing contracts
Procedures (number)	20
Time (days)	275
Cost (% of debt)	113.8

Closing a business
Time (years)	no practice
Cost (% of estate)	no practice
Recovery rate (cents on the dollar)	0.0

BOLIVIA

Ease of doing business (rank)	111	Latin America & Caribbean Lower middle income		GNI per capita (US$) Population (m)		960 8.8

Starting a business
Procedures (number)	15
Time (days)	50
Cost (% of income per capita)	154.8
Minimum capital (% of income per capita)	4.1

Dealing with licenses
Procedures (number)	13
Time (days)	187
Cost (% of income per capita)	268.2

Hiring and firing workers
Difficulty of hiring index (0–100)	61
Rigidity of hours index (0–100)	60
Difficulty of firing index (0–100)	0
Rigidity of employment index (0–100)	40
Hiring cost (% of salary)	14
Firing cost (weeks of salary)	98

Registering property
Procedures (number)	7
Time (days)	92
Cost (% of property value)	5.0

Getting credit
Strength of legal rights index (0–10)	3
Depth of credit information index (0–6)	4
Public registry coverage (% of adults)	10.3
Private bureau coverage (% of adults)	24.6

Protecting investors
Extent of disclosure index (0–10)	1
Extent of director liability index (0–10)	5
Ease of shareholder suits index (0–10)	7
Strength of investor protection index (0–10)	4.3

Paying taxes
Payments (number)	41
Time (hours per year)	1080
Total tax payable (% of gross profit)	64.0

Trading across borders
Documents for export (number)	9
Signatures for export (number)	15
Time for export (days)	43
Documents for import (number)	9
Signatures for import (number)	16
Time for import (days)	49

Enforcing contracts
Procedures (number)	47
Time (days)	591
Cost (% of debt)	10.6

Closing a business
Time (years)	2
Cost (% of estate)	15
Recovery rate (cents on the dollar)	36.9

BOSNIA AND HERZEGOVINA

Ease of doing business (rank)	87	Eastern Europe & Central Asia Lower middle income	GNI per capita (US$) Population (m)	2,040 4.1

Starting a business
Procedures (number)	12
Time (days)	54
Cost (% of income per capita)	40.9
Minimum capital (% of income per capita)	57.4

Dealing with licenses
Procedures (number)	17
Time (days)	476
Cost (% of income per capita)	8735.4

Hiring and firing workers
Difficulty of hiring index (0–100)	56
Rigidity of hours index (0–100)	40
Difficulty of firing index (0–100)	30
Rigidity of employment index (0–100)	42
Hiring cost (% of salary)	42
Firing cost (weeks of salary)	33

Registering property
Procedures (number)	7
Time (days)	331
Cost (% of property value)	6.0

Getting credit
Strength of legal rights index (0–10)	8
Depth of credit information index (0–6)	5
Public registry coverage (% of adults)	0.0
Private bureau coverage (% of adults)	19.3

Protecting investors
Extent of disclosure index (0–10)	3
Extent of director liability index (0–10)	6
Ease of shareholder suits index (0–10)	5
Strength of investor protection index (0–10)	4.7

Paying taxes
Payments (number)	73
Time (hours per year)	100
Total tax payable (% of gross profit)	19.7

Trading across borders
Documents for export (number)	9
Signatures for export (number)	15
Time for export (days)	32
Documents for import (number)	15
Signatures for import (number)	18
Time for import (days)	43

Enforcing contracts
Procedures (number)	36
Time (days)	330
Cost (% of debt)	19.6

Closing a business
Time (years)	3
Cost (% of estate)	9
Recovery rate (cents on the dollar)	32.0

BOTSWANA

Ease of doing business (rank)	40	Sub-Saharan Africa Upper middle income	GNI per capita (US$) Population (m)	4,340 1.7

Starting a business
Procedures (number)	11
Time (days)	108
Cost (% of income per capita)	10.9
Minimum capital (% of income per capita)	0.0

Dealing with licenses
Procedures (number)	42
Time (days)	160
Cost (% of income per capita)	298.8

Hiring and firing workers
Difficulty of hiring index (0–100)	11
Rigidity of hours index (0–100)	40
Difficulty of firing index (0–100)	40
Rigidity of employment index (0–100)	30
Hiring cost (% of salary)	0
Firing cost (weeks of salary)	19

Registering property
Procedures (number)	6
Time (days)	69
Cost (% of property value)	5.1

Getting credit
Strength of legal rights index (0–10)	9
Depth of credit information index (0–6)	5
Public registry coverage (% of adults)	0.0
Private bureau coverage (% of adults)	30.8

Protecting investors
Extent of disclosure index (0–10)	8
Extent of director liability index (0–10)	2
Ease of shareholder suits index (0–10)	3
Strength of investor protection index (0–10)	4.3

Paying taxes
Payments (number)	24
Time (hours per year)	140
Total tax payable (% of gross profit)	52.9

Trading across borders
Documents for export (number)	6
Signatures for export (number)	7
Time for export (days)	37
Documents for import (number)	9
Signatures for import (number)	10
Time for import (days)	42

Enforcing contracts
Procedures (number)	26
Time (days)	154
Cost (% of debt)	24.8

Closing a business
Time (years)	2
Cost (% of estate)	15
Recovery rate (cents on the dollar)	54.4

BRAZIL

Ease of doing business (rank)	119	Latin America & Caribbean Lower middle income	GNI per capita (US$) Population (m)	3,090 177.0

Starting a business
Procedures (number)	17
Time (days)	152
Cost (% of income per capita)	10.1
Minimum capital (% of income per capita)	0.0

Dealing with licenses
Procedures (number)	19
Time (days)	460
Cost (% of income per capita)	184.4

Hiring and firing workers
Difficulty of hiring index (0–100)	67
Rigidity of hours index (0–100)	80
Difficulty of firing index (0–100)	20
Rigidity of employment index (0–100)	56
Hiring cost (% of salary)	27
Firing cost (weeks of salary)	165

Registering property
Procedures (number)	15
Time (days)	47
Cost (% of property value)	4.0

Getting credit
Strength of legal rights index (0–10)	2
Depth of credit information index (0–6)	5
Public registry coverage (% of adults)	9.6
Private bureau coverage (% of adults)	53.6

Protecting investors
Extent of disclosure index (0–10)	5
Extent of director liability index (0–10)	7
Ease of shareholder suits index (0–10)	4
Strength of investor protection index (0–10)	5.3

Paying taxes
Payments (number)	23
Time (hours per year)	2600
Total tax payable (% of gross profit)	147.9

Trading across borders
Documents for export (number)	7
Signatures for export (number)	8
Time for export (days)	39
Documents for import (number)	14
Signatures for import (number)	16
Time for import (days)	43

Enforcing contracts
Procedures (number)	24
Time (days)	546
Cost (% of debt)	15.5

Closing a business
Time (years)	10
Cost (% of estate)	9
Recovery rate (cents on the dollar)	0.4

BULGARIA

		Eastern Europe & Central Asia		GNI per capita (US$)	2,740
Ease of doing business (rank)	62	Lower middle income		Population (m)	7.8

Starting a business		**Registering property**		**Trading across borders**	
Procedures (number)	11	Procedures (number)	9	Documents for export (number)	7
Time (days)	32	Time (days)	19	Signatures for export (number)	5
Cost (% of income per capita)	9.6	Cost (% of property value)	2.3	Time for export (days)	26
Minimum capital (% of income per capita)	104.2			Documents for import (number)	10
		Getting credit		Signatures for import (number)	4
Dealing with licenses		Strength of legal rights index (0–10)	6	Time for import (days)	24
Procedures (number)	24	Depth of credit information index (0–6)	3		
Time (days)	212	Public registry coverage (% of adults)	13.6	**Enforcing contracts**	
Cost (% of income per capita)	325.1	Private bureau coverage (% of adults)	0.0	Procedures (number)	34
				Time (days)	440
Hiring and firing workers		**Protecting investors**		Cost (% of debt)	14.0
Difficulty of hiring index (0–100)	61	Extent of disclosure index (0–10)	8		
Rigidity of hours index (0–100)	60	Extent of director liability index (0–10)	1	**Closing a business**	
Difficulty of firing index (0–100)	10	Ease of shareholder suits index (0–10)	7	Time (years)	3
Rigidity of employment index (0–100)	44	Strength of investor protection index (0–10)	5.3	Cost (% of estate)	9
Hiring cost (% of salary)	32			Recovery rate (cents on the dollar)	33.5
Firing cost (weeks of salary)	30	**Paying taxes**			
		Payments (number)	27		
		Time (hours per year)	616		
		Total tax payable (% of gross profit)	38.6		

BURKINA FASO

		Sub-Saharan Africa		GNI per capita (US$)	360
Ease of doing business (rank)	154	Low income		Population (m)	12.1

Starting a business		**Registering property**		**Trading across borders**	
Procedures (number)	12	Procedures (number)	8	Documents for export (number)	9
Time (days)	45	Time (days)	107	Signatures for export (number)	19
Cost (% of income per capita)	149.9	Cost (% of property value)	16.2	Time for export (days)	71
Minimum capital (% of income per capita)	483.8			Documents for import (number)	13
		Getting credit		Signatures for import (number)	37
Dealing with licenses		Strength of legal rights index (0–10)	4	Time for import (days)	66
Procedures (number)	46	Depth of credit information index (0–6)	1		
Time (days)	241	Public registry coverage (% of adults)	1.9	**Enforcing contracts**	
Cost (% of income per capita)	5002.3	Private bureau coverage (% of adults)	0.0	Procedures (number)	41
				Time (days)	446
Hiring and firing workers		**Protecting investors**		Cost (% of debt)	95.4
Difficulty of hiring index (0–100)	83	Extent of disclosure index (0–10)	6		
Rigidity of hours index (0–100)	100	Extent of director liability index (0–10)	5	**Closing a business**	
Difficulty of firing index (0–100)	70	Ease of shareholder suits index (0–10)	3	Time (years)	4
Rigidity of employment index (0–100)	84	Strength of investor protection index (0–10)	4.7	Cost (% of estate)	9
Hiring cost (% of salary)	23			Recovery rate (cents on the dollar)	6.3
Firing cost (weeks of salary)	57	**Paying taxes**			
		Payments (number)	40		
		Time (hours per year)	270		
		Total tax payable (% of gross profit)	48.3		

BURUNDI

		Sub-Saharan Africa		GNI per capita (US$)	90
Ease of doing business (rank)	143	Low income		Population (m)	7.2

Starting a business		**Registering property**		**Trading across borders**	
Procedures (number)	11	Procedures (number)	5	Documents for export (number)	11
Time (days)	43	Time (days)	94	Signatures for export (number)	29
Cost (% of income per capita)	200.7	Cost (% of property value)	18.9	Time for export (days)	67
Minimum capital (% of income per capita)	0.0			Documents for import (number)	19
		Getting credit		Signatures for import (number)	55
Dealing with licenses		Strength of legal rights index (0–10)	2	Time for import (days)	124
Procedures (number)	18	Depth of credit information index (0–6)	3		
Time (days)	302	Public registry coverage (% of adults)	0.2	**Enforcing contracts**	
Cost (% of income per capita)	10740.5	Private bureau coverage (% of adults)	0.0	Procedures (number)	47
				Time (days)	433
Hiring and firing workers		**Protecting investors**		Cost (% of debt)	32.5
Difficulty of hiring index (0–100)	67	Extent of disclosure index (0–10)	. .		
Rigidity of hours index (0–100)	80	Extent of director liability index (0–10)	. .	**Closing a business**	
Difficulty of firing index (0–100)	60	Ease of shareholder suits index (0–10)	. .	Time (years)	4
Rigidity of employment index (0–100)	69	Strength of investor protection index (0–10)	. .	Cost (% of estate)	18
Hiring cost (% of salary)	7			Recovery rate (cents on the dollar)	16.4
Firing cost (weeks of salary)	25	**Paying taxes**			
		Payments (number)	41		
		Time (hours per year)	140		
		Total tax payable (% of gross profit)	173.5		

CAMBODIA

Ease of doing business (rank)	133	East Asia & Pacific Low income		GNI per capita (US$) Population (m)	320 13.4

Starting a business

Procedures (number)	10
Time (days)	86
Cost (% of income per capita)	276.1
Minimum capital (% of income per capita)	80.7

Dealing with licenses

Procedures (number)	28
Time (days)	247
Cost (% of income per capita)	606.7

Hiring and firing workers

Difficulty of hiring index (0–100)	67
Rigidity of hours index (0–100)	80
Difficulty of firing index (0–100)	30
Rigidity of employment index (0–100)	59
Hiring cost (% of salary)	0
Firing cost (weeks of salary)	39

Registering property

Procedures (number)	7
Time (days)	56
Cost (% of property value)	4.7

Getting credit

Strength of legal rights index (0–10)	0
Depth of credit information index (0–6)	0
Public registry coverage (% of adults)	0.0
Private bureau coverage (% of adults)	0.0

Protecting investors

Extent of disclosure index (0–10)	5
Extent of director liability index (0–10)	9
Ease of shareholder suits index (0–10)	2
Strength of investor protection index (0–10)	5.3

Paying taxes

Payments (number)	27
Time (hours per year)	97
Total tax payable (% of gross profit)	31.1

Trading across borders

Documents for export (number)	8
Signatures for export (number)	10
Time for export (days)	43
Documents for import (number)	12
Signatures for import (number)	18
Time for import (days)	55

Enforcing contracts

Procedures (number)	31
Time (days)	401
Cost (% of debt)	121.3

Closing a business

Time (years)	no practice
Cost (% of estate)	no practice
Recovery rate (cents on the dollar)	0.0

CAMEROON

Ease of doing business (rank)	130	Sub-Saharan Africa Low income		GNI per capita (US$) Population (m)	800 16.1

Starting a business

Procedures (number)	12
Time (days)	37
Cost (% of income per capita)	172.8
Minimum capital (% of income per capita)	216.5

Dealing with licenses

Procedures (number)	15
Time (days)	444
Cost (% of income per capita)	1094.2

Hiring and firing workers

Difficulty of hiring index (0–100)	28
Rigidity of hours index (0–100)	60
Difficulty of firing index (0–100)	80
Rigidity of employment index (0–100)	56
Hiring cost (% of salary)	15
Firing cost (weeks of salary)	40

Registering property

Procedures (number)	5
Time (days)	93
Cost (% of property value)	19.0

Getting credit

Strength of legal rights index (0–10)	4
Depth of credit information index (0–6)	2
Public registry coverage (% of adults)	0.8
Private bureau coverage (% of adults)	0.0

Protecting investors

Extent of disclosure index (0–10)	8
Extent of director liability index (0–10)	3
Ease of shareholder suits index (0–10)	6
Strength of investor protection index (0–10)	5.7

Paying taxes

Payments (number)	51
Time (hours per year)	1300
Total tax payable (% of gross profit)	47.6

Trading across borders

Documents for export (number)	10
Signatures for export (number)	11
Time for export (days)	39
Documents for import (number)	14
Signatures for import (number)	20
Time for import (days)	53

Enforcing contracts

Procedures (number)	58
Time (days)	585
Cost (% of debt)	36.4

Closing a business

Time (years)	3
Cost (% of estate)	15
Recovery rate (cents on the dollar)	23.5

CANADA

Ease of doing business (rank)	4	OECD: High Income High income		GNI per capita (US$) Population (m)	28,390 31.6

Starting a business

Procedures (number)	2
Time (days)	3
Cost (% of income per capita)	0.9
Minimum capital (% of income per capita)	0.0

Dealing with licenses

Procedures (number)	15
Time (days)	87
Cost (% of income per capita)	123.0

Hiring and firing workers

Difficulty of hiring index (0–100)	11
Rigidity of hours index (0–100)	0
Difficulty of firing index (0–100)	30
Rigidity of employment index (0–100)	14
Hiring cost (% of salary)	12
Firing cost (weeks of salary)	28

Registering property

Procedures (number)	6
Time (days)	10
Cost (% of property value)	1.7

Getting credit

Strength of legal rights index (0–10)	7
Depth of credit information index (0–6)	6
Public registry coverage (% of adults)	0.0
Private bureau coverage (% of adults)	100.0

Protecting investors

Extent of disclosure index (0–10)	8
Extent of director liability index (0–10)	9
Ease of shareholder suits index (0–10)	9
Strength of investor protection index (0–10)	8.7

Paying taxes

Payments (number)	10
Time (hours per year)	119
Total tax payable (% of gross profit)	32.5

Trading across borders

Documents for export (number)	6
Signatures for export (number)	2
Time for export (days)	12
Documents for import (number)	7
Signatures for import (number)	1
Time for import (days)	12

Enforcing contracts

Procedures (number)	17
Time (days)	346
Cost (% of debt)	12.0

Closing a business

Time (years)	1
Cost (% of estate)	4
Recovery rate (cents on the dollar)	90.1

CENTRAL AFRICAN REPUBLIC

Ease of doing business (rank)	153	Sub-Saharan Africa	
		Low income	

GNI per capita (US$) 310
Population (m) 3.9

Starting a business
Procedures (number)	10
Time (days)	14
Cost (% of income per capita)	211.6
Minimum capital (% of income per capita)	568.1

Dealing with licenses
Procedures (number)	21
Time (days)	237
Cost (% of income per capita)	308.3

Hiring and firing workers
Difficulty of hiring index (0–100)	89
Rigidity of hours index (0–100)	80
Difficulty of firing index (0–100)	60
Rigidity of employment index (0–100)	76
Hiring cost (% of salary)	18
Firing cost (weeks of salary)	37

Registering property
Procedures (number)	3
Time (days)	69
Cost (% of property value)	17.3

Getting credit
Strength of legal rights index (0–10)	3
Depth of credit information index (0–6)	2
Public registry coverage (% of adults)	1.2
Private bureau coverage (% of adults)	0.0

Protecting investors
Extent of disclosure index (0–10)	. .
Extent of director liability index (0–10)	. .
Ease of shareholder suits index (0–10)	. .
Strength of investor protection index (0–10)	. .

Paying taxes
Payments (number)	66
Time (hours per year)	504
Total tax payable (% of gross profit)	60.9

Trading across borders
Documents for export (number)	9
Signatures for export (number)	38
Time for export (days)	116
Documents for import (number)	10
Signatures for import (number)	75
Time for import (days)	122

Enforcing contracts
Procedures (number)	45
Time (days)	660
Cost (% of debt)	72.2

Closing a business
Time (years)	5
Cost (% of estate)	76
Recovery rate (cents on the dollar)	0.0

CHAD

Ease of doing business (rank)	152	Sub-Saharan Africa	
		Low income	

GNI per capita (US$) 260
Population (m) 8.6

Starting a business
Procedures (number)	19
Time (days)	75
Cost (% of income per capita)	360.8
Minimum capital (% of income per capita)	619.1

Dealing with licenses
Procedures (number)	16
Time (days)	199
Cost (% of income per capita)	1703.1

Hiring and firing workers
Difficulty of hiring index (0–100)	67
Rigidity of hours index (0–100)	80
Difficulty of firing index (0–100)	70
Rigidity of employment index (0–100)	72
Hiring cost (% of salary)	21
Firing cost (weeks of salary)	21

Registering property
Procedures (number)	6
Time (days)	44
Cost (% of property value)	21.3

Getting credit
Strength of legal rights index (0–10)	3
Depth of credit information index (0–6)	2
Public registry coverage (% of adults)	0.2
Private bureau coverage (% of adults)	0.0

Protecting investors
Extent of disclosure index (0–10)	3
Extent of director liability index (0–10)	6
Ease of shareholder suits index (0–10)	5
Strength of investor protection index (0–10)	4.7

Paying taxes
Payments (number)	65
Time (hours per year)	122
Total tax payable (% of gross profit)	51.3

Trading across borders
Documents for export (number)	7
Signatures for export (number)	32
Time for export (days)	87
Documents for import (number)	14
Signatures for import (number)	42
Time for import (days)	111

Enforcing contracts
Procedures (number)	52
Time (days)	526
Cost (% of debt)	54.9

Closing a business
Time (years)	10
Cost (% of estate)	63
Recovery rate (cents on the dollar)	0.0

CHILE

Ease of doing business (rank)	25	Latin America & Caribbean	
		Upper middle income	

GNI per capita (US$) 4,910
Population (m) 15.8

Starting a business
Procedures (number)	9
Time (days)	27
Cost (% of income per capita)	10.3
Minimum capital (% of income per capita)	0.0

Dealing with licenses
Procedures (number)	12
Time (days)	191
Cost (% of income per capita)	125.2

Hiring and firing workers
Difficulty of hiring index (0–100)	33
Rigidity of hours index (0–100)	20
Difficulty of firing index (0–100)	20
Rigidity of employment index (0–100)	24
Hiring cost (% of salary)	3
Firing cost (weeks of salary)	51

Registering property
Procedures (number)	6
Time (days)	31
Cost (% of property value)	1.3

Getting credit
Strength of legal rights index (0–10)	4
Depth of credit information index (0–6)	6
Public registry coverage (% of adults)	45.7
Private bureau coverage (% of adults)	22.1

Protecting investors
Extent of disclosure index (0–10)	8
Extent of director liability index (0–10)	4
Ease of shareholder suits index (0–10)	5
Strength of investor protection index (0–10)	5.7

Paying taxes
Payments (number)	8
Time (hours per year)	432
Total tax payable (% of gross profit)	46.7

Trading across borders
Documents for export (number)	6
Signatures for export (number)	7
Time for export (days)	23
Documents for import (number)	8
Signatures for import (number)	8
Time for import (days)	24

Enforcing contracts
Procedures (number)	28
Time (days)	305
Cost (% of debt)	10.4

Closing a business
Time (years)	6
Cost (% of estate)	15
Recovery rate (cents on the dollar)	23.1

CHINA

Ease of doing business (rank)	91	East Asia & Pacific Lower middle income	GNI per capita (US$) 1,290 Population (m) 1,290.0

Starting a business
Procedures (number)	13
Time (days)	48
Cost (% of income per capita)	13.6
Minimum capital (% of income per capita)	946.7

Dealing with licenses
Procedures (number)	30
Time (days)	363
Cost (% of income per capita)	126.0

Hiring and firing workers
Difficulty of hiring index (0–100)	11
Rigidity of hours index (0–100)	40
Difficulty of firing index (0–100)	40
Rigidity of employment index (0–100)	30
Hiring cost (% of salary)	30
Firing cost (weeks of salary)	90

Registering property
Procedures (number)	3
Time (days)	32
Cost (% of property value)	3.1

Getting credit
Strength of legal rights index (0–10)	2
Depth of credit information index (0–6)	3
Public registry coverage (% of adults)	0.4
Private bureau coverage (% of adults)	0.0

Protecting investors
Extent of disclosure index (0–10)	10
Extent of director liability index (0–10)	1
Ease of shareholder suits index (0–10)	2
Strength of investor protection index (0–10)	4.3

Paying taxes
Payments (number)	34
Time (hours per year)	584
Total tax payable (% of gross profit)	46.9

Trading across borders
Documents for export (number)	6
Signatures for export (number)	7
Time for export (days)	20
Documents for import (number)	11
Signatures for import (number)	8
Time for import (days)	24

Enforcing contracts
Procedures (number)	25
Time (days)	241
Cost (% of debt)	25.5

Closing a business
Time (years)	2
Cost (% of estate)	22
Recovery rate (cents on the dollar)	31.5

COLOMBIA

Ease of doing business (rank)	66	Latin America & Caribbean Lower middle income	GNI per capita (US$) 2,000 Population (m) 44.6

Starting a business
Procedures (number)	12
Time (days)	43
Cost (% of income per capita)	25.3
Minimum capital (% of income per capita)	0.0

Dealing with licenses
Procedures (number)	12
Time (days)	150
Cost (% of income per capita)	697.3

Hiring and firing workers
Difficulty of hiring index (0–100)	72
Rigidity of hours index (0–100)	60
Difficulty of firing index (0–100)	40
Rigidity of employment index (0–100)	57
Hiring cost (% of salary)	28
Firing cost (weeks of salary)	44

Registering property
Procedures (number)	7
Time (days)	23
Cost (% of property value)	3.5

Getting credit
Strength of legal rights index (0–10)	4
Depth of credit information index (0–6)	4
Public registry coverage (% of adults)	0.0
Private bureau coverage (% of adults)	31.7

Protecting investors
Extent of disclosure index (0–10)	7
Extent of director liability index (0–10)	1
Ease of shareholder suits index (0–10)	9
Strength of investor protection index (0–10)	5.7

Paying taxes
Payments (number)	54
Time (hours per year)	432
Total tax payable (% of gross profit)	75.1

Trading across borders
Documents for export (number)	6
Signatures for export (number)	7
Time for export (days)	34
Documents for import (number)	11
Signatures for import (number)	12
Time for import (days)	48

Enforcing contracts
Procedures (number)	37
Time (days)	363
Cost (% of debt)	18.6

Closing a business
Time (years)	3
Cost (% of estate)	1
Recovery rate (cents on the dollar)	55.1

CONGO, DEM. REP.

Ease of doing business (rank)	155	Sub-Saharan Africa Low income	GNI per capita (US$) 120 Population (m) 53.2

Starting a business
Procedures (number)	13
Time (days)	155
Cost (% of income per capita)	503.3
Minimum capital (% of income per capita)	215.9

Dealing with licenses
Procedures (number)	16
Time (days)	306
Cost (% of income per capita)	6516.3

Hiring and firing workers
Difficulty of hiring index (0–100)	100
Rigidity of hours index (0–100)	100
Difficulty of firing index (0–100)	70
Rigidity of employment index (0–100)	90
Hiring cost (% of salary)	9
Firing cost (weeks of salary)	31

Registering property
Procedures (number)	8
Time (days)	106
Cost (% of property value)	10.2

Getting credit
Strength of legal rights index (0–10)	3
Depth of credit information index (0–6)	0
Public registry coverage (% of adults)	0.0
Private bureau coverage (% of adults)	0.0

Protecting investors
Extent of disclosure index (0–10)	3
Extent of director liability index (0–10)	4
Ease of shareholder suits index (0–10)	5
Strength of investor protection index (0–10)	4.0

Paying taxes
Payments (number)	34
Time (hours per year)	312
Total tax payable (% of gross profit)	134.7

Trading across borders
Documents for export (number)	8
Signatures for export (number)	45
Time for export (days)	50
Documents for import (number)	15
Signatures for import (number)	80
Time for import (days)	67

Enforcing contracts
Procedures (number)	51
Time (days)	909
Cost (% of debt)	256.8

Closing a business
Time (years)	5
Cost (% of estate)	22
Recovery rate (cents on the dollar)	1.6

CONGO, REP.

Ease of doing business (rank)	148	Sub-Saharan Africa Low income		GNI per capita (US$) Population (m)	770 3.8

Starting a business
Procedures (number)	8
Time (days)	67
Cost (% of income per capita)	288.8
Minimum capital (% of income per capita)	220.1

Dealing with licenses
Procedures (number)	15
Time (days)	174
Cost (% of income per capita)	1422.2

Hiring and firing workers
Difficulty of hiring index (0–100)	89
Rigidity of hours index (0–100)	80
Difficulty of firing index (0–100)	70
Rigidity of employment index (0–100)	80
Hiring cost (% of salary)	16
Firing cost (weeks of salary)	42

Registering property
Procedures (number)	6
Time (days)	103
Cost (% of property value)	22.1

Getting credit
Strength of legal rights index (0–10)	2
Depth of credit information index (0–6)	2
Public registry coverage (% of adults)	2.3
Private bureau coverage (% of adults)	0.0

Protecting investors
Extent of disclosure index (0–10)	4
Extent of director liability index (0–10)	5
Ease of shareholder suits index (0–10)	6
Strength of investor protection index (0–10)	5.0

Paying taxes
Payments (number)	94
Time (hours per year)	576
Total tax payable (% of gross profit)	66.9

Trading across borders
Documents for export (number)	8
Signatures for export (number)	42
Time for export (days)	50
Documents for import (number)	12
Signatures for import (number)	51
Time for import (days)	62

Enforcing contracts
Procedures (number)	47
Time (days)	560
Cost (% of debt)	43.0

Closing a business
Time (years)	3
Cost (% of estate)	24
Recovery rate (cents on the dollar)	19.2

COSTA RICA

Ease of doing business (rank)	89	Latin America & Caribbean Upper middle income		GNI per capita (US$) Population (m)	4,670 4.0

Starting a business
Procedures (number)	11
Time (days)	77
Cost (% of income per capita)	23.8
Minimum capital (% of income per capita)	0.0

Dealing with licenses
Procedures (number)	19
Time (days)	120
Cost (% of income per capita)	150.3

Hiring and firing workers
Difficulty of hiring index (0–100)	56
Rigidity of hours index (0–100)	60
Difficulty of firing index (0–100)	0
Rigidity of employment index (0–100)	39
Hiring cost (% of salary)	24
Firing cost (weeks of salary)	34

Registering property
Procedures (number)	6
Time (days)	21
Cost (% of property value)	3.6

Getting credit
Strength of legal rights index (0–10)	4
Depth of credit information index (0–6)	6
Public registry coverage (% of adults)	34.8
Private bureau coverage (% of adults)	4.5

Protecting investors
Extent of disclosure index (0–10)	2
Extent of director liability index (0–10)	5
Ease of shareholder suits index (0–10)	2
Strength of investor protection index (0–10)	3.0

Paying taxes
Payments (number)	41
Time (hours per year)	402
Total tax payable (% of gross profit)	54.3

Trading across borders
Documents for export (number)	7
Signatures for export (number)	8
Time for export (days)	36
Documents for import (number)	13
Signatures for import (number)	8
Time for import (days)	42

Enforcing contracts
Procedures (number)	34
Time (days)	550
Cost (% of debt)	41.2

Closing a business
Time (years)	4
Cost (% of estate)	15
Recovery rate (cents on the dollar)	18.2

COTE D'IVOIRE

Ease of doing business (rank)	145	Sub-Saharan Africa Low income		GNI per capita (US$) Population (m)	770 16.8

Starting a business
Procedures (number)	11
Time (days)	45
Cost (% of income per capita)	134.0
Minimum capital (% of income per capita)	225.2

Dealing with licenses
Procedures (number)	22
Time (days)	569
Cost (% of income per capita)	194.9

Hiring and firing workers
Difficulty of hiring index (0–100)	44
Rigidity of hours index (0–100)	80
Difficulty of firing index (0–100)	10
Rigidity of employment index (0–100)	45
Hiring cost (% of salary)	15
Firing cost (weeks of salary)	68

Registering property
Procedures (number)	7
Time (days)	369
Cost (% of property value)	14.3

Getting credit
Strength of legal rights index (0–10)	2
Depth of credit information index (0–6)	1
Public registry coverage (% of adults)	3.0
Private bureau coverage (% of adults)	0.0

Protecting investors
Extent of disclosure index (0–10)	6
Extent of director liability index (0–10)	5
Ease of shareholder suits index (0–10)	3
Strength of investor protection index (0–10)	4.7

Paying taxes
Payments (number)	71
Time (hours per year)	270
Total tax payable (% of gross profit)	46.9

Trading across borders
Documents for export (number)	7
Signatures for export (number)	11
Time for export (days)	21
Documents for import (number)	16
Signatures for import (number)	21
Time for import (days)	48

Enforcing contracts
Procedures (number)	25
Time (days)	525
Cost (% of debt)	47.6

Closing a business
Time (years)	2
Cost (% of estate)	18
Recovery rate (cents on the dollar)	14.9

CROATIA
Ease of doing business (rank)   118

Eastern Europe & Central Asia
Upper middle income

GNI per capita (US$)	6,590
Population (m)	4.4

Starting a business

Procedures (number)	12
Time (days)	49
Cost (% of income per capita)	13.4
Minimum capital (% of income per capita)	22.7

Dealing with licenses

Procedures (number)	28
Time (days)	278
Cost (% of income per capita)	1236.7

Hiring and firing workers

Difficulty of hiring index (0–100)	61
Rigidity of hours index (0–100)	60
Difficulty of firing index (0–100)	50
Rigidity of employment index (0–100)	57
Hiring cost (% of salary)	17
Firing cost (weeks of salary)	38

Registering property

Procedures (number)	5
Time (days)	956
Cost (% of property value)	5.0

Getting credit

Strength of legal rights index (0–10)	4
Depth of credit information index (0–6)	0
Public registry coverage (% of adults)	0.0
Private bureau coverage (% of adults)	0.0

Protecting investors

Extent of disclosure index (0–10)	2
Extent of director liability index (0–10)	5
Ease of shareholder suits index (0–10)	2
Strength of investor protection index (0–10)	3.0

Paying taxes

Payments (number)	39
Time (hours per year)	232
Total tax payable (% of gross profit)	47.1

Trading across borders

Documents for export (number)	9
Signatures for export (number)	10
Time for export (days)	35
Documents for import (number)	15
Signatures for import (number)	10
Time for import (days)	37

Enforcing contracts

Procedures (number)	22
Time (days)	415
Cost (% of debt)	10.0

Closing a business

Time (years)	3
Cost (% of estate)	15
Recovery rate (cents on the dollar)	28.4

CZECH REPUBLIC
Ease of doing business (rank)   41

Eastern Europe & Central Asia
Upper middle income

GNI per capita (US$)	9,150
Population (m)	10.2

Starting a business

Procedures (number)	10
Time (days)	40
Cost (% of income per capita)	9.5
Minimum capital (% of income per capita)	39.0

Dealing with licenses

Procedures (number)	31
Time (days)	245
Cost (% of income per capita)	16.1

Hiring and firing workers

Difficulty of hiring index (0–100)	33
Rigidity of hours index (0–100)	20
Difficulty of firing index (0–100)	20
Rigidity of employment index (0–100)	24
Hiring cost (% of salary)	37
Firing cost (weeks of salary)	22

Registering property

Procedures (number)	4
Time (days)	123
Cost (% of property value)	3.0

Getting credit

Strength of legal rights index (0–10)	6
Depth of credit information index (0–6)	5
Public registry coverage (% of adults)	2.8
Private bureau coverage (% of adults)	37.9

Protecting investors

Extent of disclosure index (0–10)	2
Extent of director liability index (0–10)	5
Ease of shareholder suits index (0–10)	8
Strength of investor protection index (0–10)	5.0

Paying taxes

Payments (number)	14
Time (hours per year)	930
Total tax payable (% of gross profit)	40.1

Trading across borders

Documents for export (number)	5
Signatures for export (number)	3
Time for export (days)	20
Documents for import (number)	8
Signatures for import (number)	4
Time for import (days)	22

Enforcing contracts

Procedures (number)	21
Time (days)	290
Cost (% of debt)	9.1

Closing a business

Time (years)	9
Cost (% of estate)	15
Recovery rate (cents on the dollar)	17.8

DENMARK
Ease of doing business (rank)   8

OECD: High Income
High income

GNI per capita (US$)	40,650
Population (m)	5.4

Starting a business

Procedures (number)	3
Time (days)	5
Cost (% of income per capita)	0.0
Minimum capital (% of income per capita)	47.0

Dealing with licenses

Procedures (number)	7
Time (days)	70
Cost (% of income per capita)	71.3

Hiring and firing workers

Difficulty of hiring index (0–100)	11
Rigidity of hours index (0–100)	40
Difficulty of firing index (0–100)	10
Rigidity of employment index (0–100)	20
Hiring cost (% of salary)	1
Firing cost (weeks of salary)	39

Registering property

Procedures (number)	6
Time (days)	42
Cost (% of property value)	0.6

Getting credit

Strength of legal rights index (0–10)	7
Depth of credit information index (0–6)	4
Public registry coverage (% of adults)	0.0
Private bureau coverage (% of adults)	7.7

Protecting investors

Extent of disclosure index (0–10)	7
Extent of director liability index (0–10)	5
Ease of shareholder suits index (0–10)	7
Strength of investor protection index (0–10)	6.3

Paying taxes

Payments (number)	18
Time (hours per year)	135
Total tax payable (% of gross profit)	63.4

Trading across borders

Documents for export (number)	3
Signatures for export (number)	2
Time for export (days)	5
Documents for import (number)	3
Signatures for import (number)	1
Time for import (days)	5

Enforcing contracts

Procedures (number)	15
Time (days)	83
Cost (% of debt)	5.3

Closing a business

Time (years)	3
Cost (% of estate)	9
Recovery rate (cents on the dollar)	63.0

DOMINICAN REPUBLIC
Ease of doing business (rank) 103

Latin America & Caribbean
Lower middle income

GNI per capita (US$) 2,080
Population (m) 8.7

Starting a business
Procedures (number)	10
Time (days)	75
Cost (% of income per capita)	30.9
Minimum capital (% of income per capita)	1.2

Dealing with licenses
Procedures (number)	12
Time (days)	150
Cost (% of income per capita)	255.1

Hiring and firing workers
Difficulty of hiring index (0–100)	22
Rigidity of hours index (0–100)	80
Difficulty of firing index (0–100)	30
Rigidity of employment index (0–100)	44
Hiring cost (% of salary)	14
Firing cost (weeks of salary)	77

Registering property
Procedures (number)	7
Time (days)	107
Cost (% of property value)	5.1

Getting credit
Strength of legal rights index (0–10)	4
Depth of credit information index (0–6)	5
Public registry coverage (% of adults)	19.2
Private bureau coverage (% of adults)	34.6

Protecting investors
Extent of disclosure index (0–10)	3
Extent of director liability index (0–10)	0
Ease of shareholder suits index (0–10)	9
Strength of investor protection index (0–10)	4.0

Paying taxes
Payments (number)	85
Time (hours per year)	124
Total tax payable (% of gross profit)	57.2

Trading across borders
Documents for export (number)	6
Signatures for export (number)	3
Time for export (days)	17
Documents for import (number)	11
Signatures for import (number)	6
Time for import (days)	17

Enforcing contracts
Procedures (number)	29
Time (days)	580
Cost (% of debt)	35.0

Closing a business
Time (years)	4
Cost (% of estate)	38
Recovery rate (cents on the dollar)	5.4

ECUADOR
Ease of doing business (rank) 107

Latin America & Caribbean
Lower middle income

GNI per capita (US$) 2,180
Population (m) 13.0

Starting a business
Procedures (number)	14
Time (days)	69
Cost (% of income per capita)	38.1
Minimum capital (% of income per capita)	9.2

Dealing with licenses
Procedures (number)	19
Time (days)	149
Cost (% of income per capita)	100.0

Hiring and firing workers
Difficulty of hiring index (0–100)	44
Rigidity of hours index (0–100)	60
Difficulty of firing index (0–100)	70
Rigidity of employment index (0–100)	58
Hiring cost (% of salary)	13
Firing cost (weeks of salary)	131

Registering property
Procedures (number)	10
Time (days)	21
Cost (% of property value)	6.7

Getting credit
Strength of legal rights index (0–10)	3
Depth of credit information index (0–6)	4
Public registry coverage (% of adults)	13.6
Private bureau coverage (% of adults)	0.0

Protecting investors
Extent of disclosure index (0–10)	1
Extent of director liability index (0–10)	5
Ease of shareholder suits index (0–10)	6
Strength of investor protection index (0–10)	4.0

Paying taxes
Payments (number)	33
Time (hours per year)	600
Total tax payable (% of gross profit)	33.9

Trading across borders
Documents for export (number)	12
Signatures for export (number)	4
Time for export (days)	20
Documents for import (number)	11
Signatures for import (number)	7
Time for import (days)	42

Enforcing contracts
Procedures (number)	41
Time (days)	388
Cost (% of debt)	15.3

Closing a business
Time (years)	4.3
Cost (% of estate)	18
Recovery rate (cents on the dollar)	20.7

EGYPT
Ease of doing business (rank) 141

Middle East & North Africa
Lower middle income

GNI per capita (US$) 1,310
Population (m) 67.6

Starting a business
Procedures (number)	10
Time (days)	34
Cost (% of income per capita)	104.9
Minimum capital (% of income per capita)	739.8

Dealing with licenses
Procedures (number)	30
Time (days)	263
Cost (% of income per capita)	1067.1

Hiring and firing workers
Difficulty of hiring index (0–100)	0
Rigidity of hours index (0–100)	80
Difficulty of firing index (0–100)	80
Rigidity of employment index (0–100)	53
Hiring cost (% of salary)	26
Firing cost (weeks of salary)	162

Registering property
Procedures (number)	7
Time (days)	193
Cost (% of property value)	6.1

Getting credit
Strength of legal rights index (0–10)	1
Depth of credit information index (0–6)	2
Public registry coverage (% of adults)	1.2
Private bureau coverage (% of adults)	0.0

Protecting investors
Extent of disclosure index (0–10)	5
Extent of director liability index (0–10)	2
Ease of shareholder suits index (0–10)	5
Strength of investor protection index (0–10)	4.0

Paying taxes
Payments (number)	39
Time (hours per year)	504
Total tax payable (% of gross profit)	32.1

Trading across borders
Documents for export (number)	8
Signatures for export (number)	11
Time for export (days)	27
Documents for import (number)	9
Signatures for import (number)	8
Time for import (days)	29

Enforcing contracts
Procedures (number)	55
Time (days)	410
Cost (% of debt)	18.4

Closing a business
Time (years)	4
Cost (% of estate)	22
Recovery rate (cents on the dollar)	16.1

EL SALVADOR

Ease of doing business (rank)	76

Latin America & Caribbean
Lower middle income

GNI per capita (US$)	2,350
Population (m)	6.5

Starting a business
Procedures (number)	12
Time (days)	40
Cost (% of income per capita)	118.0
Minimum capital (% of income per capita)	124.4

Dealing with licenses
Procedures (number)	22
Time (days)	144
Cost (% of income per capita)	204.2

Hiring and firing workers
Difficulty of hiring index (0–100)	44
Rigidity of hours index (0–100)	60
Difficulty of firing index (0–100)	20
Rigidity of employment index (0–100)	41
Hiring cost (% of salary)	15
Firing cost (weeks of salary)	86

Registering property
Procedures (number)	5
Time (days)	52
Cost (% of property value)	3.6

Getting credit
Strength of legal rights index (0–10)	5
Depth of credit information index (0–6)	5
Public registry coverage (% of adults)	17.3
Private bureau coverage (% of adults)	78.7

Protecting investors
Extent of disclosure index (0–10)	6
Extent of director liability index (0–10)	2
Ease of shareholder suits index (0–10)	6
Strength of investor protection index (0–10)	4.7

Paying taxes
Payments (number)	65
Time (hours per year)	224
Total tax payable (% of gross profit)	32.2

Trading across borders
Documents for export (number)	7
Signatures for export (number)	10
Time for export (days)	43
Documents for import (number)	15
Signatures for import (number)	11
Time for import (days)	54

Enforcing contracts
Procedures (number)	41
Time (days)	275
Cost (% of debt)	12.5

Closing a business
Time (years)	4
Cost (% of estate)	9
Recovery rate (cents on the dollar)	30.5

ERITREA

Ease of doing business (rank)	137

Sub-Saharan Africa
Low income

GNI per capita (US$)	180
Population (m)	4.4

Starting a business
Procedures (number)	13
Time (days)	91
Cost (% of income per capita)	128.6
Minimum capital (% of income per capita)	535.2

Dealing with licenses
Procedures (number)	19
Time (days)	187
Cost (% of income per capita)	1254.2

Hiring and firing workers
Difficulty of hiring index (0–100)	0
Rigidity of hours index (0–100)	60
Difficulty of firing index (0–100)	20
Rigidity of employment index (0–100)	27
Hiring cost (% of salary)	2
Firing cost (weeks of salary)	69

Registering property
Procedures (number)	6
Time (days)	91
Cost (% of property value)	9.1

Getting credit
Strength of legal rights index (0–10)	3
Depth of credit information index (0–6)	0
Public registry coverage (% of adults)	0.0
Private bureau coverage (% of adults)	0.0

Protecting investors
Extent of disclosure index (0–10)	4
Extent of director liability index (0–10)	5
Ease of shareholder suits index (0–10)	5
Strength of investor protection index (0–10)	4.7

Paying taxes
Payments (number)	18
Time (hours per year)	216
Total tax payable (% of gross profit)	66.3

Trading across borders
Documents for export (number)	11
Signatures for export (number)	20
Time for export (days)	69
Documents for import (number)	17
Signatures for import (number)	33
Time for import (days)	69

Enforcing contracts
Procedures (number)	27
Time (days)	385
Cost (% of debt)	19.9

Closing a business
Time (years)	NO PRACTICE
Cost (% of estate)	NO PRACTICE
Recovery rate (cents on the dollar)	0.0

ESTONIA

Ease of doing business (rank)	16

Eastern Europe & Central Asia
Upper middle income

GNI per capita (US$)	7,010
Population (m)	1.4

Starting a business
Procedures (number)	6
Time (days)	35
Cost (% of income per capita)	6.2
Minimum capital (% of income per capita)	41.4

Dealing with licenses
Procedures (number)	12
Time (days)	116
Cost (% of income per capita)	41.4

Hiring and firing workers
Difficulty of hiring index (0–100)	33
Rigidity of hours index (0–100)	80
Difficulty of firing index (0–100)	40
Rigidity of employment index (0–100)	51
Hiring cost (% of salary)	33
Firing cost (weeks of salary)	33

Registering property
Procedures (number)	4
Time (days)	65
Cost (% of property value)	0.5

Getting credit
Strength of legal rights index (0–10)	4
Depth of credit information index (0–6)	5
Public registry coverage (% of adults)	0.0
Private bureau coverage (% of adults)	12.5

Protecting investors
Extent of disclosure index (0–10)	8
Extent of director liability index (0–10)	4
Ease of shareholder suits index (0–10)	6
Strength of investor protection index (0–10)	6.0

Paying taxes
Payments (number)	11
Time (hours per year)	104
Total tax payable (% of gross profit)	39.5

Trading across borders
Documents for export (number)	5
Signatures for export (number)	2
Time for export (days)	12
Documents for import (number)	5
Signatures for import (number)	5
Time for import (days)	14

Enforcing contracts
Procedures (number)	25
Time (days)	150
Cost (% of debt)	10.6

Closing a business
Time (years)	3
Cost (% of estate)	9
Recovery rate (cents on the dollar)	39.0

ETHIOPIA

Ease of doing business (rank)	101	Sub-Saharan Africa Low income		GNI per capita (US$) Population (m)		110 68.6

Starting a business
Procedures (number)	7
Time (days)	32
Cost (% of income per capita)	65.1
Minimum capital (% of income per capita)	1532.0

Dealing with licenses
Procedures (number)	12
Time (days)	133
Cost (% of income per capita)	1746.5

Hiring and firing workers
Difficulty of hiring index (0–100)	33
Rigidity of hours index (0–100)	60
Difficulty of firing index (0–100)	30
Rigidity of employment index (0–100)	41
Hiring cost (% of salary)	0
Firing cost (weeks of salary)	40

Registering property
Procedures (number)	15
Time (days)	56
Cost (% of property value)	10.4

Getting credit
Strength of legal rights index (0–10)	5
Depth of credit information index (0–6)	0
Public registry coverage (% of adults)	0.0
Private bureau coverage (% of adults)	0.0

Protecting investors
Extent of disclosure index (0–10)	1
Extent of director liability index (0–10)	4
Ease of shareholder suits index (0–10)	3
Strength of investor protection index (0–10)	2.7

Paying taxes
Payments (number)	20
Time (hours per year)	52
Total tax payable (% of gross profit)	43.6

Trading across borders
Documents for export (number)	8
Signatures for export (number)	33
Time for export (days)	46
Documents for import (number)	13
Signatures for import (number)	45
Time for import (days)	57

Enforcing contracts
Procedures (number)	30
Time (days)	420
Cost (% of debt)	14.8

Closing a business
Time (years)	2
Cost (% of estate)	14.5
Recovery rate (cents on the dollar)	36.9

FIJI

Ease of doing business (rank)	34	East Asia & Pacific Lower middle income		GNI per capita (US$) Population (m)		2,690 0.8

Starting a business
Procedures (number)	8
Time (days)	46
Cost (% of income per capita)	28.4
Minimum capital (% of income per capita)	0.0

Dealing with licenses
Procedures (number)	29
Time (days)	117
Cost (% of income per capita)	35.3

Hiring and firing workers
Difficulty of hiring index (0–100)	22
Rigidity of hours index (0–100)	40
Difficulty of firing index (0–100)	0
Rigidity of employment index (0–100)	21
Hiring cost (% of salary)	8
Firing cost (weeks of salary)	28

Registering property
Procedures (number)	3
Time (days)	48
Cost (% of property value)	12.0

Getting credit
Strength of legal rights index (0–10)	8
Depth of credit information index (0–6)	4
Public registry coverage (% of adults)	0.0
Private bureau coverage (% of adults)	28.3

Protecting investors
Extent of disclosure index (0–10)	5
Extent of director liability index (0–10)	5
Ease of shareholder suits index (0–10)	7
Strength of investor protection index (0–10)	5.7

Paying taxes
Payments (number)	22
Time (hours per year)	140
Total tax payable (% of gross profit)	44.4

Trading across borders
Documents for export (number)	6
Signatures for export (number)	5
Time for export (days)	22
Documents for import (number)	13
Signatures for import (number)	2
Time for import (days)	22

Enforcing contracts
Procedures (number)	26
Time (days)	420
Cost (% of debt)	53.8

Closing a business
Time (years)	2
Cost (% of estate)	38
Recovery rate (cents on the dollar)	20.6

FINLAND

Ease of doing business (rank)	13	OECD: High Income High income		GNI per capita (US$) Population (m)		32,790 5.2

Starting a business
Procedures (number)	3
Time (days)	14
Cost (% of income per capita)	1.2
Minimum capital (% of income per capita)	28.0

Dealing with licenses
Procedures (number)	17
Time (days)	56
Cost (% of income per capita)	76.2

Hiring and firing workers
Difficulty of hiring index (0–100)	44
Rigidity of hours index (0–100)	60
Difficulty of firing index (0–100)	40
Rigidity of employment index (0–100)	48
Hiring cost (% of salary)	22
Firing cost (weeks of salary)	24

Registering property
Procedures (number)	3
Time (days)	14
Cost (% of property value)	4.0

Getting credit
Strength of legal rights index (0–10)	6
Depth of credit information index (0–6)	5
Public registry coverage (% of adults)	0.0
Private bureau coverage (% of adults)	14.7

Protecting investors
Extent of disclosure index (0–10)	6
Extent of director liability index (0–10)	4
Ease of shareholder suits index (0–10)	7
Strength of investor protection index (0–10)	5.7

Paying taxes
Payments (number)	19
Time (hours per year)	..
Total tax payable (% of gross profit)	52.1

Trading across borders
Documents for export (number)	4
Signatures for export (number)	3
Time for export (days)	7
Documents for import (number)	3
Signatures for import (number)	1
Time for import (days)	7

Enforcing contracts
Procedures (number)	27
Time (days)	228
Cost (% of debt)	6.5

Closing a business
Time (years)	1
Cost (% of estate)	4
Recovery rate (cents on the dollar)	89.0

FRANCE

		OECD: High Income		GNI per capita (US$)	30,090
Ease of doing business (rank)	44	High income		Population (m)	59.8

Starting a business
Procedures (number)	7
Time (days)	8
Cost (% of income per capita)	1.2
Minimum capital (% of income per capita)	0.0

Dealing with licenses
Procedures (number)	10
Time (days)	185
Cost (% of income per capita)	78.0

Hiring and firing workers
Difficulty of hiring index (0–100)	78
Rigidity of hours index (0–100)	80
Difficulty of firing index (0–100)	40
Rigidity of employment index (0–100)	66
Hiring cost (% of salary)	47
Firing cost (weeks of salary)	32

Registering property
Procedures (number)	9
Time (days)	183
Cost (% of property value)	6.5

Getting credit
Strength of legal rights index (0–10)	3
Depth of credit information index (0–6)	2
Public registry coverage (% of adults)	1.8
Private bureau coverage (% of adults)	0.0

Protecting investors
Extent of disclosure index (0–10)	10
Extent of director liability index (0–10)	1
Ease of shareholder suits index (0–10)	5
Strength of investor protection index (0–10)	5.3

Paying taxes
Payments (number)	29
Time (hours per year)	72
Total tax payable (% of gross profit)	42.8

Trading across borders
Documents for export (number)	7
Signatures for export (number)	3
Time for export (days)	22
Documents for import (number)	13
Signatures for import (number)	3
Time for import (days)	23

Enforcing contracts
Procedures (number)	21
Time (days)	75
Cost (% of debt)	11.7

Closing a business
Time (years)	2
Cost (% of estate)	9
Recovery rate (cents on the dollar)	47.6

GEORGIA

		Eastern Europe & Central Asia		GNI per capita (US$)	1,040
Ease of doing business (rank)	100	Lower middle income		Population (m)	5.1

Starting a business
Procedures (number)	8
Time (days)	21
Cost (% of income per capita)	13.7
Minimum capital (% of income per capita)	46.8

Dealing with licenses
Procedures (number)	29
Time (days)	282
Cost (% of income per capita)	144.6

Hiring and firing workers
Difficulty of hiring index (0–100)	0
Rigidity of hours index (0–100)	60
Difficulty of firing index (0–100)	70
Rigidity of employment index (0–100)	43
Hiring cost (% of salary)	31
Firing cost (weeks of salary)	4

Registering property
Procedures (number)	6
Time (days)	9
Cost (% of property value)	0.6

Getting credit
Strength of legal rights index (0–10)	7
Depth of credit information index (0–6)	0
Public registry coverage (% of adults)	0.0
Private bureau coverage (% of adults)	0.0

Protecting investors
Extent of disclosure index (0–10)	4
Extent of director liability index (0–10)	4
Ease of shareholder suits index (0–10)	4
Strength of investor protection index (0–10)	4.0

Paying taxes
Payments (number)	49
Time (hours per year)	448
Total tax payable (% of gross profit)	49.7

Trading across borders
Documents for export (number)	9
Signatures for export (number)	35
Time for export (days)	54
Documents for import (number)	15
Signatures for import (number)	42
Time for import (days)	52

Enforcing contracts
Procedures (number)	18
Time (days)	375
Cost (% of debt)	31.7

Closing a business
Time (years)	3
Cost (% of estate)	4
Recovery rate (cents on the dollar)	20.8

GERMANY

		OECD: High Income		GNI per capita (US$)	30,120
Ease of doing business (rank)	19	High income		Population (m)	82.5

Starting a business
Procedures (number)	9
Time (days)	24
Cost (% of income per capita)	4.7
Minimum capital (% of income per capita)	47.6

Dealing with licenses
Procedures (number)	11
Time (days)	165
Cost (% of income per capita)	82.8

Hiring and firing workers
Difficulty of hiring index (0–100)	44
Rigidity of hours index (0–100)	80
Difficulty of firing index (0–100)	40
Rigidity of employment index (0–100)	55
Hiring cost (% of salary)	21
Firing cost (weeks of salary)	67

Registering property
Procedures (number)	4
Time (days)	41
Cost (% of property value)	4.1

Getting credit
Strength of legal rights index (0–10)	8
Depth of credit information index (0–6)	6
Public registry coverage (% of adults)	0.6
Private bureau coverage (% of adults)	88.2

Protecting investors
Extent of disclosure index (0–10)	5
Extent of director liability index (0–10)	5
Ease of shareholder suits index (0–10)	6
Strength of investor protection index (0–10)	5.3

Paying taxes
Payments (number)	32
Time (hours per year)	105
Total tax payable (% of gross profit)	50.3

Trading across borders
Documents for export (number)	4
Signatures for export (number)	1
Time for export (days)	6
Documents for import (number)	4
Signatures for import (number)	1
Time for import (days)	6

Enforcing contracts
Procedures (number)	26
Time (days)	175
Cost (% of debt)	10.5

Closing a business
Time (years)	1
Cost (% of estate)	8
Recovery rate (cents on the dollar)	53.0

GHANA

		Sub-Saharan Africa		GNI per capita (US$)	380
Ease of doing business (rank)	82	Low income		Population (m)	20.7

Starting a business		**Registering property**		**Trading across borders**	
Procedures (number)	12	Procedures (number)	7	Documents for export (number)	6
Time (days)	81	Time (days)	382	Signatures for export (number)	11
Cost (% of income per capita)	78.6	Cost (% of property value)	3.7	Time for export (days)	47
Minimum capital (% of income per capita)	27.9			Documents for import (number)	13
		Getting credit		Signatures for import (number)	13
Dealing with licenses		Strength of legal rights index (0–10)	5	Time for import (days)	55
Procedures (number)	16	Depth of credit information index (0–6)	0		
Time (days)	127	Public registry coverage (% of adults)	0.0	**Enforcing contracts**	
Cost (% of income per capita)	1549.7	Private bureau coverage (% of adults)	0.0	Procedures (number)	23
				Time (days)	200
Hiring and firing workers		**Protecting investors**		Cost (% of debt)	14.4
Difficulty of hiring index (0–100)	11	Extent of disclosure index (0–10)	7		
Rigidity of hours index (0–100)	40	Extent of director liability index (0–10)	7	**Closing a business**	
Difficulty of firing index (0–100)	50	Ease of shareholder suits index (0–10)	4	Time (years)	2
Rigidity of employment index (0–100)	34	Strength of investor protection index (0–10)	6.0	Cost (% of estate)	22
Hiring cost (% of salary)	13			Recovery rate (cents on the dollar)	23.7
Firing cost (weeks of salary)	25	**Paying taxes**			
		Payments (number)	35		
		Time (hours per year)	304		
		Total tax payable (% of gross profit)	45.3		

GREECE

		OECD: High Income		GNI per capita (US$)	16,610
Ease of doing business (rank)	80	High income		Population (m)	11.0

Starting a business		**Registering property**		**Trading across borders**	
Procedures (number)	15	Procedures (number)	12	Documents for export (number)	7
Time (days)	38	Time (days)	23	Signatures for export (number)	6
Cost (% of income per capita)	24.6	Cost (% of property value)	13.7	Time for export (days)	29
Minimum capital (% of income per capita)	121.4			Documents for import (number)	11
		Getting credit		Signatures for import (number)	9
Dealing with licenses		Strength of legal rights index (0–10)	3	Time for import (days)	34
Procedures (number)	17	Depth of credit information index (0–6)	4		
Time (days)	176	Public registry coverage (% of adults)	0.0	**Enforcing contracts**	
Cost (% of income per capita)	71.9	Private bureau coverage (% of adults)	17.7	Procedures (number)	14
				Time (days)	151
Hiring and firing workers		**Protecting investors**		Cost (% of debt)	12.7
Difficulty of hiring index (0–100)	78	Extent of disclosure index (0–10)	1		
Rigidity of hours index (0–100)	80	Extent of director liability index (0–10)	4	**Closing a business**	
Difficulty of firing index (0–100)	40	Ease of shareholder suits index (0–10)	5	Time (years)	2
Rigidity of employment index (0–100)	66	Strength of investor protection index (0–10)	3.3	Cost (% of estate)	9
Hiring cost (% of salary)	30			Recovery rate (cents on the dollar)	45.9
Firing cost (weeks of salary)	69	**Paying taxes**			
		Payments (number)	32		
		Time (hours per year)	204		
		Total tax payable (% of gross profit)	47.9		

GUATEMALA

		Latin America & Caribbean		GNI per capita (US$)	2,130
Ease of doing business (rank)	109	Lower middle income		Population (m)	12.3

Starting a business		**Registering property**		**Trading across borders**	
Procedures (number)	15	Procedures (number)	5	Documents for export (number)	8
Time (days)	39	Time (days)	69	Signatures for export (number)	6
Cost (% of income per capita)	58.4	Cost (% of property value)	4.7	Time for export (days)	20
Minimum capital (% of income per capita)	29.3			Documents for import (number)	7
		Getting credit		Signatures for import (number)	5
Dealing with licenses		Strength of legal rights index (0–10)	4	Time for import (days)	36
Procedures (number)	22	Depth of credit information index (0–6)	5		
Time (days)	294	Public registry coverage (% of adults)	0.0	**Enforcing contracts**	
Cost (% of income per capita)	667.8	Private bureau coverage (% of adults)	9.9	Procedures (number)	37
				Time (days)	1459
Hiring and firing workers		**Protecting investors**		Cost (% of debt)	14.5
Difficulty of hiring index (0–100)	61	Extent of disclosure index (0–10)	1		
Rigidity of hours index (0–100)	40	Extent of director liability index (0–10)	3	**Closing a business**	
Difficulty of firing index (0–100)	20	Ease of shareholder suits index (0–10)	7	Time (years)	4
Rigidity of employment index (0–100)	40	Strength of investor protection index (0–10)	3.7	Cost (% of estate)	15
Hiring cost (% of salary)	13			Recovery rate (cents on the dollar)	21.2
Firing cost (weeks of salary)	101	**Paying taxes**			
		Payments (number)	50		
		Time (hours per year)	260		
		Total tax payable (% of gross profit)	53.4		

GUINEA

Ease of doing business (rank)	144	

Sub-Saharan Africa		GNI per capita (US$)	460
Low income		Population (m)	7.9

Starting a business
Procedures (number)	13
Time (days)	49
Cost (% of income per capita)	178.8
Minimum capital (% of income per capita)	405.0

Dealing with licenses
Procedures (number)	29
Time (days)	278
Cost (% of income per capita)	512.2

Hiring and firing workers
Difficulty of hiring index (0–100)	33
Rigidity of hours index (0–100)	80
Difficulty of firing index (0–100)	30
Rigidity of employment index (0–100)	48
Hiring cost (% of salary)	27
Firing cost (weeks of salary)	26

Registering property
Procedures (number)	6
Time (days)	104
Cost (% of property value)	15.6

Getting credit
Strength of legal rights index (0–10)	2
Depth of credit information index (0–6)	1
Public registry coverage (% of adults)	0.0
Private bureau coverage (% of adults)	0.0

Protecting investors
Extent of disclosure index (0–10)	5
Extent of director liability index (0–10)	6
Ease of shareholder suits index (0–10)	3
Strength of investor protection index (0–10)	4.7

Paying taxes
Payments (number)	55
Time (hours per year)	416
Total tax payable (% of gross profit)	51.2

Trading across borders
Documents for export (number)	7
Signatures for export (number)	11
Time for export (days)	43
Documents for import (number)	12
Signatures for import (number)	23
Time for import (days)	56

Enforcing contracts
Procedures (number)	44
Time (days)	306
Cost (% of debt)	27.6

Closing a business
Time (years)	4
Cost (% of estate)	8
Recovery rate (cents on the dollar)	23.3

GUYANA

Ease of doing business (rank)	105	

Latin America & Caribbean		GNI per capita (US$)	990
Lower middle income		Population (m)	0.8

Starting a business
Procedures (number)	8
Time (days)	46
Cost (% of income per capita)	101.4
Minimum capital (% of income per capita)	0.0

Dealing with licenses
Procedures (number)	17
Time (days)	202
Cost (% of income per capita)	96.7

Hiring and firing workers
Difficulty of hiring index (0–100)	..
Rigidity of hours index (0–100)	..
Difficulty of firing index (0–100)	..
Rigidity of employment index (0–100)	..
Hiring cost (% of salary)	7
Firing cost (weeks of salary)	..

Registering property
Procedures (number)	4
Time (days)	24
Cost (% of property value)	2.5

Getting credit
Strength of legal rights index (0–10)	3
Depth of credit information index (0–6)	0
Public registry coverage (% of adults)	0.0
Private bureau coverage (% of adults)	0.0

Protecting investors
Extent of disclosure index (0–10)	5
Extent of director liability index (0–10)	4
Ease of shareholder suits index (0–10)	4
Strength of investor protection index (0–10)	4.3

Paying taxes
Payments (number)	45
Time (hours per year)	288
Total tax payable (% of gross profit)	20.7

Trading across borders
Documents for export (number)	8
Signatures for export (number)	10
Time for export (days)	42
Documents for import (number)	11
Signatures for import (number)	15
Time for import (days)	54

Enforcing contracts
Procedures (number)	..
Time (days)	525
Cost (% of debt)	24.4

Closing a business
Time (years)	2
Cost (% of estate)	42
Recovery rate (cents on the dollar)	16.7

HAITI

Ease of doing business (rank)	134	

Latin America & Caribbean		GNI per capita (US$)	390
Low income		Population (m)	8.4

Starting a business
Procedures (number)	12
Time (days)	203
Cost (% of income per capita)	153.1
Minimum capital (% of income per capita)	155.0

Dealing with licenses
Procedures (number)	12
Time (days)	186
Cost (% of income per capita)	1129.6

Hiring and firing workers
Difficulty of hiring index (0–100)	11
Rigidity of hours index (0–100)	40
Difficulty of firing index (0–100)	20
Rigidity of employment index (0–100)	24
Hiring cost (% of salary)	9
Firing cost (weeks of salary)	26

Registering property
Procedures (number)	5
Time (days)	683
Cost (% of property value)	8.1

Getting credit
Strength of legal rights index (0–10)	2
Depth of credit information index (0–6)	2
Public registry coverage (% of adults)	0.3
Private bureau coverage (% of adults)	0.0

Protecting investors
Extent of disclosure index (0–10)	4
Extent of director liability index (0–10)	3
Ease of shareholder suits index (0–10)	4
Strength of investor protection index (0–10)	3.7

Paying taxes
Payments (number)	53
Time (hours per year)	..
Total tax payable (% of gross profit)	31.7

Trading across borders
Documents for export (number)	8
Signatures for export (number)	20
Time for export (days)	58
Documents for import (number)	9
Signatures for import (number)	35
Time for import (days)	60

Enforcing contracts
Procedures (number)	35
Time (days)	368
Cost (% of debt)	25.0

Closing a business
Time (years)	6
Cost (% of estate)	30
Recovery rate (cents on the dollar)	2.9

HONDURAS

Ease of doing business (rank)	112

Latin America & Caribbean
Lower middle income

GNI per capita (US$)	1,030
Population (m)	7.0

Starting a business

Procedures (number)	13
Time (days)	62
Cost (% of income per capita)	64.1
Minimum capital (% of income per capita)	34.1

Dealing with licenses

Procedures (number)	14
Time (days)	199
Cost (% of income per capita)	759.6

Hiring and firing workers

Difficulty of hiring index (0–100)	22
Rigidity of hours index (0–100)	40
Difficulty of firing index (0–100)	40
Rigidity of employment index (0–100)	34
Hiring cost (% of salary)	10
Firing cost (weeks of salary)	46

Registering property

Procedures (number)	7
Time (days)	36
Cost (% of property value)	5.8

Getting credit

Strength of legal rights index (0–10)	5
Depth of credit information index (0–6)	4
Public registry coverage (% of adults)	11.2
Private bureau coverage (% of adults)	18.7

Protecting investors

Extent of disclosure index (0–10)	1
Extent of director liability index (0–10)	5
Ease of shareholder suits index (0–10)	4
Strength of investor protection index (0–10)	3.3

Paying taxes

Payments (number)	48
Time (hours per year)	424
Total tax payable (% of gross profit)	43.2

Trading across borders

Documents for export (number)	7
Signatures for export (number)	17
Time for export (days)	34
Documents for import (number)	15
Signatures for import (number)	21
Time for import (days)	46

Enforcing contracts

Procedures (number)	36
Time (days)	545
Cost (% of debt)	33.1

Closing a business

Time (years)	4
Cost (% of estate)	8
Recovery rate (cents on the dollar)	21.9

HONG KONG, CHINA

Ease of doing business (rank)	7

East Asia & Pacific
High income

GNI per capita (US$)	26,810
Population (m)	6.8

Starting a business

Procedures (number)	5
Time (days)	11
Cost (% of income per capita)	3.4
Minimum capital (% of income per capita)	0.0

Dealing with licenses

Procedures (number)	22
Time (days)	230
Cost (% of income per capita)	38.5

Hiring and firing workers

Difficulty of hiring index (0–100)	0
Rigidity of hours index (0–100)	0
Difficulty of firing index (0–100)	0
Rigidity of employment index (0–100)	0
Hiring cost (% of salary)	5
Firing cost (weeks of salary)	13

Registering property

Procedures (number)	5
Time (days)	83
Cost (% of property value)	5.0

Getting credit

Strength of legal rights index (0–10)	10
Depth of credit information index (0–6)	5
Public registry coverage (% of adults)	0.0
Private bureau coverage (% of adults)	64.5

Protecting investors

Extent of disclosure index (0–10)	10
Extent of director liability index (0–10)	8
Ease of shareholder suits index (0–10)	8
Strength of investor protection index (0–10)	8.7

Paying taxes

Payments (number)	1
Time (hours per year)	80
Total tax payable (% of gross profit)	14.3

Trading across borders

Documents for export (number)	6
Signatures for export (number)	4
Time for export (days)	13
Documents for import (number)	8
Signatures for import (number)	3
Time for import (days)	16

Enforcing contracts

Procedures (number)	16
Time (days)	211
Cost (% of debt)	12.9

Closing a business

Time (years)	1
Cost (% of estate)	9
Recovery rate (cents on the dollar)	81.2

HUNGARY

Ease of doing business (rank)	52

Eastern Europe & Central Asia
Upper middle income

GNI per capita (US$)	8,270
Population (m)	10.1

Starting a business

Procedures (number)	6
Time (days)	38
Cost (% of income per capita)	22.4
Minimum capital (% of income per capita)	79.6

Dealing with licenses

Procedures (number)	25
Time (days)	213
Cost (% of income per capita)	279.1

Hiring and firing workers

Difficulty of hiring index (0–100)	11
Rigidity of hours index (0–100)	80
Difficulty of firing index (0–100)	20
Rigidity of employment index (0–100)	37
Hiring cost (% of salary)	34
Firing cost (weeks of salary)	34

Registering property

Procedures (number)	4
Time (days)	78
Cost (% of property value)	11.0

Getting credit

Strength of legal rights index (0–10)	6
Depth of credit information index (0–6)	5
Public registry coverage (% of adults)	0.0
Private bureau coverage (% of adults)	4.0

Protecting investors

Extent of disclosure index (0–10)	1
Extent of director liability index (0–10)	5
Ease of shareholder suits index (0–10)	8
Strength of investor protection index (0–10)	4.7

Paying taxes

Payments (number)	24
Time (hours per year)	304
Total tax payable (% of gross profit)	56.8

Trading across borders

Documents for export (number)	6
Signatures for export (number)	4
Time for export (days)	23
Documents for import (number)	10
Signatures for import (number)	5
Time for import (days)	24

Enforcing contracts

Procedures (number)	21
Time (days)	365
Cost (% of debt)	8.1

Closing a business

Time (years)	2
Cost (% of estate)	15
Recovery rate (cents on the dollar)	35.7

ICELAND

Ease of doing business (rank)	12	OECD: High Income High income		GNI per capita (US$)		38,620
				Population (m)		0.3

Starting a business		Registering property		Trading across borders	
Procedures (number)	5	Procedures (number)	3	Documents for export (number)	7
Time (days)	5	Time (days)	4	Signatures for export (number)	3
Cost (% of income per capita)	2.9	Cost (% of property value)	2.4	Time for export (days)	15
Minimum capital (% of income per capita)	17.1			Documents for import (number)	6
		Getting credit		Signatures for import (number)	2
Dealing with licenses		Strength of legal rights index (0–10)	7	Time for import (days)	15
Procedures (number)	20	Depth of credit information index (0–6)	5		
Time (days)	124	Public registry coverage (% of adults)	0.0	**Enforcing contracts**	
Cost (% of income per capita)	16.8	Private bureau coverage (% of adults)	100.0	Procedures (number)	14
				Time (days)	158
Hiring and firing workers		**Protecting investors**		Cost (% of debt)	9.3
Difficulty of hiring index (0–100)	33	Extent of disclosure index (0–10)	4		
Rigidity of hours index (0–100)	60	Extent of director liability index (0–10)	5	**Closing a business**	
Difficulty of firing index (0–100)	0	Ease of shareholder suits index (0–10)	6	Time (years)	1
Rigidity of employment index (0–100)	31	Strength of investor protection index (0–10)	5.0	Cost (% of estate)	4
Hiring cost (% of salary)	12			Recovery rate (cents on the dollar)	81.7
Firing cost (weeks of salary)	13	**Paying taxes**			
		Payments (number)	19		
		Time (hours per year)	175		
		Total tax payable (% of gross profit)	52.2		

INDIA

Ease of doing business (rank)	116	South Asia Low income		GNI per capita (US$)		620
				Population (m)		1,060.0

Starting a business		Registering property		Trading across borders	
Procedures (number)	11	Procedures (number)	6	Documents for export (number)	10
Time (days)	71	Time (days)	67	Signatures for export (number)	22
Cost (% of income per capita)	62.0	Cost (% of property value)	7.9	Time for export (days)	36
Minimum capital (% of income per capita)	0.0			Documents for import (number)	15
		Getting credit		Signatures for import (number)	27
Dealing with licenses		Strength of legal rights index (0–10)	5	Time for import (days)	43
Procedures (number)	20	Depth of credit information index (0–6)	2		
Time (days)	270	Public registry coverage (% of adults)	0.0	**Enforcing contracts**	
Cost (% of income per capita)	678.5	Private bureau coverage (% of adults)	1 7	Procedures (number)	40
				Time (days)	425
Hiring and firing workers		**Protecting investors**		Cost (% of debt)	43.1
Difficulty of hiring index (0–100)	56	Extent of disclosure index (0–10)	7		
Rigidity of hours index (0–100)	40	Extent of director liability index (0–10)	4	**Closing a business**	
Difficulty of firing index (0–100)	90	Ease of shareholder suits index (0–10)	7	Time (years)	10
Rigidity of employment index (0–100)	62	Strength of investor protection index (0–10)	6.0	Cost (% of estate)	9
Hiring cost (% of salary)	12			Recovery rate (cents on the dollar)	12.8
Firing cost (weeks of salary)	79	**Paying taxes**			
		Payments (number)	59		
		Time (hours per year)	264		
		Total tax payable (% of gross profit)	43.2		

INDONESIA

Ease of doing business (rank)	115	East Asia & Pacific Lower middle income		GNI per capita (US$)		1,140
				Population (m)		215.0

Starting a business		Registering property		Trading across borders	
Procedures (number)	12	Procedures (number)	7	Documents for export (number)	7
Time (days)	151	Time (days)	42	Signatures for export (number)	3
Cost (% of income per capita)	101.7	Cost (% of property value)	11.0	Time for export (days)	25
Minimum capital (% of income per capita)	97.8			Documents for import (number)	10
		Getting credit		Signatures for import (number)	6
Dealing with licenses		Strength of legal rights index (0–10)	5	Time for import (days)	30
Procedures (number)	19	Depth of credit information index (0–6)	3		
Time (days)	224	Public registry coverage (% of adults)	0.0	**Enforcing contracts**	
Cost (% of income per capita)	364.9	Private bureau coverage (% of adults)	0.1	Procedures (number)	34
				Time (days)	570
Hiring and firing workers		**Protecting investors**		Cost (% of debt)	126.5
Difficulty of hiring index (0–100)	61	Extent of disclosure index (0–10)	8		
Rigidity of hours index (0–100)	40	Extent of director liability index (0–10)	5	**Closing a business**	
Difficulty of firing index (0–100)	70	Ease of shareholder suits index (0–10)	3	Time (years)	6
Rigidity of employment index (0–100)	57	Strength of investor protection index (0–10)	5.3	Cost (% of estate)	18
Hiring cost (% of salary)	10			Recovery rate (cents on the dollar)	13.1
Firing cost (weeks of salary)	145	**Paying taxes**			
		Payments (number)	52		
		Time (hours per year)	560		
		Total tax payable (% of gross profit)	38.8		

IRAN

Ease of doing business (rank)	108	Middle East & North Africa Lower middle income		GNI per capita (US$) Population (m)		2,300 66.4

Starting a business

Procedures (number)	8
Time (days)	47
Cost (% of income per capita)	6.3
Minimum capital (% of income per capita)	1.7

Dealing with licenses

Procedures (number)	21
Time (days)	668
Cost (% of income per capita)	818.0

Hiring and firing workers

Difficulty of hiring index (0–100)	78
Rigidity of hours index (0–100)	60
Difficulty of firing index (0–100)	10
Rigidity of employment index (0–100)	49
Hiring cost (% of salary)	23
Firing cost (weeks of salary)	90

Registering property

Procedures (number)	9
Time (days)	36
Cost (% of property value)	5.0

Getting credit

Strength of legal rights index (0–10)	5
Depth of credit information index (0–6)	3
Public registry coverage (% of adults)	13.7
Private bureau coverage (% of adults)	0.0

Protecting investors

Extent of disclosure index (0–10)	3
Extent of director liability index (0–10)	5
Ease of shareholder suits index (0–10)	0
Strength of investor protection index (0–10)	2.7

Paying taxes

Payments (number)	28
Time (hours per year)	. .
Total tax payable (% of gross profit)	14.6

Trading across borders

Documents for export (number)	11
Signatures for export (number)	30
Time for export (days)	45
Documents for import (number)	11
Signatures for import (number)	45
Time for import (days)	51

Enforcing contracts

Procedures (number)	23
Time (days)	545
Cost (% of debt)	12.0

Closing a business

Time (years)	5
Cost (% of estate)	9
Recovery rate (cents on the dollar)	19.3

IRAQ

Ease of doing business (rank)	114	Middle East & North Africa Lower middle income		GNI per capita (US$) Population (m)		2,170 24.7

Starting a business

Procedures (number)	11
Time (days)	77
Cost (% of income per capita)	37.4
Minimum capital (% of income per capita)	31.6

Dealing with licenses

Procedures (number)	14
Time (days)	210
Cost (% of income per capita)	311.5

Hiring and firing workers

Difficulty of hiring index (0–100)	78
Rigidity of hours index (0–100)	80
Difficulty of firing index (0–100)	50
Rigidity of employment index (0–100)	69
Hiring cost (% of salary)	12
Firing cost (weeks of salary)	4

Registering property

Procedures (number)	5
Time (days)	8
Cost (% of property value)	7.7

Getting credit

Strength of legal rights index (0–10)	4
Depth of credit information index (0–6)	0
Public registry coverage (% of adults)	0.0
Private bureau coverage (% of adults)	0.0

Protecting investors

Extent of disclosure index (0–10)	4
Extent of director liability index (0–10)	5
Ease of shareholder suits index (0–10)	5
Strength of investor protection index (0–10)	4.7

Paying taxes

Payments (number)	13
Time (hours per year)	48
Total tax payable (% of gross profit)	5.6

Trading across borders

Documents for export (number)	10
Signatures for export (number)	70
Time for export (days)	105
Documents for import (number)	19
Signatures for import (number)	75
Time for import (days)	135

Enforcing contracts

Procedures (number)	65
Time (days)	320
Cost (% of debt)	10.5

Closing a business

Time (years)	. .
Cost (% of estate)	. .
Recovery rate (cents on the dollar)	. .

IRELAND

Ease of doing business (rank)	11	OECD: High Income High income		GNI per capita (US$) Population (m)		34,280 4.0

Starting a business

Procedures (number)	4
Time (days)	24
Cost (% of income per capita)	5.3
Minimum capital (% of income per capita)	0.0

Dealing with licenses

Procedures (number)	10
Time (days)	181
Cost (% of income per capita)	23.6

Hiring and firing workers

Difficulty of hiring index (0–100)	28
Rigidity of hours index (0–100)	40
Difficulty of firing index (0–100)	30
Rigidity of employment index (0–100)	33
Hiring cost (% of salary)	11
Firing cost (weeks of salary)	52

Registering property

Procedures (number)	5
Time (days)	38
Cost (% of property value)	10.3

Getting credit

Strength of legal rights index (0–10)	8
Depth of credit information index (0–6)	5
Public registry coverage (% of adults)	0.0
Private bureau coverage (% of adults)	100.0

Protecting investors

Extent of disclosure index (0–10)	9
Extent of director liability index (0–10)	5
Ease of shareholder suits index (0–10)	9
Strength of investor protection index (0–10)	7.7

Paying taxes

Payments (number)	8
Time (hours per year)	76
Total tax payable (% of gross profit)	45.3

Trading across borders

Documents for export (number)	5
Signatures for export (number)	5
Time for export (days)	14
Documents for import (number)	4
Signatures for import (number)	5
Time for import (days)	15

Enforcing contracts

Procedures (number)	16
Time (days)	217
Cost (% of debt)	21.1

Closing a business

Time (years)	0
Cost (% of estate)	9
Recovery rate (cents on the dollar)	88.0

ISRAEL

Ease of doing business (rank)	29	Middle East & North Africa High income		GNI per capita (US$) Population (m)		17,380 6.7

Starting a business

Procedures (number)	5
Time (days)	34
Cost (% of income per capita)	5.3
Minimum capital (% of income per capita)	0.0

Dealing with licenses

Procedures (number)	21
Time (days)	219
Cost (% of income per capita)	93.5

Hiring and firing workers

Difficulty of hiring index (0–100)	0
Rigidity of hours index (0–100)	80
Difficulty of firing index (0–100)	20
Rigidity of employment index (0–100)	33
Hiring cost (% of salary)	6
Firing cost (weeks of salary)	90

Registering property

Procedures (number)	7
Time (days)	144
Cost (% of property value)	7.5

Getting credit

Strength of legal rights index (0–10)	8
Depth of credit information index (0–6)	5
Public registry coverage (% of adults)	0.0
Private bureau coverage (% of adults)	0.7

Protecting investors

Extent of disclosure index (0–10)	8
Extent of director liability index (0–10)	8
Ease of shareholder suits index (0–10)	9
Strength of investor protection index (0–10)	8.3

Paying taxes

Payments (number)	33
Time (hours per year)	210
Total tax payable (% of gross profit)	57.5

Trading across borders

Documents for export (number)	5
Signatures for export (number)	2
Time for export (days)	10
Documents for import (number)	5
Signatures for import (number)	4
Time for import (days)	13

Enforcing contracts

Procedures (number)	27
Time (days)	585
Cost (% of debt)	22.1

Closing a business

Time (years)	4
Cost (% of estate)	23
Recovery rate (cents on the dollar)	42.8

ITALY

Ease of doing business (rank)	70	OECD: High Income High income		GNI per capita (US$) Population (m)		26,120 57.6

Starting a business

Procedures (number)	9
Time (days)	13
Cost (% of income per capita)	15.7
Minimum capital (% of income per capita)	10.8

Dealing with licenses

Procedures (number)	17
Time (days)	284
Cost (% of income per capita)	147.3

Hiring and firing workers

Difficulty of hiring index (0–100)	61
Rigidity of hours index (0–100)	80
Difficulty of firing index (0–100)	30
Rigidity of employment index (0–100)	57
Hiring cost (% of salary)	33
Firing cost (weeks of salary)	47

Registering property

Procedures (number)	8
Time (days)	27
Cost (% of property value)	0.9

Getting credit

Strength of legal rights index (0–10)	3
Depth of credit information index (0–6)	6
Public registry coverage (% of adults)	6.1
Private bureau coverage (% of adults)	59.9

Protecting investors

Extent of disclosure index (0–10)	7
Extent of director liability index (0–10)	2
Ease of shareholder suits index (0–10)	5
Strength of investor protection index (0–10)	4.7

Paying taxes

Payments (number)	20
Time (hours per year)	360
Total tax payable (% of gross profit)	59.8

Trading across borders

Documents for export (number)	8
Signatures for export (number)	5
Time for export (days)	28
Documents for import (number)	16
Signatures for import (number)	10
Time for import (days)	38

Enforcing contracts

Procedures (number)	18
Time (days)	1390
Cost (% of debt)	17.6

Closing a business

Time (years)	1
Cost (% of estate)	22
Recovery rate (cents on the dollar)	40.0

JAMAICA

Ease of doing business (rank)	43	Latin America & Caribbean Lower middle income		GNI per capita (US$) Population (m)		2,900 2.6

Starting a business

Procedures (number)	6
Time (days)	9
Cost (% of income per capita)	8.3
Minimum capital (% of income per capita)	0.0

Dealing with licenses

Procedures (number)	13
Time (days)	242
Cost (% of income per capita)	526.1

Hiring and firing workers

Difficulty of hiring index (0–100)	11
Rigidity of hours index (0–100)	0
Difficulty of firing index (0–100)	20
Rigidity of employment index (0–100)	10
Hiring cost (% of salary)	12
Firing cost (weeks of salary)	60

Registering property

Procedures (number)	5
Time (days)	54
Cost (% of property value)	13.5

Getting credit

Strength of legal rights index (0–10)	6
Depth of credit information index (0–6)	0
Public registry coverage (% of adults)	0.0
Private bureau coverage (% of adults)	0.0

Protecting investors

Extent of disclosure index (0–10)	3
Extent of director liability index (0–10)	8
Ease of shareholder suits index (0–10)	5
Strength of investor protection index (0–10)	5.3

Paying taxes

Payments (number)	72
Time (hours per year)	414
Total tax payable (% of gross profit)	49.4

Trading across borders

Documents for export (number)	5
Signatures for export (number)	7
Time for export (days)	20
Documents for import (number)	8
Signatures for import (number)	7
Time for import (days)	26

Enforcing contracts

Procedures (number)	18
Time (days)	202
Cost (% of debt)	27.8

Closing a business

Time (years)	1
Cost (% of estate)	18
Recovery rate (cents on the dollar)	63.9

JAPAN

Ease of doing business (rank)	10

OECD: High Income
High income

GNI per capita (US$)	37,180
Population (m)	128.0

Starting a business

Procedures (number)	11
Time (days)	31
Cost (% of income per capita)	10.7
Minimum capital (% of income per capita)	75.3

Dealing with licenses

Procedures (number)	11
Time (days)	87
Cost (% of income per capita)	19.7

Hiring and firing workers

Difficulty of hiring index (0–100)	17
Rigidity of hours index (0–100)	40
Difficulty of firing index (0–100)	0
Rigidity of employment index (0–100)	19
Hiring cost (% of salary)	13
Firing cost (weeks of salary)	21

Registering property

Procedures (number)	6
Time (days)	14
Cost (% of property value)	4.1

Getting credit

Strength of legal rights index (0–10)	6
Depth of credit information index (0–6)	6
Public registry coverage (% of adults)	0.0
Private bureau coverage (% of adults)	61.2

Protecting investors

Extent of disclosure index (0–10)	6
Extent of director liability index (0–10)	7
Ease of shareholder suits index (0–10)	7
Strength of investor protection index (0–10)	6.7

Paying taxes

Payments (number)	26
Time (hours per year)	315
Total tax payable (% of gross profit)	34.6

Trading across borders

Documents for export (number)	5
Signatures for export (number)	3
Time for export (days)	11
Documents for import (number)	7
Signatures for import (number)	3
Time for import (days)	11

Enforcing contracts

Procedures (number)	16
Time (days)	60
Cost (% of debt)	8.6

Closing a business

Time (years)	1
Cost (% of estate)	4
Recovery rate (cents on the dollar)	92.6

JORDAN

Ease of doing business (rank)	74

Middle East & North Africa
Lower middle income

GNI per capita (US$)	2,140
Population (m)	5.3

Starting a business

Procedures (number)	11
Time (days)	36
Cost (% of income per capita)	45.9
Minimum capital (% of income per capita)	1011.6

Dealing with licenses

Procedures (number)	17
Time (days)	122
Cost (% of income per capita)	506.3

Hiring and firing workers

Difficulty of hiring index (0–100)	11
Rigidity of hours index (0–100)	40
Difficulty of firing index (0–100)	50
Rigidity of employment index (0–100)	34
Hiring cost (% of salary)	11
Firing cost (weeks of salary)	90

Registering property

Procedures (number)	8
Time (days)	22
Cost (% of property value)	10.0

Getting credit

Strength of legal rights index (0–10)	6
Depth of credit information index (0–6)	2
Public registry coverage (% of adults)	0.6
Private bureau coverage (% of adults)	0.0

Protecting investors

Extent of disclosure index (0–10)	5
Extent of director liability index (0–10)	2
Ease of shareholder suits index (0–10)	4
Strength of investor protection index (0–10)	3.7

Paying taxes

Payments (number)	10
Time (hours per year)	101
Total tax payable (% of gross profit)	39.8

Trading across borders

Documents for export (number)	7
Signatures for export (number)	6
Time for export (days)	28
Documents for import (number)	12
Signatures for import (number)	5
Time for import (days)	28

Enforcing contracts

Procedures (number)	43
Time (days)	342
Cost (% of debt)	8.8

Closing a business

Time (years)	4
Cost (% of estate)	9
Recovery rate (cents on the dollar)	27.9

KAZAKHSTAN

Ease of doing business (rank)	86

Eastern Europe & Central Asia
Lower middle income

GNI per capita (US$)	2,260
Population (m)	14.9

Starting a business

Procedures (number)	7
Time (days)	24
Cost (% of income per capita)	8.6
Minimum capital (% of income per capita)	26.6

Dealing with licenses

Procedures (number)	32
Time (days)	258
Cost (% of income per capita)	68.3

Hiring and firing workers

Difficulty of hiring index (0–100)	0
Rigidity of hours index (0–100)	60
Difficulty of firing index (0–100)	10
Rigidity of employment index (0–100)	23
Hiring cost (% of salary)	22
Firing cost (weeks of salary)	8

Registering property

Procedures (number)	8
Time (days)	52
Cost (% of property value)	1.6

Getting credit

Strength of legal rights index (0–10)	5
Depth of credit information index (0–6)	0
Public registry coverage (% of adults)	0.0
Private bureau coverage (% of adults)	0.0

Protecting investors

Extent of disclosure index (0–10)	7
Extent of director liability index (0–10)	2
Ease of shareholder suits index (0–10)	6
Strength of investor protection index (0–10)	5.0

Paying taxes

Payments (number)	34
Time (hours per year)	156
Total tax payable (% of gross profit)	41.6

Trading across borders

Documents for export (number)	14
Signatures for export (number)	15
Time for export (days)	93
Documents for import (number)	18
Signatures for import (number)	17
Time for import (days)	87

Enforcing contracts

Procedures (number)	47
Time (days)	380
Cost (% of debt)	8.5

Closing a business

Time (years)	3
Cost (% of estate)	18
Recovery rate (cents on the dollar)	19.9

KENYA

Ease of doing business (rank)	68	Sub-Saharan Africa Low income		GNI per capita (US$) Population (m)		460 31.9

Starting a business		Registering property		Trading across borders	
Procedures (number)	13	Procedures (number)	8	Documents for export (number)	8
Time (days)	54	Time (days)	73	Signatures for export (number)	15
Cost (% of income per capita)	48.2	Cost (% of property value)	4.1	Time for export (days)	45
Minimum capital (% of income per capita)	0.0			Documents for import (number)	13
		Getting credit		Signatures for import (number)	20
Dealing with licenses		Strength of legal rights index (0–10)	8	Time for import (days)	62
Procedures (number)	11	Depth of credit information index (0–6)	5		
Time (days)	170	Public registry coverage (% of adults)	0.0	**Enforcing contracts**	
Cost (% of income per capita)	40.0	Private bureau coverage (% of adults)	0.1	Procedures (number)	25
				Time (days)	360
Hiring and firing workers		**Protecting investors**		Cost (% of debt)	41.3
Difficulty of hiring index (0–100)	33	Extent of disclosure index (0–10)	4		
Rigidity of hours index (0–100)	20	Extent of director liability index (0–10)	2	**Closing a business**	
Difficulty of firing index (0–100)	30	Ease of shareholder suits index (0–10)	10	Time (years)	5
Rigidity of employment index (0–100)	28	Strength of investor protection index (0–10)	5.3	Cost (% of estate)	22
Hiring cost (% of salary)	5			Recovery rate (cents on the dollar)	15.0
Firing cost (weeks of salary)	47	**Paying taxes**			
		Payments (number)	17		
		Time (hours per year)	372		
		Total tax payable (% of gross profit)	68.2		

KIRIBATI

Ease of doing business (rank)	45	East Asia & Pacific Lower middle income		GNI per capita (US$) Population (m)		970 0.1

Starting a business		Registering property		Trading across borders	
Procedures (number)	6	Procedures (number)	4	Documents for export (number)	6
Time (days)	21	Time (days)	58	Signatures for export (number)	5
Cost (% of income per capita)	71.0	Cost (% of property value)	0.1	Time for export (days)	31
Minimum capital (% of income per capita)	38.4			Documents for import (number)	11
		Getting credit		Signatures for import (number)	6
Dealing with licenses		Strength of legal rights index (0–10)	6	Time for import (days)	32
Procedures (number)	. .	Depth of credit information index (0–6)	0		
Time (days)	. .	Public registry coverage (% of adults)	0.0	**Enforcing contracts**	
Cost (% of income per capita)	. .	Private bureau coverage (% of adults)	0.0	Procedures (number)	18
				Time (days)	440
Hiring and firing workers		**Protecting investors**		Cost (% of debt)	71.0
Difficulty of hiring index (0–100)	0	Extent of disclosure index (0–10)	6		
Rigidity of hours index (0–100)	0	Extent of director liability index (0–10)	5	**Closing a business**	
Difficulty of firing index (0–100)	50	Ease of shareholder suits index (0–10)	8	Time (years)	3
Rigidity of employment index (0–100)	17	Strength of investor protection index (0–10)	6.3	Cost (% of estate)	38
Hiring cost (% of salary)	8			Recovery rate (cents on the dollar)	14.1
Firing cost (weeks of salary)	46	**Paying taxes**			
		Payments (number)	16		
		Time (hours per year)	. .		
		Total tax payable (% of gross profit)	15.6		

KOREA

Ease of doing business (rank)	27	East Asia & Pacific High income		GNI per capita (US$) Population (m)		13,980 47.9

Starting a business		Registering property		Trading across borders	
Procedures (number)	12	Procedures (number)	7	Documents for export (number)	5
Time (days)	22	Time (days)	11	Signatures for export (number)	3
Cost (% of income per capita)	15.2	Cost (% of property value)	6.3	Time for export (days)	12
Minimum capital (% of income per capita)	308.8			Documents for import (number)	8
		Getting credit		Signatures for import (number)	5
Dealing with licenses		Strength of legal rights index (0–10)	6	Time for import (days)	12
Procedures (number)	14	Depth of credit information index (0–6)	5		
Time (days)	60	Public registry coverage (% of adults)	0.0	**Enforcing contracts**	
Cost (% of income per capita)	232.6	Private bureau coverage (% of adults)	80.7	Procedures (number)	29
				Time (days)	75
Hiring and firing workers		**Protecting investors**		Cost (% of debt)	5.4
Difficulty of hiring index (0–100)	44	Extent of disclosure index (0–10)	7		
Rigidity of hours index (0–100)	60	Extent of director liability index (0–10)	2	**Closing a business**	
Difficulty of firing index (0–100)	30	Ease of shareholder suits index (0–10)	5	Time (years)	2
Rigidity of employment index (0–100)	45	Strength of investor protection index (0–10)	4.7	Cost (% of estate)	4
Hiring cost (% of salary)	17			Recovery rate (cents on the dollar)	81.7
Firing cost (weeks of salary)	90	**Paying taxes**			
		Payments (number)	26		
		Time (hours per year)	290		
		Total tax payable (% of gross profit)	29.6		

KUWAIT

Ease of doing business (rank)	47

Middle East & North Africa
High income

GNI per capita (US$)	17,970
Population (m)	2.4

Starting a business

Procedures (number)	13
Time (days)	35
Cost (% of income per capita)	2.2
Minimum capital (% of income per capita)	133.8

Dealing with licenses

Procedures (number)	26
Time (days)	149
Cost (% of income per capita)	278.9

Hiring and firing workers

Difficulty of hiring index (0–100)	0
Rigidity of hours index (0–100)	60
Difficulty of firing index (0–100)	0
Rigidity of employment index (0–100)	20
Hiring cost (% of salary)	11
Firing cost (weeks of salary)	42

Registering property

Procedures (number)	8
Time (days)	75
Cost (% of property value)	0.6

Getting credit

Strength of legal rights index (0–10)	5
Depth of credit information index (0–6)	4
Public registry coverage (% of adults)	0.0
Private bureau coverage (% of adults)	16.1

Protecting investors

Extent of disclosure index (0–10)	5
Extent of director liability index (0–10)	5
Ease of shareholder suits index (0–10)	5
Strength of investor protection index (0–10)	5.0

Paying taxes

Payments (number)	14
Time (hours per year)	..
Total tax payable (% of gross profit)	8.2

Trading across borders

Documents for export (number)	5
Signatures for export (number)	10
Time for export (days)	30
Documents for import (number)	11
Signatures for import (number)	12
Time for import (days)	39

Enforcing contracts

Procedures (number)	52
Time (days)	390
Cost (% of debt)	13.3

Closing a business

Time (years)	4
Cost (% of estate)	1
Recovery rate (cents on the dollar)	38.3

KYRGYZ REPUBLIC

Ease of doing business (rank)	84

Eastern Europe & Central Asia
Low income

GNI per capita (US$)	400
Population (m)	5.1

Starting a business

Procedures (number)	8
Time (days)	21
Cost (% of income per capita)	10.4
Minimum capital (% of income per capita)	0.6

Dealing with licenses

Procedures (number)	16
Time (days)	152
Cost (% of income per capita)	325.2

Hiring and firing workers

Difficulty of hiring index (0–100)	33
Rigidity of hours index (0–100)	40
Difficulty of firing index (0–100)	40
Rigidity of employment index (0–100)	38
Hiring cost (% of salary)	27
Firing cost (weeks of salary)	21

Registering property

Procedures (number)	7
Time (days)	10
Cost (% of property value)	5.3

Getting credit

Strength of legal rights index (0–10)	8
Depth of credit information index (0–6)	2
Public registry coverage (% of adults)	0.0
Private bureau coverage (% of adults)	0.2

Protecting investors

Extent of disclosure index (0–10)	8
Extent of director liability index (0–10)	1
Ease of shareholder suits index (0–10)	8
Strength of investor protection index (0–10)	5.7

Paying taxes

Payments (number)	95
Time (hours per year)	204
Total tax payable (% of gross profit)	59.4

Trading across borders

Documents for export (number)	..
Signatures for export (number)	..
Time for export (days)	..
Documents for import (number)	18
Signatures for import (number)	27
Time for import (days)	127

Enforcing contracts

Procedures (number)	46
Time (days)	492
Cost (% of debt)	47.9

Closing a business

Time (years)	4
Cost (% of estate)	4
Recovery rate (cents on the dollar)	19.7

LAO PDR

Ease of doing business (rank)	147

East Asia & Pacific
Low income

GNI per capita (US$)	390
Population (m)	5.7

Starting a business

Procedures (number)	9
Time (days)	198
Cost (% of income per capita)	15.1
Minimum capital (% of income per capita)	23.4

Dealing with licenses

Procedures (number)	24
Time (days)	208
Cost (% of income per capita)	224.5

Hiring and firing workers

Difficulty of hiring index (0–100)	11
Rigidity of hours index (0–100)	60
Difficulty of firing index (0–100)	80
Rigidity of employment index (0–100)	50
Hiring cost (% of salary)	5
Firing cost (weeks of salary)	36

Registering property

Procedures (number)	9
Time (days)	135
Cost (% of property value)	4.2

Getting credit

Strength of legal rights index (0–10)	2
Depth of credit information index (0–6)	0
Public registry coverage (% of adults)	0.0
Private bureau coverage (% of adults)	0.0

Protecting investors

Extent of disclosure index (0–10)	4
Extent of director liability index (0–10)	2
Ease of shareholder suits index (0–10)	4
Strength of investor protection index (0–10)	3.3

Paying taxes

Payments (number)	31
Time (hours per year)	180
Total tax payable (% of gross profit)	24.7

Trading across borders

Documents for export (number)	12
Signatures for export (number)	17
Time for export (days)	66
Documents for import (number)	16
Signatures for import (number)	28
Time for import (days)	78

Enforcing contracts

Procedures (number)	53
Time (days)	443
Cost (% of debt)	30.3

Closing a business

Time (years)	5
Cost (% of estate)	76
Recovery rate (cents on the dollar)	0.0

LATVIA

Ease of doing business (rank)	26	Eastern Europe & Central Asia Upper middle income		GNI per capita (US$) Population (m)	5,460 2.3

Starting a business
Procedures (number)	7
Time (days)	18
Cost (% of income per capita)	4.2
Minimum capital (% of income per capita)	31.8

Dealing with licenses
Procedures (number)	21
Time (days)	160
Cost (% of income per capita)	43.9

Hiring and firing workers
Difficulty of hiring index (0–100)	67
Rigidity of hours index (0–100)	40
Difficulty of firing index (0–100)	70
Rigidity of employment index (0–100)	59
Hiring cost (% of salary)	22
Firing cost (weeks of salary)	17

Registering property
Procedures (number)	9
Time (days)	54
Cost (% of property value)	2.1

Getting credit
Strength of legal rights index (0–10)	8
Depth of credit information index (0–6)	3
Public registry coverage (% of adults)	1.1
Private bureau coverage (% of adults)	0.0

Protecting investors
Extent of disclosure index (0–10)	5
Extent of director liability index (0–10)	4
Ease of shareholder suits index (0–10)	8
Strength of investor protection index (0–10)	5.7

Paying taxes
Payments (number)	39
Time (hours per year)	320
Total tax payable (% of gross profit)	38.7

Trading across borders
Documents for export (number)	9
Signatures for export (number)	6
Time for export (days)	18
Documents for import (number)	13
Signatures for import (number)	7
Time for import (days)	21

Enforcing contracts
Procedures (number)	20
Time (days)	186
Cost (% of debt)	10.4

Closing a business
Time (years)	1
Cost (% of estate)	4
Recovery rate (cents on the dollar)	83.1

LEBANON

Ease of doing business (rank)	95	Middle East & North Africa Upper middle income		GNI per capita (US$) Population (m)	4,980 4.5

Starting a business
Procedures (number)	6
Time (days)	46
Cost (% of income per capita)	110.6
Minimum capital (% of income per capita)	68.5

Dealing with licenses
Procedures (number)	16
Time (days)	275
Cost (% of income per capita)	214.6

Hiring and firing workers
Difficulty of hiring index (0–100)	33
Rigidity of hours index (0–100)	0
Difficulty of firing index (0–100)	40
Rigidity of employment index (0–100)	24
Hiring cost (% of salary)	22
Firing cost (weeks of salary)	17

Registering property
Procedures (number)	8
Time (days)	25
Cost (% of property value)	5.9

Getting credit
Strength of legal rights index (0–10)	4
Depth of credit information index (0–6)	4
Public registry coverage (% of adults)	3.5
Private bureau coverage (% of adults)	0.0

Protecting investors
Extent of disclosure index (0–10)	8
Extent of director liability index (0–10)	1
Ease of shareholder suits index (0–10)	4
Strength of investor protection index (0–10)	4.3

Paying taxes
Payments (number)	33
Time (hours per year)	208
Total tax payable (% of gross profit)	30.4

Trading across borders
Documents for export (number)	6
Signatures for export (number)	15
Time for export (days)	22
Documents for import (number)	12
Signatures for import (number)	35
Time for import (days)	34

Enforcing contracts
Procedures (number)	39
Time (days)	721
Cost (% of debt)	26.7

Closing a business
Time (years)	4
Cost (% of estate)	22
Recovery rate (cents on the dollar)	18.6

LESOTHO

Ease of doing business (rank)	97	Sub-Saharan Africa Low income		GNI per capita (US$) Population (m)	740 1.8

Starting a business
Procedures (number)	9
Time (days)	92
Cost (% of income per capita)	56.1
Minimum capital (% of income per capita)	16.4

Dealing with licenses
Procedures (number)	12
Time (days)	254
Cost (% of income per capita)	134.2

Hiring and firing workers
Difficulty of hiring index (0–100)	56
Rigidity of hours index (0–100)	60
Difficulty of firing index (0–100)	10
Rigidity of employment index (0–100)	42
Hiring cost (% of salary)	0
Firing cost (weeks of salary)	47

Registering property
Procedures (number)	6
Time (days)	101
Cost (% of property value)	8.5

Getting credit
Strength of legal rights index (0–10)	5
Depth of credit information index (0–6)	0
Public registry coverage (% of adults)	0.0
Private bureau coverage (% of adults)	0.0

Protecting investors
Extent of disclosure index (0–10)	2
Extent of director liability index (0–10)	2
Ease of shareholder suits index (0–10)	8
Strength of investor protection index (0–10)	4.0

Paying taxes
Payments (number)	19
Time (hours per year)	564
Total tax payable (% of gross profit)	37.7

Trading across borders
Documents for export (number)	. .
Signatures for export (number)	. .
Time for export (days)	. .
Documents for import (number)	10
Signatures for import (number)	15
Time for import (days)	50

Enforcing contracts
Procedures (number)	49
Time (days)	285
Cost (% of debt)	23.9

Closing a business
Time (years)	3
Cost (% of estate)	8
Recovery rate (cents on the dollar)	35.9

LITHUANIA

Ease of doing business (rank)	15

Eastern Europe & Central Asia
Upper middle income

GNI per capita (US$)	5,740
Population (m)	3.5

Starting a business

Procedures (number)	8
Time (days)	26
Cost (% of income per capita)	3.3
Minimum capital (% of income per capita)	57.3

Dealing with licenses

Procedures (number)	14
Time (days)	151
Cost (% of income per capita)	17.5

Hiring and firing workers

Difficulty of hiring index (0–100)	33
Rigidity of hours index (0–100)	60
Difficulty of firing index (0–100)	40
Rigidity of employment index (0–100)	44
Hiring cost (% of salary)	28
Firing cost (weeks of salary)	34

Registering property

Procedures (number)	3
Time (days)	3
Cost (% of property value)	0.8

Getting credit

Strength of legal rights index (0–10)	4
Depth of credit information index (0–6)	6
Public registry coverage (% of adults)	2.5
Private bureau coverage (% of adults)	12.1

Protecting investors

Extent of disclosure index (0–10)	5
Extent of director liability index (0–10)	4
Ease of shareholder suits index (0–10)	7
Strength of investor protection index (0–10)	5.3

Paying taxes

Payments (number)	13
Time (hours per year)	162
Total tax payable (% of gross profit)	41.6

Trading across borders

Documents for export (number)	5
Signatures for export (number)	5
Time for export (days)	6
Documents for import (number)	12
Signatures for import (number)	4
Time for import (days)	17

Enforcing contracts

Procedures (number)	17
Time (days)	154
Cost (% of debt)	9.1

Closing a business

Time (years)	1
Cost (% of estate)	7
Recovery rate (cents on the dollar)	53.6

MACEDONIA, FYR

Ease of doing business (rank)	81

Eastern Europe & Central Asia
Lower middle income

GNI per capita (US$)	2,350
Population (m)	2.1

Starting a business

Procedures (number)	13
Time (days)	48
Cost (% of income per capita)	11.3
Minimum capital (% of income per capita)	145.2

Dealing with licenses

Procedures (number)	18
Time (days)	214
Cost (% of income per capita)	67.5

Hiring and firing workers

Difficulty of hiring index (0–100)	61
Rigidity of hours index (0–100)	60
Difficulty of firing index (0–100)	40
Rigidity of employment index (0–100)	54
Hiring cost (% of salary)	33
Firing cost (weeks of salary)	41

Registering property

Procedures (number)	6
Time (days)	74
Cost (% of property value)	3.6

Getting credit

Strength of legal rights index (0–10)	6
Depth of credit information index (0–6)	3
Public registry coverage (% of adults)	1.9
Private bureau coverage (% of adults)	0.0

Protecting investors

Extent of disclosure index (0–10)	5
Extent of director liability index (0–10)	7
Ease of shareholder suits index (0–10)	6
Strength of investor protection index (0–10)	6.0

Paying taxes

Payments (number)	54
Time (hours per year)	96
Total tax payable (% of gross profit)	40.1

Trading across borders

Documents for export (number)	10
Signatures for export (number)	8
Time for export (days)	32
Documents for import (number)	10
Signatures for import (number)	11
Time for import (days)	35

Enforcing contracts

Procedures (number)	27
Time (days)	509
Cost (% of debt)	32.8

Closing a business

Time (years)	4
Cost (% of estate)	28
Recovery rate (cents on the dollar)	15.4

MADAGASCAR

Ease of doing business (rank)	131

Sub-Saharan Africa
Low income

GNI per capita (US$)	300
Population (m)	16.9

Starting a business

Procedures (number)	11
Time (days)	38
Cost (% of income per capita)	54.3
Minimum capital (% of income per capita)	2158.0

Dealing with licenses

Procedures (number)	19
Time (days)	356
Cost (% of income per capita)	447.8

Hiring and firing workers

Difficulty of hiring index (0–100)	67
Rigidity of hours index (0–100)	60
Difficulty of firing index (0–100)	50
Rigidity of employment index (0–100)	59
Hiring cost (% of salary)	18
Firing cost (weeks of salary)	41

Registering property

Procedures (number)	8
Time (days)	134
Cost (% of property value)	11.0

Getting credit

Strength of legal rights index (0–10)	4
Depth of credit information index (0–6)	2
Public registry coverage (% of adults)	0.3
Private bureau coverage (% of adults)	0.0

Protecting investors

Extent of disclosure index (0–10)	5
Extent of director liability index (0–10)	6
Ease of shareholder suits index (0–10)	6
Strength of investor protection index (0–10)	5.7

Paying taxes

Payments (number)	29
Time (hours per year)	400
Total tax payable (% of gross profit)	58.9

Trading across borders

Documents for export (number)	7
Signatures for export (number)	15
Time for export (days)	50
Documents for import (number)	9
Signatures for import (number)	18
Time for import (days)	59

Enforcing contracts

Procedures (number)	29
Time (days)	280
Cost (% of debt)	22.8

Closing a business

Time (years)	no practice
Cost (% of estate)	no practice
Recovery rate (cents on the dollar)	0.0

MALAWI
Ease of doing business (rank)	96		Sub-Saharan Africa		GNI per capita (US$)	170
			Low income		Population (m)	11.0

Starting a business
Procedures (number)	10
Time (days)	35
Cost (% of income per capita)	139.6
Minimum capital (% of income per capita)	0.0

Dealing with licenses
Procedures (number)	23
Time (days)	205
Cost (% of income per capita)	244.7

Hiring and firing workers
Difficulty of hiring index (0–100)	22
Rigidity of hours index (0–100)	20
Difficulty of firing index (0–100)	20
Rigidity of employment index (0–100)	21
Hiring cost (% of salary)	1
Firing cost (weeks of salary)	90

Registering property
Procedures (number)	6
Time (days)	118
Cost (% of property value)	3.4

Getting credit
Strength of legal rights index (0–10)	7
Depth of credit information index (0–6)	0
Public registry coverage (% of adults)	0.0
Private bureau coverage (% of adults)	0.0

Protecting investors
Extent of disclosure index (0–10)	4
Extent of director liability index (0–10)	7
Ease of shareholder suits index (0–10)	5
Strength of investor protection index (0–10)	5.3

Paying taxes
Payments (number)	33
Time (hours per year)	782
Total tax payable (% of gross profit)	56.5

Trading across borders
Documents for export (number)	9
Signatures for export (number)	12
Time for export (days)	41
Documents for import (number)	6
Signatures for import (number)	20
Time for import (days)	61

Enforcing contracts
Procedures (number)	16
Time (days)	277
Cost (% of debt)	136.5

Closing a business
Time (years)	3
Cost (% of estate)	30
Recovery rate (cents on the dollar)	12.3

MALAYSIA
Ease of doing business (rank)	21		East Asia & Pacific		GNI per capita (US$)	4,650
			Upper middle income		Population (m)	24.8

Starting a business
Procedures (number)	9
Time (days)	30
Cost (% of income per capita)	20.9
Minimum capital (% of income per capita)	0.0

Dealing with licenses
Procedures (number)	25
Time (days)	226
Cost (% of income per capita)	82.7

Hiring and firing workers
Difficulty of hiring index (0–100)	0
Rigidity of hours index (0–100)	20
Difficulty of firing index (0–100)	10
Rigidity of employment index (0–100)	10
Hiring cost (% of salary)	13
Firing cost (weeks of salary)	65

Registering property
Procedures (number)	4
Time (days)	143
Cost (% of property value)	2.3

Getting credit
Strength of legal rights index (0–10)	8
Depth of credit information index (0–6)	6
Public registry coverage (% of adults)	33.7
Private bureau coverage (% of adults)	. .

Protecting investors
Extent of disclosure index (0–10)	10
Extent of director liability index (0–10)	9
Ease of shareholder suits index (0–10)	7
Strength of investor protection index (0–10)	8.7

Paying taxes
Payments (number)	28
Time (hours per year)	. .
Total tax payable (% of gross profit)	11.6

Trading across borders
Documents for export (number)	6
Signatures for export (number)	3
Time for export (days)	20
Documents for import (number)	12
Signatures for import (number)	5
Time for import (days)	22

Enforcing contracts
Procedures (number)	31
Time (days)	300
Cost (% of debt)	20.2

Closing a business
Time (years)	2
Cost (% of estate)	15
Recovery rate (cents on the dollar)	38.8

MALDIVES
Ease of doing business (rank)	31		South Asia		GNI per capita (US$)	2,510
			Lower middle income		Population (m)	0.3

Starting a business
Procedures (number)	6
Time (days)	12
Cost (% of income per capita)	12.4
Minimum capital (% of income per capita)	6.6

Dealing with licenses
Procedures (number)	9
Time (days)	131
Cost (% of income per capita)	40.3

Hiring and firing workers
Difficulty of hiring index (0–100)	0
Rigidity of hours index (0–100)	20
Difficulty of firing index (0–100)	0
Rigidity of employment index (0–100)	7
Hiring cost (% of salary)	0
Firing cost (weeks of salary)	20

Registering property
Procedures (number)	. .
Time (days)	. .
Cost (% of property value)	. .

Getting credit
Strength of legal rights index (0–10)	4
Depth of credit information index (0–6)	0
Public registry coverage (% of adults)	0.0
Private bureau coverage (% of adults)	0.0

Protecting investors
Extent of disclosure index (0–10)	0
Extent of director liability index (0–10)	8
Ease of shareholder suits index (0–10)	8
Strength of investor protection index (0–10)	5.3

Paying taxes
Payments (number)	1
Time (hours per year)	0
Total tax payable (% of gross profit)	5.5

Trading across borders
Documents for export (number)	7
Signatures for export (number)	4
Time for export (days)	24
Documents for import (number)	12
Signatures for import (number)	4
Time for import (days)	29

Enforcing contracts
Procedures (number)	28
Time (days)	434
Cost (% of debt)	8.7

Closing a business
Time (years)	7
Cost (% of estate)	4
Recovery rate (cents on the dollar)	18.0

MALI

Ease of doing business (rank)	146	Sub-Saharan Africa Low income		GNI per capita (US$)		360
				Population (m)		11.7

Starting a business
Procedures (number)	13
Time (days)	42
Cost (% of income per capita)	190.7
Minimum capital (% of income per capita)	490.8

Dealing with licenses
Procedures (number)	17
Time (days)	260
Cost (% of income per capita)	4903.0

Hiring and firing workers
Difficulty of hiring index (0–100)	78
Rigidity of hours index (0–100)	60
Difficulty of firing index (0–100)	60
Rigidity of employment index (0–100)	66
Hiring cost (% of salary)	24
Firing cost (weeks of salary)	81

Registering property
Procedures (number)	5
Time (days)	44
Cost (% of property value)	20.0

Getting credit
Strength of legal rights index (0–10)	3
Depth of credit information index (0–6)	1
Public registry coverage (% of adults)	2.3
Private bureau coverage (% of adults)	0.0

Protecting investors
Extent of disclosure index (0–10)	6
Extent of director liability index (0–10)	5
Ease of shareholder suits index (0–10)	3
Strength of investor protection index (0–10)	4.7

Paying taxes
Payments (number)	60
Time (hours per year)	270
Total tax payable (% of gross profit)	44.0

Trading across borders
Documents for export (number)	10
Signatures for export (number)	33
Time for export (days)	67
Documents for import (number)	16
Signatures for import (number)	60
Time for import (days)	61

Enforcing contracts
Procedures (number)	28
Time (days)	340
Cost (% of debt)	34.6

Closing a business
Time (years)	4
Cost (% of estate)	18
Recovery rate (cents on the dollar)	6.3

MARSHALL ISLANDS

Ease of doing business (rank)	48	East Asia & Pacific Lower middle income		GNI per capita (US$)		2,370
				Population (m)		0.1

Starting a business
Procedures (number)	7
Time (days)	22
Cost (% of income per capita)	27.4
Minimum capital (% of income per capita)	0.0

Dealing with licenses
Procedures (number)	6
Time (days)	76
Cost (% of income per capita)	36.9

Hiring and firing workers
Difficulty of hiring index (0–100)	33
Rigidity of hours index (0–100)	0
Difficulty of firing index (0–100)	0
Rigidity of employment index (0–100)	11
Hiring cost (% of salary)	11
Firing cost (weeks of salary)	0

Registering property
Procedures (number)	4
Time (days)	12
Cost (% of property value)	1.7

Getting credit
Strength of legal rights index (0–10)	6
Depth of credit information index (0–6)	0
Public registry coverage (% of adults)	0.0
Private bureau coverage (% of adults)	0.0

Protecting investors
Extent of disclosure index (0–10)	2
Extent of director liability index (0–10)	0
Ease of shareholder suits index (0–10)	8
Strength of investor protection index (0–10)	3.3

Paying taxes
Payments (number)	20
Time (hours per year)	160
Total tax payable (% of gross profit)	42.6

Trading across borders
Documents for export (number)	. .
Signatures for export (number)	. .
Time for export (days)	. .
Documents for import (number)	6
Signatures for import (number)	6
Time for import (days)	14

Enforcing contracts
Procedures (number)	34
Time (days)	440
Cost (% of debt)	95.9

Closing a business
Time (years)	5
Cost (% of estate)	38
Recovery rate (cents on the dollar)	4.0

MAURITANIA

Ease of doing business (rank)	127	Sub-Saharan Africa Low income		GNI per capita (US$)		420
				Population (m)		2.9

Starting a business
Procedures (number)	11
Time (days)	82
Cost (% of income per capita)	143.6
Minimum capital (% of income per capita)	877.5

Dealing with licenses
Procedures (number)	19
Time (days)	152
Cost (% of income per capita)	987.1

Hiring and firing workers
Difficulty of hiring index (0–100)	100
Rigidity of hours index (0–100)	60
Difficulty of firing index (0–100)	60
Rigidity of employment index (0–100)	73
Hiring cost (% of salary)	17
Firing cost (weeks of salary)	31

Registering property
Procedures (number)	4
Time (days)	49
Cost (% of property value)	6.8

Getting credit
Strength of legal rights index (0–10)	7
Depth of credit information index (0–6)	1
Public registry coverage (% of adults)	0.2
Private bureau coverage (% of adults)	0.0

Protecting investors
Extent of disclosure index (0–10)	. .
Extent of director liability index (0–10)	. .
Ease of shareholder suits index (0–10)	. .
Strength of investor protection index (0–10)	. .

Paying taxes
Payments (number)	61
Time (hours per year)	696
Total tax payable (% of gross profit)	75.8

Trading across borders
Documents for export (number)	9
Signatures for export (number)	13
Time for export (days)	42
Documents for import (number)	7
Signatures for import (number)	25
Time for import (days)	40

Enforcing contracts
Procedures (number)	28
Time (days)	410
Cost (% of debt)	29.3

Closing a business
Time (years)	8
Cost (% of estate)	9
Recovery rate (cents on the dollar)	8.1

MAURITIUS

Ease of doing business (rank)	23	Sub-Saharan Africa Upper middle income		GNI per capita (US$) Population (m)		4,640 1.2

Starting a business
Procedures (number)	6
Time (days)	46
Cost (% of income per capita)	8.8
Minimum capital (% of income per capita)	0.0

Dealing with licenses
Procedures (number)	21
Time (days)	132
Cost (% of income per capita)	16.7

Hiring and firing workers
Difficulty of hiring index (0–100)	0
Rigidity of hours index (0–100)	60
Difficulty of firing index (0–100)	50
Rigidity of employment index (0–100)	37
Hiring cost (% of salary)	7
Firing cost (weeks of salary)	15

Registering property
Procedures (number)	5
Time (days)	210
Cost (% of property value)	16.5

Getting credit
Strength of legal rights index (0–10)	7
Depth of credit information index (0–6)	0
Public registry coverage (% of adults)	0.0
Private bureau coverage (% of adults)	0.0

Protecting investors
Extent of disclosure index (0–10)	6
Extent of director liability index (0–10)	8
Ease of shareholder suits index (0–10)	9
Strength of investor protection index (0–10)	7.7

Paying taxes
Payments (number)	7
Time (hours per year)	158
Total tax payable (% of gross profit)	38.2

Trading across borders
Documents for export (number)	5
Signatures for export (number)	4
Time for export (days)	16
Documents for import (number)	7
Signatures for import (number)	4
Time for import (days)	16

Enforcing contracts
Procedures (number)	17
Time (days)	367
Cost (% of debt)	8.6

Closing a business
Time (years)	2
Cost (% of estate)	14.5
Recovery rate (cents on the dollar)	31.1

MEXICO

Ease of doing business (rank)	73	Latin America & Caribbean Upper middle income		GNI per capita (US$) Population (m)		6,770 102.0

Starting a business
Procedures (number)	9
Time (days)	58
Cost (% of income per capita)	15.6
Minimum capital (% of income per capita)	13.9

Dealing with licenses
Procedures (number)	12
Time (days)	222
Cost (% of income per capita)	159.0

Hiring and firing workers
Difficulty of hiring index (0–100)	33
Rigidity of hours index (0–100)	60
Difficulty of firing index (0–100)	60
Rigidity of employment index (0–100)	51
Hiring cost (% of salary)	24
Firing cost (weeks of salary)	75

Registering property
Procedures (number)	5
Time (days)	74
Cost (% of property value)	5.3

Getting credit
Strength of legal rights index (0–10)	2
Depth of credit information index (0–6)	6
Public registry coverage (% of adults)	0.0
Private bureau coverage (% of adults)	49.4

Protecting investors
Extent of disclosure index (0–10)	6
Extent of director liability index (0–10)	0
Ease of shareholder suits index (0–10)	5
Strength of investor protection index (0–10)	3.7

Paying taxes
Payments (number)	49
Time (hours per year)	536
Total tax payable (% of gross profit)	31.3

Trading across borders
Documents for export (number)	6
Signatures for export (number)	4
Time for export (days)	18
Documents for import (number)	8
Signatures for Import (number)	11
Time for import (days)	26

Enforcing contracts
Procedures (number)	37
Time (days)	421
Cost (% of debt)	20.0

Closing a business
Time (years)	2
Cost (% of estate)	18
Recovery rate (cents on the dollar)	64.1

MICRONESIA

Ease of doing business (rank)	56	East Asia & Pacific Lower middle income		GNI per capita (US$) Population (m)		1,990 0.1

Starting a business
Procedures (number)	7
Time (days)	36
Cost (% of income per capita)	27.7
Minimum capital (% of income per capita)	50.3

Dealing with licenses
Procedures (number)	6
Time (days)	53
Cost (% of income per capita)	41.4

Hiring and firing workers
Difficulty of hiring index (0–100)	33
Rigidity of hours index (0–100)	0
Difficulty of firing index (0–100)	0
Rigidity of employment index (0–100)	11
Hiring cost (% of salary)	6
Firing cost (weeks of salary)	0

Registering property
Procedures (number)	3
Time (days)	8
Cost (% of property value)	1.1

Getting credit
Strength of legal rights index (0–10)	6
Depth of credit information index (0–6)	0
Public registry coverage (% of adults)	0.0
Private bureau coverage (% of adults)	0.0

Protecting investors
Extent of disclosure index (0–10)	0
Extent of director liability index (0–10)	0
Ease of shareholder suits index (0–10)	8
Strength of investor protection index (0–10)	2.7

Paying taxes
Payments (number)	8
Time (hours per year)	128
Total tax payable (% of gross profit)	32.1

Trading across borders
Documents for export (number)	. .
Signatures for export (number)	. .
Time for export (days)	. .
Documents for import (number)	14
Signatures for import (number)	5
Time for import (days)	33

Enforcing contracts
Procedures (number)	28
Time (days)	410
Cost (% of debt)	124.4

Closing a business
Time (years)	5
Cost (% of estate)	38
Recovery rate (cents on the dollar)	3.3

MOLDOVA

Ease of doing business (rank)	83	

Eastern Europe & Central Asia	
Low income	

GNI per capita (US$)	710
Population (m)	4.2

Starting a business

Procedures (number)	10
Time (days)	30
Cost (% of income per capita)	17.1
Minimum capital (% of income per capita)	22.0

Dealing with licenses

Procedures (number)	20
Time (days)	122
Cost (% of income per capita)	215.0

Hiring and firing workers

Difficulty of hiring index (0–100)	33
Rigidity of hours index (0–100)	100
Difficulty of firing index (0–100)	70
Rigidity of employment index (0–100)	68
Hiring cost (% of salary)	30
Firing cost (weeks of salary)	21

Registering property

Procedures (number)	6
Time (days)	48
Cost (% of property value)	1.5

Getting credit

Strength of legal rights index (0–10)	6
Depth of credit information index (0–6)	0
Public registry coverage (% of adults)	0.0
Private bureau coverage (% of adults)	0.0

Protecting investors

Extent of disclosure index (0–10)	7
Extent of director liability index (0–10)	1
Ease of shareholder suits index (0–10)	6
Strength of investor protection index (0–10)	4.7

Paying taxes

Payments (number)	44
Time (hours per year)	250
Total tax payable (% of gross profit)	44.7

Trading across borders

Documents for export (number)	7
Signatures for export (number)	12
Time for export (days)	33
Documents for import (number)	7
Signatures for import (number)	13
Time for import (days)	35

Enforcing contracts

Procedures (number)	37
Time (days)	340
Cost (% of debt)	16.2

Closing a business

Time (years)	3
Cost (% of estate)	9
Recovery rate (cents on the dollar)	27.3

MONGOLIA

Ease of doing business (rank)	61	

East Asia & Pacific	
Low income	

GNI per capita (US$)	590
Population (m)	2.5

Starting a business

Procedures (number)	8
Time (days)	20
Cost (% of income per capita)	6.2
Minimum capital (% of income per capita)	140.2

Dealing with licenses

Procedures (number)	18
Time (days)	96
Cost (% of income per capita)	58.8

Hiring and firing workers

Difficulty of hiring index (0–100)	11
Rigidity of hours index (0–100)	80
Difficulty of firing index (0–100)	10
Rigidity of employment index (0–100)	34
Hiring cost (% of salary)	19
Firing cost (weeks of salary)	17

Registering property

Procedures (number)	5
Time (days)	11
Cost (% of property value)	2.3

Getting credit

Strength of legal rights index (0–10)	5
Depth of credit information index (0–6)	3
Public registry coverage (% of adults)	4.7
Private bureau coverage (% of adults)	0.0

Protecting investors

Extent of disclosure index (0–10)	. .
Extent of director liability index (0–10)	. .
Ease of shareholder suits index (0–10)	. .
Strength of investor protection index (0–10)	. .

Paying taxes

Payments (number)	43
Time (hours per year)	. .
Total tax payable (% of gross profit)	45.3

Trading across borders

Documents for export (number)	11
Signatures for export (number)	21
Time for export (days)	66
Documents for import (number)	10
Signatures for import (number)	27
Time for import (days)	74

Enforcing contracts

Procedures (number)	26
Time (days)	314
Cost (% of debt)	22.6

Closing a business

Time (years)	4
Cost (% of estate)	8
Recovery rate (cents on the dollar)	17.0

MOROCCO

Ease of doing business (rank)	102	

Middle East & North Africa	
Lower middle income	

GNI per capita (US$)	1,520
Population (m)	30.1

Starting a business

Procedures (number)	5
Time (days)	11
Cost (% of income per capita)	12.0
Minimum capital (% of income per capita)	700.3

Dealing with licenses

Procedures (number)	21
Time (days)	217
Cost (% of income per capita)	1302.8

Hiring and firing workers

Difficulty of hiring index (0–100)	100
Rigidity of hours index (0–100)	40
Difficulty of firing index (0–100)	40
Rigidity of employment index (0–100)	60
Hiring cost (% of salary)	18
Firing cost (weeks of salary)	83

Registering property

Procedures (number)	3
Time (days)	82
Cost (% of property value)	6.1

Getting credit

Strength of legal rights index (0–10)	2
Depth of credit information index (0–6)	1
Public registry coverage (% of adults)	2.0
Private bureau coverage (% of adults)	0.0

Protecting investors

Extent of disclosure index (0–10)	6
Extent of director liability index (0–10)	5
Ease of shareholder suits index (0–10)	1
Strength of investor protection index (0–10)	4.0

Paying taxes

Payments (number)	28
Time (hours per year)	690
Total tax payable (% of gross profit)	54.8

Trading across borders

Documents for export (number)	7
Signatures for export (number)	13
Time for export (days)	31
Documents for import (number)	11
Signatures for import (number)	17
Time for import (days)	33

Enforcing contracts

Procedures (number)	17
Time (days)	240
Cost (% of debt)	17.7

Closing a business

Time (years)	2
Cost (% of estate)	18
Recovery rate (cents on the dollar)	35.1

MOZAMBIQUE

Ease of doing business (rank)	110	

Sub-Saharan Africa
Low income

GNI per capita (US$)	250
Population (m)	18.8

Starting a business

Procedures (number)	14
Time (days)	153
Cost (% of income per capita)	95.0
Minimum capital (% of income per capita)	12.0

Dealing with licenses

Procedures (number)	14
Time (days)	212
Cost (% of income per capita)	148.6

Hiring and firing workers

Difficulty of hiring index (0–100)	83
Rigidity of hours index (0–100)	80
Difficulty of firing index (0–100)	20
Rigidity of employment index (0–100)	61
Hiring cost (% of salary)	4
Firing cost (weeks of salary)	141

Registering property

Procedures (number)	8
Time (days)	42
Cost (% of property value)	5.2

Getting credit

Strength of legal rights index (0–10)	4
Depth of credit information index (0–6)	4
Public registry coverage (% of adults)	0.8
Private bureau coverage (% of adults)	0.0

Protecting investors

Extent of disclosure index (0–10)	..
Extent of director liability index (0–10)	..
Ease of shareholder suits index (0–10)	..
Strength of investor protection index (0–10)	..

Paying taxes

Payments (number)	35
Time (hours per year)	230
Total tax payable (% of gross profit)	50.9

Trading across borders

Documents for export (number)	6
Signatures for export (number)	12
Time for export (days)	41
Documents for import (number)	16
Signatures for import (number)	12
Time for import (days)	41

Enforcing contracts

Procedures (number)	38
Time (days)	580
Cost (% of debt)	16.0

Closing a business

Time (years)	5
Cost (% of estate)	9
Recovery rate (cents on the dollar)	13.3

NAMIBIA

Ease of doing business (rank)	33	

Sub-Saharan Africa
Lower middle income

GNI per capita (US$)	2,370
Population (m)	2.0

Starting a business

Procedures (number)	10
Time (days)	95
Cost (% of income per capita)	18.8
Minimum capital (% of income per capita)	0.0

Dealing with licenses

Procedures (number)	11
Time (days)	169
Cost (% of income per capita)	892.0

Hiring and firing workers

Difficulty of hiring index (0–100)	0
Rigidity of hours index (0–100)	60
Difficulty of firing index (0–100)	20
Rigidity of employment index (0–100)	27
Hiring cost (% of salary)	0
Firing cost (weeks of salary)	24

Registering property

Procedures (number)	9
Time (days)	28
Cost (% of property value)	9.3

Getting credit

Strength of legal rights index (0–10)	5
Depth of credit information index (0–6)	5
Public registry coverage (% of adults)	0.0
Private bureau coverage (% of adults)	35.2

Protecting investors

Extent of disclosure index (0–10)	8
Extent of director liability index (0–10)	5
Ease of shareholder suits index (0–10)	7
Strength of investor protection index (0–10)	6.7

Paying taxes

Payments (number)	23
Time (hours per year)	50
Total tax payable (% of gross profit)	43.9

Trading across borders

Documents for export (number)	9
Signatures for export (number)	7
Time for export (days)	32
Documents for import (number)	14
Signatures for import (number)	7
Time for import (days)	25

Enforcing contracts

Procedures (number)	31
Time (days)	270
Cost (% of debt)	28.3

Closing a business

Time (years)	1
Cost (% of estate)	15
Recovery rate (cents on the dollar)	45.3

NEPAL

Ease of doing business (rank)	55	

South Asia
Low income

GNI per capita (US$)	260
Population (m)	24.7

Starting a business

Procedures (number)	7
Time (days)	21
Cost (% of income per capita)	69.9
Minimum capital (% of income per capita)	0.0

Dealing with licenses

Procedures (number)	12
Time (days)	147
Cost (% of income per capita)	314.7

Hiring and firing workers

Difficulty of hiring index (0–100)	56
Rigidity of hours index (0–100)	20
Difficulty of firing index (0–100)	90
Rigidity of employment index (0–100)	55
Hiring cost (% of salary)	0
Firing cost (weeks of salary)	90

Registering property

Procedures (number)	2
Time (days)	2
Cost (% of property value)	6.2

Getting credit

Strength of legal rights index (0–10)	4
Depth of credit information index (0–6)	3
Public registry coverage (% of adults)	0.0
Private bureau coverage (% of adults)	0.1

Protecting investors

Extent of disclosure index (0–10)	4
Extent of director liability index (0–10)	1
Ease of shareholder suits index (0–10)	9
Strength of investor protection index (0–10)	4.7

Paying taxes

Payments (number)	23
Time (hours per year)	408
Total tax payable (% of gross profit)	31.8

Trading across borders

Documents for export (number)	7
Signatures for export (number)	12
Time for export (days)	44
Documents for import (number)	10
Signatures for import (number)	24
Time for import (days)	38

Enforcing contracts

Procedures (number)	28
Time (days)	350
Cost (% of debt)	25.8

Closing a business

Time (years)	5
Cost (% of estate)	9
Recovery rate (cents on the dollar)	23.9

NETHERLANDS

Ease of doing business (rank)	24	

OECD: High Income	GNI per capita (US$)	31,700
High income	Population (m)	16.2

Starting a business

Procedures (number)	7
Time (days)	11
Cost (% of income per capita)	13.0
Minimum capital (% of income per capita)	64.6

Dealing with licenses

Procedures (number)	18
Time (days)	184
Cost (% of income per capita)	142.7

Hiring and firing workers

Difficulty of hiring index (0–100)	28
Rigidity of hours index (0–100)	60
Difficulty of firing index (0–100)	60
Rigidity of employment index (0–100)	49
Hiring cost (% of salary)	16
Firing cost (weeks of salary)	16

Registering property

Procedures (number)	2
Time (days)	2
Cost (% of property value)	6.2

Getting credit

Strength of legal rights index (0–10)	8
Depth of credit information index (0–6)	5
Public registry coverage (% of adults)	0.0
Private bureau coverage (% of adults)	68.9

Protecting investors

Extent of disclosure index (0–10)	4
Extent of director liability index (0–10)	3
Ease of shareholder suits index (0–10)	6
Strength of investor protection index (0–10)	4.3

Paying taxes

Payments (number)	22
Time (hours per year)	700
Total tax payable (% of gross profit)	53.3

Trading across borders

Documents for export (number)	5
Signatures for export (number)	3
Time for export (days)	7
Documents for import (number)	4
Signatures for import (number)	1
Time for import (days)	8

Enforcing contracts

Procedures (number)	22
Time (days)	48
Cost (% of debt)	17.0

Closing a business

Time (years)	2
Cost (% of estate)	1
Recovery rate (cents on the dollar)	86.7

NEW ZEALAND

Ease of doing business (rank)	1	

OECD: High Income	GNI per capita (US$)	20,310
High income	Population (m)	4.0

Starting a business

Procedures (number)	2
Time (days)	12
Cost (% of income per capita)	0.2
Minimum capital (% of income per capita)	0.0

Dealing with licenses

Procedures (number)	7
Time (days)	65
Cost (% of income per capita)	29.3

Hiring and firing workers

Difficulty of hiring index (0–100)	11
Rigidity of hours index (0–100)	0
Difficulty of firing index (0–100)	10
Rigidity of employment index (0–100)	7
Hiring cost (% of salary)	0
Firing cost (weeks of salary)	0

Registering property

Procedures (number)	2
Time (days)	2
Cost (% of property value)	0.1

Getting credit

Strength of legal rights index (0–10)	9
Depth of credit information index (0–6)	5
Public registry coverage (% of adults)	0.0
Private bureau coverage (% of adults)	95.8

Protecting investors

Extent of disclosure index (0–10)	10
Extent of director liability index (0–10)	9
Ease of shareholder suits index (0–10)	10
Strength of investor protection index (0–10)	9.7

Paying taxes

Payments (number)	8
Time (hours per year)	70
Total tax payable (% of gross profit)	44.2

Trading across borders

Documents for export (number)	5
Signatures for export (number)	2
Time for export (days)	8
Documents for import (number)	9
Signatures for import (number)	2
Time for import (days)	13

Enforcing contracts

Procedures (number)	19
Time (days)	50
Cost (% of debt)	4.8

Closing a business

Time (years)	2
Cost (% of estate)	4
Recovery rate (cents on the dollar)	71.0

NICARAGUA

Ease of doing business (rank)	59	

Latin America & Caribbean	GNI per capita (US$)	790
Low income	Population (m)	5.5

Starting a business

Procedures (number)	8
Time (days)	42
Cost (% of income per capita)	139.1
Minimum capital (% of income per capita)	0.0

Dealing with licenses

Procedures (number)	12
Time (days)	192
Cost (% of income per capita)	1243.8

Hiring and firing workers

Difficulty of hiring index (0–100)	11
Rigidity of hours index (0–100)	80
Difficulty of firing index (0–100)	50
Rigidity of employment index (0–100)	47
Hiring cost (% of salary)	17
Firing cost (weeks of salary)	24

Registering property

Procedures (number)	7
Time (days)	65
Cost (% of property value)	6.5

Getting credit

Strength of legal rights index (0–10)	4
Depth of credit information index (0–6)	4
Public registry coverage (% of adults)	8.1
Private bureau coverage (% of adults)	0.0

Protecting investors

Extent of disclosure index (0–10)	4
Extent of director liability index (0–10)	5
Ease of shareholder suits index (0–10)	6
Strength of investor protection index (0–10)	5.0

Paying taxes

Payments (number)	64
Time (hours per year)	240
Total tax payable (% of gross profit)	54.3

Trading across borders

Documents for export (number)	6
Signatures for export (number)	4
Time for export (days)	38
Documents for import (number)	7
Signatures for import (number)	5
Time for import (days)	38

Enforcing contracts

Procedures (number)	20
Time (days)	155
Cost (% of debt)	16.3

Closing a business

Time (years)	2
Cost (% of estate)	14.5
Recovery rate (cents on the dollar)	33.8

NIGER

Ease of doing business (rank)	150	Sub-Saharan Africa		Low income	GNI per capita (US$)	230
					Population (m)	11.8

Starting a business
Procedures (number)	13
Time (days)	35
Cost (% of income per capita)	465.4
Minimum capital (% of income per capita)	760.8

Dealing with licenses
Procedures (number)	27
Time (days)	165
Cost (% of income per capita)	2920.3

Hiring and firing workers
Difficulty of hiring index (0–100)	100
Rigidity of hours index (0–100)	100
Difficulty of firing index (0–100)	70
Rigidity of employment index (0–100)	90
Hiring cost (% of salary)	16
Firing cost (weeks of salary)	76

Registering property
Procedures (number)	5
Time (days)	49
Cost (% of property value)	14.0

Getting credit
Strength of legal rights index (0–10)	4
Depth of credit information index (0–6)	1
Public registry coverage (% of adults)	0.9
Private bureau coverage (% of adults)	0.0

Protecting investors
Extent of disclosure index (0–10)	6
Extent of director liability index (0–10)	5
Ease of shareholder suits index (0–10)	3
Strength of investor protection index (0–10)	4.7

Paying taxes
Payments (number)	44
Time (hours per year)	270
Total tax payable (% of gross profit)	49.4

Trading across borders
Documents for export (number)	. .
Signatures for export (number)	. .
Time for export (days)	. .
Documents for import (number)	19
Signatures for import (number)	52
Time for import (days)	89

Enforcing contracts
Procedures (number)	33
Time (days)	330
Cost (% of debt)	42.0

Closing a business
Time (years)	5
Cost (% of estate)	18
Recovery rate (cents on the dollar)	2.6

NIGERIA

Ease of doing business (rank)	94	Sub-Saharan Africa		Low income	GNI per capita (US$)	390
					Population (m)	136.0

Starting a business
Procedures (number)	9
Time (days)	43
Cost (% of income per capita)	73.8
Minimum capital (% of income per capita)	43.3

Dealing with licenses
Procedures (number)	16
Time (days)	465
Cost (% of income per capita)	355.8

Hiring and firing workers
Difficulty of hiring index (0–100)	33
Rigidity of hours index (0–100)	60
Difficulty of firing index (0–100)	20
Rigidity of employment index (0–100)	38
Hiring cost (% of salary)	8
Firing cost (weeks of salary)	4

Registering property
Procedures (number)	21
Time (days)	274
Cost (% of property value)	27.1

Getting credit
Strength of legal rights index (0–10)	7
Depth of credit information index (0–6)	3
Public registry coverage (% of adults)	0.0
Private bureau coverage (% of adults)	0.3

Protecting investors
Extent of disclosure index (0–10)	6
Extent of director liability index (0–10)	7
Ease of shareholder suits index (0–10)	4
Strength of investor protection index (0–10)	5.7

Paying taxes
Payments (number)	36
Time (hours per year)	1120
Total tax payable (% of gross profit)	27.1

Trading across borders
Documents for export (number)	11
Signatures for export (number)	39
Time for export (days)	41
Documents for import (number)	13
Signatures for import (number)	71
Time for import (days)	53

Enforcing contracts
Procedures (number)	23
Time (days)	730
Cost (% of debt)	37.2

Closing a business
Time (years)	2
Cost (% of estate)	22
Recovery rate (cents on the dollar)	31.1

NORWAY

Ease of doing business (rank)	5	OECD: High Income		High income	GNI per capita (US$)	52,030
					Population (m)	4.6

Starting a business
Procedures (number)	4
Time (days)	13
Cost (% of income per capita)	2.7
Minimum capital (% of income per capita)	27.0

Dealing with licenses
Procedures (number)	13
Time (days)	97
Cost (% of income per capita)	53.9

Hiring and firing workers
Difficulty of hiring index (0–100)	44
Rigidity of hours index (0–100)	40
Difficulty of firing index (0–100)	30
Rigidity of employment index (0–100)	38
Hiring cost (% of salary)	14
Firing cost (weeks of salary)	12

Registering property
Procedures (number)	1
Time (days)	1
Cost (% of property value)	2.5

Getting credit
Strength of legal rights index (0–10)	6
Depth of credit information index (0–6)	4
Public registry coverage (% of adults)	0.0
Private bureau coverage (% of adults)	100.0

Protecting investors
Extent of disclosure index (0–10)	7
Extent of director liability index (0–10)	6
Ease of shareholder suits index (0–10)	7
Strength of investor protection index (0–10)	6.7

Paying taxes
Payments (number)	3
Time (hours per year)	87
Total tax payable (% of gross profit)	60.1

Trading across borders
Documents for export (number)	4
Signatures for export (number)	3
Time for export (days)	7
Documents for import (number)	4
Signatures for import (number)	3
Time for import (days)	7

Enforcing contracts
Procedures (number)	14
Time (days)	87
Cost (% of debt)	4.2

Closing a business
Time (years)	1
Cost (% of estate)	1
Recovery rate (cents on the dollar)	91.1

OMAN

| | | Middle East & North Africa | | GNI per capita (US$) | 7,890 |
| Ease of doing business (rank) | 51 | Upper middle income | | Population (m) | 2.6 |

Starting a business
Procedures (number)	9
Time (days)	34
Cost (% of income per capita)	4.8
Minimum capital (% of income per capita)	97.3

Dealing with licenses
Procedures (number)	16
Time (days)	271
Cost (% of income per capita)	1014.0

Hiring and firing workers
Difficulty of hiring index (0–100)	44
Rigidity of hours index (0–100)	60
Difficulty of firing index (0–100)	0
Rigidity of employment index (0–100)	35
Hiring cost (% of salary)	9
Firing cost (weeks of salary)	13

Registering property
Procedures (number)	4
Time (days)	16
Cost (% of property value)	3.0

Getting credit
Strength of legal rights index (0–10)	3
Depth of credit information index (0–6)	0
Public registry coverage (% of adults)	0.0
Private bureau coverage (% of adults)	0.0

Protecting investors
Extent of disclosure index (0–10)	8
Extent of director liability index (0–10)	6
Ease of shareholder suits index (0–10)	3
Strength of investor protection index (0–10)	5.7

Paying taxes
Payments (number)	13
Time (hours per year)	52
Total tax payable (% of gross profit)	5.2

Trading across borders
Documents for export (number)	9
Signatures for export (number)	7
Time for export (days)	23
Documents for import (number)	13
Signatures for import (number)	9
Time for import (days)	27

Enforcing contracts
Procedures (number)	41
Time (days)	455
Cost (% of debt)	10.0

Closing a business
Time (years)	7
Cost (% of estate)	4
Recovery rate (cents on the dollar)	24.9

PAKISTAN

| | | South Asia | | GNI per capita (US$) | 600 |
| Ease of doing business (rank) | 60 | Low income | | Population (m) | 148.0 |

Starting a business
Procedures (number)	11
Time (days)	24
Cost (% of income per capita)	18.6
Minimum capital (% of income per capita)	0.0

Dealing with licenses
Procedures (number)	12
Time (days)	218
Cost (% of income per capita)	1170.7

Hiring and firing workers
Difficulty of hiring index (0–100)	67
Rigidity of hours index (0–100)	40
Difficulty of firing index (0–100)	30
Rigidity of employment index (0–100)	46
Hiring cost (% of salary)	12
Firing cost (weeks of salary)	90

Registering property
Procedures (number)	5
Time (days)	49
Cost (% of property value)	3.2

Getting credit
Strength of legal rights index (0–10)	4
Depth of credit information index (0–6)	4
Public registry coverage (% of adults)	0.3
Private bureau coverage (% of adults)	0.9

Protecting investors
Extent of disclosure index (0–10)	6
Extent of director liability index (0–10)	6
Ease of shareholder suits index (0–10)	7
Strength of investor protection index (0–10)	6.3

Paying taxes
Payments (number)	32
Time (hours per year)	560
Total tax payable (% of gross profit)	57.4

Trading across borders
Documents for export (number)	8
Signatures for export (number)	10
Time for export (days)	33
Documents for import (number)	12
Signatures for import (number)	15
Time for import (days)	39

Enforcing contracts
Procedures (number)	46
Time (days)	395
Cost (% of debt)	35.2

Closing a business
Time (years)	3
Cost (% of estate)	4
Recovery rate (cents on the dollar)	44.3

PALAU

| | | East Asia & Pacific | | GNI per capita (US$) | 6,870 |
| Ease of doing business (rank) | 50 | Upper middle income | | Population (m) | 0.0 |

Starting a business
Procedures (number)	8
Time (days)	33
Cost (% of income per capita)	10.2
Minimum capital (% of income per capita)	7.3

Dealing with licenses
Procedures (number)	6
Time (days)	67
Cost (% of income per capita)	18.8

Hiring and firing workers
Difficulty of hiring index (0–100)	0
Rigidity of hours index (0–100)	0
Difficulty of firing index (0–100)	0
Rigidity of employment index (0–100)	0
Hiring cost (% of salary)	6
Firing cost (weeks of salary)	0

Registering property
Procedures (number)	3
Time (days)	14
Cost (% of property value)	0.3

Getting credit
Strength of legal rights index (0–10)	5
Depth of credit information index (0–6)	0
Public registry coverage (% of adults)	0.0
Private bureau coverage (% of adults)	0.0

Protecting investors
Extent of disclosure index (0–10)	0
Extent of director liability index (0–10)	0
Ease of shareholder suits index (0–10)	8
Strength of investor protection index (0–10)	2.7

Paying taxes
Payments (number)	17
Time (hours per year)	128
Total tax payable (% of gross profit)	40.0

Trading across borders
Documents for export (number)	7
Signatures for export (number)	3
Time for export (days)	20
Documents for import (number)	9
Signatures for import (number)	4
Time for import (days)	26

Enforcing contracts
Procedures (number)	34
Time (days)	465
Cost (% of debt)	34.7

Closing a business
Time (years)	7
Cost (% of estate)	38
Recovery rate (cents on the dollar)	3.5

PANAMA

Ease of doing business (rank)	57	Latin America & Caribbean Upper middle income		GNI per capita (US$) Population (m)	4,450 3.0	

Starting a business
Procedures (number)	7
Time (days)	19
Cost (% of income per capita)	24.8
Minimum capital (% of income per capita)	0.0

Dealing with licenses
Procedures (number)	22
Time (days)	128
Cost (% of income per capita)	114.3

Hiring and firing workers
Difficulty of hiring index (0–100)	78
Rigidity of hours index (0–100)	40
Difficulty of firing index (0–100)	70
Rigidity of employment index (0–100)	63
Hiring cost (% of salary)	14
Firing cost (weeks of salary)	47

Registering property
Procedures (number)	7
Time (days)	44
Cost (% of property value)	2.4

Getting credit
Strength of legal rights index (0–10)	6
Depth of credit information index (0–6)	6
Public registry coverage (% of adults)	0.0
Private bureau coverage (% of adults)	40.2

Protecting investors
Extent of disclosure index (0–10)	3
Extent of director liability index (0–10)	4
Ease of shareholder suits index (0–10)	7
Strength of investor protection index (0–10)	4.7

Paying taxes
Payments (number)	45
Time (hours per year)	424
Total tax payable (% of gross profit)	32.9

Trading across borders
Documents for export (number)	8
Signatures for export (number)	3
Time for export (days)	30
Documents for import (number)	12
Signatures for import (number)	3
Time for import (days)	32

Enforcing contracts
Procedures (number)	45
Time (days)	355
Cost (% of debt)	37.0

Closing a business
Time (years)	2
Cost (% of estate)	30
Recovery rate (cents on the dollar)	25.8

PAPUA NEW GUINEA

Ease of doing business (rank)	64	East Asia & Pacific Low income		GNI per capita (US$) Population (m)	580 5.5	

Starting a business
Procedures (number)	8
Time (days)	56
Cost (% of income per capita)	30.2
Minimum capital (% of income per capita)	0.0

Dealing with licenses
Procedures (number)	20
Time (days)	218
Cost (% of income per capita)	124.7

Hiring and firing workers
Difficulty of hiring index (0–100)	22
Rigidity of hours index (0–100)	20
Difficulty of firing index (0–100)	20
Rigidity of employment index (0–100)	21
Hiring cost (% of salary)	8
Firing cost (weeks of salary)	38

Registering property
Procedures (number)	4
Time (days)	72
Cost (% of property value)	5.2

Getting credit
Strength of legal rights index (0–10)	6
Depth of credit information index (0–6)	0
Public registry coverage (% of adults)	0.0
Private bureau coverage (% of adults)	0.0

Protecting investors
Extent of disclosure index (0–10)	5
Extent of director liability index (0–10)	5
Ease of shareholder suits index (0–10)	8
Strength of investor protection index (0–10)	6.0

Paying taxes
Payments (number)	43
Time (hours per year)	198
Total tax payable (% of gross profit)	36.7

Trading across borders
Documents for export (number)	5
Signatures for export (number)	5
Time for export (days)	30
Documents for import (number)	10
Signatures for import (number)	6
Time for import (days)	32

Enforcing contracts
Procedures (number)	22
Time (days)	440
Cost (% of debt)	110.3

Closing a business
Time (years)	3
Cost (% of estate)	38
Recovery rate (cents on the dollar)	13.0

PARAGUAY

Ease of doing business (rank)	88	Latin America & Caribbean Lower middle income		GNI per capita (US$) Population (m)	1,170 5.6	

Starting a business
Procedures (number)	17
Time (days)	74
Cost (% of income per capita)	147.8
Minimum capital (% of income per capita)	0.0

Dealing with licenses
Procedures (number)	15
Time (days)	273
Cost (% of income per capita)	544.5

Hiring and firing workers
Difficulty of hiring index (0–100)	56
Rigidity of hours index (0–100)	60
Difficulty of firing index (0–100)	60
Rigidity of employment index (0–100)	59
Hiring cost (% of salary)	17
Firing cost (weeks of salary)	99

Registering property
Procedures (number)	7
Time (days)	48
Cost (% of property value)	2.0

Getting credit
Strength of legal rights index (0–10)	3
Depth of credit information index (0–6)	6
Public registry coverage (% of adults)	8.7
Private bureau coverage (% of adults)	52.2

Protecting investors
Extent of disclosure index (0–10)	6
Extent of director liability index (0–10)	5
Ease of shareholder suits index (0–10)	6
Strength of investor protection index (0–10)	5.7

Paying taxes
Payments (number)	33
Time (hours per year)	328
Total tax payable (% of gross profit)	37.9

Trading across borders
Documents for export (number)	9
Signatures for export (number)	7
Time for export (days)	34
Documents for import (number)	13
Signatures for import (number)	11
Time for import (days)	31

Enforcing contracts
Procedures (number)	46
Time (days)	285
Cost (% of debt)	30.4

Closing a business
Time (years)	4
Cost (% of estate)	9
Recovery rate (cents on the dollar)	13.3

PERU

		Latin America & Caribbean		GNI per capita (US$)	2,360
Ease of doing business (rank)	71	Lower middle income		Population (m)	27.1

Starting a business		**Registering property**		**Trading across borders**	
Procedures (number)	10	Procedures (number)	5	Documents for export (number)	8
Time (days)	102	Time (days)	33	Signatures for export (number)	10
Cost (% of income per capita)	38.0	Cost (% of property value)	3.2	Time for export (days)	24
Minimum capital (% of income per capita)	0.0			Documents for import (number)	13
		Getting credit		Signatures for import (number)	13
Dealing with licenses		Strength of legal rights index (0–10)	2	Time for import (days)	31
Procedures (number)	19	Depth of credit information index (0–6)	6		
Time (days)	201	Public registry coverage (% of adults)	30.2	**Enforcing contracts**	
Cost (% of income per capita)	366.3	Private bureau coverage (% of adults)	27.8	Procedures (number)	35
				Time (days)	381
Hiring and firing workers		**Protecting investors**		Cost (% of debt)	34.7
Difficulty of hiring index (0–100)	44	Extent of disclosure index (0–10)	7		
Rigidity of hours index (0–100)	60	Extent of director liability index (0–10)	5	**Closing a business**	
Difficulty of firing index (0–100)	40	Ease of shareholder suits index (0–10)	7	Time (years)	3
Rigidity of employment index (0–100)	48	Strength of investor protection index (0–10)	6.3	Cost (% of estate)	7
Hiring cost (% of salary)	10			Recovery rate (cents on the dollar)	31.3
Firing cost (weeks of salary)	56	**Paying taxes**			
		Payments (number)	53		
		Time (hours per year)	424		
		Total tax payable (% of gross profit)	50.7		

PHILIPPINES

		East Asia & Pacific		GNI per capita (US$)	1,170
Ease of doing business (rank)	113	Lower middle income		Population (m)	81.5

Starting a business		**Registering property**		**Trading across borders**	
Procedures (number)	11	Procedures (number)	8	Documents for export (number)	6
Time (days)	48	Time (days)	33	Signatures for export (number)	5
Cost (% of income per capita)	20.3	Cost (% of property value)	5.7	Time for export (days)	19
Minimum capital (% of income per capita)	2.0			Documents for import (number)	8
		Getting credit		Signatures for import (number)	7
Dealing with licenses		Strength of legal rights index (0–10)	3	Time for import (days)	22
Procedures (number)	23	Depth of credit information index (0–6)	2		
Time (days)	197	Public registry coverage (% of adults)	0.0	**Enforcing contracts**	
Cost (% of income per capita)	121.0	Private bureau coverage (% of adults)	3.7	Procedures (number)	25
				Time (days)	360
Hiring and firing workers		**Protecting investors**		Cost (% of debt)	50.7
Difficulty of hiring index (0–100)	56	Extent of disclosure index (0–10)	1		
Rigidity of hours index (0–100)	40	Extent of director liability index (0–10)	2	**Closing a business**	
Difficulty of firing index (0–100)	40	Ease of shareholder suits index (0–10)	7	Time (years)	6
Rigidity of employment index (0–100)	45	Strength of investor protection index (0–10)	3.3	Cost (% of estate)	38
Hiring cost (% of salary)	9			Recovery rate (cents on the dollar)	4.1
Firing cost (weeks of salary)	90	**Paying taxes**			
		Payments (number)	62		
		Time (hours per year)	94		
		Total tax payable (% of gross profit)	46.4		

POLAND

		Eastern Europe & Central Asia		GNI per capita (US$)	6,090
Ease of doing business (rank)	54	Upper middle income		Population (m)	38.2

Starting a business		**Registering property**		**Trading across borders**	
Procedures (number)	10	Procedures (number)	6	Documents for export (number)	6
Time (days)	31	Time (days)	197	Signatures for export (number)	5
Cost (% of income per capita)	22.2	Cost (% of property value)	1.6	Time for export (days)	19
Minimum capital (% of income per capita)	220.1			Documents for import (number)	7
		Getting credit		Signatures for import (number)	8
Dealing with licenses		Strength of legal rights index (0–10)	3	Time for import (days)	26
Procedures (number)	25	Depth of credit information index (0–6)	4		
Time (days)	322	Public registry coverage (% of adults)	0.0	**Enforcing contracts**	
Cost (% of income per capita)	83.1	Private bureau coverage (% of adults)	38.1	Procedures (number)	41
				Time (days)	980
Hiring and firing workers		**Protecting investors**		Cost (% of debt)	8.7
Difficulty of hiring index (0–100)	11	Extent of disclosure index (0–10)	7		
Rigidity of hours index (0–100)	60	Extent of director liability index (0–10)	4	**Closing a business**	
Difficulty of firing index (0–100)	40	Ease of shareholder suits index (0–10)	8	Time (years)	1
Rigidity of employment index (0–100)	37	Strength of investor protection index (0–10)	6.3	Cost (% of estate)	22
Hiring cost (% of salary)	26			Recovery rate (cents on the dollar)	64.0
Firing cost (weeks of salary)	25	**Paying taxes**			
		Payments (number)	43		
		Time (hours per year)	175		
		Total tax payable (% of gross profit)	55.6		

PORTUGAL

Ease of doing business (rank)	42

OECD: High Income
High income

GNI per capita (US$)	14,350
Population (m)	10.4

Starting a business

Procedures (number)	11
Time (days)	54
Cost (% of income per capita)	13.4
Minimum capital (% of income per capita)	39.4

Dealing with licenses

Procedures (number)	20
Time (days)	327
Cost (% of income per capita)	57.7

Hiring and firing workers

Difficulty of hiring index (0–100)	33
Rigidity of hours index (0–100)	80
Difficulty of firing index (0–100)	60
Rigidity of employment index (0–100)	58
Hiring cost (% of salary)	24
Firing cost (weeks of salary)	98

Registering property

Procedures (number)	5
Time (days)	83
Cost (% of property value)	7.4

Getting credit

Strength of legal rights index (0–10)	5
Depth of credit information index (0–6)	4
Public registry coverage (% of adults)	64.3
Private bureau coverage (% of adults)	9.8

Protecting investors

Extent of disclosure index (0–10)	7
Extent of director liability index (0–10)	5
Ease of shareholder suits index (0–10)	6
Strength of investor protection index (0–10)	6.0

Paying taxes

Payments (number)	7
Time (hours per year)	328
Total tax payable (% of gross profit)	45.4

Trading across borders

Documents for export (number)	6
Signatures for export (number)	4
Time for export (days)	18
Documents for import (number)	7
Signatures for import (number)	5
Time for import (days)	18

Enforcing contracts

Procedures (number)	24
Time (days)	320
Cost (% of debt)	17.5

Closing a business

Time (years)	2
Cost (% of estate)	9
Recovery rate (cents on the dollar)	74.7

PUERTO RICO

Ease of doing business (rank)	22

Latin America & Caribbean
High income

GNI per capita (US$)	10,950
Population (m)	3.9

Starting a business

Procedures (number)	7
Time (days)	7
Cost (% of income per capita)	1.0
Minimum capital (% of income per capita)	0.0

Dealing with licenses

Procedures (number)	20
Time (days)	137
Cost (% of income per capita)	103.3

Hiring and firing workers

Difficulty of hiring index (0–100)	56
Rigidity of hours index (0–100)	20
Difficulty of firing index (0–100)	30
Rigidity of employment index (0–100)	35
Hiring cost (% of salary)	16
Firing cost (weeks of salary)	0

Registering property

Procedures (number)	8
Time (days)	15
Cost (% of property value)	1.6

Getting credit

Strength of legal rights index (0–10)	6
Depth of credit information index (0–6)	5
Public registry coverage (% of adults)	0.0
Private bureau coverage (% of adults)	63.6

Protecting investors

Extent of disclosure index (0–10)	. .
Extent of director liability index (0–10)	. .
Ease of shareholder suits index (0–10)	. .
Strength of investor protection index (0–10)	. .

Paying taxes

Payments (number)	41
Time (hours per year)	140
Total tax payable (% of gross profit)	17.8

Trading across borders

Documents for export (number)	9
Signatures for export (number)	3
Time for export (days)	15
Documents for import (number)	10
Signatures for import (number)	3
Time for import (days)	19

Enforcing contracts

Procedures (number)	43
Time (days)	270
Cost (% of debt)	21.0

Closing a business

Time (years)	4
Cost (% of estate)	8
Recovery rate (cents on the dollar)	61.4

ROMANIA

Ease of doing business (rank)	78

Eastern Europe & Central Asia
Lower middle income

GNI per capita (US$)	2,920
Population (m)	21.7

Starting a business

Procedures (number)	5
Time (days)	11
Cost (% of income per capita)	5.3
Minimum capital (% of income per capita)	0.0

Dealing with licenses

Procedures (number)	15
Time (days)	291
Cost (% of income per capita)	187.7

Hiring and firing workers

Difficulty of hiring index (0–100)	67
Rigidity of hours index (0–100)	60
Difficulty of firing index (0–100)	50
Rigidity of employment index (0–100)	59
Hiring cost (% of salary)	34
Firing cost (weeks of salary)	98

Registering property

Procedures (number)	8
Time (days)	170
Cost (% of property value)	2.0

Getting credit

Strength of legal rights index (0–10)	4
Depth of credit information index (0–6)	4
Public registry coverage (% of adults)	1.4
Private bureau coverage (% of adults)	1.0

Protecting investors

Extent of disclosure index (0–10)	8
Extent of director liability index (0–10)	5
Ease of shareholder suits index (0–10)	4
Strength of investor protection index (0–10)	5.7

Paying taxes

Payments (number)	62
Time (hours per year)	188
Total tax payable (% of gross profit)	51.1

Trading across borders

Documents for export (number)	7
Signatures for export (number)	6
Time for export (days)	27
Documents for import (number)	15
Signatures for import (number)	10
Time for import (days)	28

Enforcing contracts

Procedures (number)	43
Time (days)	335
Cost (% of debt)	12.4

Closing a business

Time (years)	5
Cost (% of estate)	9
Recovery rate (cents on the dollar)	17.5

RUSSIA

Ease of doing business (rank)	79	Eastern Europe & Central Asia Upper middle income		GNI per capita (US$) Population (m)		3,410 143.0

Starting a business

Procedures (number)	8
Time (days)	33
Cost (% of income per capita)	5.0
Minimum capital (% of income per capita)	4.4

Dealing with licenses

Procedures (number)	22
Time (days)	528
Cost (% of income per capita)	353.7

Hiring and firing workers

Difficulty of hiring index (0–100)	0
Rigidity of hours index (0–100)	60
Difficulty of firing index (0–100)	30
Rigidity of employment index (0–100)	30
Hiring cost (% of salary)	36
Firing cost (weeks of salary)	17

Registering property

Procedures (number)	6
Time (days)	52
Cost (% of property value)	0.4

Getting credit

Strength of legal rights index (0–10)	3
Depth of credit information index (0–6)	0
Public registry coverage (% of adults)	0.0
Private bureau coverage (% of adults)	0.0

Protecting investors

Extent of disclosure index (0–10)	7
Extent of director liability index (0–10)	3
Ease of shareholder suits index (0–10)	5
Strength of investor protection index (0–10)	5.0

Paying taxes

Payments (number)	27
Time (hours per year)	256
Total tax payable (% of gross profit)	40.8

Trading across borders

Documents for export (number)	8
Signatures for export (number)	8
Time for export (days)	29
Documents for import (number)	8
Signatures for import (number)	10
Time for import (days)	35

Enforcing contracts

Procedures (number)	29
Time (days)	330
Cost (% of debt)	20.3

Closing a business

Time (years)	4
Cost (% of estate)	9
Recovery rate (cents on the dollar)	27.6

RWANDA

Ease of doing business (rank)	139	Sub-Saharan Africa Low income		GNI per capita (US$) Population (m)		220 8.4

Starting a business

Procedures (number)	9
Time (days)	21
Cost (% of income per capita)	280.2
Minimum capital (% of income per capita)	0.0

Dealing with licenses

Procedures (number)	17
Time (days)	252
Cost (% of income per capita)	510.9

Hiring and firing workers

Difficulty of hiring index (0–100)	56
Rigidity of hours index (0–100)	60
Difficulty of firing index (0–100)	60
Rigidity of employment index (0–100)	59
Hiring cost (% of salary)	8
Firing cost (weeks of salary)	54

Registering property

Procedures (number)	5
Time (days)	371
Cost (% of property value)	9.6

Getting credit

Strength of legal rights index (0–10)	1
Depth of credit information index (0–6)	2
Public registry coverage (% of adults)	0.1
Private bureau coverage (% of adults)	0.0

Protecting investors

Extent of disclosure index (0–10)	. .
Extent of director liability index (0–10)	. .
Ease of shareholder suits index (0–10)	. .
Strength of investor protection index (0–10)	. .

Paying taxes

Payments (number)	42
Time (hours per year)	168
Total tax payable (% of gross profit)	53.9

Trading across borders

Documents for export (number)	14
Signatures for export (number)	27
Time for export (days)	63
Documents for import (number)	19
Signatures for import (number)	46
Time for import (days)	92

Enforcing contracts

Procedures (number)	27
Time (days)	310
Cost (% of debt)	43.2

Closing a business

Time (years)	no practice
Cost (% of estate)	no practice
Recovery rate (cents on the dollar)	0.0

SAMOA

Ease of doing business (rank)	39	East Asia & Pacific Lower middle income		GNI per capita (US$) Population (m)		1,860 0.2

Starting a business

Procedures (number)	7
Time (days)	68
Cost (% of income per capita)	18.8
Minimum capital (% of income per capita)	0.0

Dealing with licenses

Procedures (number)	19
Time (days)	88
Cost (% of income per capita)	107.3

Hiring and firing workers

Difficulty of hiring index (0–100)	11
Rigidity of hours index (0–100)	20
Difficulty of firing index (0–100)	0
Rigidity of employment index (0–100)	10
Hiring cost (% of salary)	6
Firing cost (weeks of salary)	42

Registering property

Procedures (number)	5
Time (days)	147
Cost (% of property value)	1.9

Getting credit

Strength of legal rights index (0–10)	7
Depth of credit information index (0–6)	0
Public registry coverage (% of adults)	0.0
Private bureau coverage (% of adults)	0.0

Protecting investors

Extent of disclosure index (0–10)	5
Extent of director liability index (0–10)	6
Ease of shareholder suits index (0–10)	8
Strength of investor protection index (0–10)	6.3

Paying taxes

Payments (number)	35
Time (hours per year)	224
Total tax payable (% of gross profit)	35.8

Trading across borders

Documents for export (number)	6
Signatures for export (number)	4
Time for export (days)	12
Documents for import (number)	8
Signatures for import (number)	6
Time for import (days)	13

Enforcing contracts

Procedures (number)	21
Time (days)	505
Cost (% of debt)	25.0

Closing a business

Time (years)	3
Cost (% of estate)	38
Recovery rate (cents on the dollar)	15.2

SAO TOME AND PRINCIPE

Ease of doing business (rank)	123	Sub-Saharan Africa	
		Low income	

GNI per capita (US$)	370
Population (m)	0.2

Starting a business
Procedures (number)	9
Time (days)	192
Cost (% of income per capita)	97.0
Minimum capital (% of income per capita)	0.0

Dealing with licenses
Procedures (number)	13
Time (days)	259
Cost (% of income per capita)	1737.1

Hiring and firing workers
Difficulty of hiring index (0–100)	61
Rigidity of hours index (0–100)	60
Difficulty of firing index (0–100)	60
Rigidity of employment index (0–100)	60
Hiring cost (% of salary)	6
Firing cost (weeks of salary)	108

Registering property
Procedures (number)	6
Time (days)	51
Cost (% of property value)	12.6

Getting credit
Strength of legal rights index (0–10)	. .
Depth of credit information index (0–6)	0
Public registry coverage (% of adults)	0.0
Private bureau coverage (% of adults)	0.0

Protecting investors
Extent of disclosure index (0–10)	6
Extent of director liability index (0–10)	1
Ease of shareholder suits index (0–10)	6
Strength of investor protection index (0–10)	4.3

Paying taxes
Payments (number)	29
Time (hours per year)	1008
Total tax payable (% of gross profit)	27.4

Trading across borders
Documents for export (number)	7
Signatures for export (number)	8
Time for export (days)	31
Documents for import (number)	9
Signatures for import (number)	12
Time for import (days)	40

Enforcing contracts
Procedures (number)	67
Time (days)	240
Cost (% of debt)	69.5

Closing a business
Time (years)	NO PRACTICE
Cost (% of estate)	NO PRACTI CE
Recovery rate (cents on the dollar)	0.0

SAUDI ARABIA

Ease of doing business (rank)	38	Middle East & North Africa	
		High income	

GNI per capita (US$)	10,430
Population (m)	22.5

Starting a business
Procedures (number)	13
Time (days)	64
Cost (% of income per capita)	68.5
Minimum capital (% of income per capita)	1236.9

Dealing with licenses
Procedures (number)	18
Time (days)	131
Cost (% of income per capita)	82.1

Hiring and firing workers
Difficulty of hiring index (0–100)	0
Rigidity of hours index (0–100)	40
Difficulty of firing index (0–100)	0
Rigidity of employment index (0–100)	13
Hiring cost (% of salary)	11
Firing cost (weeks of salary)	79

Registering property
Procedures (number)	4
Time (days)	4
Cost (% of property value)	0.0

Getting credit
Strength of legal rights index (0–10)	4
Depth of credit information index (0–6)	5
Public registry coverage (% of adults)	0.2
Private bureau coverage (% of adults)	10.2

Protecting investors
Extent of disclosure index (0–10)	8
Extent of director liability index (0–10)	4
Ease of shareholder suits index (0–10)	3
Strength of investor protection index (0–10)	5.0

Paying taxes
Payments (number)	13
Time (hours per year)	70
Total tax payable (% of gross profit)	1.4

Trading across borders
Documents for export (number)	5
Signatures for export (number)	12
Time for export (days)	36
Documents for import (number)	9
Signatures for import (number)	18
Time for import (days)	44

Enforcing contracts
Procedures (number)	44
Time (days)	360
Cost (% of debt)	20.0

Closing a business
Time (years)	3
Cost (% of estate)	22
Recovery rate (cents on the dollar)	28.4

SENEGAL

Ease of doing business (rank)	132	Sub-Saharan Africa	
		Low income	

GNI per capita (US$)	670
Population (m)	10.2

Starting a business
Procedures (number)	9
Time (days)	57
Cost (% of income per capita)	108.7
Minimum capital (% of income per capita)	260.4

Dealing with licenses
Procedures (number)	18
Time (days)	185
Cost (% of income per capita)	175.9

Hiring and firing workers
Difficulty of hiring index (0–100)	61
Rigidity of hours index (0–100)	60
Difficulty of firing index (0–100)	70
Rigidity of employment index (0–100)	64
Hiring cost (% of salary)	23
Firing cost (weeks of salary)	38

Registering property
Procedures (number)	6
Time (days)	114
Cost (% of property value)	18.0

Getting credit
Strength of legal rights index (0–10)	3
Depth of credit information index (0–6)	1
Public registry coverage (% of adults)	4.3
Private bureau coverage (% of adults)	0.0

Protecting investors
Extent of disclosure index (0–10)	7
Extent of director liability index (0–10)	1
Ease of shareholder suits index (0–10)	3
Strength of investor protection index (0–10)	3.7

Paying taxes
Payments (number)	59
Time (hours per year)	696
Total tax payable (% of gross profit)	45.0

Trading across borders
Documents for export (number)	6
Signatures for export (number)	8
Time for export (days)	6
Documents for import (number)	10
Signatures for import (number)	12
Time for import (days)	26

Enforcing contracts
Procedures (number)	33
Time (days)	485
Cost (% of debt)	23.8

Closing a business
Time (years)	3
Cost (% of estate)	7
Recovery rate (cents on the dollar)	19.0

SERBIA AND MONTENEGRO

| | | Eastern Europe & Central Asia | | GNI per capita (US$) | 2,620 |
| Ease of doing business (rank) | 92 | Lower middle income | | Population (m) | 8.1 |

Starting a business
Procedures (number)	10
Time (days)	15
Cost (% of income per capita)	6.0
Minimum capital (% of income per capita)	9.5

Dealing with licenses
Procedures (number)	21
Time (days)	212
Cost (% of income per capita)	2195.0

Hiring and firing workers
Difficulty of hiring index (0–100)	44
Rigidity of hours index (0–100)	0
Difficulty of firing index (0–100)	40
Rigidity of employment index (0–100)	28
Hiring cost (% of salary)	25
Firing cost (weeks of salary)	21

Registering property
Procedures (number)	6
Time (days)	111
Cost (% of property value)	5.3

Getting credit
Strength of legal rights index (0–10)	5
Depth of credit information index (0–6)	1
Public registry coverage (% of adults)	0.1
Private bureau coverage (% of adults)	0.0

Protecting investors
Extent of disclosure index (0–10)	7
Extent of director liability index (0–10)	6
Ease of shareholder suits index (0–10)	4
Strength of investor protection index (0–10)	5.7

Paying taxes
Payments (number)	41
Time (hours per year)	168
Total tax payable (% of gross profit)	46.3

Trading across borders
Documents for export (number)	9
Signatures for export (number)	15
Time for export (days)	32
Documents for import (number)	15
Signatures for import (number)	17
Time for import (days)	44

Enforcing contracts
Procedures (number)	33
Time (days)	635
Cost (% of debt)	18.1

Closing a business
Time (years)	3
Cost (% of estate)	23
Recovery rate (cents on the dollar)	20.3

SIERRA LEONE

| | | Sub-Saharan Africa | | GNI per capita (US$) | 200 |
| Ease of doing business (rank) | 136 | Low income | | Population (m) | 5.3 |

Starting a business
Procedures (number)	9
Time (days)	26
Cost (% of income per capita)	835.4
Minimum capital (% of income per capita)	0.0

Dealing with licenses
Procedures (number)	48
Time (days)	236
Cost (% of income per capita)	268.9

Hiring and firing workers
Difficulty of hiring index (0–100)	89
Rigidity of hours index (0–100)	80
Difficulty of firing index (0–100)	70
Rigidity of employment index (0–100)	80
Hiring cost (% of salary)	10
Firing cost (weeks of salary)	188

Registering property
Procedures (number)	8
Time (days)	58
Cost (% of property value)	15.4

Getting credit
Strength of legal rights index (0–10)	5
Depth of credit information index (0–6)	0
Public registry coverage (% of adults)	0.0
Private bureau coverage (% of adults)	0.0

Protecting investors
Extent of disclosure index (0–10)	3
Extent of director liability index (0–10)	6
Ease of shareholder suits index (0–10)	5
Strength of investor protection index (0–10)	4.7

Paying taxes
Payments (number)	20
Time (hours per year)	399
Total tax payable (% of gross profit)	163.9

Trading across borders
Documents for export (number)	7
Signatures for export (number)	8
Time for export (days)	36
Documents for import (number)	7
Signatures for import (number)	22
Time for import (days)	39

Enforcing contracts
Procedures (number)	58
Time (days)	305
Cost (% of debt)	31.0

Closing a business
Time (years)	3
Cost (% of estate)	42
Recovery rate (cents on the dollar)	9.0

SINGAPORE

| | | East Asia & Pacific | | GNI per capita (US$) | 24,220 |
| Ease of doing business (rank) | 2 | High income | | Population (m) | 4.3 |

Starting a business
Procedures (number)	6
Time (days)	6
Cost (% of income per capita)	1.1
Minimum capital (% of income per capita)	0.0

Dealing with licenses
Procedures (number)	11
Time (days)	129
Cost (% of income per capita)	24.0

Hiring and firing workers
Difficulty of hiring index (0–100)	0
Rigidity of hours index (0–100)	0
Difficulty of firing index (0–100)	0
Rigidity of employment index (0–100)	0
Hiring cost (% of salary)	13
Firing cost (weeks of salary)	4

Registering property
Procedures (number)	3
Time (days)	9
Cost (% of property value)	2.8

Getting credit
Strength of legal rights index (0–10)	10
Depth of credit information index (0–6)	4
Public registry coverage (% of adults)	0.0
Private bureau coverage (% of adults)	38.6

Protecting investors
Extent of disclosure index (0–10)	10
Extent of director liability index (0–10)	9
Ease of shareholder suits index (0–10)	9
Strength of investor protection index (0–10)	9.3

Paying taxes
Payments (number)	16
Time (hours per year)	30
Total tax payable (% of gross profit)	19.5

Trading across borders
Documents for export (number)	5
Signatures for export (number)	2
Time for export (days)	6
Documents for import (number)	6
Signatures for import (number)	2
Time for import (days)	8

Enforcing contracts
Procedures (number)	23
Time (days)	69
Cost (% of debt)	9.0

Closing a business
Time (years)	1
Cost (% of estate)	1
Recovery rate (cents on the dollar)	91.3

SLOVAKIA
Ease of doing business (rank)	37	Eastern Europe & Central Asia Upper middle income		GNI per capita (US$) Population (m)		6,480 5.4

Starting a business
Procedures (number)	9
Time (days)	25
Cost (% of income per capita)	5.1
Minimum capital (% of income per capita)	41.0

Dealing with licenses
Procedures (number)	13
Time (days)	272
Cost (% of income per capita)	18.0

Hiring and firing workers
Difficulty of hiring index (0–100)	17
Rigidity of hours index (0–100)	60
Difficulty of firing index (0–100)	40
Rigidity of employment index (0–100)	39
Hiring cost (% of salary)	35
Firing cost (weeks of salary)	13

Registering property
Procedures (number)	3
Time (days)	17
Cost (% of property value)	0.1

Getting credit
Strength of legal rights index (0–10)	9
Depth of credit information index (0–6)	2
Public registry coverage (% of adults)	0.5
Private bureau coverage (% of adults)	18.1

Protecting investors
Extent of disclosure index (0–10)	2
Extent of director liability index (0–10)	4
Ease of shareholder suits index (0–10)	6
Strength of investor protection index (0–10)	4.0

Paying taxes
Payments (number)	31
Time (hours per year)	344
Total tax payable (% of gross profit)	39.5

Trading across borders
Documents for export (number)	9
Signatures for export (number)	8
Time for export (days)	20
Documents for import (number)	8
Signatures for import (number)	10
Time for import (days)	21

Enforcing contracts
Procedures (number)	27
Time (days)	565
Cost (% of debt)	15.0

Closing a business
Time (years)	5
Cost (% of estate)	18.
Recovery rate (cents on the dollar)	38.6

SLOVENIA
Ease of doing business (rank)	63	Eastern Europe & Central Asia High income		GNI per capita (US$) Population (m)		14,810 2.0

Starting a business
Procedures (number)	9
Time (days)	60
Cost (% of income per capita)	10.1
Minimum capital (% of income per capita)	17.0

Dealing with licenses
Procedures (number)	14
Time (days)	207
Cost (% of income per capita)	128.7

Hiring and firing workers
Difficulty of hiring index (0–100)	61
Rigidity of hours index (0–100)	80
Difficulty of firing index (0–100)	50
Rigidity of employment index (0–100)	64
Hiring cost (% of salary)	17
Firing cost (weeks of salary)	43

Registering property
Procedures (number)	6
Time (days)	391
Cost (% of property value)	2.0

Getting credit
Strength of legal rights index (0–10)	6
Depth of credit information index (0–6)	3
Public registry coverage (% of adults)	2.7
Private bureau coverage (% of adults)	0.0

Protecting investors
Extent of disclosure index (0–10)	3
Extent of director liability index (0–10)	8
Ease of shareholder suits index (0–10)	6
Strength of investor protection index (0–10)	5.7

Paying taxes
Payments (number)	29
Time (hours per year)	272
Total tax payable (% of gross profit)	47.3

Trading across borders
Documents for export (number)	9
Signatures for export (number)	7
Time for export (days)	20
Documents for import (number)	11
Signatures for import (number)	9
Time for import (days)	24

Enforcing contracts
Procedures (number)	25
Time (days)	913
Cost (% of debt)	15.2

Closing a business
Time (years)	4
Cost (% of estate)	15
Recovery rate (cents on the dollar)	27.9

SOLOMON ISLANDS
Ease of doing business (rank)	53	East Asia & Pacific Low income		GNI per capita (US$) Population (m)		550 0.5

Starting a business
Procedures (number)	5
Time (days)	35
Cost (% of income per capita)	48.4
Minimum capital (% of income per capita)	0.0

Dealing with licenses
Procedures (number)	..
Time (days)	..
Cost (% of income per capita)	..

Hiring and firing workers
Difficulty of hiring index (0–100)	11
Rigidity of hours index (0–100)	20
Difficulty of firing index (0–100)	20
Rigidity of employment index (0–100)	17
Hiring cost (% of salary)	8
Firing cost (weeks of salary)	52

Registering property
Procedures (number)	6
Time (days)	86
Cost (% of property value)	10.2

Getting credit
Strength of legal rights index (0–10)	6
Depth of credit information index (0–6)	0
Public registry coverage (% of adults)	0.0
Private bureau coverage (% of adults)	0.0

Protecting investors
Extent of disclosure index (0–10)	5
Extent of director liability index (0–10)	6
Ease of shareholder suits index (0–10)	8
Strength of investor protection index (0–10)	6.3

Paying taxes
Payments (number)	33
Time (hours per year)	80
Total tax payable (% of gross profit)	13.5

Trading across borders
Documents for export (number)	..
Signatures for export (number)	..
Time for export (days)	..
Documents for import (number)	7
Signatures for import (number)	5
Time for import (days)	24

Enforcing contracts
Procedures (number)	30
Time (days)	455
Cost (% of debt)	140.8

Closing a business
Time (years)	4
Cost (% of estate)	38
Recovery rate (cents on the dollar)	7.1

SOUTH AFRICA

Ease of doing business (rank)	28	Sub-Saharan Africa Upper middle income		GNI per capita (US$) Population (m)	3,630 45.8	

Starting a business
Procedures (number)	9
Time (days)	38
Cost (% of income per capita)	8.6
Minimum capital (% of income per capita)	0.0

Dealing with licenses
Procedures (number)	18
Time (days)	176
Cost (% of income per capita)	38.0

Hiring and firing workers
Difficulty of hiring index (0–100)	56
Rigidity of hours index (0–100)	40
Difficulty of firing index (0–100)	60
Rigidity of employment index (0–100)	52
Hiring cost (% of salary)	3
Firing cost (weeks of salary)	38

Registering property
Procedures (number)	6
Time (days)	23
Cost (% of property value)	11.0

Getting credit
Strength of legal rights index (0–10)	5
Depth of credit information index (0–6)	5
Public registry coverage (% of adults)	0.0
Private bureau coverage (% of adults)	63.4

Protecting investors
Extent of disclosure index (0–10)	8
Extent of director liability index (0–10)	8
Ease of shareholder suits index (0–10)	8
Strength of investor protection index (0–10)	8.0

Paying taxes
Payments (number)	32
Time (hours per year)	350
Total tax payable (% of gross profit)	43.8

Trading across borders
Documents for export (number)	5
Signatures for export (number)	7
Time for export (days)	31
Documents for import (number)	9
Signatures for import (number)	9
Time for import (days)	34

Enforcing contracts
Procedures (number)	26
Time (days)	277
Cost (% of debt)	11.5

Closing a business
Time (years)	2
Cost (% of estate)	18
Recovery rate (cents on the dollar)	33.9

SPAIN

Ease of doing business (rank)	30	OECD: High Income High income		GNI per capita (US$) Population (m)	21,210 41.1	

Starting a business
Procedures (number)	10
Time (days)	47
Cost (% of income per capita)	16.5
Minimum capital (% of income per capita)	15.7

Dealing with licenses
Procedures (number)	12
Time (days)	277
Cost (% of income per capita)	77.1

Hiring and firing workers
Difficulty of hiring index (0–100)	67
Rigidity of hours index (0–100)	80
Difficulty of firing index (0–100)	50
Rigidity of employment index (0–100)	66
Hiring cost (% of salary)	32
Firing cost (weeks of salary)	56

Registering property
Procedures (number)	3
Time (days)	25
Cost (% of property value)	7.2

Getting credit
Strength of legal rights index (0–10)	5
Depth of credit information index (0–6)	6
Public registry coverage (% of adults)	42.1
Private bureau coverage (% of adults)	6.5

Protecting investors
Extent of disclosure index (0–10)	4
Extent of director liability index (0–10)	6
Ease of shareholder suits index (0–10)	4
Strength of investor protection index (0–10)	4.7

Paying taxes
Payments (number)	7
Time (hours per year)	56
Total tax payable (% of gross profit)	48.4

Trading across borders
Documents for export (number)	4
Signatures for export (number)	3
Time for export (days)	9
Documents for import (number)	5
Signatures for import (number)	3
Time for import (days)	10

Enforcing contracts
Procedures (number)	23
Time (days)	169
Cost (% of debt)	14.1

Closing a business
Time (years)	1
Cost (% of estate)	15
Recovery rate (cents on the dollar)	77.8

SRI LANKA

Ease of doing business (rank)	75	South Asia Lower middle income		GNI per capita (US$) Population (m)	1,010 19.2	

Starting a business
Procedures (number)	8
Time (days)	50
Cost (% of income per capita)	10.4
Minimum capital (% of income per capita)	0.0

Dealing with licenses
Procedures (number)	18
Time (days)	167
Cost (% of income per capita)	144.0

Hiring and firing workers
Difficulty of hiring index (0–100)	0
Rigidity of hours index (0–100)	40
Difficulty of firing index (0–100)	80
Rigidity of employment index (0–100)	40
Hiring cost (% of salary)	16
Firing cost (weeks of salary)	176

Registering property
Procedures (number)	8
Time (days)	63
Cost (% of property value)	5.1

Getting credit
Strength of legal rights index (0–10)	3
Depth of credit information index (0–6)	3
Public registry coverage (% of adults)	0.0
Private bureau coverage (% of adults)	2.2

Protecting investors
Extent of disclosure index (0–10)	4
Extent of director liability index (0–10)	5
Ease of shareholder suits index (0–10)	7
Strength of investor protection index (0–10)	5.3

Paying taxes
Payments (number)	42
Time (hours per year)	..
Total tax payable (% of gross profit)	49.4

Trading across borders
Documents for export (number)	8
Signatures for export (number)	10
Time for export (days)	25
Documents for import (number)	13
Signatures for import (number)	15
Time for import (days)	27

Enforcing contracts
Procedures (number)	17
Time (days)	440
Cost (% of debt)	21.3

Closing a business
Time (years)	2
Cost (% of estate)	18
Recovery rate (cents on the dollar)	33.8

SUDAN

| | | Sub-Saharan Africa | | GNI per capita (US$) | 530 |
| Ease of doing business (rank) | 151 | Low income | | Population (m) | 33.5 |

Starting a business		**Registering property**		**Trading across borders**	
Procedures (number)	10	Procedures (number)	. .	Documents for export (number)	9
Time (days)	38	Time (days)	. .	Signatures for export (number)	35
Cost (% of income per capita)	68.1	Cost (% of property value)	. .	Time for export (days)	82
Minimum capital (% of income per capita)	0.0			Documents for import (number)	15
		Getting credit		Signatures for import (number)	50
Dealing with licenses		Strength of legal rights index (0–10)	5	Time for import (days)	111
Procedures (number)	. .	Depth of credit information index (0–6)	0		
Time (days)	. .	Public registry coverage (% of adults)	0.0	**Enforcing contracts**	
Cost (% of income per capita)	. .	Private bureau coverage (% of adults)	0.0	Procedures (number)	67
				Time (days)	915
Hiring and firing workers		**Protecting investors**		Cost (% of debt)	30.0
Difficulty of hiring index (0–100)	0	Extent of disclosure index (0–10)	. .		
Rigidity of hours index (0–100)	60	Extent of director liability index (0–10)	. .	**Closing a business**	
Difficulty of firing index (0–100)	70	Ease of shareholder suits index (0–10)	. .	Time (years)	no practice
Rigidity of employment index (0–100)	43	Strength of investor protection index (0–10)	. .	Cost (% of estate)	no practice
Hiring cost (% of salary)	19			Recovery rate (cents on the dollar)	0.0
Firing cost (weeks of salary)	37	**Paying taxes**			
		Payments (number)	. .		
		Time (hours per year)	. .		
		Total tax payable (% of gross profit)	. .		

SWEDEN

| | | OECD: High Income | | GNI per capita (US$) | 35,770 |
| Ease of doing business (rank) | 14 | High income | | Population (m) | 9.0 |

Starting a business		**Registering property**		**Trading across borders**	
Procedures (number)	3	Procedures (number)	1	Documents for export (number)	4
Time (days)	16	Time (days)	2	Signatures for export (number)	1
Cost (% of income per capita)	0.7	Cost (% of property value)	3.0	Time for export (days)	6
Minimum capital (% of income per capita)	35.0			Documents for import (number)	3
		Getting credit		Signatures for import (number)	1
Dealing with licenses		Strength of legal rights index (0–10)	6	Time for import (days)	6
Procedures (number)	8	Depth of credit information index (0–6)	5		
Time (days)	116	Public registry coverage (% of adults)	0.0	**Enforcing contracts**	
Cost (% of income per capita)	119.6	Private bureau coverage (% of adults)	100.0	Procedures (number)	23
				Time (days)	208
Hiring and firing workers		**Protecting investors**		Cost (% of debt)	5.9
Difficulty of hiring index (0–100)	28	Extent of disclosure index (0–10)	2		
Rigidity of hours index (0–100)	60	Extent of director liability index (0–10)	5	**Closing a business**	
Difficulty of firing index (0–100)	40	Ease of shareholder suits index (0–10)	7	Time (years)	2
Rigidity of employment index (0–100)	43	Strength of investor protection index (0–10)	4.7	Cost (% of estate)	9
Hiring cost (% of salary)	33			Recovery rate (cents on the dollar)	74.9
Firing cost (weeks of salary)	24	**Paying taxes**			
		Payments (number)	5		
		Time (hours per year)	122		
		Total tax payable (% of gross profit)	52.6		

SWITZERLAND

| | | OECD: High Income | | GNI per capita (US$) | 48,230 |
| Ease of doing business (rank) | 17 | High income | | Population (m) | 7.4 |

Starting a business		**Registering property**		**Trading across borders**	
Procedures (number)	6	Procedures (number)	4	Documents for export (number)	8
Time (days)	20	Time (days)	16	Signatures for export (number)	5
Cost (% of income per capita)	8.7	Cost (% of property value)	0.4	Time for export (days)	21
Minimum capital (% of income per capita)	31.3			Documents for import (number)	13
		Getting credit		Signatures for import (number)	5
Dealing with licenses		Strength of legal rights index (0–10)	6	Time for import (days)	22
Procedures (number)	15	Depth of credit information index (0–6)	5		
Time (days)	152	Public registry coverage (% of adults)	0.0	**Enforcing contracts**	
Cost (% of income per capita)	59.2	Private bureau coverage (% of adults)	23.3	Procedures (number)	22
				Time (days)	170
Hiring and firing workers		**Protecting investors**		Cost (% of debt)	5.2
Difficulty of hiring index (0–100)	0	Extent of disclosure index (0–10)	1		
Rigidity of hours index (0–100)	40	Extent of director liability index (0–10)	5	**Closing a business**	
Difficulty of firing index (0–100)	10	Ease of shareholder suits index (0–10)	6	Time (years)	3
Rigidity of employment index (0–100)	17	Strength of investor protection index (0–10)	4.0	Cost (% of estate)	4
Hiring cost (% of salary)	14			Recovery rate (cents on the dollar)	46.9
Firing cost (weeks of salary)	12	**Paying taxes**			
		Payments (number)	25		
		Time (hours per year)	63		
		Total tax payable (% of gross profit)	22.0		

SYRIA

Ease of doing business (rank)	121

Middle East & North Africa
Lower middle income

GNI per capita (US$)	1,190
Population (m)	17.4

Starting a business

Procedures (number)	12
Time (days)	47
Cost (% of income per capita)	34.5
Minimum capital (% of income per capita)	5111.9

Dealing with licenses

Procedures (number)	20
Time (days)	134
Cost (% of income per capita)	359.8

Hiring and firing workers

Difficulty of hiring index (0–100)	11
Rigidity of hours index (0–100)	60
Difficulty of firing index (0–100)	50
Rigidity of employment index (0–100)	40
Hiring cost (% of salary)	17
Firing cost (weeks of salary)	79

Registering property

Procedures (number)	4
Time (days)	34
Cost (% of property value)	30.4

Getting credit

Strength of legal rights index (0–10)	5
Depth of credit information index (0–6)	0
Public registry coverage (% of adults)	0.0
Private bureau coverage (% of adults)	0.0

Protecting investors

Extent of disclosure index (0–10)	5
Extent of director liability index (0–10)	7
Ease of shareholder suits index (0–10)	1
Strength of investor protection index (0–10)	4.3

Paying taxes

Payments (number)	22
Time (hours per year)	336
Total tax payable (% of gross profit)	20.8

Trading across borders

Documents for export (number)	12
Signatures for export (number)	19
Time for export (days)	49
Documents for import (number)	18
Signatures for import (number)	47
Time for import (days)	63

Enforcing contracts

Procedures (number)	47
Time (days)	672
Cost (% of debt)	34.3

Closing a business

Time (years)	4
Cost (% of estate)	9
Recovery rate (cents on the dollar)	28.5

TAIWAN, CHINA

Ease of doing business (rank)	35

East Asia & Pacific
High income

GNI per capita (US$)	14,630
Population (m)	22.6

Starting a business

Procedures (number)	8
Time (days)	48
Cost (% of income per capita)	6.0
Minimum capital (% of income per capita)	216.3

Dealing with licenses

Procedures (number)	32
Time (days)	235
Cost (% of income per capita)	250.9

Hiring and firing workers

Difficulty of hiring index (0–100)	78
Rigidity of hours index (0–100)	60
Difficulty of firing index (0–100)	30
Rigidity of employment index (0–100)	56
Hiring cost (% of salary)	10
Firing cost (weeks of salary)	90

Registering property

Procedures (number)	3
Time (days)	5
Cost (% of property value)	6.2

Getting credit

Strength of legal rights index (0–10)	4
Depth of credit information index (0–6)	5
Public registry coverage (% of adults)	0.0
Private bureau coverage (% of adults)	57.1

Protecting investors

Extent of disclosure index (0–10)	8
Extent of director liability index (0–10)	4
Ease of shareholder suits index (0–10)	4
Strength of investor protection index (0–10)	5.3

Paying taxes

Payments (number)	15
Time (hours per year)	296
Total tax payable (% of gross profit)	23.6

Trading across borders

Documents for export (number)	8
Signatures for export (number)	9
Time for export (days)	14
Documents for import (number)	8
Signatures for import (number)	11
Time for import (days)	14

Enforcing contracts

Procedures (number)	28
Time (days)	210
Cost (% of debt)	7.7

Closing a business

Time (years)	1
Cost (% of estate)	4
Recovery rate (cents on the dollar)	89.4

TANZANIA

Ease of doing business (rank)	140

Sub-Saharan Africa
Low income

GNI per capita (US$)	330
Population (m)	35.9

Starting a business

Procedures (number)	13
Time (days)	35
Cost (% of income per capita)	161.3
Minimum capital (% of income per capita)	6.0

Dealing with licenses

Procedures (number)	26
Time (days)	313
Cost (% of income per capita)	4110.2

Hiring and firing workers

Difficulty of hiring index (0–100)	67
Rigidity of hours index (0–100)	80
Difficulty of firing index (0–100)	60
Rigidity of employment index (0–100)	69
Hiring cost (% of salary)	16
Firing cost (weeks of salary)	38

Registering property

Procedures (number)	12
Time (days)	61
Cost (% of property value)	12.2

Getting credit

Strength of legal rights index (0–10)	5
Depth of credit information index (0–6)	0
Public registry coverage (% of adults)	0.0
Private bureau coverage (% of adults)	0.0

Protecting investors

Extent of disclosure index (0–10)	3
Extent of director liability index (0–10)	3
Ease of shareholder suits index (0–10)	0
Strength of investor protection index (0–10)	2.0

Paying taxes

Payments (number)	48
Time (hours per year)	248
Total tax payable (% of gross profit)	51.3

Trading across borders

Documents for export (number)	7
Signatures for export (number)	10
Time for export (days)	30
Documents for import (number)	13
Signatures for import (number)	16
Time for import (days)	51

Enforcing contracts

Procedures (number)	21
Time (days)	242
Cost (% of debt)	35.3

Closing a business

Time (years)	3
Cost (% of estate)	22
Recovery rate (cents on the dollar)	22.3

THAILAND

| East Asia & Pacific | GNI per capita (US$) | 2,540 |
| Lower middle income | Population (m) | 62.0 |

| Ease of doing business (rank) | 20 |

Starting a business

Procedures (number)	8
Time (days)	33
Cost (% of income per capita)	6.1
Minimum capital (% of income per capita)	0.0

Dealing with licenses

Procedures (number)	9
Time (days)	147
Cost (% of income per capita)	17.3

Hiring and firing workers

Difficulty of hiring index (0–100)	33
Rigidity of hours index (0–100)	20
Difficulty of firing index (0–100)	0
Rigidity of employment index (0–100)	18
Hiring cost (% of salary)	5
Firing cost (weeks of salary)	47

Registering property

Procedures (number)	2
Time (days)	2
Cost (% of property value)	6.3

Getting credit

Strength of legal rights index (0–10)	5
Depth of credit information index (0–6)	4
Public registry coverage (% of adults)	0.0
Private bureau coverage (% of adults)	18.4

Protecting investors

Extent of disclosure index (0–10)	10
Extent of director liability index (0–10)	2
Ease of shareholder suits index (0–10)	6
Strength of investor protection index (0–10)	6.0

Paying taxes

Payments (number)	44
Time (hours per year)	52
Total tax payable (% of gross profit)	29.2

Trading across borders

Documents for export (number)	9
Signatures for export (number)	10
Time for export (days)	23
Documents for import (number)	14
Signatures for import (number)	10
Time for import (days)	25

Enforcing contracts

Procedures (number)	26
Time (days)	390
Cost (% of debt)	13.4

Closing a business

Time (years)	3
Cost (% of estate)	36
Recovery rate (cents on the dollar)	43.9

TIMOR-LESTE

| East Asia & Pacific | GNI per capita (US$) | 550 |
| Low income | Population (m) | 0.9 |

| Ease of doing business (rank) | 142 |

Starting a business

Procedures (number)	10
Time (days)	92
Cost (% of income per capita)	125.4
Minimum capital (% of income per capita)	909.1

Dealing with licenses

Procedures (number)	24
Time (days)	192
Cost (% of income per capita)	51.0

Hiring and firing workers

Difficulty of hiring index (0–100)	67
Rigidity of hours index (0–100)	20
Difficulty of firing index (0–100)	50
Rigidity of employment index (0–100)	46
Hiring cost (% of salary)	0
Firing cost (weeks of salary)	21

Registering property

Procedures (number)	7
Time (days)	71
Cost (% of property value)	10.0

Getting credit

Strength of legal rights index (0–10)	3
Depth of credit information index (0–6)	0
Public registry coverage (% of adults)	0.0
Private bureau coverage (% of adults)	0.0

Protecting investors

Extent of disclosure index (0–10)	7
Extent of director liability index (0–10)	1
Ease of shareholder suits index (0–10)	3
Strength of investor protection index (0–10)	3.7

Paying taxes

Payments (number)	15
Time (hours per year)	640
Total tax payable (% of gross profit)	34.9

Trading across borders

Documents for export (number)	6
Signatures for export (number)	9
Time for export (days)	32
Documents for import (number)	11
Signatures for import (number)	12
Time for import (days)	37

Enforcing contracts

Procedures (number)	69
Time (days)	990
Cost (% of debt)	183.1

Closing a business

Time (years)	no practice
Cost (% of estate)	no practice
Recovery rate (cents on the dollar)	0.0

TOGO

| Sub-Saharan Africa | GNI per capita (US$) | 380 |
| Low income | Population (m) | 4.9 |

| Ease of doing business (rank) | 149 |

Starting a business

Procedures (number)	13
Time (days)	53
Cost (% of income per capita)	218.3
Minimum capital (% of income per capita)	459.9

Dealing with licenses

Procedures (number)	14
Time (days)	273
Cost (% of income per capita)	1223.4

Hiring and firing workers

Difficulty of hiring index (0–100)	78
Rigidity of hours index (0–100)	80
Difficulty of firing index (0–100)	80
Rigidity of employment index (0–100)	79
Hiring cost (% of salary)	25
Firing cost (weeks of salary)	66

Registering property

Procedures (number)	6
Time (days)	212
Cost (% of property value)	7.5

Getting credit

Strength of legal rights index (0–10)	2
Depth of credit information index (0–6)	1
Public registry coverage (% of adults)	3.5
Private bureau coverage (% of adults)	0.0

Protecting investors

Extent of disclosure index (0–10)	4
Extent of director liability index (0–10)	3
Ease of shareholder suits index (0–10)	5
Strength of investor protection index (0–10)	4.0

Paying taxes

Payments (number)	51
Time (hours per year)	270
Total tax payable (% of gross profit)	50.9

Trading across borders

Documents for export (number)	8
Signatures for export (number)	8
Time for export (days)	34
Documents for import (number)	11
Signatures for import (number)	14
Time for import (days)	43

Enforcing contracts

Procedures (number)	37
Time (days)	535
Cost (% of debt)	24.3

Closing a business

Time (years)	3
Cost (% of estate)	15
Recovery rate (cents on the dollar)	15.9

TONGA

		East Asia & Pacific		GNI per capita (US$)	1,830
Ease of doing business (rank)	36	Lower middle income		Population (m)	0.1

Starting a business		**Registering property**		**Trading across borders**	
Procedures (number)	4	Procedures (number)	4	Documents for export (number)	6
Time (days)	32	Time (days)	108	Signatures for export (number)	4
Cost (% of income per capita)	11.7	Cost (% of property value)	10.3	Time for export (days)	11
Minimum capital (% of income per capita)	0.0			Documents for import (number)	9
		Getting credit		Signatures for import (number)	5
Dealing with licenses		Strength of legal rights index (0–10)	5	Time for import (days)	11
Procedures (number)	15	Depth of credit information index (0–6)	0		
Time (days)	81	Public registry coverage (% of adults)	0.0	**Enforcing contracts**	
Cost (% of income per capita)	198.0	Private bureau coverage (% of adults)	0.0	Procedures (number)	30
				Time (days)	510
Hiring and firing workers		**Protecting investors**		Cost (% of debt)	47.0
Difficulty of hiring index (0–100)	0	Extent of disclosure index (0–10)	3		
Rigidity of hours index (0–100)	40	Extent of director liability index (0–10)	6	**Closing a business**	
Difficulty of firing index (0–100)	0	Ease of shareholder suits index (0–10)	8	Time (years)	3
Rigidity of employment index (0–100)	13	Strength of investor protection index (0–10)	5.7	Cost (% of estate)	22
Hiring cost (% of salary)	0			Recovery rate (cents on the dollar)	25.0
Firing cost (weeks of salary)	0	**Paying taxes**			
		Payments (number)	11		
		Time (hours per year)	156		
		Total tax payable (% of gross profit)	32.0		

TUNISIA

		Middle East & North Africa		GNI per capita (US$)	2,630
Ease of doing business (rank)	58	Lower middle income		Population (m)	9.9

Starting a business		**Registering property**		**Trading across borders**	
Procedures (number)	9	Procedures (number)	5	Documents for export (number)	5
Time (days)	14	Time (days)	57	Signatures for export (number)	8
Cost (% of income per capita)	10.0	Cost (% of property value)	6.1	Time for export (days)	25
Minimum capital (% of income per capita)	29.8			Documents for import (number)	8
		Getting credit		Signatures for import (number)	12
Dealing with licenses		Strength of legal rights index (0–10)	4	Time for import (days)	33
Procedures (number)	21	Depth of credit information index (0–6)	2		
Time (days)	154	Public registry coverage (% of adults)	8.2	**Enforcing contracts**	
Cost (% of income per capita)	340.0	Private bureau coverage (% of adults)	0.0	Procedures (number)	14
				Time (days)	27
Hiring and firing workers		**Protecting investors**		Cost (% of debt)	12.0
Difficulty of hiring index (0–100)	61	Extent of disclosure index (0–10)	0		
Rigidity of hours index (0–100)	0	Extent of director liability index (0–10)	4	**Closing a business**	
Difficulty of firing index (0–100)	100	Ease of shareholder suits index (0–10)	6	Time (years)	1
Rigidity of employment index (0–100)	54	Strength of investor protection index (0–10)	3.3	Cost (% of estate)	7
Hiring cost (% of salary)	19			Recovery rate (cents on the dollar)	51.5
Firing cost (weeks of salary)	29	**Paying taxes**			
		Payments (number)	31		
		Time (hours per year)	112		
		Total tax payable (% of gross profit)	52.7		

TURKEY

		Eastern Europe & Central Asia		GNI per capita (US$)	3,750
Ease of doing business (rank)	93	Upper middle income		Population (m)	70.7

Starting a business		**Registering property**		**Trading across borders**	
Procedures (number)	8	Procedures (number)	8	Documents for export (number)	9
Time (days)	9	Time (days)	9	Signatures for export (number)	10
Cost (% of income per capita)	27.7	Cost (% of property value)	3.2	Time for export (days)	20
Minimum capital (% of income per capita)	20.9			Documents for import (number)	13
		Getting credit		Signatures for import (number)	20
Dealing with licenses		Strength of legal rights index (0–10)	1	Time for import (days)	25
Procedures (number)	32	Depth of credit information index (0–6)	5		
Time (days)	232	Public registry coverage (% of adults)	4.9	**Enforcing contracts**	
Cost (% of income per capita)	368.7	Private bureau coverage (% of adults)	27.6	Procedures (number)	22
				Time (days)	330
Hiring and firing workers		**Protecting investors**		Cost (% of debt)	12.5
Difficulty of hiring index (0–100)	44	Extent of disclosure index (0–10)	8		
Rigidity of hours index (0–100)	80	Extent of director liability index (0–10)	3	**Closing a business**	
Difficulty of firing index (0–100)	40	Ease of shareholder suits index (0–10)	4	Time (years)	6
Rigidity of employment index (0–100)	55	Strength of investor protection index (0–10)	5.0	Cost (% of estate)	7
Hiring cost (% of salary)	22			Recovery rate (cents on the dollar)	7.2
Firing cost (weeks of salary)	112	**Paying taxes**			
		Payments (number)	18		
		Time (hours per year)	254		
		Total tax payable (% of gross profit)	51.1		

UGANDA

Ease of doing business (rank)	72

Sub-Saharan Africa
Low income

GNI per capita (US$)	270
Population (m)	25.3

Starting a business	
Procedures (number)	17
Time (days)	36
Cost (% of income per capita)	117.8
Minimum capital (% of income per capita)	0.0

Dealing with licenses	
Procedures (number)	19
Time (days)	155
Cost (% of income per capita)	861.8

Hiring and firing workers	
Difficulty of hiring index (0–100)	0
Rigidity of hours index (0–100)	20
Difficulty of firing index (0–100)	20
Rigidity of employment index (0–100)	13
Hiring cost (% of salary)	10
Firing cost (weeks of salary)	12

Registering property	
Procedures (number)	8
Time (days)	48
Cost (% of property value)	5.1

Getting credit	
Strength of legal rights index (0–10)	5
Depth of credit information index (0–6)	0
Public registry coverage (% of adults)	0.0
Private bureau coverage (% of adults)	0.0

Protecting investors	
Extent of disclosure index (0–10)	7
Extent of director liability index (0–10)	5
Ease of shareholder suits index (0–10)	4
Strength of investor protection index (0–10)	5.3

Paying taxes	
Payments (number)	31
Time (hours per year)	237
Total tax payable (% of gross profit)	42.9

Trading across borders	
Documents for export (number)	13
Signatures for export (number)	18
Time for export (days)	58
Documents for import (number)	17
Signatures for import (number)	27
Time for import (days)	73

Enforcing contracts	
Procedures (number)	15
Time (days)	209
Cost (% of debt)	22.3

Closing a business	
Time (years)	2
Cost (% of estate)	30
Recovery rate (cents on the dollar)	39.8

UKRAINE

Ease of doing business (rank)	124

Eastern Europe & Central Asia
Lower middle income

GNI per capita (US$)	1,260
Population (m)	48.4

Starting a business	
Procedures (number)	15
Time (days)	34
Cost (% of income per capita)	10.6
Minimum capital (% of income per capita)	183.0

Dealing with licenses	
Procedures (number)	18
Time (days)	265
Cost (% of income per capita)	229.4

Hiring and firing workers	
Difficulty of hiring index (0–100)	44
Rigidity of hours index (0–100)	60
Difficulty of firing index (0–100)	80
Rigidity of employment index (0–100)	61
Hiring cost (% of salary)	36
Firing cost (weeks of salary)	17

Registering property	
Procedures (number)	10
Time (days)	93
Cost (% of property value)	3.8

Getting credit	
Strength of legal rights index (0–10)	8
Depth of credit information index (0–6)	0
Public registry coverage (% of adults)	0.0
Private bureau coverage (% of adults)	0.0

Protecting investors	
Extent of disclosure index (0–10)	1
Extent of director liability index (0–10)	3
Ease of shareholder suits index (0–10)	4
Strength of investor protection index (0–10)	2.7

Paying taxes	
Payments (number)	84
Time (hours per year)	2185
Total tax payable (% of gross profit)	51.0

Trading across borders	
Documents for export (number)	6
Signatures for export (number)	9
Time for export (days)	34
Documents for import (number)	10
Signatures for import (number)	10
Time for import (days)	46

Enforcing contracts	
Procedures (number)	28
Time (days)	269
Cost (% of debt)	11.0

Closing a business	
Time (years)	3
Cost (% of estate)	42
Recovery rate (cents on the dollar)	8.4

UNITED ARAB EMIRATES

Ease of doing business (rank)	69

Middle East & North Africa
High income

GNI per capita (US$)	18,060
Population (m)	4.0

Starting a business	
Procedures (number)	12
Time (days)	54
Cost (% of income per capita)	44.3
Minimum capital (% of income per capita)	416.9

Dealing with licenses	
Procedures (number)	21
Time (days)	125
Cost (% of income per capita)	2.1

Hiring and firing workers	
Difficulty of hiring index (0–100)	0
Rigidity of hours index (0–100)	80
Difficulty of firing index (0–100)	20
Rigidity of employment index (0–100)	33
Hiring cost (% of salary)	13
Firing cost (weeks of salary)	96

Registering property	
Procedures (number)	3
Time (days)	9
Cost (% of property value)	2.0

Getting credit	
Strength of legal rights index (0–10)	4
Depth of credit information index (0–6)	2
Public registry coverage (% of adults)	1.5
Private bureau coverage (% of adults)	0.0

Protecting investors	
Extent of disclosure index (0–10)	4
Extent of director liability index (0–10)	8
Ease of shareholder suits index (0–10)	2
Strength of investor protection index (0–10)	4.7

Paying taxes	
Payments (number)	15
Time (hours per year)	12
Total tax payable (% of gross profit)	8.9

Trading across borders	
Documents for export (number)	6
Signatures for export (number)	3
Time for export (days)	18
Documents for import (number)	6
Signatures for import (number)	3
Time for import (days)	18

Enforcing contracts	
Procedures (number)	53
Time (days)	614
Cost (% of debt)	16.0

Closing a business	
Time (years)	5
Cost (% of estate)	30
Recovery rate (cents on the dollar)	5.5

UNITED KINGDOM
Ease of doing business (rank)   9

OECD: High Income	
High income	

GNI per capita (US$)	33,940
Population (m)	59.3

Starting a business

Procedures (number)	6
Time (days)	18
Cost (% of income per capita)	0.7
Minimum capital (% of income per capita)	0.0

Dealing with licenses

Procedures (number)	19
Time (days)	115
Cost (% of income per capita)	70.2

Hiring and firing workers

Difficulty of hiring index (0–100)	11
Rigidity of hours index (0–100)	20
Difficulty of firing index (0–100)	10
Rigidity of employment index (0–100)	14
Hiring cost (% of salary)	9
Firing cost (weeks of salary)	34

Registering property

Procedures (number)	2
Time (days)	21
Cost (% of property value)	4.1

Getting credit

Strength of legal rights index (0–10)	10
Depth of credit information index (0–6)	6
Public registry coverage (% of adults)	0.0
Private bureau coverage (% of adults)	76.2

Protecting investors

Extent of disclosure index (0–10)	10
Extent of director liability index (0–10)	7
Ease of shareholder suits index (0–10)	7
Strength of investor protection index (0–10)	8.0

Paying taxes

Payments (number)	22
Time (hours per year)	. .
Total tax payable (% of gross profit)	52.9

Trading across borders

Documents for export (number)	5
Signatures for export (number)	5
Time for export (days)	16
Documents for import (number)	4
Signatures for import (number)	5
Time for import (days)	16

Enforcing contracts

Procedures (number)	14
Time (days)	288
Cost (% of debt)	17.2

Closing a business

Time (years)	1
Cost (% of estate)	6
Recovery rate (cents on the dollar)	85.3

UNITED STATES
Ease of doing business (rank)   3

OECD: High Income	
High income	

GNI per capita (US$)	41,400
Population (m)	291.0

Starting a business

Procedures (number)	5
Time (days)	5
Cost (% of income per capita)	0.5
Minimum capital (% of income per capita)	0.0

Dealing with licenses

Procedures (number)	19
Time (days)	70
Cost (% of income per capita)	16.9

Hiring and firing workers

Difficulty of hiring index (0–100)	0
Rigidity of hours index (0–100)	0
Difficulty of firing index (0–100)	10
Rigidity of employment index (0–100)	3
Hiring cost (% of salary)	8
Firing cost (weeks of salary)	0

Registering property

Procedures (number)	4
Time (days)	12
Cost (% of property value)	0.5

Getting credit

Strength of legal rights index (0–10)	7
Depth of credit information index (0–6)	6
Public registry coverage (% of adults)	0.0
Private bureau coverage (% of adults)	100.0

Protecting investors

Extent of disclosure index (0–10)	7
Extent of director liability index (0–10)	9
Ease of shareholder suits index (0–10)	9
Strength of investor protection index (0–10)	8.3

Paying taxes

Payments (number)	9
Time (hours per year)	325
Total tax payable (% of gross profit)	21.5

Trading across borders

Documents for export (number)	6
Signatures for export (number)	5
Time for export (days)	9
Documents for import (number)	5
Signatures for import (number)	4
Time for import (days)	9

Enforcing contracts

Procedures (number)	17
Time (days)	250
Cost (% of debt)	7.5

Closing a business

Time (years)	2
Cost (% of estate)	7
Recovery rate (cents on the dollar)	76.2

URUGUAY
Ease of doing business (rank)   85

Latin America & Caribbean	
Upper middle income	

GNI per capita (US$)	3,950
Population (m)	3.4

Starting a business

Procedures (number)	11
Time (days)	45
Cost (% of income per capita)	43.9
Minimum capital (% of income per capita)	151.7

Dealing with licenses

Procedures (number)	17
Time (days)	146
Cost (% of income per capita)	95.0

Hiring and firing workers

Difficulty of hiring index (0–100)	33
Rigidity of hours index (0–100)	60
Difficulty of firing index (0–100)	0
Rigidity of employment index (0–100)	31
Hiring cost (% of salary)	20
Firing cost (weeks of salary)	26

Registering property

Procedures (number)	8
Time (days)	66
Cost (% of property value)	7.1

Getting credit

Strength of legal rights index (0–10)	4
Depth of credit information index (0–6)	5
Public registry coverage (% of adults)	5.5
Private bureau coverage (% of adults)	80.0

Protecting investors

Extent of disclosure index (0–10)	3
Extent of director liability index (0–10)	4
Ease of shareholder suits index (0–10)	8
Strength of investor protection index (0–10)	5.0

Paying taxes

Payments (number)	54
Time (hours per year)	300
Total tax payable (% of gross profit)	80.2

Trading across borders

Documents for export (number)	9
Signatures for export (number)	10
Time for export (days)	22
Documents for import (number)	9
Signatures for import (number)	12
Time for import (days)	25

Enforcing contracts

Procedures (number)	39
Time (days)	620
Cost (% of debt)	25.8

Closing a business

Time (years)	2
Cost (% of estate)	7
Recovery rate (cents on the dollar)	30.6

UZBEKISTAN

Ease of doing business (rank)	138

Eastern Europe & Central Asia
Low income

GNI per capita (US$)	460
Population (m)	25.6

Starting a business

Procedures (number)	9
Time (days)	35
Cost (% of income per capita)	15.5
Minimum capital (% of income per capita)	20.2

Dealing with licenses

Procedures (number)	..
Time (days)	..
Cost (% of income per capita)	..

Hiring and firing workers

Difficulty of hiring index (0–100)	33
Rigidity of hours index (0–100)	40
Difficulty of firing index (0–100)	30
Rigidity of employment index (0–100)	34
Hiring cost (% of salary)	36
Firing cost (weeks of salary)	31

Registering property

Procedures (number)	12
Time (days)	97
Cost (% of property value)	10.5

Getting credit

Strength of legal rights index (0–10)	5
Depth of credit information index (0–6)	0
Public registry coverage (% of adults)	0.0
Private bureau coverage (% of adults)	0.0

Protecting investors

Extent of disclosure index (0–10)	4
Extent of director liability index (0–10)	6
Ease of shareholder suits index (0–10)	3
Strength of investor protection index (0–10)	4.3

Paying taxes

Payments (number)	118
Time (hours per year)	152
Total tax payable (% of gross profit)	75.6

Trading across borders

Documents for export (number)	..
Signatures for export (number)	..
Time for export (days)	..
Documents for import (number)	18
Signatures for import (number)	32
Time for import (days)	139

Enforcing contracts

Procedures (number)	35
Time (days)	368
Cost (% of debt)	18.1

Closing a business

Time (years)	4
Cost (% of estate)	4
Recovery rate (cents on the dollar)	12.5

VANUATU

Ease of doing business (rank)	49

East Asia & Pacific
Lower middle income

GNI per capita (US$)	1,340
Population (m)	0.2

Starting a business

Procedures (number)	8
Time (days)	39
Cost (% of income per capita)	65.6
Minimum capital (% of income per capita)	0.0

Dealing with licenses

Procedures (number)	7
Time (days)	82
Cost (% of income per capita)	427.1

Hiring and firing workers

Difficulty of hiring index (0–100)	39
Rigidity of hours index (0–100)	40
Difficulty of firing index (0–100)	10
Rigidity of employment index (0–100)	30
Hiring cost (% of salary)	6
Firing cost (weeks of salary)	55

Registering property

Procedures (number)	2
Time (days)	188
Cost (% of property value)	7.0

Getting credit

Strength of legal rights index (0–10)	6
Depth of credit information index (0–6)	0
Public registry coverage (% of adults)	0.0
Private bureau coverage (% of adults)	0.0

Protecting investors

Extent of disclosure index (0–10)	5
Extent of director liability index (0–10)	6
Ease of shareholder suits index (0–10)	8
Strength of investor protection index (0–10)	6.3

Paying taxes

Payments (number)	32
Time (hours per year)	120
Total tax payable (% of gross profit)	28.1

Trading across borders

Documents for export (number)	9
Signatures for export (number)	6
Time for export (days)	7
Documents for import (number)	14
Signatures for import (number)	9
Time for import (days)	9

Enforcing contracts

Procedures (number)	24
Time (days)	430
Cost (% of debt)	64.0

Closing a business

Time (years)	3
Cost (% of estate)	38
Recovery rate (cents on the dollar)	15.8

VENEZUELA

Ease of doing business (rank)	120

Latin America & Caribbean
Upper middle income

GNI per capita (US$)	4,020
Population (m)	25.7

Starting a business

Procedures (number)	13
Time (days)	116
Cost (% of income per capita)	15.7
Minimum capital (% of income per capita)	0.0

Dealing with licenses

Procedures (number)	13
Time (days)	276
Cost (% of income per capita)	547.2

Hiring and firing workers

Difficulty of hiring index (0–100)	33
Rigidity of hours index (0–100)	80
Difficulty of firing index (0–100)	0
Rigidity of employment index (0–100)	38
Hiring cost (% of salary)	15
Firing cost (weeks of salary)	46

Registering property

Procedures (number)	7
Time (days)	33
Cost (% of property value)	2.1

Getting credit

Strength of legal rights index (0–10)	4
Depth of credit information index (0–6)	4
Public registry coverage (% of adults)	16.8
Private bureau coverage (% of adults)	0.0

Protecting investors

Extent of disclosure index (0–10)	3
Extent of director liability index (0–10)	2
Ease of shareholder suits index (0–10)	2
Strength of investor protection index (0–10)	2.3

Paying taxes

Payments (number)	68
Time (hours per year)	864
Total tax payable (% of gross profit)	48.9

Trading across borders

Documents for export (number)	8
Signatures for export (number)	6
Time for export (days)	34
Documents for import (number)	13
Signatures for import (number)	9
Time for import (days)	42

Enforcing contracts

Procedures (number)	41
Time (days)	445
Cost (% of debt)	28.7

Closing a business

Time (years)	4
Cost (% of estate)	38
Recovery rate (cents on the dollar)	6.1

VIETNAM

Ease of doing business (rank)	99

East Asia & Pacific	
Low income	

GNI per capita (US$)	550
Population (m)	81.3

Starting a business

Procedures (number)	11
Time (days)	50
Cost (% of income per capita)	50.6
Minimum capital (% of income per capita)	0.0

Dealing with licenses

Procedures (number)	14
Time (days)	143
Cost (% of income per capita)	64.1

Hiring and firing workers

Difficulty of hiring index (0–100)	44
Rigidity of hours index (0–100)	40
Difficulty of firing index (0–100)	70
Rigidity of employment index (0–100)	51
Hiring cost (% of salary)	17
Firing cost (weeks of salary)	98

Registering property

Procedures (number)	5
Time (days)	67
Cost (% of property value)	1.2

Getting credit

Strength of legal rights index (0–10)	3
Depth of credit information index (0–6)	3
Public registry coverage (% of adults)	1.1
Private bureau coverage (% of adults)	0.0

Protecting investors

Extent of disclosure index (0–10)	4
Extent of director liability index (0–10)	1
Ease of shareholder suits index (0–10)	2
Strength of investor protection index (0–10)	2.3

Paying taxes

Payments (number)	44
Time (hours per year)	1050
Total tax payable (% of gross profit)	31.5

Trading across borders

Documents for export (number)	6
Signatures for export (number)	12
Time for export (days)	35
Documents for import (number)	9
Signatures for import (number)	15
Time for import (days)	36

Enforcing contracts

Procedures (number)	37
Time (days)	343
Cost (% of debt)	30.1

Closing a business

Time (years)	5
Cost (% of estate)	15
Recovery rate (cents on the dollar)	19.2

WEST BANK AND GAZA

Ease of doing business (rank)	125

Middle East & North Africa	
Lower middle income	

GNI per capita (US$)	1,110
Population (m)	3.4

Starting a business

Procedures (number)	11
Time (days)	106
Cost (% of income per capita)	275.4
Minimum capital (% of income per capita)	1409.8

Dealing with licenses

Procedures (number)	18
Time (days)	144
Cost (% of income per capita)	779.2

Hiring and firing workers

Difficulty of hiring index (0–100)	33
Rigidity of hours index (0–100)	60
Difficulty of firing index (0–100)	20
Rigidity of employment index (0–100)	38
Hiring cost (% of salary)	13
Firing cost (weeks of salary)	90

Registering property

Procedures (number)	7
Time (days)	58
Cost (% of property value)	4.7

Getting credit

Strength of legal rights index (0–10)	5
Depth of credit information index (0–6)	0
Public registry coverage (% of adults)	0.0
Private bureau coverage (% of adults)	0.0

Protecting investors

Extent of disclosure index (0–10)	. .
Extent of director liability index (0–10)	. .
Ease of shareholder suits index (0–10)	. .
Strength of investor protection index (0–10)	. .

Paying taxes

Payments (number)	49
Time (hours per year)	. .
Total tax payable (% of gross profit)	42

Trading across borders

Documents for export (number)	6
Signatures for export (number)	10
Time for export (days)	27
Documents for import (number)	9
Signatures for import (number)	18
Time for import (days)	42

Enforcing contracts

Procedures (number)	26
Time (days)	465
Cost (% of debt)	21.4

Closing a business

Time (years)	. .
Cost (% of estate)	. .
Recovery rate (cents on the dollar)	. .

YEMEN

Ease of doing business (rank)	90

Middle East & North Africa	
Low income	

GNI per capita (US$)	570
Population (m)	19.2

Starting a business

Procedures (number)	12
Time (days)	63
Cost (% of income per capita)	240.2
Minimum capital (% of income per capita)	2703.2

Dealing with licenses

Procedures (number)	13
Time (days)	131
Cost (% of income per capita)	274.4

Hiring and firing workers

Difficulty of hiring index (0–100)	0
Rigidity of hours index (0–100)	80
Difficulty of firing index (0–100)	30
Rigidity of employment index (0–100)	37
Hiring cost (% of salary)	17
Firing cost (weeks of salary)	17

Registering property

Procedures (number)	6
Time (days)	21
Cost (% of property value)	3.9

Getting credit

Strength of legal rights index (0–10)	2
Depth of credit information index (0–6)	2
Public registry coverage (% of adults)	0.1
Private bureau coverage (% of adults)	0.0

Protecting investors

Extent of disclosure index (0–10)	6
Extent of director liability index (0–10)	4
Ease of shareholder suits index (0–10)	3
Strength of investor protection index (0–10)	4.3

Paying taxes

Payments (number)	32
Time (hours per year)	248
Total tax payable (% of gross profit)	128.8

Trading across borders

Documents for export (number)	6
Signatures for export (number)	8
Time for export (days)	33
Documents for import (number)	9
Signatures for import (number)	20
Time for import (days)	31

Enforcing contracts

Procedures (number)	37
Time (days)	360
Cost (% of debt)	10.5

Closing a business

Time (years)	3
Cost (% of estate)	8
Recovery rate (cents on the dollar)	28.2

ZAMBIA

		Sub-Saharan Africa		GNI per capita (US$)	450
Ease of doing business (rank)	67	Low income		Population (m)	10.4

Starting a business

Procedures (number)	6
Time (days)	35
Cost (% of income per capita)	18.1
Minimum capital (% of income per capita)	2.1

Dealing with licenses

Procedures (number)	16
Time (days)	165
Cost (% of income per capita)	1671.2

Hiring and firing workers

Difficulty of hiring index (0–100)	0
Rigidity of hours index (0–100)	20
Difficulty of firing index (0–100)	10
Rigidity of employment index (0–100)	10
Hiring cost (% of salary)	9
Firing cost (weeks of salary)	176

Registering property

Procedures (number)	6
Time (days)	70
Cost (% of property value)	9.6

Getting credit

Strength of legal rights index (0–10)	6
Depth of credit information index (0–6)	0
Public registry coverage (% of adults)	0.0
Private bureau coverage (% of adults)	0.0

Protecting investors

Extent of disclosure index (0–10)	10
Extent of director liability index (0–10)	4
Ease of shareholder suits index (0–10)	8
Strength of investor protection index (0–10)	7.3

Paying taxes

Payments (number)	36
Time (hours per year)	132
Total tax payable (% of gross profit)	38.6

Trading across borders

Documents for export (number)	16
Signatures for export (number)	25
Time for export (days)	60
Documents for import (number)	19
Signatures for import (number)	28
Time for import (days)	62

Enforcing contracts

Procedures (number)	16
Time (days)	274
Cost (% of debt)	28.7

Closing a business

Time (years)	3
Cost (% of estate)	9
Recovery rate (cents on the dollar)	20.0

ZIMBABWE

		Sub-Saharan Africa		GNI per capita (US$)	480
Ease of doing business (rank)	126	Low income		Population (m)	13.1

Starting a business

Procedures (number)	10
Time (days)	96
Cost (% of income per capita)	1442.5
Minimum capital (% of income per capita)	53.0

Dealing with licenses

Procedures (number)	21
Time (days)	481
Cost (% of income per capita)	1509.6

Hiring and firing workers

Difficulty of hiring index (0–100)	11
Rigidity of hours index (0–100)	40
Difficulty of firing index (0–100)	20
Rigidity of employment index (0–100)	24
Hiring cost (% of salary)	6
Firing cost (weeks of salary)	29

Registering property

Procedures (number)	4
Time (days)	30
Cost (% of property value)	22.6

Getting credit

Strength of legal rights index (0–10)	7
Depth of credit information index (0–6)	0
Public registry coverage (% of adults)	0
Private bureau coverage (% of adults)	0.0

Protecting investors

Extent of disclosure index (0–10)	8
Extent of director liability index (0–10)	1
Ease of shareholder suits index (0–10)	4
Strength of investor protection index (0–10)	4.3

Paying taxes

Payments (number)	59
Time (hours per year)	216
Total tax payable (% of gross profit)	48.6

Trading across borders

Documents for export (number)	9
Signatures for export (number)	18
Time for export (days)	52
Documents for import (number)	15
Signatures for import (number)	19
Time for import (days)	66

Enforcing contracts

Procedures (number)	33
Time (days)	350
Cost (% of debt)	19.1

Closing a business

Time (years)	2
Cost (% of estate)	22
Recovery rate (cents on the dollar)	2.1

Acknowledgments

Contact details for local partners are available
on the Doing Business website at
http://www.doingbusiness.org

Doing Business in 2006 was prepared by a team led by Simeon Djankov and Caralee McLiesh under the general direction of Michael Klein. The team also comprised Ziad Azar, Ghanem-Redouane Benamadi, Vivian Callaghan, Marie Delion, Penelope Fidas, Melissa Johns, Joanna Kata-Blackman, Marcelo Lu, Darshini Manraj, Facundo Martin, Nikolay Naumovich, Rita Ramalho, Sylvia Solf, Donaji Valencia and Lihong Wang. Additional assistance in the months prior to publication was provided by Olufunmilola Akintan, Tim Ganser, Michael Gilbert, Franck Kpomalegni and Amine Taha.

Mihir Desai, Oliver Hart, Rafael La Porta and Andrei Shleifer provided academic advice on the project. The paying taxes project was conducted in partnership with PricewaterhouseCoopers, led by Robert Morris with Kelly Murray and Penny Vaughn. The protecting investors and enforcing contracts projects were conducted in partnership with the Lex Mundi association, led by Carl Anduri and Sam Nolen. Data collection for the trading across borders project was assisted by AP Moller–Maersk, led by Soren Hansen; Bolloré Group, led by Jean Marcel Gariador and Denis Cordel; Freightnet, led by Phil Morrison; Panalpina Inc., led by Mike Krieg; and the World Customs Organization, led by Franck Lecoindre. Jean-François Gerard and Bianca Kingdon from Ius Laboris contributed to data collection on hiring and firing workers. Tony Burns wrote a background paper for the registering property chapter. Uma Subramanian designed the trading across borders survey. Several other organizations and individual experts provided input to survey design, as detailed in the Data notes. Alison Strong and Paul Holtz edited the manuscript. Timothy Harford and Suzanne Smith provided additional editorial advice. Gerry Quinn designed the report and the figures.

Individual chapters were refereed by a panel of experts comprising Hamid Alavi, Magdi Amin, Nagavalli Annamalai, Pauline Aranda, Jean Francois Arvis, Irina Astrakhan, Paul Barbour, Lubomira Beardsley, Alexander Berg, Christina Biebesheimer, Paul Brenton, John Bruce, Tony Burns, Mierta Capaul, Stijn Claessens, Jacqueline Coolidge, Asli Demirguc-Kunt, Amanda Ellis, Aurora Ferrari, Carsten Fink, Luke Haggarty, Su Lin Han, Leora Klapper, Arvo Kuddo, Oscar Madeddu, William Mako, Varsha Marathe, Gerard McLinden, Richard Messick, Margaret Miller, Claudio Montenegro, Tatiana Nenova, Richard Newfarmer, Carmen Pages, Jose Manuel Palli, Vincent Palmade, John Panzer, Sue Rutledge, Jolyne Sanjak, Phil Schuler, Sevi Simavi, Warrick Smith, Peer Stein, Richard Stern, Stefano Stoppani, Uma Subramanian, Richard Symonds, Vijay Tata, Agata Waclawik, John Wilson and Luc De Wulf.

The full draft report was reviewed by Hormoz Aghdaey, Simon Bell, Harry Broadman, Philip Keefer, Steven Knack, Cornelis Kruk, Khalid Mirza, Anand Rajaram, Stefano Scarpetta, Sandor Sipos, Andrew Stone, Nigel Twose and Marilou Uy. We are grateful for comments and review provided by the World Bank Group's country teams.

The online service of the Doing Business database is managed by the Rapid Response Unit of the World Bank Group. The team was led by Suzanne Smith and comprised Vadim Gorbach, Graeme Littler, Vandana Mathur, Victor Robinson and Leila Search-Zalmai.

The report was made possible by the generous contribution of more than 3,500 lawyers, accountants, judges, business-people and public officials in 155 economies. Quotations in this report are from local partners unless otherwise indicated. The names of those wishing to be acknowledged individually are listed on the following pages and contact details are posted on the Doing Business website at http://www.doingbusiness.org.

GLOBAL CONTRIBUTORS

BAKER & MCKENZIE

INTERNATIONAL BAR ASSOCIATION

LEX MUNDI, ASSOCIATION OF INDEPENDENT LAW FIRMS (MEMBER FIRMS IDENTIFIED BY *)

PANALPINA

PRICEWATERHOUSECOOPERS

SDV INTERNATIONAL LOGISTICS

TRANSUNION INTERNATIONAL

AFGHANISTAN

Gaurav Kukreja
ACTCO-AFGHAN COUNTAINER TRANSPORT CO.

Parwana Hasan
AWLPA

Shafic Gawhari
MINISTRY OF COMMERCE

Rashid Ibrahim
A.F. FERGUSON & CO.

Soli Parakh
PRICEWATERHOUSECOOPERS

Hamid Qaderi
AFGHANISTAN INTERNATIONAL CHAMBER OF COMMERCE

Azam Kargar
ASSOCIATION OF AFGHANISTAN FREIGHT FORWARDING CO.S

Najibullah-Rahimi
EXPORTS & INDUSTRIES

Amin Karim Zada
KABUL CHAMBER OF COMMERCE & INDUSTRIES

Mohammad Naim Maimanagi
NAIL LTD. CO.

Charles Clinton
ALTAI CONSULTING

Zaid Mohseni
ZAMOH

ALBANIA

Genc Boga
BOGA & ASSOCIATES

Victor Chimienti
BOGA & ASSOCIATES

Sokol Elmazi
BOGA & ASSOCIATES

Kreshnik Spahiu
CITIZEN ADVOCACY OFFICE

Andi Memi
HOXHA, MEMI & HOXHA

Shpati Hoxha
HOXHA, MEMI & HOXHA

Spyridon Tsakalis
IKRP ROKAS & PARTNERS

Shkelqim Kerluku
IKRP ROKAS & PARTNERS

Marsela Kokoshi
IKRP ROKAS & PARTNERS

Elisa Stamo
IKRP ROKAS & PARTNERS

Merilda Nina
IKRP ROKAS & PARTNERS

Ina Aleksi
KALO & ASSOCIATES

Jola Gjuzi
KALO & ASSOCIATES

Anisa Rrumbullaku
KALO & ASSOCIATES

Genci Krasniqi
KALO & ASSOCIATES

Alban Caushi
KALO & ASSOCIATES

Vilma Gjyshi
KALO & ASSOCIATES

Loreta Peci
PRICEWATERHOUSECOOPERS

Laura Qorlaze
PRICEWATERHOUSECOOPERS

Artur Asllani
STUDIO LEGALE TONUCCI

Robert Brugger
PANALPINA WELTTRANSPORT GMBH

ALGERIA

Mourad Dubert
CABINET D'ARCHITECT MOURAD DUBERT

Adnane Bouchaib
BOUCHAIB LAW FIRM

Nabiha Zerigui
CABINET SAMIR HAMOUDA

Samir Hamouda
CABINET SAMIR HAMOUDA

Mohamed El Amine Haddad
GHELLAL & MEKERBA

Amine Ghellal, Esq.
GHELLAL & MEKERBA

Mustapha Hamza
HAMZALAW OFFICE

Yamina Kebir
LAW OFFICE OF YAMINA KEBIR

Sid Ahmed Hasbellaou
MAERSK LOGISTICS ALGÉRIE SPA

Fares Ouzegdouh
MAERSK LOGISTICS ALGÉRIE SPA

Jérôme Le Hec
LANDWELL & ASSOCIÉS

Gerard Morin
LANDWELL & ASSOCIÉS

Dominique Rolland
LANDWELL & ASSOCIÉS

Michel Lecerf
LANDWELL & ASSOCIÉS

ANGOLA

Alexandre Do Rêgo Pinto Pegado
ALEXANDRE PEGADO LAW FIRM

Teresinha Lopes
FARIA DE BASTOS, SEBASTIÃO & LOPES

Fatima Freitas
FATIMA FREITAS ADVOGADOS

Katila Machado
FÁTIMA FREITAS ADVOGADOS

Nahary Cardoso
FÁTIMA FREITAS ADVOGADOS

Jorge Leao Peres
NATIONAL BANK OF ANGOLA

Judith De Fatima Dos Santos Lima
NATIONAL BANK OF ANGOLA

Douglas Pillinger
PANALPINA

Pedro Calixto
PRICEWATERHOUSECOOPERS

Julian Ince
PRICEWATERHOUSECOOPERS

Fernando Barros
PRICEWATERHOUSECOOPERS

Aymeric Frisch
SDV AMI ANGOLA - BOLLORE GROUP

ARGENTINA

Diego Turcato
ALFARO ABOGADOS

Mariana Morelli
ALFARO ABOGADOS

Federico Augusto Brandt
ALFARO ABOGADOS

Juan Arocena
ALLENDE & BREA

Octavio Miguel Zenarruza
ALVAREZ PRADO & ASOCIADOS

Lisandro A. Allende
BRONS & SALAS

Oscar Alberto del Rio
CENTRAL BANK OF ARGENTINA

Mariano Carricart
FORNIELES ABOGADOS

Ignacio Funes de Rioja
FUNES DE RIOJA & ASOCIADOS, MEMBER OF IUS LABORIS

Angelica Sola
MARVAL, O'FARRELL & MAIRAL*

Ignacio L. Triolo
MARVAL, O'FARRELL & MAIRAL

Santiago Laclau
MARVAL, O'FARRELL & MAIRAL

Alejandro D. Fiuza
MARVAL, O'FARRELL & MAIRAL

Patricia Ruhman Seggiaro
MARVAL, O'FARRELL & MAIRAL

Alfredo Miguel O'Farrell
MARVAL, O'FARRELL & MAIRAL

Miguel P. Murray
MURRAY, d´ANDRÉ, ISASMENDI & SIRITO DE ZAVALIA

Sean McCormick
MURRAY, d´ANDRÉ, ISASMENDI & SIRITO DE ZAVALIA

María Fraguas
NICHOLSON Y CANO

Santiago Nicholson
NICHOLSON Y CANO

Roberto Laterza
ORGANIZACION VERAZ

Enrique Pugliano
ORGANIZACION VERAZ

Ricardo Andia
PANALPINA TRANSPORTES MUNDIALES S.A.

Axel Kreutzmann
PANALPINA TRANSPORTES MUNDIALES S.A.

Carlos Zima
PRICEWATERHOUSECOOPERS

Andres M. Edelstein
PRICEWATERHOUSECOOPERS

Ignacio Rodriguez
PRICEWATERHOUSECOOPERS

Liliana Segade
QUATTRINI, LAPRIDA & ASOCIADOS

Javier Valle Zayas
URÍA & MENÉNDEZ

Vanesa Balda
VITALE, MANOFF & FEILBOGEN

ARMENIA

Mher Grigoryan

Arsen Matikyan
ALFATRANS LTD.

Ashot Poghosyan
ARAX CONSULTING GROUP

Thomas J. Samuelian
ARLEX INTERNATIONAL LTD.

Artak Arzoyan
CENTRAL BANK OF ARMENIA

Hakob Tadevosyan
GRANT THORNTON AMYOT

Aram Poghosyan
GRANT THORNTON AMYOT

Artashes F. Kakoyan
INVESTMENT LAW GROUP LLC

Hayk Hovhannisyan
INVESTMENT LAW GROUP LLC

Edward Mesropyan
JINJ CO.

Suren Melikyan
KPMG ARMENIA

Alan Kuchukyan
KPMG ARMENIA

Arno Mosikyan
KPMG ARMENIA

Tigran Serobyan
KPMG ARMENIA

Ara Markosyan
KPMG ARMENIA

Ashot Petrosyan
MINISTRY OF TRADE AND ECONOMICAL DEVELOPMENT

Hayk Sahakyan
STATE COMMITTEE OF THE REAL PROPERTY CADASTRE

Armen Ter-Tachatyan
TER-TACHATYAN LEGAL AND BUSINESS CONSULTING

Mikayel Tovmassian
TER-TACHATYAN LEGAL AND BUSINESS CONSULTING

Artur Tunyan
TUNYAN & ASSOCIATES

Maria Livinska
PRICEWATERHOUSECOOPERS

Jorge Intriago
PRICEWATERHOUSECOOPERS

Svetlana Bilyk
PRICEWATERHOUSECOOPERS

AUSTRALIA

David Cross
ALLENS ARTHUR ROBINSON

Michael Quinlan
ALLENS ARTHUR ROBINSON

Steven Fleming
ALLENS ARTHUR ROBINSON

Sarah Bergin
ALLENS ARTHUR ROBINSON

Mark Pistilli
ATANASKOVIC HARTNELL

Amelia Horvath
ATANASKOVIC HARTNELL

Basil Sawczuk
AUSTRALIAN CUSTOMS SERVICE

Jane Wilson
BAYCORP ADVANTAGE

John Lobban
BLAKE DAWSON WALDRON

Paul James
CLAYTON UTZ*

Penny Grau
CLAYTON UTZ

Luke Nicholls
CLAYTON UTZ

Ron Schaffer
CLAYTON UTZ

Christopher Davie
CLAYTON UTZ

Doug Jones AM
CLAYTON UTZ

Lucinda Girdlestone
COWLEY HEARNE LAWYERS

David Zwi
COWLEY HEARNE LAWYERS

David Buda
COWLEY HEARNE LAWYERS

Petrea Draper
COWLEY HEARNE LAWYERS

Greg Channell
DEPARTMENT OF LANDS

Des Mooney
DEPARTMENT OF LANDS

Lyn Thomson
DEPARTMENT OF LANDS

Peter Gemell
EVANS & PECK

Robert Riddell
GADENS LAWYERS

Boris Hristovski
GADENS LAWYERS

Andrew Smith
MALLESONS STEPHEN JAQUES

Eric Herding
PANALPINA WORLD TRANSPORT

Michael Croker
PRICEWATERHOUSECOOPERS

Ann Previtera
PRICEWATERHOUSECOOPERS

Lynda Brumm
PRICEWATERHOUSECOOPERS

Phil Rosser
SYDNEY PORTS CORPORATION

AUSTRIA

Irene Mandl
AUSTRIAN INSTITUTE FOR SME RESEARCH

Christian Lettmayr
AUSTRIAN INSTITUTE FOR SME RESEARCH

Walter Bornett
AUSTRIAN INSTITUTE FOR SME RESEARCH

Andreas Hable
BINDER GRÖSSWANG RECHTSANWÄLTE

Doris Buxbaum
BINDER GRÖSSWANG RECHTSANWÄLTE

Johannes Barbist
BINDER GRÖSSWANG RECHTSANWÄLTE

Tibor Fabian
BINDER GRÖSSWANG RECHTSANWÄLTE

Georg Brandstetter
BRANDSTETTER PRITZ & PARTNER

Alexander Klauser
BRAUNEIS, KLAUSER & PRANDL

Gregor Maderbacher
BRAUNEIS, KLAUSER & PRANDL

Thomas Trettnak
*CERHA HEMPEL & SPIEGELFELD**

Julian Feichtinger
CERHA HEMPEL & SPIEGELFELD

Angela Zaffalon
CERHA HEMPEL & SPIEGELFELD

Benedikt Spiegelfeld
CERHA HEMPEL & SPIEGELFELD

Martin Eckel
EISELSBERG NATLACEN WALDERDORFF CANCOLA

Georg Bahn
FRESHFIELDS BRUCKHAUS DERINGER

Edgar Langeder
FRIEDERS TASSUL & PARTNER

Georg Tuppa
GRAF, MAXL & PITKOWITZ

Ferdinand Graf
GRAF, MAXL & PITKOWITZ

Harald Heschl
KREDITSCHUTZVERBAND VON 1870

Georg Schima
KUNZ SCHIMA WALLENTIN, MEMBER OF IUS LABORIS

Wolfgang Messeritsch
NATIONAL BANK OF AUSTRIA

Günther Horvàth
OPPENHEIM ÉS TÁRSAI, FRESHFIELDS BRUCKHAUS DERING

Robert Brugger
PANALPINA WELTTRANSPORT GMBH

Ernst Biebl
PRICEWATERHOUSECOOPERS

Friedrich Roedler
PRICEWATERHOUSECOOPERS

Peter Madl
SCHOENHERR RECHTSANWAELTE

Ulrike Langwallner
SCHOENHERR RECHTSANWAELTE

Lothar Wachter
WOLF THEISS

AZERBAIJAN

Abbas Atakishi
"AZLEKS" INTERNATIONAL LAW FIRM

Tahira Shokorova
"AZLEKS" INTERNATIONAL LAW FIRM

Nadir Huseynbayov
AGENCY FOR SUPPORT TO THE DEVELOPMENT OF AGRICULTURAL PRIVATE SECTOR

Sergio Purin
AHLERS

Gunduz Karimov
BAKER & MCKENZIE

Daniel Matthews
BAKER & MCKENZIE

Abdullayev Sabit
BAKER & MCKENZIE

Natik Mamedov
BAKER & MCKENZIE

Farrukh Gassimov
BAKER BOTTS

Mark Rowley
BAKER BOTTS

Bakhtiyar Mammadov
BAKER BOTTS

Valery Sidnev
BAKER BOTTS

Namik Novruzov
BM INTERNATIONAL LLC

Vadim Shneyer
BM INTERNATIONAL LLC

Farhad Mirzayev
BM INTERNATIONAL LLC

Kanan Safarov
LEDINGHAM CHALMERS

Michael Walsh
LEDINGHAM CHALMERS

Aida Badalova
LEDINGHAM CHALMERS

Ismayil Askerov
LEDINGHAM CHALMERS

Elchin Hagverdiyev
LEDINGHAM CHALMERS

Rufat Aslanli
NATIONAL BANK OF AZERBAIJAN

Arif Guliyev
PRICEWATERHOUSECOOPERS

Rizvan Gubiyev
PRICEWATERHOUSECOOPERS

Mushfig Aliyev
PRICEWATERHOUSECOOPERS

Bob Jurik
PRICEWATERHOUSECOOPERS

Vagif Ahmadov
SALANS HERTZFELD & HEILBRONN LAW FIRM

Alum Bati
SALANS HERTZFELD & HEILBRONN LAW FIRM

Farhad Hajizade
SALANS HERTZFELD & HEILBRONN LAW FIRM

BANGLADESH

Sohel Kasem
A. QASEM & CO. / PRICEWATERHOUSECOOPERS

Badrul Ahsan
A. QASEM & CO. / PRICEWATERHOUSECOOPERS

Jasim U. Ahmed
BANGLADESH CONTAINER LINES LTD.

Jasim Uddin Ahmad
BANK OF BANGLADESH

Nasirul Doulah
DOULAH & DOULAH ADVOCATES

Shamsud Doulah
DOULAH & DOULAH ADVOCATES

A.B.M. Badrud Doulah
DOULAH & DOULAH ADVOCATES

Karishma Jahan
DR. KAMAL HOSSAIN & ASSOCIATES

Kamal Hossain
DR. KAMAL HOSSAIN & ASSOCIATES

Ashfaq Amin
INTEGRATED TRANSPORTATION SERVICES LTD. AS AGENT OF PANALPINA

Halim Bepari
SUPREME COURT OF BANGLADESH

M.D. Asadujjaman
SYED ISHTIAQ AHMED AND ASSOCIATES

Amir-Ul Islam
*THE LAW ASSOCIATES**

Shamsul Hasan
THE LAW ASSOCIATES

Shirin Chaudhury
THE LAW ASSOCIATES

Mohammed Razack
THE LAW ASSOCIATES

Nahid Afreen
THE LAW ASSOCIATES

Abdur Razzaq
THE LAW COUNSEL

BELARUS

Alexander Korneiko
AHLERS

Ilya Latyshev
APICES JURIS

Anna T. Rusetskaya
BELJURBUREAU

Vladimir G. Biruk
BELORUSSIAN COMMUNITY OF PROFESSIONALS IN CRISIS MANAGEMENT AND BANKRUPTCY

Vassili I. Salei
BOROVTSOV & SALEI

Alexander Botian
BOROVTSOV & SALEI

Vasily Volozinets
BUSINESSCONSULT LAW OFFICE

Galina Syromiadmikova
DICSA INTERNATIONAL GROUP OF LAWYERS

Gennadiy Glinskiy
DICSA INTERNATIONAL GROUP OF LAWYERS

Vitaliy Sevrukevich
DICSA INTERNATIONAL GROUP OF LAWYERS

Olga Podverbnaya
DICSA INTERNATIONAL GROUP OF LAWYERS

Igor Maziarchuk
INSTAR LOGISTICS

Anastasia Bondar
INSTAR LOGISTICS

Eugene Lazarenkov
LAW COMPANY TRUST

Ivan Zhiznevsky
MIKHEL AND PARTNERS

Kanstantsin Mikhel
MIKHEL AND PARTNERS

Ivan Alievich
MIKHEL AND PARTNERS

Andrei Baiko
NATIONAL BANK OF THE REPUBLIC OF BELARUS

Alexander Vasilevsky
VALEX CONSULT

Ekaterina Zabello
VLASOVA AND PARTNERS

Maria Livinska
PRICEWATERHOUSECOOPERS

Svetlana Bilyk
PRICEWATERHOUSECOOPERS

Jorge Intriago
PRICEWATERHOUSECOOPERS

BELGIUM

Sophie Rutten
ALLEN & OVERY

Louis H. Verbeke
ALLEN & OVERY

Dirk de Backer
ALLEN & OVERY

Jan Van Celst
ALLEN & OVERY

Fannia Polet
ALTIUS

Tom Vantroyen
ALTIUS

Carl Meyntjens
ASHURST

David Du Pont
ASHURST

Olivier Debray
CLAEYS & ENGELS, MEMBER OF IUS LABORIS

Isabelle De Stobbeleir
CUSTOMS ADMINISTRATION OF BELGIUM

Stephan Legein
CUSTOMS ADMINISTRATION OF BELGIUM

Hugo Callens
ELEGIS

Tim Roelans
ELEGIS

Ludo Cornelis
EUBELIUS ATTORNEYS

Alain Francois
EUBELIUS ATTORNEYS

Pamela R. Gonzales de Cordova
LOYENS

Dheedene Lode
MAERSK BENELUX

Hubert Andre-Dumont
MCGUIREWOODS LLP

Didier Muraille
NATIONAL BANK OF BELGIUM

Jean Philippe Lebeau
PALAIS DE JUSTICE

Ivan Verougstraete
PALAIS DE JUSTICE

Frank Dierckx
PRICEWATERHOUSECOOPERS

Koen Cooreman
PRICEWATERHOUSECOOPERS

Aurore Mons delle Roche
PRICEWATERHOUSECOOPERS

Luc Legon
PRICEWATERHOUSECOOPERS

Bart Vanham
PRICEWATERHOUSECOOPERS

Pierrette Fraisse
SERVICE PUBLIC FEDERAL FINANCES

Leo Peeters
SIMMONS & SIMMONS

Sandrine Hirsch
SIMONT BRAUN

Steven de Schrijver
VAN BAEL & BELLIS

Marie-Rose Roussety
WORLD CUSTOMS ORGANIZATION

BENIN

Veronique Akankossi Duguenon
CABINET D'AVOCATS AKANKOSSI-DUGUENON

Elisha Victoire
CABINET AGBANRIN-ELISHA VICTOIRE

Alice Codjia-Sohouenou
CABINET AGBANTOU SAIDOU

Saïdou Agbantou
CABINET AGBANTOU SAIDOU

Serge Pognon
CABINET D'AVOCATS A. POGNON

Agnes A. Campbell
CABINET D'AVOCATS CAMPELL & ASSOCIES

Edgar-Yves Monnou
CABINET EDGAR-YVES MONNOU

Rafikou Alabi
CABINET MAÎTRE ALABI

Zachari Baba Body
CABINET SPA BABA BODY QUENUM

Luc-M. C. Gnacadja
IMOTEPH

Jacques Migan
JACQUES MIGAN LAW FIRM

Jean Sourou Agossou
ORDRE NATIONAL DES ARCHITECTES ET URBANISTES

Hans De Lille
SAGA BENIN S.A.

Jacques Chareyre
FIDAFRICA / PRICEWATERHOUSECOOPERS

Dominique Taty
FIDAFRICA / PRICEWATERHOUSECOOPERS

Edouard Messou
FIDAFRICA / PRICEWATERHOUSECOOPERS

Denis Cordel
BOLLORÉ DTI - SDV

Jean Marcel Gariador
BOLLORÉ DTI - SDV

François Nare
CENTRALE DES RISQUES DE L'UNION MONÉTAIRE OUEST AFRICAINE

BHUTAN

Tshering Dorji
UNITED GROUP

Prakash Rasaily
CITY LEGAL UNIT

N. B. Gurung
DHL/GLOBAL PACKERS FORWARDERS AND CLEARING AGENT

Sonam P. Wangdi
MINISTRY OF TRADE & INDUSTRY

Dawa Sherpa
SHERPA CONSULTANCY

BOLIVIA

Pablo Ybarnegaray Ponce
BOLIVIAN CUSTOMS

Milenka Saavedra Muñoz
BUFETE AGUIRRE

Carolina Aguiree Urioste
BUFETE AGUIRRE

Fernando Aguirre
BUFETE AGUIRRE

Carlos Ferreira
C.R. & F. ROJAS*

Diego Rojas
C.R. & F. ROJAS

Alejandra Bernal Mercado
C.R. & F. ROJAS

Paula Bauer Velasco
C.R. & F. ROJAS

Fernando Rojas
C.R. & F. ROJAS

Sandra Salinas
C.R. & F. ROJAS

Manfredo Kempff
C.R. & F. ROJAS

María Eugenia Antezana V.
CRIALES, URCULLO & ANTEZANA

Jose A. Criales
CRIALES, URCULLO & ANTEZANA

Jaime Urcullo Reyes
CRIALES, URCULLO & ANTEZANA

Adrián Barrenechea
Bazoberry
CRIALES, URCULLO & ANTEZANA

Jorge Subirana Castellos
*ENTIDAD DE SERVICIOS DE
INFORMACIÓN ENSERBIC S.A.*

Francisco Bollini Roca
*GUEVARA & GUTIÉRREZ S.C.
SERVICIOS LEGALES*

Primitivo Gutiérrez
*GUEVARA & GUTIÉRREZ S.C.
SERVICIOS LEGALES*

Renato Goitia Machicado
HERMES GROUP

Mariana Pereira Nava
INDACOCHEA & ASOCIADOS

Ricardo Indacochea San
Martin
INDACOCHEA & ASOCIADOS

Ana Maria Luna Yañez
INDEPENDENT

Jorge Paz
INFOCENTER

Miguel Angel Jemio
MORENO-BALDIVIESO

Rodrigo Garrón
MORENO-BALDIVIESO

Maria Cecilia Agreda Gómez
MORENO-BALDIVIESO

Miguel Vertiz
PRICEWATERHOUSECOOPERS

Fabian Rabinovich
PRICEWATERHOUSECOOPERS

Liliana Ching
PRICEWATERHOUSECOOPERS

Cintya Burgoa
PRICEWATERHOUSECOOPERS

A. Mauricio Torrico Galindo
QUINTANILLA & SORIA

Sergio Salazar-Machicado
*SALAZAR & ASOCIADOS, SOC.
CIV*

Enrique Hurtado
*SUPERINTENDENCY OF BANKS
AND FINANCIAL ENTITIES*

BOSNIA AND HERZEGOVINA

Robert Brugger
*PANALPINA WELTTRANSPORT
GMBH*

Kerim Karabdic
*ADVOKATI SALIH & KERIM
KARABDIC*

Branko Maric
BRANKO & VLADIMIR MARIC

Nedzida Salihovic-Whalen
DLA WEISS-TESSBACH

Emir Kovačevič
EMIR KOVACEVIC LAW FIRM

Kemal Jogic
*FEDERAL MINISTRY OF LABOUR
AND SOCIAL POLICY*

Tom Kyriakopoulos
IKRP ROKAS & PARTNERS

Emina Adembegovic
IKRP ROKAS & PARTNERS

Mira Todorovic-Symeonidis
IKRP ROKAS & PARTNERS

Selver Zaimovic
LANSKY & PARTNER ATTORNEYS

Nikola Jankovic
LANSKY, GANZGER & PARTNER

Bojana Tkalcic-Dulic
*LAWYERS' OFFICE TKALCIC-
DULIC & PREBANIC*

Adnan Hrenovica
LRC CREDIT BUREAU

Senada Havic
LRC CREDIT BUREAU

Ruzica Topic
RUZIKA TOPIC

Katerina Carceva
PRICEWATERHOUSECOOPERS

Rudi Lazarevski
PRICEWATERHOUSECOOPERS

BOTSWANA

Angelica Waibale-Muganga
ARMSTRONGS ATTORNEYS*

Neill Armstrong
ARMSTRONGS ATTORNEYS

S. A. Ziga
ARMSTRONGS ATTORNEYS

Kwadwo Osei-Ofei
ARMSTRONGS ATTORNEYS

Sharon Quansah
*CHIBANDA, MAKGALEMELE &
COMPANY*

Mercia Makgalemele
*CHIBANDA, MAKGALEMELE &
COMPANY*

Elizabeth Macharia
*CHIBANDA, MAKGALEMELE &
COMPANY*

Outule Bale
KNIGHT FRANK

Colin McVey
*LANDFLOW SOLUTIONS (PTY)
LTD.*

Edward W. Fashole-Luke II
LUKE & ASSOCIATES

Akheel Jinabhai
MAGANG & COMPANY

Nigel Haynes
MANICA BOTSWANA (PTY) LTD.

Claude Mojafi
*MINISTRY OF LABOUR AND
HOME AFFAIRS*

T.M Bakwena
*MINISTRY OF LABOUR AND
HOME AFFAIRS*

Max Gunasekera
PRICEWATERHOUSECOOPERS

Uttum Corea
PRICEWATERHOUSECOOPERS

Mark Badenhorst
PRICEWATERHOUSECOOPERS

Thata Tshukudu
ROSCOE BONNA VALUERS

Alfred Ngowi
UNIVERSITY OF BOTSWANA

Victor Mesquita
MANICA AFRICA

BRAZIL

Esther Jerussalmy
*ARAÚJO E POLICASTRO
ADVOGADOS*

Alvir Alberto Hoffman
BANCO CENTRAL DO BRASIL

Rodrigo Matos
CARGO LOGISTICS DO BRASIL

Julia Dinamarco
*DEMAREST E ALMEIDA -
ADVOGADOS**

Maria Lucia Silva Mauricio
Costa
*DEMAREST E ALMEIDA -
ADVOGADOS*

Nadine Baleeiro Teixeira
*DEMAREST E ALMEIDA -
ADVOGADOS*

Karina Romano
*DEMAREST E ALMEIDA -
ADVOGADOS*

Monica Arruda de Toledo Piza
*DEMAREST E ALMEIDA -
ADVOGADOS*

Isabel Franco
*DEMAREST E ALMEIDA -
ADVOGADOS*

Altimiro Boscoli
*DEMAREST E ALMEIDA -
ADVOGADOS*

Eliane Ribeiro Gago
*DUARTE GARCIA, CASELLI
GUIMARÃES E TERRA
ADVOGADOS*

Silvia Poggi de Carvalho
*DUARTE GARCIA, CASELLI
GUIMARÃES E TERRA
ADVOGADOS*

Duarte Garcia
*DUARTE GARCIA, CASELLI
GUIMARÃES E TERRA
ADVOGADOS*

Heloisa Bonciani Nader di
Cunto
*DUARTE GARCIA, CASELLI
GUIMARÃES E TERRA
ADVOGADOS*

Pedro Vitor Araujo da Costa
*ESCRITORIO DE ADVOCACIA
GOUVÊA VIEIRA*

Thomas Benes Felsberg
FELSBERG E ASSOCIADOS

Andrea Acerbi
FELSBERG E ASSOCIADOS

Beatriz Ryoko Yamashita
*FISCHER & FORSTER
ADVOGADOS*

Rui Ramos de Oliveira
*INTERCARRIER - TRANSPORTE
INTERNACIONAL LTDA.*

Caio Julius Bolina
LAZZARESCHI ADVOGADOS

Cássio Mesquita Barros
*MESQUITA BARROS ADVOGADOS,
MEMBER OF IUS LABORIS*

Joao Montandon Borges
*MONTANDON BORGES -
ADVOCACIA E CONSULTORIA*

Cacilda Pedrosa Vieira
NASCIMENTO IMOVEIS

Laercio Nascimento
NASCIMENTO IMOVEIS

Marcus Harwardt
PANALPINA LTDA.

Josef Zech
PANALPINA LTDA.

Carlos Iacia
PRICEWATERHOUSECOOPERS

Leonardo Soares de Oliveira
*SECRETARIA DE INSPECAO DO
TRABALHO*

Tania Mara Coelho de
Almeida Costa
*SECRETARIA DE INSPECAO DO
TRABALHO*

Ricardo Loureiro
SERASA S.A.

Paulo Sergio Vaz Pedro
TRANSCARGO INTERNACIONAL

Marcos Tiraboschi
*VEIRANO ADVOGADOS
ASSOCIADOS*

Flavia Bailone Marcilio
*VEIRANO ADVOGADOS
ASSOCIADOS*

Maria Fernanda Pecora
*VEIRANO ADVOGADOS
ASSOCIADOS*

Andrea Oricchio Kirsh
*VISEU, CASTRO, CUNHA E
ORICCHIO ADVOGADOS*

Adriano Borges
*VISEU, CASTRO, CUNHA E
ORICCHIO ADVOGADOS*

Andrea Francolin
*VISEU, CASTRO, CUNHA E
ORICCHIO ADVOGADOS*

Andrea Pulici
*VISEU, CASTRO, CUNHA E
ORICCHIO ADVOGADOS*

BULGARIA

Dessislava Loukarova
ARSIV, NATCHEV, GANEVA

Vladimir Natchev
ARSIV, NATCHEV, GANEVA

Yordan Naydenov
BORISLAV BOYANOV & CO.

Georgi Kalinov
BORISLAV BOYANOV & CO.

Jordan Manahilov
BULGARIAN NATIONAL BANK

George Dimitrov
DIMITROV, PETROV & CO.

Kalina Tchakarova
*DJINGOV, GOUGINSKI,
KYUTCHUKOV & VELICHKOV*

Marius A. Velichkov
*DJINGOV, GOUGINSKI,
KYUTCHUKOV & VELICHKOV*

Stefaniya Nikolova
*DJINGOV, GOUGINSKI,
KYUTCHUKOV & VELICHKOV*

Stephan Kyutchukov
*DJINGOV, GOUGINSKI,
KYUTCHUKOV & VELICHKOV*

Jasmina Uzova
*DJINGOV, GOUGINSKI,
KYUTCHUKOV & VELICHKOV*

Alexander Georgiev
*DOBREV, KINKIN, LYUTSKANOV
& PARTNERS*

Darina Oresharova
EXPERIAN-SCOREX BULGARIA

Dimitar Danailov
GEORGIEV, TODOROV & CO.

Alexander Pachamanov
GEORGIEV, TODOROV & CO.

Marina Marinova
GEORGIEV, TODOROV & CO.

Bogdan Drenski
GEORGIEV, TODOROV & CO.

Stefan Tzakov
KAMBOUROV & PARTNERS

Dessislava Fessenko
KAMBOUROV & PARTNERS

Polina Ganeva
LANDWELL BULGARIA

Ivan Markov
*LEGA INTERCONSULT - PENKOV,
MARKOV AND PARTNERS**

Svetlin Adrianov
*LEGA INTERCONSULT - PENKOV,
MARKOV AND PARTNERS*

Vladimir Penkov
*LEGA INTERCONSULT - PENKOV,
MARKOV AND PARTNERS*

Svilen Todorov
LEGACOM ANTOV & PARTNERS

Totju Mladenov
*MINISTRY OF LABOUR AND
SOCIAL POLICY*

Irina Tsvetkova
PRICEWATERHOUSECOOPERS

Krasimir Merdzhov
PRICEWATERHOUSECOOPERS

Mina Kapsazova
PRICEWATERHOUSECOOPERS

Ginka Iskrova
PRICEWATERHOUSECOOPERS

Radostina Krasteva
PRICEWATERHOUSECOOPERS

Nikolai Bozhilov
UNIMASTERS LOGISTICS GROUP

BURKINA FASO

Hamidou Savadogo
*CABINET D'AVOCATS HAMIDOU
SAVADOGO*

Marie Ouedraogo
BARREAU DU BURKINA FASO

Barthélémy Kere
CABINET D'AVOCATS
BARTHÉLÉMY KERE

Titinga Frédéric Pacere
CABINET D'AVOCATS TITINGA
FREDERIC PACERE

Jean-Pierre Bassole
CABINET D'AVOCATS TITINGA
FREDERIC PACERE

Mamadou Savadogo
CABINET D'AVOCATS MAMADOU
SAVADOGO

Farima Diarra
CABINET FARIMA DIARRA

Anna T. Ouattara-Sory
CABINET MAÎTRE PAULIN
SALAMBÉRÉ

Dieudonne Bonkoungou
CABINET OUEDRAOGO &
BONKOUNGOU

Oumarou Ouedraogo
CABINET OUEDRAOGO &
BONKOUNGOU

Evelyne Mandessi Bell
CABINET OUEDRAOGO &
BONKOUNGOU

Gilles Yameogo
CABINET YAMEOGO

Ignace Sawadogo
CICAD

Bernardin Dabire
DABIRE SORGHO & TOE

Frank Didier Toe
DABIRE SORGHO & TOE

Barterlé Mathieu Some
LAWYER

Thierry Compaore
ORDRE NATIONAL DES
ARCHITECTES DU BURKINA FASO

Messan Lawson
SNTB SAGA - BOLLORE GROUP

Bouba Yaguibou
YAGUIBOU & YANOGO

Jacques Chareyre
FIDAFRICA /
PRICEWATERHOUSECOOPERS

Dominique Taty
FIDAFRICA /
PRICEWATERHOUSECOOPERS

Edouard Messou
FIDAFRICA /
PRICEWATERHOUSECOOPERS

Denis Cordel
BOLLORÉ DTI - SDV

Jean Marcel Gariador
BOLLORÉ DTI - SDV

BURUNDI

François Nyamoya
CABINET D'AVOCATS FRANÇOIS
NYAMOYA

Gabriel Sinarinzi
CABINET D'AVOCATS GABRIEL
SINARINZI

Yves Ntivumbura
BANQUE DE LA RÉPUBLIQUE DU
BURUNDI

Severin Kagabo
BANQUE DE LA RÉPUBLIQUE DU
BURUNDI

Rubeya Willy
BARREAU DU BURUNDI

Anatole Miburo
CABINET ANATOLE MIBURO

Tharcisse Ntakiyica
CABINET THARCISSE NTAKIYICA

Fabien Segatwa
ETUDE MAÎTRE SEGATWA

Sylvestre Banzubaze
S&P BANZUBAZE - CABINET
D'AVOCATS

Salvator Sindayihebura
SDV TRANSAMI - GROUPE
BOLLORE

Antoine Ntsigana
SODETRA LTD.

Denis Cordel
BOLLORÉ DTI - SDV

Jean Marcel Gariador
BOLLORÉ DTI - SDV

CAMBODIA

Seakirin Neak
B.N.G. - ADVOCATES &
SOLICITORS

Naryth H. Hem
B.N.G. - ADVOCATES &
SOLICITORS

Ouk Ry
BOU NOU OUK & PARTNERS

Rot Mony Rath
CAMBODIAN CONSTRUCTION
WORKERS TRADE UNION
FEDERATON

Tyseng Ly
DFDL MEKONG LAW GROUP

Esther Lau
DFDL MEKONG LAW GROUP

Edward Nicholas
DFDL MEKONG LAW GROUP

Avy Kong Putheavy
DIRKSEN FLIPSE DORAN & LE

Rany Chung
FIDES SERVICES CAMBODIA

David King
KPMG CAMBODIA

Ham Phea
MINISTRY OF LABOR AND
VOCATIONAL TRAINING

Jean Loi
PRICEWATERHOUSECOOPERS

Ngov Chong
PRICEWATERHOUSECOOPERS

Richard Irwin
PRICEWATERHOUSECOOPERS

Denora Sarin
SARIN & ASSOCIATES

Matthew Rendall
SCIARONI & ASSOCIATES

Christine Soutif
SDV CAMBODGE LTD.

Janvibol Tip
TIP & PARTNERS

Ang Udom
UDOM LAW CHAMBERS

CAMEROON

Roland Abeng
ABENG LAW FIRM

Jean Aimet Kounga
ABENG LAW FIRM

Idrissou
BEAC - HEADQUARTERS

Pierre Talom
BEAC - HEADQUARTERS

Emmanuel Ekobo
CABINET EKOBO

Isabelle Fomukong
CABINET FOMUKONG

Pierre Henri Makon
CABINET PIERRE HENRI MAKON
(MAPIH - CONSEIL)

Ernestine Mbong Samba
ETA BESONG LAW CHAMBERS

D. Etah Akoh
ETAH-NAN & C. SOCIÉTÉ
D'AVOCATS, BARRISTERS &
SOLICITORS

Jean-Jacques Kotto
GAA - GROUPEMENT
D'ARCHITECTES AFRICAINS

Jacques Kuete
GENERAL ADMINISTRATION
OF CUSTOMS

Feh H. Baaboh
HENRY SAMUELSON & CO.

Paul Jing
JING & PARTNERS

David Boyo
JING & PARTNERS

Kumfa Jude Kwenyui
JURIS CONSUL LAW FIRM

Uffe Doessing Andreasen
MAERSK CAMEROUN SA

Christian O'Jeanson
MAERSK CAMEROUN SA

Tognia Djanko
ORDRE NATIONAL DES
ARCHITECTES DU CAMEROUN

Buergi Marcel
PANALPINA WORLD TRANSPORT
LTD.

Eric Melet
SDV CAMEROON

Jacques Chareyre
FIDAFRICA / ERS

CANADA

Leonid Gorelik
BAKER & MCKENZIE

Pamela S. Hughes
BLAKE, CASSELS & GRAYDON*

Paul Schabas
BLAKE, CASSELS & GRAYDON

Courtney Harris
BLAKE, CASSELS & GRAYDON

Erica Young
BLAKE, CASSELS & GRAYDON

Jason Koskela
BLAKE, CASSELS & GRAYDON

Dera Nevin
BLAKE, CASSELS & GRAYDON

David Epstein
GARDINER ROBERTS

Yoine Goldstein
GOLDSTEIN FLANZ & FISHMAN

David Bish
GOODMANS LLP

Jay A. Carfagnini
GOODMANS LLP

Mathias Link
HEENAN BLAIKIE LLP, MEMBER
OF IUS LABORIS

John Craig
HEENAN BLAIKIE LLP, MEMBER
OF IUS LABORIS

Gian Fortuna
KENAIDAN CONTRACTING LTD.

Paul Avis
MCMILLAN BINCH LLP

Shelley Munro
OSLER, HOSKIN & HARCOURT
LLP

Susan Clifford
OSLER, HOSKIN & HARCOURT
LLP

Michael Davies
OSLER, HOSKIN & HARCOURT
LLP

Uwe Wicke
PANALPINA IND.

Richard Marcovitz
PRICEWATERHOUSECOOPERS

Michael S. Bondy
PRICEWATERHOUSECOOPERS

Grace Lee
PRICEWATERHOUSECOOPERS

Larry Chapman
PRICEWATERHOUSECOOPERS

Melanie N. Laskey
PRICEWATERHOUSECOOPERS

Heather Paterson
SHIBLEY RIGHTON LLP

Harris M. Rosen
SHIBLEY RIGHTON LLP

Karen Grant
TRANSUNION

**CENTRAL AFRICAN
REPUBLIC**

Pierre Talom
BEAC - HEADQUARTERS

Jean Noel Bangue

Sylvia Pauline Yawet
Kengueleoua
BARREAU DE LA RÉPUBLIQUE
CENTRAFRICAINE

Maurice Dibert- Dollet
MINISTÈRE DE LA JUSTICE,
MAÎTRE NDENGOU

Emile Bizon
NICOLAS TIANGAYE LAW FIRM

Noel Kelembho
SDV CENTRAFRIQUE - GROUPE
BOLLORE

Denis Cordel
SDV CENTRAFRIQUE - GROUPE
BOLLORE

Jean Marcel Gariador
SDV CENTRAFRIQUE - GROUPE
BOLLORE

CHAD

Pierre Talom
BEAC - HEADQUARTERS

Nathé Amady
BAKER & MCKENZIE, WONG &
LEOW

Thomas Dingamgoto
CABINET THOMAS DINGAMGOTO

Jacques Chareyre
FIDAFRICA /
PRICEWATERHOUSECOOPERS

Matthias Hubert
FIDAFRICA /
PRICEWATERHOUSECOOPERS

Gerard Leclaire
INGÉNIERIE & ARCHITECTURE

Charles Ngueyara
MOSCOW INTERBANK CURRENCY
EXCHANGE

Bechir Madet
OFFICE NOTARIAL

Sobdibe Zoua
SCI PADARE

CHILE

Alfonso Reymond Larrain
ALDUNATE Y CIA ABOGADOS

Fernando Jamarne
ALESSANDRI & COMPAÑIA

Camilo Cortés
ALESSANDRI & COMPAÑIA

Andrés Jana Linetzky
ALVAREZ, HINZPETER, JANA &
VALLE

Leon Larrain
BAKER & MCKENZIE

Cristián Boetsch
BAKER & MCKENZIE

Eduardo Torreti
BARROS COURT & CORREA

Daniela Peña Fergadiott
BARROS COURT & CORREA

Miguel Capo Valdez
BESALCO S.A.

Claudio Ortiz Tello
BOLETIN COMERCIAL

Carmen Paz Cruz Lozano
CAMARA CHILENA DE LA
CONSTRUCCION

Fernando Echeverria
CAMARA CHILENA DE LA
CONSTRUCCION

Alejandra Mejía G.
CAREY Y CIA LAW FIRM

Ricardo Escobar
CAREY Y CIA LAW FIRM

Jeronimo Carcelen
CARIOLA DIEZ PEREZ-COPATOS
& CIA

Sebastian Obach
CARIOLA DIEZ PEREZ-COPATOS
& CIA

Juan Pablo Matus
CARIOLA DIEZ PEREZ-COPATOS
& CIA

Juan Esteban Montero
CARIOLA DIEZ PEREZ-COPATOS
& CIA

Felipe Ossa
CLARO & CIA.*

Cristian Eyzaguirre
CLARO & CIA.

Ricardo Riesco
CLARO & CIA.

Edmundo Rojas García
CONSERVADOR DE BIENES RAICES
DE SANTIAGO

Silvio Figari Napoli
DATABUSINESS

María Ester Feres Nazarala
DIRECCIÓN DEL TRABAJO,
MINISTERIO DEL TRABAJO Y DE
PREVISIÓN SOCIAL

Jimena Bronfman
GUERRERO, OLIVOS NOVOA Y
ERRAZURIZ

Sebastián Yunge
GUERRERO, OLIVOS NOVOA Y ERRAZURIZ

Diego Ramirez
PANALPINA CHILE

Sebastian Diaz
PRICEWATERHOUSECOOPERS

María Eugenia Sandoval Gouet
PRICEWATERHOUSECOOPERS

Roberto Carlos Rivas
PRICEWATERHOUSECOOPERS

Hector Carrasco Reyes
SUPERINTENDENCIA DE BANCOS E INSTITUCIONES FINANCIERAS

Enrique Benitez Urrutia
URRUTIA & CIA

Jorge Benitez Urrutia
URRUTIA & CIA

Juan Eduardo Palma Jr.
VIAL Y PALMA ABOGADOS

Martín del Río
VIAL Y PALMA ABOGADOS

CHINA

Rico Chan
BAKER & MCKENZIE

Brian Barron
BAKER & MCKENZIE

Alexander Gong
BAKER & MCKENZIE

Wei Lei
CHEN & CO.

Ye Hong
COUDERT BROTHERS - BEIJING

Jie Tang
COUDERT BROTHERS - BEIJING

Han Shen
DAVIS POLK & WARDWELL

Li Wang
DEHENG LAW OFFICE

Kejun Guo
DEHENG LAW OFFICE

He Jun
DEHENG LAW OFFICE

Hongli Ma
*JUN HE LAW OFFICE**

Li Leon
JUN HE LAW OFFICE

Linfei Liu
JUN HE LAW OFFICE

Yingdong Wang
JUN HE LAW OFFICE

Jin Zhong
JUN HE LAW OFFICE

Yanjua Rebecca Chao
JUN HE LAW OFFICE

Tianpeng Wang
KING AND WOOD PRC LAWYERS

Harry Duprey
KING AND WOOD PRC LAWYERS

Hanzhou Huang
KONFILL SHIPPING CO. LTD.

Rocky Qian
LEHMAN, LEE & XU

Edward E. Lehman
LEHMAN, LEE & XU

Jack Zhu
MAERSK (CHINA) SHIPPING CO. LTD., XIAMEN BRANCH

Ive Van Nuffelen
PANALPINA CHINA LTD.

Zhang Hongsheng
PEOPLE'S BANK OF CHINA

Xiaochuan Yang
PRICEWATERHOUSECOOPERS

Rex Chan
PRICEWATERHOUSECOOPERS

Maggie Jiang
PRICEWATERHOUSECOOPERS

Cassie Wong
PRICEWATERHOUSECOOPERS

Sharon Wang
THROUGHWAY LOGISTICS(SHANGHAI) CO. LTD.

COLOMBIA

Juan Pablo Moreno-Piñeros
*BRIGARD & URRUTIA**

Carlos Urrutia Jr.
BRIGARD & URRUTIA

Bernardo Salazar
BRIGARD & URRUTIA

Pablo Barraquer-Uprimny
BRIGARD & URRUTIA

Carlos Fradique-Méndez
BRIGARD & URRUTIA

Carlos Umaña
BRIGARD & URRUTIA

Margarita Llorente
BRIGARD & URRUTIA

Dario Cardenas Navas
CARDENAS & CARDENAS

Gabriela Mancero
CAVELIER ABOGADOS

Natalia Tobón
CAVELIER ABOGADOS

Leonardo Calderón
COLEGIO DE REGISTRADORES DE INSTRUMENTOS PÚBLICOS DE COLOMBIA

Juan Pablo Ortiz Bravo
COLOMBIAN CUSTOMS

Juan Manuel Villaveces Hollmann
COMPUTEC - DATACRÉDITO

Ignacio Durán
COMPUTEC - DATACRÉDITO

Paula Samper Salazar
GÓMEZ-PINZÓN ABOGADOS

Patricia Arrázola Bustillo
GOMEZ-PINZON LINARES SAMPER SUAREZ VILLAMIL

Felipe Sandoval Villamil
GOMEZ-PINZON LINARES SAMPER SUAREZ VILLAMIL

Jinni Pastrana
JOSÉ LLOREDA CAMACHO & CO.

Enrique Alvarez
JOSÉ LLOREDA CAMACHO & CO.

Gustavo Tamayo
JOSÉ LLOREDA CAMACHO & CO.

Santiago Gutiérrez
JOSÉ LLOREDA CAMACHO & CO.

Mónica Rolong
JOSÉ LLOREDA CAMACHO & CO.

Camilo Cortés Guarín
LEWIN & WILLS, ABOGADOS

Luis E. Nieto
NIETO & CHALELA ABOGADOS

Olga Lucia Ruiz
PANALPINA S.A.

Rodrigo Prieto Martinez
PINILLA, GONZÁLEZ & PRIETO

Felipe Arbouin
PINILLA, GONZÁLEZ & PRIETO

Carlos Felipe Pinilla Acevedo
PINILLA, GONZÁLEZ & PRIETO

Carlos Lafaurie
PRICEWATERHOUSECOOPERS

Jean Pierre Lenaerts
PRICEWATERHOUSECOOPERS

Javier Gonzalez
PRICEWATERHOUSECOOPERS

Lucero Rodriguez
PRICEWATERHOUSECOOPERS

Antonio Jose Lafaurie
PRICEWATERHOUSECOOPERS

Juan Carlos Rocha
PRIETO & CARRIZOSA S.A.

Felipe Cuberos
PRIETO & CARRIZOSA S.A.

Cristina Rueda
RAISBECK, LARA, RODRIGUEZ & RUEDA affiliate of BAKER & MCKENZIE

Jorge Lara
RAISBECK, LARA, RODRIGUEZ & RUEDA affiliate of BAKER & MCKENZIE

Gustavo Flores
SOCIEDAD PORTUARIA REGIONAL DE CARTAGENA

Jaime Robledo-Vasquez
ZULETA SUAREZ ARAQUE & JARAMILLO ABOGADOS

Gustavo Suárez Camacho
ZULETA SUAREZ ARAQUE & JARAMILLO ABOGADOS

CONGO, DEM. REP.

G. Le Dourain
AGETRAF SDV RD CONGO GROUPE BOLLORÉ

R. Rigo
GTS EXPRESS

Babala Man Gala
GTS EXPRESS

Paul Kabongo Tshibangu
CABINET PAUL KABONGO

David Guarnieri
FIDAFRICA / PRICEWATERHOUSECOOPERS

Jacques Chareyre
FIDAFRICA / PRICEWATERHOUSECOOPERS

Leon Nzimbi
FIDAFRICA / PRICEWATERHOUSECOOPERS

Fabienne De Greef
CABINET D'AVOCATS FABIENNE DE GREEF

Bernard Claude
CABINET DE MAÎTRE MBU NE LETANG

Jean Claude Mbaki Siluzaku
CABINET MBAKI ET ASSOCIÉS

Marie-Antoinette Mbombo Ngoyi
CABINET MBOMBO

Louman Mpoy
CABINET ML & A

Jacques Munday
CABINET NTOTO

Ambroise Kamukuny
CABINET TSHIBANGU ET ASSOCIES

Lambert S. Djunga
DJUNGA & RISASI

CONGO, REP.

Philippe Jarry
SAGA CONGO - BOLLORE GROUP

Denis Cordel
SDV - BOLLORÉ DTI

Jean Marcel Gariador
SDV - BOLLORÉ DTI

Jean Petro
CABINET D'AVOCATS JEAN PETRO

Jean-Philippe Esseau
CABINET ESSEAU

Gerard Devillers
CABINET GERARD DEVILLERS

Françoise Mpongo
CABINET MPONGO

COSTA RICA

Silvia Chacon Bolanos
ALFREDO FOURNIER & ASOCIADOS

Carlos Ayon Lacayo
ALFREDO FOURNIER & ASOCIADOS

Octavio Fournier
ALFREDO FOURNIER & ASOCIADOS

Alfredo Fournier Beeche
ALFREDO FOURNIER & ASOCIADOS

Roger Petersen
ALLIANCE LAW GROUP, SRL

Luis Manuel Castro
BLP ABOGADOS

Mariano Jimenez
BLP ABOGADOS

Eduardo Calderón
BUFETE FACIO & CAÑAS

Manuel Gonzalez Sanz
BUFETE FACIO & CAÑAS

Rodrigo Oreamuno
BUFETE FACIO & CAÑAS

Kathya Araya
BUFETE FACIO & CAÑAS

Tomás F. Guardia
BUFETE FACIO & CAÑAS

Alejandro Bettoni Traube
DONINELLI & DONINELLI - ASESORES JURÍDICOS ASOCIADOS

Mario Quintana
DONINELLI & DONINELLI - ASESORES JURÍDICOS ASOCIADOS

Frederico Peralta
*FACIO & CAÑAS**

Carlos Urrego Silva
INDUSTRIAS SAFRAN SA

Daniel de LaGarza
J. DE CANO ESTUDIO LEGAL

Walter Anderson Salomons
JAPDEVA - PORT LIMON

Abraham Stern
LEXINCORP

Ivannia Méndez Rodríguez
OLLER ABOGADOS

Adrián Obando Agüero
OLLER ABOGADOS

Pedro Oller
OLLER ABOGADOS

Freddy Fachler
PACHECO COTO

Alejandro Antillon
PACHECO COTO

Ramon Ortega
PRICEWATERHOUSECOOPERS

Alejandro Fernandez
PRICEWATERHOUSECOOPERS

Victor Andrés Gómez
PRICEWATERHOUSECOOPERS

Ludovino Colón Sánchez
PRICEWATERHOUSECOOPERS

Dagoberto Sibaja Morales
REGISTRO NACIONAL DE COSTA RICA

Eduardo Montoya Solano
SUPERINTENDENCIA GENERAL DE ENTIDADES FINANCIERAS

Luis Monge Sancho
TELETEC

Mainor Quesada
TELETEC

Alex Grossmann
PANALPINA

COTE D'IVOIRE

Patricia N'guessan
CABINET JEAN-FRANÇOIS CHAUVEAU

Jean-François Chauveau
CABINET JEAN-FRANÇOIS CHAUVEAU

Nadia Vanie
CABINET N'GOAN, ASMAN & ASSOCIÉS

Georges N'Goan
CABINET N'GOAN, ASMAN & ASSOCIÉS

Jean-Pierre Elisha
ELISHA & ASSOCIÉS

Nathalie Assou
ELISHA & ASSOCIÉS

Colette Kacoutie
FADIKA-DELAFOSSE-KACOUTIE ANTHONY

Simon Silue Dognima
FADIKA-DELAFOSSE-KACOUTIE ANTHONY

Jacques Chareyre
FIDAFRICA / PRICEWATERHOUSECOOPERS

Dominique Taty
FIDAFRICA / PRICEWATERHOUSECOOPERS

Edouard Messou
FIDAFRICA / PRICEWATERHOUSECOOPERS

Alice Anthony-Diomande
M. FADIKA-DELAFOSSE, K. FADIKA ET C. KACOUTIÉ

Fadika Karim
M. FADIKA-DELAFOSSE, K. FADIKA ET C. KACOUTIÉ

Léon Désiré Zalo
MINISTÈRE D'ETAT, MINISTÈRE DE L'AGRICULTURE

Jerome Beseme
SAGA CI

Ghislane Moise - Bazie
SCPA Konate, Moise-Bazie & Koyo

Gerard Kone Dogbenin
SCPA Nambeya-Dogbemin et Associés

Denis Cordel
Bolloré DTI

Jean Marcel Gariador
Bolloré DTI

François Nare
Centrale des Risques de l'Union Monétaire Ouest Africaine

CROATIA

Robert Brugger
Panalpina Welttransport GmbH

Stefan Stockinger
Wolf Theiss

Zoran Bohacek
Croatian Banking Association

Dunja Hitrec
Ernst & Young

Eugen Zadravec
Eugen Zadravec Law Firm

Marijan Hanzekovic
*Hanzekovic & Radakovic**

Lidija Hanzek
HROK

Stefanija Cukman
Juric Law Offices

Sanja Juric
Juric Law Offices

Marija Haramija
Korper & Haramija

Irina Jelcic Hüsein
Law Firm Hanzekovic, Radakovic & Partners

Hrvoje Vidan
Law Office Vidan, in cooperation with Wolf Theiss

Zvonko Nogolica
Law Offices Nogolica

Fran Marovic
Ministry of Economy, Labour and Entrepreneurship

Zlatko Grabar
Ministry of Finance

Margita Kis
Porobija & Porobija Law Firm

Iva Torik
Porobija & Porobija Law Firm

Sanja Porobija
Porobija & Porobija Law Firm

Iain McGuire
PricewaterhouseCoopers

Tatjana Arapinac
PricewaterhouseCoopers

Gordan Rotkvič
PricewaterhouseCoopers

Ivo Bijelič
PricewaterhouseCoopers

Mirna Kette
PricewaterhouseCoopers

Ana Sihtar
Sihtar Attorneys at Law

Lidija Stopfer
Vukmir Law Office

Tarja Krehic-Duranovic
Wolf Theiss

Bojan Fras
Žurič i Partneri

Ivan Vukas
Žurič i Partneri

Beata Glinska Kovac
Žurič i Partneri

CZECH REPUBLIC

Miroslava Kybalova
Ambruz & Dark advokati v.o.s.

Libor Basl
Baker & McKenzie

Andrea Korpasova
Baker & McKenzie

Jana Muchyova
Baker & McKenzie

Petr Kucera
CCB - Czech banking Credit Bureau

Jarmila Musilova
Czech National Bank

Jörg Nürnberger
DLA Weiss-Tessbach

Vít Horáček
Glatzová & Co. Law Offices Prague

Katerina Wlodarczykova
Glatzová & Co. Law Offices Prague

Růžena Trojánková
Linklaters & Alliance

Ludek Vrána
Linklaters & Alliance

Martina Pavelkova
Panalpina Czech s.r.o.

Robert Brugger
Panalpina Welttransport GmbH

Vladimir Ambruz
Peterka & Partners v.o.s.

Pavla Prikrylova
Peterka & Partners v.o.s.

Gabriela Hájková
Peterka & Partners v.o.s.

Jiri Cerny
Peterka & Partners v.o.s.

David Hora
PricewaterhouseCoopers

Tomas Liptak
PricewaterhouseCoopers

Lenka Mrazova
PricewaterhouseCoopers

Stephen B. Booth
PricewaterhouseCoopers

Martin Divis
PricewaterhouseCoopers

Natasa Randlová
Procházka Randl Kubr, *member of Ius Laboris*

Sarka Jandova
Procházka Randl Kubr, member of Ius Laboris

Jarmila Hanzalova
Procházka Randl Kubr, member of Ius Laboris

Daniel Rosicky
Procházka Randl Kubr, member of Ius Laboris

Jarmila Bilkova
Procházka Randl Kubr, member of Ius Laboris

Dagmar Novakova
Procházka Randl Kubr, member of Ius Laboris

Zdenek Rosicky
Squire, Sanders & Dempsey

Michal Koranda
Vejmelka & Wünsch

Erik Steger
Wolf Theiss

DENMARK

Ole Borch
Bech-Bruun Dragsted Law Firm

Ulla Trolle
Central Customs and Tax Administration

Jonas Bøgelund
Gorrissen Federspiel Kierkegaard

Mogens Ebeling
Jonas Bruun

Christian Andersen
Jonas Bruun

Christian Guldmann
*Kromann Reumert**

Louise Krarup Simonsen
Kromann Reumert

Mette Hedelund Thomasen
Kromann Reumert

Jørgen B. Jepsen
Kromann Reumert

Henrik Stenbjerre
Kromann Reumert

Jeppe Buskov
Kromann Reumert

Jørgen Kjærgaard Madsen
Kromann Reumert

Kurt Skovlund
Kromann Reumert

Jens Steen Jensen
Kromann Reumert

Knud Villemoes Hansen
National Survey and Cadastre - Denmark / Kort-og Matrikelstyrelsen

Elsebeth Aaes-Jørgensen
Norbom & Vinding, member of Ius Laboris

Thomas Olsen
Panalpina Denmark

Jakob Hüttel Larsen
Philip & Partnere

Claus Kaare Pedersen
Philip & Partnere

Eivind Einersen
Philip & Partnere

Mikael Stenstrup
PricewaterhouseCoopers

Carsten Melgaard
PricewaterhouseCoopers

Anette Henriksen
PricewaterhouseCoopers

Karin L. Nielsen
PricewaterhouseCoopers

Arne Gehring
PricewaterhouseCoopers

Torben Wolsted
PricewaterhouseCoopers

Bente Skovgaard Risvig
RKI Kredit Information A/S (Experian Denmark)

Joern S. Hansen
RKI Kredit Information A/S (Experian Denmark)

DOMINICAN REPUBLIC

Cecilio Santana Silvestre
Juan Suero
Aaron Suero & Pedersini

José Antonio Logroño Morales
Adams Guzman & Asociados

Pablo Gonzalez Tapia
Biaggi & Messina

Maria Portes
Castillo y Castillo

Praxedes J. Castillo Baez
Castillo y Castillo

Juan C. Miranda
Covadonga

Xavier Marra
Dhimes & Marra

Fabio Guzman
Guzman Ariza

Sarah de León
Headrick Rizik Alvarez & Fernandez

Claudia Roca
Headrick Rizik Alvarez & Fernandez

Wilfredo Senior
Headrick Rizik Alvarez & Fernandez

Mary Fernández Rodríguez
Headrick Rizik Alvarez & Fernandez

Juan Carlos De Moya Chico
Langa & Abinader

Carolina Almonte
Maersk Dominicana

Philippe Lescuras
Panalpina

Hipolito Herrera V.
*Pellerano & Herrera**

Luis Pellerano
Pellerano & Herrera

Eduardo Trueba
Pellerano & Herrera

Flavia Baez de George
Pellerano & Herrera

Ludovino Colón Sánchez
PricewaterhouseCoopers

Alejandro Fernandez
PricewaterhouseCoopers

Ramon Ortega
PricewaterhouseCoopers

Robinson Cuello Shanlate
Programa de Modernización de la Jurisdicción de Tierras

Armando P. Henriquez
Steel Hector Davis Peña Prieto & Gamundi, Ltd.

Joanna M. Bonnelly Ginebra
Steel Hector Davis Peña Prieto & Gamundi, Ltd.

Luis Andres Montes De Oca
Superintendencia de Bancos

Elisa Pimentel
Superintendencia de Bancos

Wilson Gomez Ramirez
Suprema Corte de Justicia

Wendy Sanchez
Transunion

ECUADOR

Mauricio Acosta
ACOS

Diego Cabezas-Klaere
Cabezas & Cabezas-Klaere

Ines Baldeon
Consultores Estrategicos Asociados

Xavier Amador Pino
Estidio Juridico Amador

Ricardo Velasco Cuesta
Fabara & Compañia Abogados

Maria de los Angeles Roman
Fabara & Compañia Abogados

Lucía Cordero-Ledergerber
Falconi Puig Abogados

Falconi Puig
Falconi Puig Abogados

Juan Carlos Gallegos
Gallegos & Valarezo

Paulina Montesdeoca De Bustamante
Macias Hurtado & Macias

Carlos Enriquez
MODA

Heinz Moeller Freile
Moeller, Gómez-Lince & Cia

Jose Duran
Moeller, Gómez-Lince & Cia

Santiago Terán Muñoz
Moeller, Gómez-Lince & Cia

Fernando Coral
Panalpina

Jorge Paz Durini
Paz & Horowitz

Sandra Reed
*Pérez Bustamente & Ponce**

Jacob R. Hidrowoh
Pérez, Bustamante y Ponce

Hernan Santacruz
Pérez, Bustamante y Ponce

Jose Rumazo Arcos
Pérez, Bustamante y Ponce

Rodrigo Jijon
Pérez, Bustamante y Ponce

José M. Pérez
Pérez, Bustamante y Ponce

Silvia Hidalgo-Pallares
Pérez, Bustamante y Ponce

Bruno Pineda-Cordero
Pérez, Bustamante y Ponce

Juan Manuel Marchan
Pérez, Bustamante y Ponce

Luciano Almeida
PricewaterhouseCoopers

Pablo Aguirre
PricewaterhouseCoopers

Rodrigo Espinosa
Superintendencia de Bancos e Seguros

Miriam Rosales
SUPERINTENDENCIA DE BANCOS E SEGUROS

EGYPT

Adel Kheir
ADEL KHEIR LAW OFFICE

Abdel Aal Aly
AFIFI WORLD TRANSPORT

Maha Hassan
AFIFI WORLD TRANSPORT

Egyptian Customs Authority
Claude Huet
PANALPINA

Karim Adel Kamel
ADEL KAMEL & ASSOCIATES

Tarek El-Marsafawy
ADEL KAMEL & ASSOCIATES

Nabila Mohamed Habashy Ali
CENTRAL BANK OF EGYPT

Yehia H El Bably
EL BABLY LAW FIRM

Ashraf Elibrachy
IBRACHY & DERMARKAR

Ingy Rasekh
MENA ASSOCIATES

Reinhard Klarmann
MENA ASSOCIATES

Sadeyaa Ibrahim
MINISTRY OF MANPOWER AND MIGRATION

Alaa Amer
MINISTRY OF MANPOWER AND MIGRATION

Samir El Tagy
MINISTRY OF MANPOWER AND MIGRATION

Ashraf Nadoury
NADOURY & NAHAS LAW OFFICES

Ahmed Abdel Reheem
NADOURY & NAHAS LAW OFFICES

Amr ElMonayer
PRICEWATERHOUSECOOPERS / MANSOUR & CO.

Mohamed Fahim
PRICEWATERHOUSECOOPERS / MANSOUR & CO.

Heather Carpenter
PRICEWATERHOUSECOOPERS / MANSOUR & CO.

Sherif Mansour
PRICEWATERHOUSECOOPERS / MANSOUR & CO.

Rania Bata
SARWAT A. SHAHID LAW FIRM

Girgis Abd El-Shahid
SARWAT A. SHAHID LAW FIRM

Mahmoud Shedid
SHALAKANY LAW OFFICE*

Mohamed Serry
SHALAKANY LAW OFFICE

Mona Zulficar
SHALAKANY LAW OFFICE

Sara Hinton
TROWERS & HAMLINS

Daniel MacSweeney
TROWERS & HAMLINS

Stephan Jäger
KRAUSS AMERELLER HENKENBORG

EL SALVADOR

Maria Eugenia Olmedo de Castaneda
ACZALAW

Monica Guadalupe Pineda Machuca
ACZALAW

Francisco Eduardo Portillo
COMISIÓN EJECUTIVA PORTUARIA AUTÁNOMA

Ricardo A. Cevallos
DELGADO & CEVALLOS

Carlos Oviedo
DELGADO & CEVALLOS

Danilo Rodríguez Villamil
ESPINO, NIETO, UMAÑA & ASSOCIADOS

Luis Miguel Espino
ESPINO, NIETO, UMAÑA & ASSOCIADOS

Francisco Armando Arias Rivera
F.A. ARIAS & MUÑOZ

Roberta Gallardo
F.A. ARIAS & MUÑOZ

Juan Carlos Herrera
F.A. ARIAS & MUÑOZ

Miriam Eleana Mixco Reyna
GOLD SERVICE S.A. DE C.V.

Mauricio Melhado
GOLD SERVICE S.A. DE C.V.

Ana Patricia Portillo Reyes
GUANDIQUE SEGOVIA QUINTANILLA

Manuel Telles Suvillaga
LEXINCORP

Alex Grossmann
PANALPINA

Alejandro Fernandez
PRICEWATERHOUSECOOPERS

Ludovino Colón Sánchez
PRICEWATERHOUSECOOPERS

Ramon Ortega
PRICEWATERHOUSECOOPERS

Jose Romero
ROMERO PINEDA & ASOCIADOS*

Antonio R Mendez Llort
ROMERO PINEDA & ASOCIADOS

Thelma Dinora Lizama de Osorio
SUPERINTENDENCIA DEL SISTEMA FINANCIERO

Astrud María Meléndez
TRANSUNION

ERITREA

Berhane Gila-Michael
BERHANE GILA-MICHAEL LAW FIRM

Rahel Abera
BERHANE GILA-MICHAEL LAW FIRM

Tekeste Mesghenna
MTD ENTERPRISES PLC

Michael Joseph
PRICEWATERHOUSECOOPERS

ESTONIA

Aleksei Pali
CHR. JENSEN EESTI AS

Risto Koovit
CORVUS GRUPP TRANSPORT

Andres Juss
ESTONIAN LAND BOARD

Imanta Hütt
HOUGH, HÜBNER, HÜTT & PARTNERS

Igr Kostjuk
HOUGH, HÜBNER, HÜTT & PARTNERS

Veiko Meos
KREDIIDIINFO AS

Silja Holsmer
LAW FIRM MODY & HÄÄL GLIMSTEDT

Jaan Lindmäe
LAW OFFICE TARK & CO.

Kristi Kullerkup
LAW OFFICE TARK & CO.

Marko Mehilane
LEPIK & LUHAÄÄR*

Peeter Lepik
LEPIK & LUHAÄÄR

Anton Sigal
LEPIK & LUHAÄÄR

Vesse Võhma
LEPIK & LUHAÄÄR

Karolina Ullman
MAGNUSSON WAHLIN QVIST STANBROOK ADVOKATBYRÅ EESTI FILIAAL

Heili Haabu
MOQUET BORDE & ASSOCIÉS RAIDLA & PARTNERS

Sven Papp
MOQUET BORDE & ASSOCIÉS RAIDLA & PARTNERS

Villi Tõntson
PRICEWATERHOUSECOOPERS

Aare Kurist
PRICEWATERHOUSECOOPERS

Cameron Greaves
PRICEWATERHOUSECOOPERS

Raino Paron
RAIDLA & PARTNERS

Marit Toom
RAIDLA & PARTNERS

Kristi Reinson
RAIDLA & PARTNERS

Toomas Vaher
RAIDLA & PARTNERS

Karin Madisson
SORAINEN LAW OFFICES

Katrin Sarap
SORAINEN LAW OFFICES

Lea Liigus
SORAINEN LAW OFFICES

Jane Eespõld
SORAINEN LAW OFFICES

Kaido Loor
SORAINEN LAW OFFICES

ETHIOPIA

Bekure Assefa
BEKURE ASSEFA LAW OFFICE

Berhane Ghebray
BERHANE GHEBRAY AND ASSOCIATES

Mekuria Tafassa
FITANRARI TAFASSA LEGAL FIRM

Habtu Wolde Kiros
HABTU AND ASSOCIATES

Solomon Gizaw
HST, CHARTERED CERTIFIED ACCOUNTANTS

Shimelise Eshete
MIDROC CONSTRUCTION ETHIOPIA PLC

Damtew Demiss
ETHIOPIAN CUSTOMS AUTHORITY

Dawit Melaku
ZEREYAD GROUP TRANSIT AND FORWARDING PLC

Tadesse Kiros
TADESS, GETACHEW & ABATE LAW OFFICE

Aberra Ketsela
TAMERU WONDM AGEGNEHU LAW OFFICES

Tameru Wondm Agegnehu
TAMERU WONDM AGEGNEHU LAW OFFICES

Teshome Gabre-Mariam Bokan
TESHOME GABRE-MARIAM LAW FIRM

FIJI

Anthea S. Fong
CROMPTONS

Mohini Prasad
CROMPTONS

Paul McDonnell
CROMPTONS

Delores Elliott
DATABUREAU, BAYCORP ADVANTAGE

Williams Wylie Clarke
HOWARDS LAW

Ana Rasovo
HOWARDS LAW

Ramesh Prakash
HOWARDS LAW

Shayne Sorby
HOWARDS LAW

Mitchel Keil
MITCHELL, KEIL & ASSOCIATES

Richard Krishnan Naidu
MUNRO LEYS

Nehla Basawaiya
MUNRO LEYS

Florence Fenton
MUNRO LEYS

John Ridgway
PACIFIC LEGAL NETWORK

Chirk Yam
PRICEWATERHOUSECOOPERS

Jenny Seeto
PRICEWATERHOUSECOOPERS

Abdul Hassan
UNIVERSITY OF THE SOUTH PACIFIC

Krishn Shah
UNIVERSITY OF THE SOUTH PACIFIC

Spike Boydell
UNIVERSITY OF THE SOUTH PACIFIC

FINLAND

Sami Rautiainen
CASTREN & SNELLMAN

Claudio Busi
CASTREN & SNELLMAN

Pekka Jaatinen
CASTREN & SNELLMAN

Jenni Hupli
CASTREN & SNELLMAN

Jyri Makela
CONFEDERATION OF FINNISH CONSTRUCTION INDUSTRIES

Markku Aaltonen
CONFEDERATION OF FINNISH CONSTRUCTION INDUSTRIES

Jukka-Pekka Miettinen
FINNISH NATIONAL BOARD OF CUSTOMS

Irmeli Timonen
HANNES SNELLMAN

Janne Simula
HANNES SNELLMAN

Patrik Lindfors
HANNES SNELLMAN

Andrei Novitsky
HEDMAN OSBORNE CLARKE ALLIANCE

Mikko Mali
KROGERUS & CO.

Marja Ramm-Schmidt
KROGERUS & CO.

Tuomas Lukkarinen
NATIONAL LAND SURVEY OF FINLAND

Pekka Halme
NATIONAL LAND SURVEY OF FINLAND

Ville Sulonen
PANALPINA FINLAND

Kai Koivula
PANALPINA FINLAND

Ilkka Kajas
PRICEWATERHOUSECOOPERS OY - SVH

Markku Hakkarainen
PRICEWATERHOUSECOOPERS OY - SVH

Susanna Tiihonen
ROSCHIER HOLMBERG ATTORNEYS LTD.,* MEMBER OF IUS LABORIS

Eva Nordman
ROSCHIER HOLMBERG ATTORNEYS LTD., MEMBER OF IUS LABORIS

Sami Pauni
ROSCHIER HOLMBERG ATTORNEYS LTD., MEMBER OF IUS LABORIS

Micaela Thorström
ROSCHIER HOLMBERG ATTORNEYS LTD., MEMBER OF IUS LABORIS

Carita Wallgren
ROSCHIER HOLMBERG ATTORNEYS LTD., MEMBER OF IUS LABORIS

Gunnar Westerlund
ROSCHIER-HOLMBERG & WASELIUS

Tomas Lindholm
ROSCHIER-HOLMBERG & WASELIUS

Sini Sioni
ROSCHIER-HOLMBERG & WASELIUS

Gisela Knuts
ROSCHIER-HOLMBERG & WASELIUS

Bernt Juthstrom
ROSCHIER-HOLMBERG &
WASELIUS

Helena Viita
ROSCHIER-HOLMBERG &
WASELIUS

Juuso Jokela
SUOMEN ASIAKASTIETO OY -
FINSKA

Mikko Parjanne
SUOMEN ASIAKASTIETO OY -
FINSKA

Pauline Koskelo
THE SUPREME COURT OF
FINLAND

Mikko Eerola
WASELIUS & WIST

FRANCE

Bertrand Delaunay
ASHURST MORRIS CRISP

Nicolas Barberis
ASHURST MORRIS CRISP

Laurent Barbara
BAKER & MCKENZIE

Philippe Prevost
BANQUE DE FRANCE

Philippe Chapuis
BARTHÉLÉMY ET ASSOCIÉS,
MEMBER OF IUS LABORIS

Daniel Laprès
CABINET D'AVOCATS

Safouen Ben Abdallah
CABINET D'AVOCATS SERRES &
ASSOCIATES

Florence Grillier-Rousseau
DELOITTE & TOUCHE JURIDIQUE
ET FISCAL

Stéphanie Chatelon
DELOITTE & TOUCHE JURIDIQUE
ET FISCAL

Delphine Legras
DUBARRY LE DOUARIN VEIL

Frédérique Chifflot Bourgeois
ETIENNE PICHAT
ALLEZ & ASSOCIES

François Fauvet
FAUVET, LA GIRAUDIÈRE &
ASSOCIÉS

Nadia Gourlais
FOLIA

Anne Delerable
GIDE LOYRETTE NOUEL*

David Malamed
GIDE LOYRETTE NOUEL

Bertrand Barrier
GIDE LOYRETTE NOUEL

Philippe Xavier-Bender
GIDE LOYRETTE NOUEL

François Zimeray
JEANTET ASSOCIES

Marc Jobert
JOBERT & ASSOCIÉS

Carol Khoury
JONES DAY

Jean-Louis Martin
JONES DAY

Geraldine Malinge
KLEIN-GODDARD ASSOCIÉS

Christophe Leclere
LANDWELL & ASSOCIÉS

Aurélie Besloin
LANDWELL & ASSOCIÉS

Jennifer Juvenal
LANDWELL & ASSOCIÉS

Albane Henry de Villeneuve
LANDWELL & ASSOCIÉS

Arnaud Chastel
LANDWELL & ASSOCIÉS

Jean-Pierre Fiquet
LANDWELL & ASSOCIÉS

Odile Lautard
MINISTÈRE DES AFFAIRES
SOCIALES, DU TRAVAIL ET DE LA
SOLIDARIÉ

Patrick Le Moal
MINISTÈRE DES AFFAIRES
SOCIALES, DU TRAVAIL ET DE LA
SOLIDARIÉ

Andrew Booth
RIBA DUAOB

Christopher Baker
SKADDEN, ARPS, SLATE,
MEAGHER & FLOM LLP

Anne Creelman
VATIER & ASSOCIÉS

Bernard Piot
VICE PRESIDENT HONORAIRE DU
TRIBUNAL DE COMMERCE DE
PARIS

Xavier-Philippe Gruwez
XP LEGAL INTERNATIONAL LAW
FIRM

GEORGIA

Sergio Purin
AHLERS

Giorgi Begiashvili
BEGIASHVILI & CO.

Avto Namicheishvili
BEGIASHVILI & CO.

Zaza Bibilashvili
BGI LEGAL

Tamara Tevdoradze
BGI LEGAL

Eka Aleksidze
EY LAW

Irakli Adeishuvili
GEORGIAN LEGAL PARTNERSHIP

Dimitri Kitoshvili
GEORGIAN LEGAL PARTNERSHIP

Irina Gordeladze
GEORGIAN LEGAL PARTNERSHIP

Aieti Kukava
JSC CREDITINFO GEORGIA

Joseph Salukvadze
KFW FINANCED "CADASTRE AND
LAND REGISTER PROJECT"

Roin Migriauli
LAW OFFICE "MIGRIAULI &
PARTNERS"

Victor Kipiani
MGALOBLISHVILI, KIPIANI,
DZIDZIGURI

Vakhtang Shevardnadze
MGALOBLISHVILI, KIPIANI,
DZIDZIGURI

Lela Shatirishvili
TBILISI TITLE COMPANY

Lia Gogilashvili
TRANSWAYS LTD. AS AGENT FOR
P&O NEDLLOYD

Arif Guliyev
PRICEWATERHOUSECOOPERS

Bob Jurik
PRICEWATERHOUSECOOPERS

Rizvan Gubiyev
PRICEWATERHOUSECOOPERS

Mushfig Aliyev
PRICEWATERHOUSECOOPERS

Dave Sharp
REGISTERS OF SCOTLAND

GERMANY

Oliver Waldburg
ALLEN & OVERY

Peter Hoegen
ALLEN & OVERY

Andrea Hosenfeld
ASHURST

Günter Schneiders
BUNDESAMT FÜR FINANZEN

Bernd Oberbossel
BUNDESAMT FÜR FINANZEN

Werner M. Mues
C·B·H RECHTSANWÄLTE,
MEMBER OF IUS LABORIS

Manfred Heinrich
DEUTSCHE BUNDESBANK

Jennifer Bierly-Seipp
GASSNER STOCKMANN &
KOLLEGEN

Christof Kautzsch
HAARMANN HEMMELRATH &
PARTNER

Friedrich Tobias Schoene
HOGAN & HARTSON RAUE LLP

Silke Wollgarten
HOGAN & HARTSON RAUE LLP

Michael Unkelbach
KANZLEI UNKELBACH

Thomas Miller
KROHN RECHTSANWÄLTE

Götz-Sebastian Hök
LAW FIRM DR. HÖK,
STIEGLMEIER & KOLLEGEN

Manon Brindöpke
LINKLATERS OPPENHOFF &
RÄDLER

Klaus Günther
LINKLATERS OPPENHOFF &
RÄDLER

Bernard Khun
LOVELLS

Klaus Berner
NÖRR STIEFENHOFER LUTZ LAW
FIRM*

Stefan Heyder
NÖRR STIEFENHOFER LUTZ LAW
FIRM

Thomas Schulz
NÖRR STIEFENHOFER LUTZ LAW
FIRM

Markus Stadler
NÖRR STIEFENHOFER LUTZ LAW
FIRM

Heike Pospiech
NÖRR STIEFENHOFER LUTZ LAW
FIRM

Michael Molitoris
NÖRR STIEFENHOFER LUTZ LAW
FIRM

Heiko Vogt
PANALPINA WELTTRANSPORT
GMBH

Raphael Söhlke
PÖLLATH & PARTNERS

Dieter Endres
PRICEWATERHOUSECOOPERS
AG WPG

Dirk Baumgardt
PRICEWATERHOUSECOOPERS
AG WPG

Pia Dorfmueller
PRICEWATERHOUSECOOPERS
AG WPG

Wulf Bach
SCHUFA

Holger Thomas
SJ BERWIN KNOPF TULLOCH
STEININGER

Markus Jakoby
VELTEN FRANZ JAKOBY

Wolfgang Jakob
WEITNAUER

Henning Berger
WHITE & CASE

Wilhelm Zeddies
WORKING COMMITTEE OF THE
SURVEYING AUTHORITIES

GHANA

Kojo Bentsi-Enchill
BENTSI-ENCHILL & LETSA*

Rosa Kudoadzi
BENTSI-ENCHILL & LETSA

Reginald Bannerman
BRUCE-LYLE BANNERMAN &
THOMPSON

D.A.K. Mensah
CENTRAL DATABANK

Lawrence Otto
FUGAR & COMPANY

William E. Fugar
FUGAR & COMPANY

David A. Hesse
HESSE & LARSEY LAW FIRM

Stella Acwerth
LAND TITLE REGISTRY

Wilfred Anim-Odame
LAND VALUATION BOARD

Kenneth D. Laryea
LARYEA, LARYEA & CO. P.C.

Larry Adjetey
LAW TRUST COMPANY

Mary Mitchelle Gounder
MAERSK LOGISTICS GHANA LTD.

Fred Quarshie
MINISTRY OF FINANCE &
ECONOMIC PLANNING

Stefan Peter
PANALPINA GHANA LTD.

George Kwatia
PRICEWATERHOUSECOOPERS

Darcy White
PRICEWATERHOUSECOOPERS

Charles Egan
PRICEWATERHOUSECOOPERS

Shaira Adamali
PRICEWATERHOUSECOOPERS

Nene Amegatcher
SAM OKUDZETO & ASSOCIATES

Sam Okudzeto
SAM OKUDZETO & ASSOCIATES

Samuel L'Quartey
SAMLON CONSTRUCTION GH.
LTD.

Issac Quarshie
UNATRAC c/o TRACTOR &
EQUIPMENT GHANA LTD.

George Ahiafor
XDSDATA GHANA LTD.

GREECE

Georgios B. Bazinas
ANAGNOSTOPOULOS BAZINAS
FIFIS

Yanos Gramatidis
BAHAS, GRAMATIDIS &
PARTNERS

Dimitris E. Paraskevas
ELIAS SP. PARASKEVAS

Spyridon Tsallas
IKRP ROKAS & PARTNERS

Maira Galani
IKRP ROKAS & PARTNERS

Alkistis Christofilou
IKRP ROKAS & PARTNERS

Vasiliki Tsoumelea
KARATZAS & PARTNERS

John C. Kyriakides
KYRIAKIDES - GEOGROPOULOS
LAW FIRM

Effie G. Mitsopoulou
KYRIAKIDES - GEOGROPOULOS
LAW FIRM

Poulakou Chryssiis
KYRIAKIDES - GEOGROPOULOS
LAW FIRM

Vicky Xourafa
KYRIAKIDES - GEORGOPOULOS
LAW FIRM

Panayotis Bernitsas
M. & P. BERNITSAS LAW OFFICES

Yannis Kourniotis
M. & P. BERNITSAS LAW OFFICES

Dimitris Katsadakis
ORPHEE BEINOGLOU INTL.
FORWARDERS

Anna Kazantzidou
PANAGOPOULOS, VAINANIDIS,
SCHINA, ECONOMOU

George Samothrakis
PRICEWATERHOUSECOOPERS

Freddy Yatracou
PRICEWATERHOUSECOOPERS

Eirini Eleftheria Galinou
PROFESSOR K. KREMALIS &
PARTNERS, MEMBER OF IUS
LABORIS

Vassiliki Strantzia
PWC BUSINESS SOLUTIONS S.A.

Kleanthis Roussos
ROUSSOS LAW FIRM

Georgios Ladogiannis
ROUSSOS LAW FIRM

Ennie Dodou
SARANTITIS & PARTNERS

Konstantinos Mellios
SARANTITIS & PARTNERS

Victoria Zachopoulou
TIRESIAS

Athina Skolarikou
ZEPOS & YANNOPOULOS*

Nicholas Kontizas
ZEPOS & YANNOPOULOS

Vassiliki Lazarakou
ZEPOS & YANNOPOULOS

Emmanuela Truli
ZEPOS & YANNOPOULOS

Ilias Koimtzoglou
ZEPOS & YANNOPOULOS

Sonia Melengou
ZEPOS & YANNOPOULOS

GUATEMALA

Ruby Asturias
ACZALAW

Jorge Rolando Barrios
BONILLA, MONTANO & TORIELLO

Luis Rene Pellecer Lopez
CARRILLO & ASOCIADOS

Alfonso Carrillo
CARRILLO & ASOCIADOS

Rodrigo Callejas Aquino
CARRILLO & ASOCIADOS

Juan Pablo Cardenas Villamar
DHV CONSULTANTS

Mario Adolfo Búcaro F.
DÍAZ-DURAN & ASOCIADOS

Juan Pablo Carrasco de Groote
DÍAZ-DURÁN & ASOCIADOS

Juan Manuel Díaz-Durán
DÍAZ-DURÁN & ASOCIADOS

Gabriela Tenenbaum
LEXINCORP

Edgar Ruiz
LEXINCORP

Claudia Pereira
MAYORA & MAYORA*

Vanessa Castro Mirón
MAYORA & MAYORA

Ana Rosa Alfaro Altuve
MAYORA & MAYORA

Eduardo Mayora Dawe
MAYORA & MAYORA

Eduardo Dawe
MAYORA & MAYORA

Ana Lucía Umaña
MAYORA & MAYORA

Victor Orantes
PRESA, POLANCO, QUEVEDO, ORANTES & SISNIEGA

Diego Polanco
PRESA, POLANCO, QUEVEDO, ORANTES & SISNIEGA

Ludovino Colón Sánchez
PRICEWATERHOUSECOOPERS

Alejandro Fernandez
PRICEWATERHOUSECOOPERS

Ramon Ortega
PRICEWATERHOUSECOOPERS

Rodolfo Fuentes
PROTECTORA DE CREDITO COMERCIAL

Julio Eduardo Camey Silva
REGISTRO GENERAL DE LA PROPIEDAD DE GUATEMALA

Alfredo Rodriguez-Mahuad
RODRÍGUEZ, ARCHILA, CASTELLANOS, SOLARES & AGUILAR, S.C.

Carlos González Castellanos
RODRÍGUEZ, ARCHILA, CASTELLANOS, SOLARES & AGUILAR, S.C.

Sylvia Ruiz Hochstetter
RUIZ SKINNER-KLEE & RUIZ

Juan Pedro Falla
RUIZ SKINNER-KLEE & RUIZ

Aída Ruíz
TEXTILES AMATITLÁN

GUINEA

Jacques Chareyre
FIDAFRICA / PRICEWATERHOUSECOOPERS

Dominique Taty
FIDAFRICA / PRICEWATERHOUSECOOPERS

Koly Kourouma

Cheick Mohamed Tidjane Sylla
BANQUE CENTRALE - B.C.R.G.

Boubacar Barry
BOUBACAR BARRY LAW FIRM

Alpha Bakar Barry
CABINET ME ALPHA BAKAR BARRY

Alpha Abdoulaye Diallo
DIALLO ET DIALLO

Ibrahima Diakite
LANDNET

Robert Bal
MAERSK GUINEE S.A.

Paphiah Selvakumar
MAERSK LOGISTICS GUINEE SA

Alpha Ibrahima
MAERSK LOGISTICS GUINEE SA

GUYANA

Roger Yearwood
BRITTON, HAMILTON & ADAMS

Josephine Whitehead
CAMERON & SHEPHERD

Raphael Trotman
CHAPMAN & TROTMAN

Desmond Correia
CORREIA & CORREIA LTD.

G. Thomside
GUYANA NATIONAL SHIPPING CORPORATION LTD.

Robin S. Stoby
HUGHES, FIELD AND STOBY

Colin Murray
COASTAL CONSTRUCTION SERVICES

K.A. Juman-Yessi
K. A. JUMAN-YASSIN JUMAN-YASSIN & ASSOCIATES

William Sampson
LINCOLN CHAMBERS & ASSOCIATES (WILLIAM H. SAMPSON)

Christopher Ram
RAM & MCRAE

Rexford Jackson
SINGH, DOODNAUTH LAW FIRM

HAITI

Gaylor Esper
Marc Hebert Ignace
BANQUE DE LA RÉPUBLIQUE D'HAITI

Jean Baptiste Brown
BROWN LAW FIRM

Steve Christian Brown
BROWN LAW FIRM

Enedland Jabouin
CABINET JABOIN REGIS DESCARDES

Robert Laforest
CABINET LAFOREST

Salim Succar
CABINET LISSADE

Louis Gary Lissade
CABINET LISSADE

Jean Frederic Sales
CABINET SALES

Marc Hebert Ignace
BANQUE DE LA RÉPUBLIQUE D'HAITI

Chantal Hudicourt-Ewald
HUDICOURT-WOOLLEY

Joseph Nadal
LES ENTREPRISES COMMERCIALES J. NADAL S.A.

Raoul Celestin
LES ENTREPRISES COMMERCIALES J. NADAL S.A.

HONDURAS

Enrique Rodriguez Burchard
ABOGADOS Y ASESORES SRL

Armida Maria Lopez de Arguello
ACZALAW

Gustavo Martin Arguello
ACZALAW

Jorge Omar Casco
BUFETE CASCO & ASOCIADOS

Tania Casco
BUFETE CASCO & ASOCIADOS

Francisco Guillermo Durón Lopez
BUFETE DURÓN

Laureano Gutierrez Falla
BUFETE GUTIERREZ FALLA*

José Dolores Tijerino
BUFETE TIJERINO Y ASOCIADOS

Dino Rietti
COLEGIO DE ARQUITECTOS DE HONDURAS

Carmen Chavez
COMISION NACIONAL DE BANCOS Y SEGUROS

Janeth Castañeda
CROPA PANALPINA TEGUCIGALPA HONDURAS

Dennis Matamoros Batson
F.A. ARIAS & MUÑOZ

Juan Carlos Mejia Cotto
INSTITUTO DE LA PROPIEDAD

Jose Ramon Paz
J. R. PAZ & ASOCIADOS

José Rafael Rivera Ferrari
J.R. PAZ & ASOCIADOS

Allan Elvir
LEXINCORP

Rene Lopez Rodezno
LOPEZ RODEZNO & ASOCIADOS

Arturo Medrano
MEDRANO Y MEDRANO ABOGADOS Y NOTARIOS

Enrique Ortez Sequeira
ORTEZ SEQUEIRA & ASSOCIATES

Maria Elena Matute Cruz
PALACIO DE JUSTICIA

Alejandro Fernandez
PRICEWATERHOUSECOOPERS

Ramon Ortega
PRICEWATERHOUSECOOPERS

Ludovino Colón Sánchez
PRICEWATERHOUSECOOPERS

Estela Chavez
TRANSUNION

Roberto Zacarias Jr.
ZACARIAS AGUILAR & ASOCIADOS

HONG KONG, CHINA

Ranbir Singh
FIRST CARGO (HK) LTD.

Cliff Chow
MAERSK HONG KONG LIMITED

Alex Liu
THE GOVERNMENT OF THE HONG KONG SPECIAL ADMINISTRATIVE REGION OF THE PEOPLE'S REPUBLIC OF CHINA

Stephen Vine
ANGELA WANG & CO.

Brian Barron
BAKER & MCKENZIE

Patrick Wong
JOHNSON STOKES & MASTER*

Tammy Goh
JOHNSON STOKES & MASTER

F.K. Au
JOHNSON STOKES & MASTER

Glenda Fung
JOHNSON STOKES & MASTER

Thomas So
JOHNSON STOKES & MASTER

Raymond Wong
JOHNSON STOKES & MASTER

Nina Sze
JOHNSON STOKES & MASTER

Rod Houng-Lee
PRICEWATERHOUSECOOPERS

Raymond Wong
PRICEWATERHOUSECOOPERS

Nicholas Chan
SQUIRE, SANDERS & DEMPSEY

Sara Tong
TEMPLE CHAMBERS

Paul Fox
THE HONG KONG POLYTECHNIC UNIVERSITY, HUNG HOM

Albert P.C. Chan
THE HONG KONG POLYTECHNIC UNIVERSITY, HUNG HOM

James Wong
THE HONG KONG POLYTECHNIC UNIVERSITY, HUNG HOM

Cindy Lam
THE LAND REGISTRY

Magdalena Kwan
TRANSUNION INFORMATION SERVICES LIMITED

Charles D. Booth
UNIVERSITY OF HONG KONG

HUNGARY

Zsuzsanna Cseri
BARD CSERI AND PARTNERS

Adam Petho
BISZ RT.

Csaba Szőke
BOGSCH & PARTNERS

Anna Gaspar
BUILD & ECON HUNGARY

Zoltan Krausz
BUILD & ECON HUNGARY

Tamas Saad
BUILD & ECON HUNGARY

Csaba Szabó
DESSEWFFY, DÁVID ÉS TÁRSAI ÜGYVÉDI IRODA

Andrea Jádi Németh
HAARMANN HEMMELRATH & PARTNER

Krisztián Bácsi
HUNGARIAN CUSTOMS AND FINANCE GUARD

Gábor Felsen
KÖVES CLIFFORD CHANCE

András Bekes
MINISTRY OF EMPLOYMENT AND LABOUR

Péter Berethalmi
NAGY ÉS TRÓCSÁNYI LAW OFFICE*

Csaba Pigler
NAGY ÉS TRÓCSÁNYI LAW OFFICE

Túri Melinda
NAGY ÉS TRÓCSÁNYI LAW OFFICE

Gábor Tóth
OPPENHEIM ÉS TÁRSAI, FRESHFIELDS BRUCKHAUS DERING

Klara Oppenheim
OPPENHEIM ÉS TÁRSAI, FRESHFIELDS BRUCKHAUS DERING

Robert Brugger
PANALPINA WELTTRANSPORT GMBH

Atilla Katkics
PANALPINA MAGYARORSZÁG KFT.

Dora Mathe
PRICEWATERHOUSECOOPERS

Peter Mihaly
PRICEWATERHOUSECOOPERS

Gabriella Erdos
PRICEWATERHOUSECOOPERS

Tibor Torok
PRICEWATERHOUSECOOPERS

Peter Gerendasi
PRICEWATERHOUSECOOPERS

Agnes Szent-Ivány
SÁNDOR SZEGEDI SZENT-IVÁNY & KOMÁROMI

András Szecskay
SZECSKAY

ICELAND

Bragi Ragnarsson
EIMSKIPAFÉLAG ÍSLANDS EHF

Margrét Hauksdóttir
FASTEIGNAMAT RIKISINS - THE LAND REGISTRY OF ICELAND

Skuli Th. Fjeldsted
FJELDSTED, BLÖNDAL & FJELDSTED

Karl F. Garðarsson
ICELAND CUSTOMS

Kolbeinn Kolbeinsson
ISTAK

Loftur Árnason
ISTAK

Gunnar Jonsson
JONSSON & HALL

Kari Hrafn Kjartansson
LANDWELL

Reynir Grétarsson
LÁNSTRAUST LTD.

Birgir Már Ragnarsson
LEX-NESTOR

Vifill Harouarson hdl
LEX–NESTOR

Tómas J. Jónsson
LÖGFRAEDISTOFU REYKJAVÍKUR

Guorún Björk Bjarnadóttir
hdl.
LOGOS LEGAL SERVICES*

Gunnar Sturluson
LOGOS LEGAL SERVICES

Erlendur Gislason
LOGOS LEGAL SERVICES

Heidar Asberg Atlason
LOGOS LEGAL SERVICES

Asta Kristjansdottir
PRICEWATERHOUSECOOPERS

Fridgeir Sigurdsson
PRICEWATERHOUSECOOPERS

INDIA

Shardul S. Shroff
AMARCHAND MANGALDAS*

Raj Pal Arora
BUILDERS' ASSOCIATION OF
INDIA

Vipender Mann
CHAWLA & CO.

Harminder Chawla
CHAWLA & CO.

P.R. Viswanathan
CREDIT INFORMATION BUREAU
INDIA

Harshala Chandorkar
CREDIT INFORMATION BUREAU
INDIA

Ashish Bhasin
CROSSPORT ALLIANCES INDIA
LIMITED

V. C. Augustine
DEPARTMENT OF BANKING
SUPERVISION

Shreyas Patel
FOX MANDAL

Saurabh Misra
FOX MANDAL

Toral Jhaveri
FOX MANDAL

Anshoo Nayar
FOX MANDAL

Radhika Sankaran
FOX MANDAL

Som Mandal
FOX MANDAL

Vishal Gandhi
GANDHI & ASSOCIATES

Manish Madhukar
INFINI JURIDIQUE

Abhishek Saket
INFINI JURIDIQUE

Vasanth Rajasekaran
KACHWAHA & PARTNERS

Anuradha Sharma
KACHWAHA & PARTNERS

Prachi Puri Malhotra
KACHWAHA & PARTNERS

Sumeet Kachwaha
KACHWAHA & PARTNERS

K. V. Ramesh
KOCHHAR & CO.

Dara Mehta
LITTLE & CO.

Nirmala Gill
LITTLE & CO.

Joseph Sandiav
MAERSK INDIA PVT. LTD.

Akil Hirani
MAJMUDAR & CO.

Satish Murthi
MURTI AND MURTI
INTERNATIONAL LAW PRACTICE

Tapas Sen
NATIONAL INSTITUTE OF PUBLIC
FINANCE AND POLICY

Vikram Shroff
NISHITH DESAI ASSOCIATES

Ravi Mathur
PANALPINA WORLD TRANSPORT
INDIA PVT. LTD.

Nityanand Gupta
PRICEWATERHOUSECOOPERS

Ashutosh Chaturvedi
PRICEWATERHOUSECOOPERS

Amit Bahl
PRICEWATERHOUSECOOPERS

Rahul Garg
PRICEWATERHOUSECOOPERS

Dipak Rao
SINGHANIA & PARTNERS

Ravi Singhania
SINGHANIA & PARTNERS

D.C. Singhania
SINGHANIA & PARTNERS

Vikas Goel
SINGHANIA & PARTNERS

Sameer Rastogi
SINGHANIA & PARTNERS

S.N. Variava
SUPREME COURT OF INDIA

Vinod Khotari
VINOD KOTHARI & CO.,
COMPANY SECRETARIES

Samik Mukherjee
VINOD KOTHARI & CO.,
COMPANY SECRETARIES

INDONESIA

Ernst G. Tehuteru
ALI BUDIARDJO, NUGROHO,
REKSODIPUTRO*

Ayik Candrawulan Gunadi
ALI BUDIARDJO, NUGROHO,
REKSODIPUTRO

Indra Setiawan Jamin
ALI BUDIARDJO, NUGROHO,
REKSODIPUTRO

Theodoor Bakker
ALI BUDIARDJO, NUGROHO,
REKSODIPUTRO

John Andre Panggabean
ALI BUDIARDJO, NUGROHO,
REKSODIPUTRO

Brian J. Wesol
ALI BUDIARDJO, NUGROHO,
REKSODIPUTRO

Ferry Madian
ALI BUDIARDJO, NUGROHO,
REKSODIPUTRO

Kevin O. Sidharta
ALI BUDIARDJO, NUGROHO,
REKSODIPUTRO

Herry N. Kurniawan
ALI BUDIARDJO, NUGROHO,
REKSODIPUTRO

Hamud M. Balfas
ALI BUDIARDJO, NUGROHO,
REKSODIPUTRO

Bruce Johnston
ALLENS ARTHUR ROBINSON

Riza Haryadi
BANK INDONESIA

Hartono Parbudi
BIRO KREDIT INDONESIA

Almer Apon
BMCL INDONESIA

Brigitta I. Rahayoe
BRIGITTA I. RAHAYOE &
SYAMSUDDIN

Christian Teo
CHRISTIAN TEO & ASSOCIATES

Anton Budiman
GEORGE WIDJOJO & PARTNERS

Stephanus Jonathan
HADROMI & PARTNERS LAW
FIRM

Yulian Hadromi
HADROMI & PARTNERS LAW
FIRM

Fabian Buddy Pascoal
HANAFIAH PONGGAWA BANGUN

Benjamin Abrams
JAKARTA ADVISORY SERVICES

Winita E. Kusnandar
KUSNANDAR & CO.

Eman Achmad Sulaeman
LUBIS, SANTOSA & MAULANA

Pudji Wahjuni Purbo
MAKARIM & TAIRA S.

Helen Sunarjo
MAKARIM & TAIRA S.

Andreas Hartono
MAKARIM & TAIRA S.

Jenny Budiman
MAKARIM & TAIRA S.

Inge Resdiano
MAKARIM & TAIRA S.

Galinar Kartakusuma
MAKARIM & TAIRA S.

Bill MacDonald
PRICEWATERHOUSECOOPERS

Paul O'Brien
PRICEWATERHOUSECOOPERS

Robertus Winarto
PRICEWATERHOUSECOOPERS

Ray Headifen
PRICEWATERHOUSECOOPERS

Krisman Damanik
P.T. PANALPINA NUSAJAYA
TRANSPORT

Arfidea Dwi Saraswati
SSEK INDONESIAN LEGAL
CONSULTANTS

Ira A. Eddymurthy
SSEK INDONESIAN LEGAL
CONSULTANTS

Darrell R. Johnson
SSEK INDONESIAN LEGAL
CONSULTANTS

Bambang Soelaksono
THE SMERU RESEARCH
INSTITUTE

IRAN

Faraz Nikoukar Shahir
CHAIN INTERNATIONAL
TRANSPORTATION

Mozaffar Mohammadian
POUYA BAR INTERNATIONAL
TRANSPORT COMPANY

Mohammad Adib
ADIB LAW FIRM

Albert Bernardi
ALBERT BERNARDI & ASSOCIATES

Mohammad Reza Shojaedinni
CENTRAL BANK OF IRAN

Behrooz Akhlaghi
DR. BEHROOZ AKHLAGHI &
ASSOCIATES

Ali Hatami
DR. BEHROOZ AKHLAGHI &
ASSOCIATES

Mir Shahbiz Shafe'e
DR. JAMAL SEIFI & ASSOCIATES

Jamal Seifi
DR. JAMAL SEIFI & ASSOCIATES

Sirin Ozra Entezari
DR. SHIRIN O.EENTEZARI &
ASSOCIATES

Reza Askari
FOREGIN LEGAL AFFAIRS GROUP

Hassan Badamchi
HASSAN BADAMCHI &
ASSOCIATES

Rasoul Dorri Esfahani
IRAN MOSHAR CO.

Yahya Rayegani
RAYEGANI LAW OFFICE

Shahla Pournazeri
SHAHLA POURNAZERI -
ATTORNEY AT LAW

M. Shahabi
TAVAKOLI & SHAHABI

IRAQ

Munthir Hasan Mahmoud
AL FADHAA CO. LTD.

Imad Makki Mohmoud
AL QARYA GROUP

Adil Sinjakli
AL TAMIMI & COMPANY

Farquad Al-Salman
F.H. AL-SALMAN & CO.

Hisham Katurji
GEZAIRI TRANSPORT IRAQI
COMPANY LTD.

Hadeel Salih Abboud Al-
Janabi
MENA ASSOCIATES

Blund Najeb
PRIVATE ATTORNEY

Munaf Hammed Muhammed
Al-Abbas
PRIVATE LAWYER

IRELAND

William Johnston
ARTHUR COX*

Michael Meghen
ARTHUR COX

David O'Donohoe
ARTHUR COX

Daniel Boland
ARTHUR COX

Jonathan Sheehan
ARTHUR COX

Melissa Jennings
ARTHUR COX

Gillian Woods
ARTHUR COX

Ted Williams
ARTHUR COX

Steven Hegarty
ARTHUR COX

Gerard Coll
EUGENE F. COLLINS SOLICITORS

Gavin Doherty
EUGENE F. COLLINS SOLICITORS

Gavin Simons
EUGENE F. COLLINS SOLICITORS

Barry O'Neill
EUGENE F. COLLINS SOLICITORS

Sinead Power
IRISH CREDIT BUREAU

Seamus Tighearnaigh
IRISH CREDIT BUREAU

Patricia McGovern
L. K. SHIELDS, SOLICITORS,
MEMBER OF IUS LABORIS

Alan Browning
L. K. SHIELDS, SOLICITORS,
MEMBER OF IUS LABORIS

Fiona Thornton
LK SHIELDS SOLICITORS,
MEMBER OF IUS LABORIS

Gillian Dully
LK SHIELDS SOLICITORS,
MEMBER OF IUS LABORIS

Declan Black
MASON HAYES & CURRAN

Tanya Colbert
MASON HAYES & CURRAN

Maurice Phelan
MASON HAYES & CURRAN

Colm Kelly
PRICEWATERHOUSECOOPERS

Lynne Rae
PRICEWATERHOUSECOOPERS

Matt O'Keeffe
PRICEWATERHOUSECOOPERS

Michael Treacy
LAND REGISTRY

Sandro Knecht
PANALPINA

ISRAEL

Avie Arenson
A. ARENSON LTD.

Ron Berry
AMIT LTD

Amnon Altman
BDI BUSINESS DATA ISRAEL AND
PERSONAL CHECK

Daniel Singerman
BDI BUSINESS DATA ISRAEL AND
PERSONAL CHECK

Gideon Koren
BEN ZVI KOREN

Jakob Melcer
E.S. SHIMRON, I. MOLHO, PERSKY & CO.

Dina Brown
ELCHANAN LANDAU LAW OFFICES

Ron Storch
GLOBAL CREDIT SERVICES

Gerry Seligman
KESSELMAN & KESSELMAN / PRICEWATERHOUSECOOPERS

Shilomi Zehaui
KESSELMAN & KESSELMAN / PRICEWATERHOUSECOOPERS

Vered Kirshner
KESSELMAN & KESSELMAN / PRICEWATERHOUSECOOPERS

Clifford Davis
*S. HOROWITZ & CO.**

Michelle Liberman
S. HOROWITZ & CO.

Ofer Bar-On
SAVIT BAR-ON GAL-ON TZIN NOV YAGUR LAW OFFICES

Orna Kornreich-Cohen
SAVIT BAR-ON GAL-ON TZIN NOV YAGUR LAW OFFICES

Zeev Weiss
WEISS-PORAT & CO. LAW OFFICES

Ronen Bar-Even
WEISS-PORAT & CO. LAW OFFICES

Noa Solomon
YEHUDA RAVEH & CO. LAW OFFICES

Aaron Jaffe
YIGAL ARNON & CO.

Paul Baris
YIGAL ARNON & CO.

Galit Rozovsky
YUVAL LEVY & CO., LAW OFFICES AND NOTARY

ITALY

Antonella Tanico
Giovanni Izzo
ABBATESCIANNI

Roberto Donnini
ALLEN & OVERY

Ida Marotta
ALLEN & OVERY

Kathleen Lemmens
ALLEN & OVERY

Vincenzo Giannantonio
ASHURST

Eva Maschietto
ASHURST

Carlo Bruno
ASHURST

Maria Pia Ascenzo
BANK OF ITALY

Gian Bruno Bruni
BRUNI GRAMELLINI E ASSOCIATI

Pier Andrea Fré Torelli Massini
CARNELUTTI

Filippo Cecchetti
*CHIOMENTI STUDIO LEGALE**

Enrico Lodi
CRIF S.P.A.

Beatrice Rubini
CRIF S.P.A.

Frederica La Chioma
GRIECO E ASSOCIATI

Alessandro Cardia
GRIECO E ASSOCIATI

Antonio Grieco
GRIECO E ASSOCIATI

ITALIAN CUSTOMS

Luisa Cucchi
JONES DAY

Stefano Macchi di Cellere
JONES DAY

Silvio Tersilla
LOVELLS STUDIO LEGALE

Sergio Calderara
NUNZIANTE MAGRONE

Massimiliano Silvetti
NUNZIANTE MAGRONE

Norberto Pala
PANALPINA TRASPORTI MONDIALI S.P.A.

Domenico Colella
PORTOLANO COLELLA CAVALLO PROSPERETTI STUDIO LEGALE

Daniela Marrani
PORTOLANO COLELLA CAVALLO PROSPERETTI STUDIO LEGALE

Barbara Corsetti
PORTOLANO COLELLA CAVALLO PROSPERETTI STUDIO LEGALE

Ignazio la Candia
STUDIO PIROLA

Massimo Cremona
STUDIO PIROLA

Daniela Sgro
SPASARO MISURACA & ASSOCIATES

Antonio de Martinis
SPASARO MISURACA & ASSOCIATES

Piervincenzo Spasaro
SPASARO MISURACA & ASSOCIATES

Francesco Misuraca
SPASARO MISURACA & ASSOCIATES

Fabrizio Mariotti
STUDIO LEGALE BELTRAMO

Marco Sella
STUDIO LEGALE MACCHI DI CELLERE E GANGEMI

Linda Frigo
STUDIO LEGALE MACCHI DI CELLERE E GANGEMI

Luigi Walter Veroi
STUDIO LEGALE VEROI

Franco Toffoletto
TOFFOLETTO E SOCI LAW FIRM, MEMBER OF IUS LABORIS

Valeria Morossini
TOFFOLETTO E SOCI LAW FIRM, MEMBER OF IUS LABORIS

Giovanni Crenna
VARRENTI BASSAN LENZI ASSOCIATI

Fabrizio Colonna
VARRENTI BASSAN LENZI ASSOCIATI

Giovanni Verusio
VERUSIO E COSMELLI STUDIO LEGALE

Maria Grazia Medici
VERUSIO E COSMELLI STUDIO LEGALE

Enrico Bugielli
VERUSIO E COSMELLI STUDIO LEGALE

JAMAICA

Janet Morgan
DUNNCOX

Nicole Foga
FOGA DALEY & CO.

Jackie Cole
GRACE KENNEDY & COMPANY LTD.

Rosie Plant
INCORPORATED MASTERBUILDERS ASSOCIATION OF JAMAICA

Strachan Fitzpatrick
KIER CONSTRUCTION LTD.

Jerome Spencer
*MYERS, FLETCHER & GORDON**

Suzette Moss
MYERS, FLETCHER & GORDON

Peter Goldson
MYERS, FLETCHER & GORDON

Dave García
MYERS, FLETCHER & GORDON

Tamara Green
MYERS, FLETCHER & GORDON

Stuart Stimpson
MYERS, FLETCHER & GORDON

Norman Minott
MYERS, FLETCHER & GORDON

Viveen Morrison
PRICEWATERHOUSECOOPERS

Eric Crawford
PRICEWATERHOUSECOOPERS

Michael Hall
PRICEWATERHOUSECOOPERS

Karen Wilson
RATTRAY, PATTERSON, RATTRAY

Humprey Taylor
TAYLOR CONSTRUCTION LTD.

JAPAN

Toshio Miyatake
ADACHI, HENDERSON, MIYATAKE & FUJITA

Takaya Konishi
*ASAHI KOMA LAW OFFICES**

Yuji Onuki
ASAHI KOMA LAW OFFICES

Kaoru Hattori
ASAHI KOMA LAW OFFICES

Tetsuro Sato
ASAHI KOMA LAW OFFICES

Alvin Hiromasa Shiozaki
ASAHI KOMA LAW OFFICES

Setsuko Yufu
ATSUMI & PARTNERS

Shinichiro Abe
BINGHAM MCCUTCHEN

Tomoe Sato
CREDIT INFORMATION CENTER CORP

Aki Takahashi
CREDIT INFORMATION CENTER CORP

Tamotsu Hatasawa
HATASAWA & WAKAI LAW FIRM

Takafumi Suzuki
JAPAN CUSTOMS

Akio Yamamoto
KAJIMA CORPORATION

Masahiko Shira
MAERSK K.K.

Kenji Utsumi
NAGASHIMA OHNO & TSUNEMATSU

Takafumi Nihei
NISHIMURA & PARTNERS

Takanobu Takehara
NISHIMURA & PARTNERS

Kenji Nakajima
PANALPINA WORLD TRANSPORT JAPAN LTD.

Kotaku Kimu
PRICEWATERHOUSECOOPERS / ZEIRISHI-HOJIN CHUOAOYAMA

Hiroyuki Suzuki
PRICEWATERHOUSECOOPERS / ZEIRISHI-HOJIN CHUOAOYAMA

Nobuaki Matsuoka
YAMAGUCHI INTERNATIONAL

JORDAN

Sahar Anani
*ALI SHARIF ZU'BI & SHARIF ALI ZU'BI**

Fadi Kawar
ALI SHARIF ZU'BI & SHARIF ALI ZU'BI

Ali Sharif Zu'bi
ALI SHARIF ZU'BI & SHARIF ALI ZU'BI

Hani Kurdi
ALI SHARIF ZU'BI & SHARIF ALI ZU'BI

Masoud Sakfal Hait
ALI SHARIF ZU'BI & SHARIF ALI ZU'BI

Shireen Okkeh
ALI SHARIF ZU'BI & SHARIF ALI ZU'BI

Saleh Abd El-Ati
ALI SHARIF ZU'BI & SHARIF ALI ZU'BI

Ola Al Kadi
ALI SHARIF ZU'BI & SHARIF ALI ZU'BI

Basel Kawar
AMIN KAWAR & SONS

Arafat Alfayoumi
CENTRAL BANK OF JORDAN

Shadi Zghoul
DAJANI & ASSOCIATES

Eman M. Al-Dabbas
INTERNATIONAL BUSINESS LEGAL ASSOCIATES

Firas Malhas
INTERNATIONAL BUSINESS LEGAL ASSOCIATES

Nissreen Haram
INTERNATIONAL BUSINESS LEGAL ASSOCIATES

Naif Salem
JORDANIAN CONSTRUCTION CONTRACTORS ASSOCIATION

Sa'ed Karajah
KARAJAH & ASSOCIATES LAW FIRM

Ahmad Masa'deh
KHALAF MASA'DEH & PARTNERS

Khaldoun Nazer
KHALIFEH & PARTNERS

Alá Khalifeh
KHALIFEH & PARTNERS

Ibrahim Abunameh
LAW AND ARBITRATION CENTRE

Micheal T. Dabit
MICHEAL DABIT & ASSOCIATES ATTORNEYS AT LAW

Francis J. Bawab
PRICEWATERHOUSECOOPERS

Stephan Stephan
PRICEWATERHOUSECOOPERS

Ala'a Abdel-Hadi
RAHHAL AND ASSOCIATES

Youssef Khalilieh
RAJAI DAJANI & ASSOCIATES LAW OFFICE

Rasha Laswi
ZALLOUM & LASWI LAW FIRM

KAZAKHSTAN

Tatyana Suleyeva
AEQUITAS LAW FIRM

Aiman Yerenova
AEQUITAS LAW FIRM

Sanzhan N. Burambayev
AEQUITAS LAW FIRM

Zhibek Karamanova
BRACEWELL & GIULIANI, LLP

Aidar Yegeubayev
BRACEWELL & GIULIANI, LLP

Marla Valdez
DENTON WILDE SAPTE

Aidar Kashkarbayev
DENTON WILDE SAPTE

Thomas Johnson
DENTON WILDE SAPTE

Anvar Akhmedov
FIRST CREDIT BUREAU

Sabina Barayeva
JSC KAZKOMMERTSBANK

Semyon Issyk
LAW FIRM AEQUITAS

Kamilya T. Nurpeissova
LEBOEUF, LAMB, GREENE & MACRAE, LLP

Marat Kh. Muzdubaev
LEBOEUF, LAMB, GREENE & MACRAE, LLP

Elvis Roberts
M&M LOGISTICS

Dinara Jarmukhanova
MCGUIREWOODS KAZAKHSTAN LLP

John W. Barnum
MCGUIREWOODS KAZAKHSTAN LLP

Berik Imashev
MCGUIREWOODS KAZAKHSTAN LLP

Richard Remias
MCGUIREWOODS KAZAKHSTAN LLP

Snezhana V. Popova
MCGUIREWOODS KAZAKHSTAN LLP

Ivan A. Zaitsev
McGuireWoods Kazakhstan LLP

Sanzhar Shaimardanov
McGuireWoods Kazakhstan LLP

Assel Tokusheva
McGuireWoods Kazakhstan LLP

Bakhytzhan Kadyrov
McGuireWoods Kazakhstan LLP

Alexander Baruskov
McGuireWoods Kazakhstan LLP

Carter Younger
McGuireWoods Kazakhstan LLP

Yuri Bolotov
McGuireWoods Kazakhstan LLP

Maxim Telemtayev
McLeod Dixon LLP

Rosa Abirova
McLeod Dixon LLP

Vsevolod Markov
Michael Wilson & Partners Ltd.

Michael Wilson
Michael Wilson & Partners Ltd.

Yekaterina Kim
Michael Wilson & Partners Ltd.

Natalya Revenko
PricewaterhouseCoopers

Elena Kaeva
PricewaterhouseCoopers

Matthew Tallarovic
PricewaterhouseCoopers

Katherine Garkavets
PricewaterhouseCoopers

Courtney Fowler
PricewaterhouseCoopers

Rima Zhakupova
Salans

Dina Khakimzhanova
Salans

Zhomart Sarsenbay
Salans

Yerlanbek Zhussupov
Zanger Law Firm

Natalie Yelizarova
Zhakenov & Partners, in partnership with White & Jones LLP

Valerie A. Zhakenov
Zhakenov & Partners, in partnership with White & Jones LLP

KENYA

Anthony Mwangi
Ameritrans Freight International

Sonal Sejpal
Anjarwalla & Khanna Advocates

Janet Mutua
B. M. Musau & Co. Advocates

Morris Kimuli
B. M. Musau & Co. Advocates

Benson Njiru
B. M. Musau & Co. Advocates

Gladys Mwariri
B. M. Musau & Co. Advocates

Benjamin Musau
B. M. Musau & Co. Advocates

Virginia Nzioka
B. M. Musau & Co. Advocates

Morris Kimuli
B. M. Musau & Co. Advocates

Fiona Fox
Chunga Associates

Wachira Ndege
Credit Reference Bureau Africa Ltd.

Julius Wako
Daly & Figgis Advocates

Hamish Keith
Daly & Figgis Advocates

Richard Omwela
Hamilton Harrison & Mathews Law Firm

Henry M. Kissinger
Infocell Risk Managers Ltd.

Samuel Momanyi
Interfreight East Africa Limited

William Maema
Iseme, Kamau & Maema Advocates

James Kamau
Iseme, Kamau & Maema Advocates

Kamau Karori
Iseme, Kamau & Maema Advocates

Peter Gachuhi
*Kaplan & Stratton**

Oliver Fowler
Kaplan & Stratton

Jack Ranguma
Kenya Revenue Authority

Amoyo Andibo
Metropol East Africa Limited

Tom Onyango
Ochieng, Onyango, Kibet & Ohaga

Anne Kimotho
PricewaterhouseCoopers

Shaira Adamali
PricewaterhouseCoopers

Gavin McEwen
PricewaterhouseCoopers

Dipak Shah
PricewaterhouseCoopers

Mansoor A. Mohamed
Ruman Limited

Meshack Kipturgo
Siginon Freight Limited

Alexandra Kontos
Walker Kontos Advocates

Rina Thakar
Walker Kontos Advocates

KIRIBATI

John Ridgway
Pacific Legal Network

KOREA

Hansen Han
Maersk Korea Ltd.

Keunyeop Kim
Panalpina IAF (Korea) Ltd.

Sung Whan Lee
Ahnse Law Offices

Eui Jong Chung
Bae, Kim & Lee

Sung-Ho Moon
Horizon Law Group

Gee Hong Kim
Horizon Law Group

Ju Myung Hwang
*Hwang Mok Park**

Sang Il Park
Hwang Mok Park

Joshua Margolis
Hwang Mok Park

James Rim
Jungmin Law Offices

Jin Kim
Jungmin Law Offices

Dean Fealk
Kim & Chang

C. W. Hyun
Kim & Chang

Ae-Ryun Rho
Kim & Chang

Shin Hi-Taek
Kim & Chang

Jisung Park
Korea Information Service - KIS

Ando Yun
PricewaterhouseCoopers

Mina Yoo
PricewaterhouseCoopers

Mi-Sook Yoon
PricewaterhouseCoopers

Dong-Bum Kim
PricewaterhouseCoopers

Dae-Geun Kim
PricewaterhouseCoopers

Hongnam Lim
PricewaterhouseCoopers

Daniel Y. Kim
Sojong Partners

Yong S. Bae
Sojong Partners

Sung Jin Kim
Woo Yun Kang Jeong & Han

Young-Cheol Jeong
Woo Yun Kang Jeong & Han

KUWAIT

Abdullah Al-Ayoub
*Abdullah Kh. Al-Ayoub & Associates**

Rafiq Jaffer
Abdullah Kh. Al-Ayoub & Associates

Sam Habbas
Al Sarraf & Al Ruwayeh, in association with Stephenson Harwood

Reema Ali
Ali & Partners

Nazih Abdul Hameed
Al-Saleh & Partners

Eyad Omar Al-Serri
Credit Information Network

Paul Fardy
Kuwait Transcontinental Shipping Company

Mishare M. Al-Ghazali
Mishare M. Al-Ghazali & Partners

Adel Sami
Mishari Al-Ghazali & Partners

Labeed M. A. Abdal
The Law Firm of Labeed Abdal

KYRGYZ REPUBLIC

Sergio Purin
Ahlers

Alexander Korchagin
Baker & McKenzie, Central Asia

Curtis Masters
Baker & McKenzie, Central Asia

Akjoltoy Elebesova
Association of credit and financing organizations Credit Information Bureau

Gulnara Kalikova
Dignitas Law Firm

Bakytbek Saparaliev
Dignitas Law Firm

Tania Chogai
Dignitas Law Firm

Anna Fomina
In affiliation with Dignitas

Elmurat Abdraimov
In affiliation with Dignitas

Aisuluu Subanbekova
In affiliation with Dignitas

Temir Kazy
In affiliation with Dignitas

Sarsen Omrkulov
Kyrgyz Republic Customs Authority

Asel Kenenbaeva
Law Firm "Partner"

Julia Bulatova
Law Firm "Partner"

Mirgul Smanalieva
Law Firm "Partner"

Elena Kaeva
PricewaterhouseCoopers

Courtney Fowler
PricewaterhouseCoopers

Matthew Tallarovic
PricewaterhouseCoopers

Natalya Revenko
PricewaterhouseCoopers

Katherine Garkavets
PricewaterhouseCoopers

Ainura Abdyrakunova
USAID Legal Infrastructure for a Market Economy Project, implemented by ARD/Checchi

LAO PDR

Prasith Phommarath

Simmaly Vongsack
Bank of Lao PDR

Tyseng Ly
DFDL Mekong Law Group

Edward Nicholas
DFDL Mekong Law Group

Esther Lau
DFDL Mekong Law Group

Isabelle Robineau
DFDL Mekong Law Group

Lasonexay Chanthavong
DFDL Mekong Law Group

Louis-Martin Desautels
DFDL Mekong Law Group

Audray Souche
DFDL Mekong Law Group

Phivath Vorachak
Lao Bar Association

Vichit Sadettan
Lao Freight Forwarder Co. Ltd.

Siri Sayavong
Lao Trademark Agency

Maligna Saignavongs
Private Lawyer

John Biddle
PricewaterhouseCoopers

Richard Irwin
PricewaterhouseCoopers

Intong Oudom
Seneoudom Trading Co. Ltd.

LATVIA

Daina Zvirgzde
Ace Logistics Sia

Ivars Pommers
Advokatfirman Glimstedt

Kristine Stege
Baltmane & Bitans

Ilze Baltmane
Baltmane & Bitans

Laura Viksna
Bank of Latvia

Andis Conka
Bank of Latvia

Ludmila Kornijenko
Blueger & Plaude

Baiba Plaude
Blueger & Plaude

Dace Jenava
Jenava Birojs

Anita Tamberga-Salmane
Klavins, Slaidins & Loze

Jevgueni Jesilevskis
KPMG Latvia

Ivars Grunte
Law firm Grunte & Cers

Inese Rendeniece
Law firm Grunte & Cers

Daiga Zivtina
*Law Offices of Klavins & Slaidins**

Mikus Buls
Law Offices of Klavins & Slaidins

Filip Klavins
Law Offices of Klavins & Slaidins

Dace Silava-Tomsone
Lejins, Torgans & Vonsovics

Romualds Vonsovics
Lejins, Torgans & Vonsovics

Indrikis Liepa
LIEPA, SKOPINA, BORENIUS

Zane Stalberga - Markvarte
MARKVARTE & PARTNERI LAW OFFICE

Cameron Greaves
PRICEWATERHOUSECOOPERS

Zlata Elksnina
PRICEWATERHOUSECOOPERS

Ilze Abika
SKUDRA & UDRIS

Ziedonis Udris
SKUDRA & UDRIS

Edgars Briedis
SORAINEN LAW OFFICES

Eva Berlaus-Gulbe
SORAINEN LAW OFFICES

Janis Bite
SORAINEN LAW OFFICES

Gints Vilgerts
SORAINEN LAW OFFICES

Brigita Terauda
SORAINEN LAW OFFICES

Girts Ruda
SORAINEN LAW OFFICES

Edvins Kapostins
STATE LAND SERVICE OF THE REPUBLIC OF LATVIA

LEBANON

Salim El Meouchi
BADRI & SALIM EL MEOUCHI LAW FIRM

Nada Abusamra
BADRI & SALIM EL MEOUCHI LAW FIRM

Mazen Rasamny
BADRI & SALIM EL MEOUCHI LAW FIRM

Ramy Aoun
BADRI & SALIM EL MEOUCHI LAW FIRM

Choucair Najib
BANQUE DU LIBAN

Samir Baroudi
BAROUDI & ASSOCIATES

Jean Baroudi
BAROUDI & ASSOCIATES

Georges Jureidini
COSERV SARL PANALPINA AGENTS

Samir Francis
FREIGHT LEADER SARL

Mario Mohanna
GEORGE JABRE & ASSOCIATES

George Jabre
GEORGE JABRE & ASSOCIATES

Nabil Mallat
HYAM MALLAT LAW OFFICES

Georges Mallat
HYAM MALLAT LAW OFFICES

Fady Jamaleddine
JAMALEDDINE LAW FIRM

Georges Kadige
KADIGE & KADIGE LAW FIRM

Albert Laham
LAW OFFICE OF ALBERT LAHAM

Toufic Nehme
LAW OFFICE OF ALBERT LAIIAM

Fadi Moghaizel
MOGHAIZEL LAW OFFICES*

Reem Abou Fadel
MOGHAIZEL LAW OFFICES

Katia Bou
MOGHAIZEL LAW OFFICES

Dania George
PRICEWATERHOUSECOOPERS

Bassel Habiby
PRICEWATERHOUSECOOPERS

Nady Tyan
THE LAW OFFICES OF TYAN & ZGHEIB

LESOTHO

Theodore Ntlatlapa
DNT ARCHITECTS

Thabo Michael Letjama
LESOTHO REVENUE AUTHORITY

Pieter La Grange
MANICA AFRICA (PTY) LTD.

Qhalehang Letsika
MEI & MEI ATTORNEYS INC. / NATIONAL UNIVERSITY OF LESOTHO

Relebohile Ntene
MINISTRY OF EMPLOYMENT AND LABOR

Tseliso Daniel Makhaphela
MINISTRY OF LOCAL GOVERNMENT

Deborah Mofolo
MOFOLO, TAU - THABANE AND COMPANY

Thabo Mpaka
MPAKA CHAMBERS

Keketso Maleka
NALEDI CHAMBERS INCORPORATED

Thakane Chimombe
NALEDI CHAMBERS INCORPORATED

Palesa Khabele
NATIONAL UNIVERSITY OF LESOTHO

Thabiso Ramokoena
NEDBANK

T. Ntaopane
NEDBANK

Lindiwe Sephomolo
ORGANIZATION ASSOCIATION OF LESOTHO EMPLOYERS AND BUSINESS

Thuso Green
SECHABA CONSULTANTS

Borenahabokhethe Sekoneyla
SEKOYELA CHAMBERS & ASSOCIATES

Mathias Sheeran
SHEERAN AND ASSOCIATES

Vuyelwa Kotelo
VVM KOTELO AND CO.

Lebohang Molete
WEBBER NEWDIGATE

Victor Mesquita
MANICA AFRICA

Erle Koomets
PRICEWATERHOUSECOOPERS

Mark Badenhorst
PRICEWATERHOUSECOOPERS

Mathias Sheeran
SHEERAN & ASSOCIATES

LITHUANIA

Marius Jakulis Jason
AAA LAW FIRM

Ignas Puluikis
ACE LOGISTICS UAB

Kazimieras Ramonas
BANK OF LITHUANIA

Marius Navickas
FORESTA BUSINESS LAW GROUP

Agnes Zironaite
FORESTA BUSINESS LAW GROUP

Jurgita Rotomskiene
INFOBANKAS UAB

Giedre Domkute
J. JASINSKIO 16 B, VICTORIA BUILDING

Audrius Zvybas
LAW FIRM "BERNOTAS & DOMINAS GLIMSTEDT

Egidijus Bernotas
LAW FIRM "BERNOTAS & DOMINAS GLIMSTEDT

Dainius Stasiulis
LAW FIRM "BERNOTAS & DOMINAS GLIMSTEDT

Dalia Foigt
LAW FIRM D.FOIGT AND PARTNERS / REGIJA

Mindaugas Vaiciunas
LAW FIRM D. FOIGT AND PARTNERS / REGIJA

Darius Zabiela
LAW FIRM ZABIELA, ZABIELAITE & PARTNERS

Indre Jonaityte
LIDEIKA, PETRAUSKAS, VALIUNAS IR PARTNERIAI*

Rolandas Valiunas
LIDEIKA, PETRAUSKAS, VALIUNAS IR PARTNERIAI

Ramunas Petravicius
LIDEIKA, PETRAUSKAS, VALIUNAS IR PARTNERIAI

Rolandas Galvenas
LIDEIKA, PETRAUSKAS, VALIUNAS IR PARTNERIAI

Mindaugas Kiskis
LIDEIKA, PETRAUSKAS, VALIUNAS IR PARTNERIAI

Laimonas Skibarka
LIDEIKA, PETRAUSKAS, VALIUNAS IR PARTNERIAI

Vilija Vaitkute Pavan
LIDEIKA, PETRAUSKAS, VALIUNAS IR PARTNERIAI

Dovile Burgiene
LIDEIKA, PETRAUSKAS, VALIUNAS IR PARTNERIAI

Sarune Smeleviciute
PRICEWATERHOUSECOOPERS

Egidijus Kundelis
PRICEWATERHOUSECOOPERS

Lina Mockeliunaite
PRICEWATERHOUSECOOPERS

Kristina Bartuseviciene
PRICEWATERHOUSECOOPERS

Jurate Stulgyte
PRICEWATERHOUSECOOPERS

Marius Urbelis
SORAINEN LAW OFFICES

Tomas Davidonis
SORAINEN LAW OFFICES

Kestutis Adamonis
SORAINEN LAW OFFICES

Renata Berzanskiene
SORAINEN LAW OFFICES

Bronislovas Mikuta
STATE ENTERPRISE CENTRE OF REGISTERS

Edita Sumskiene
STATE ENTERPRISE CENTRE OF REGISTERS

Rasa Lubauskaite
THE CUSTOMS DEPARTMENT UNDER THE MINISTRY OF FINANCE

MACEDONIA, FYR

Zlatko Veterovski
CUSTOMS ADMINISTRATION

Marija Petroska
ECONOMIC CHAMBER OF MACEDONIA

Theodoros Giannitsakis
IKRP ROKAS & PARTNERS

Biljana Joanidis
LAW & PATENT OFFICE JOANIDIS

Dejan Knezovic, Esq.
LAW OFFICE KNEZOVIC & ASSOCIATES

Maja Drakulovska
LAW OFFICE PEPELJUGOSKI

Valentin Pepeljugoski
LAW OFFICE PEPELJUGOSKI

Zoran Andonovski
LAW OFFICE POLENAK

Kristijan Poolenak
LAW OFFICE POLENAK

Tatjana Popovski
LAW OFFICE POLENAK

Zlatko Antevski
LAWYERS ANTEVSKI

Irena Petkovska
LAWYERS ANTEVSKI

Ljubica Ruben
MENS LEGIS

Biljana Cakmakova
MENS LEGIS

Valerjan Monevski
MONEVSKI LAW FIRM

Sanja Iliovska Madzovska
NATIONAL BANK OF THE REPUBLIC OF MACEDONIA

Frosina Celeska
NATIONAL BANK OF THE REPUBLIC OF MACEDONIA

Rudi Lazarevski
PRICEWATERHOUSECOOPERS

Katerina Carceva
PRICEWATERHOUSECOOPERS

Zoran Cvetanoski
STATE AUTHORITY FOR GEODETIC WORKS

Charapich Sinisha
TIR - INTERNATIONAL FREIGHT FORWARDERS

MADAGASCAR

Allain Hubert Rajoelina
MAÎTRE ALLAIN HUBERT RAJOELINA

Jacques Chareyre
FIDAFRICA / PRICEWATERHOUSECOOPERS

Olivier Ribot
FIDAFRICA / PRICEWATERHOUSECOOPERS

Michel Pain
CABINET MAITRE MICHEL PAIN

Njiva Razanantsoa
BANQUE CENTRALE DE MADAGASCAR

Zakazo Ranaivoson
CABINET DE CONSEILS D'ENTREPRISES

Raphaël Jakoba
CABINET MADAGASCAR CONSEIL INTERNATIONAL

Justin Radilofe
CABINET RADILOFE

Thomas Reynders
CHECCHI AND COMPANY CONSULTING, INC.

Jean Moutton
FTL MADAGASCAR

Hanta Radilofe
HANTA RADILOFE LAW OFFICES

Rakotomanantsoa
MCI (MADAGASCAR CONSEIL INTERNATIONAL)

Danielle Rakotomanana
RAKOTOMANANA ADVOCAT AU BUREAU DE MADAGASCAR

Jules Raf
SDV MADAGASCAR

MALAWI

Krishna Savjani
—

Stuart Forster
BRITISH HIGH COMMISSION

Anthony Kamanga
MINISTRY OF JUSTICE

Temwa Nyirenda
NYIRENDA & MSISHA

Mark Badenhorst
PRICEWATERHOUSECOOPERS

Jim Ghobede
PRICEWATERHOUSECOOPERS

Kevin M. Carpenter
PRICEWATERHOUSECOOPERS

Jai Banda
SACRANIE, GOW & CO.

Roseline Gramani
SAVJANI & ASSOCIATES LAW FIRM

Ben Ndau
SAVJANI & ASSOCIATES LAW FIRM

Duncan Singano
SAVJANI & ASSOCIATES LAW FIRM

Krishna Savjani
SAVJANI & ASSOCIATES LAW FIRM

Andrews Katuya
SAVJANI & ASSOCIATES LAW FIRM

Shabir Latif
SCRANIE, GOW & CO.

Bansri Lakhani
SCRANIE, GOW & CO.

John Deans
SDV MALAWI

Eggrey Mpango
STUTTSFORDS INTERNATIONAL REMOVALS

Samuel Tembenu
TEMBENU MASUMBU & CO.

Marshal Chilenga
TF& PARTNERS

Ralph Kasambara
UNIVERSITY OF MALAWI

Alan Chinula
WILLIAM FAULKNER

D. A. Ravel
WILSON & MORGAN

MALAYSIA

Khoo Liong Chuan
ALLIED WAREHOUSES SDN. BHD.

Rajendra Navaratnam
AZMAN, DAVIDSON & CO.

Francis Tan
AZMAN, DAVIDSON & CO.

Jamie Lee
AZMI & ASSOCIATES

Hendun Abd Rahman
AZMI & ASSOCIATES

Azmi Mohd Ali
AZMI & ASSOCIATES

Chew Siew Kheam
CENTRAL BANK OF MALAYSIA

Chung Tze Keong
CTOS SDN BHD

Tharminder Singh
LOGAN SABAPATHY & CO.

Loganath Sabapathy
LOGAN SABAPATHY & CO.

Grace Yeo
MAERSK MALAYSIA SDN BHD

Shameer Bin Othman
NIK SAGHIR & ISMAIL

Vibhu Prakash
PANALPINA

Chuan Keat Khoo
PRICEWATERHOUSECOOPERS

Theresa Lim
PRICEWATERHOUSECOOPERS

Wan Heng Choon
PRICEWATERHOUSECOOPERS

Peter Wee
PRICEWATERHOUSECOOPERS

Wynnee Tan
PRICEWATERHOUSECOOPERS

Chin Sin Lan
RASLAN - LOONG

Caesar Loong
RASLAN - LOONG

Melina Yong
RASLAN - LOONG

Ng Swee Kee
SHEARN DELAMORE & CO.

Jong Yon Tzan
SHEARN DELAMORE & CO.

Lim Koon Huan
SKRINE*

Elaine Ho
SKRINE

Wong Chong Wah
SKRINE

Yun Chang
TAY & PARTNERS

Leonard Yeoh
TAY & PARTNERS

Chia Chee Hoong
ZAIN & CO.

J.Wilfred Durai
ZAIN & CO.

Wilfred Abraham
ZUL RAFIQUE & PARTNERS, ADVOCATE & SOLICITORS

MALDIVES

Mohamed Hameed
ANTRAC MALDIVES PVT. LTD

Abdul Rashees Ibrahim
MALDIVES CUSTOMS SERVICE

Ahmed Muizzu
MUIZZU, SUOOD & CO..

Sriyani Perera
PRICEWATERHOUSECOOPERS

Shuaib M. Shah
SHAH, HUSSAIN & CO. BARRISTERS AND ATTORNEYS

MALI

Mamadou Keita-Kanda
CHAMBER OF NOTARIES

Jacques Chareyre
FIDAFRICA / PRICEWATERHOUSECOOPERS

Dominique Taty
FIDAFRICA / PRICEWATERHOUSECOOPERS

Edouard Messou
FIDAFRICA / PRICEWATERHOUSECOOPERS

Dembele Fatoumata Kone
ASSOCIATION DES ANCIENS PARTICIPANTS DE L'IDLO AU MALI

Malick Badara Sow
ATELIER D'ARCHITECTURE ET D'URBANISME

Ahmadou Toure
ETUDE DE MAÎTRE AHMADOU TOURE

Amadou Camara
ETUDE DE MAÎTRE AMADOU CAMARA

Alassne Diallo
ETUDE MAIRE DIALLO ALASSANE

Djibril Guindo
JURIFIS CONSULT SCPA

Aida Niare-Toure
JURIFIS CONSULT SCPA

Diop Mohamed Abdoulaye
SDV MALI

M. Domptail
SDV MALI

François Nare
CENTRALE DES RISQUES DE L'UNION MONÉTAIRE OUEST AFRICAINE

Jean Marcel Gariador
SDV - BOLLORÉ DTI

Denis Cordel
SDV - BOLLORÉ DTI

MARSHALL ISLANDS

Philip Welch
MICRONESIAN SHIPPING AGENCIES

Kenneth Barden
MINISTRY OF FINANCE

MAURITANIA

Moulaye El Ghali Ould
Aliou Sall
ASSURIM

Menna Ould Hamoni
BANQUE CENTRALE DE MAURITANIE

Ahmed Salem Ould Bouhoubeyni
CABINET BOUHOUBEYNI

Cheikhani Jules
CABINET MAÎTRE JULES

Oumar Mohamed Moctar
CABINET MAÎTRE OUMAR MOHAMED MOCTAR

Sidi Mohamed Ould Mohamed Lemine
CHAMBRE COMMERCIALE PRES DE LA COUR D'APPEL DE NOUAKCHOTT

Maouloud Vall Hady Seyid
ETUDE MAITRE HADY

Jacques Chareyre
FIDAFRICA / PRICEWATERHOUSECOOPERS

Aly Ould Salihi
MAERSK MAURTITANIE SA

Saliou Niang
FIDAFRICA / PRICEWATERHOUSECOOPERS

MAURITIUS

Urmila Boolell
BANYMANDHUB BOOLELL CHAMBERS

Clarel Benoit
CLAREL BENOIT, M.A.

Tenuja Ghose
CLAREL BENOIT, M.A.

Afzal Delbar
CUSTOMS HOUSE BROKER ASSOCIATION

Martine de Fleuriot de la Colinière
DE COMARMOND & KOENIG*

Thierry Koenig
DE COMARMOND & KOENIG

Jean-Pierre Montocchio
ETUDE JEAN-PIERRE MONTOCCHIO & BERNARD D'HOTMAN DE VILLIERS

Catherine de Rosnay
LEGIS & PARTNERS

Robert Ferrat
LEGIS & PARTNERS

Parikshat Teeluck
MAERSK LOGISTICS MAURITIUS LTD.

Yeung Yin In David
MAERSK LOGISTICS MAURITIUS LTD.

Wong Chung Toi
MAURITIUS PORTS AUTHORITY

Bert C. Cunningham
MINISTRY OF FINANCE/CUSTOMS AND EXCISE DEPARTMENT

Shakeel Mohamed
MOHAMED CHAMBERS LAW OFFICES

Robert Bigaignon
PRICEWATERHOUSECOOPERS

Didier Lenette
PRICEWATERHOUSECOOPERS

MEXICO

Oscar O. Cano
ADEATH LOGISTICS SA DE CV

Perez Martinez Alfonso
ADMINISTRACIÓN PORTUARIA INTEGRAL DE MANZANILLO S.A DE C.V.

Hector Alejandro Gutierrez Fuentes
ADMINISTRATION GENERAL OF CUSTOMS

Ignacio Diaque
BAKER & MCKENZIE

Carlos Grimm
BAKER & MCKENZIE

María Casas Lopez
BAKER & MCKENZIE

Mariano Enriquez-Mejia
BAKER & MCKENZIE

Gerardo Garreto-Chavez
BARRERA, SIQUEIROS Y TORRES LANDA

Juan Francisco Torres-Landa
BARRERA, SIQUEIROS Y TORRES LANDA

Oscar de la Vega
BASHAM, RINGE Y CORREA, MEMBER OF IUS LABORIS

Monica Schiaffino Pérez
BASHAM, RINGE Y CORREA, MEMBER OF IUS LABORIS

Jorge Videgaray Verdad
CAMARA MEXICANA DE LA INDUSTRIA DE LA CONSTRUCCION

Rafael Licea Alvarez
CAMARA MEXICANA DE LA INDUSTRIA DE LA CONSTRUCCION

Roberto Hernandez Garcia
COMAD SC

Adrián Salgado Morante
COMAD SC

Enrique Nort
COMISION NACIONAL BANCARIA Y DE VALORES

Arturo Pedromo
GALICIA Y ROBLES

Héctor Kuri
GALICIA Y ROBLES

Carlos Chávez
GALICIA Y ROBLES

Juan Manuel Rincon
GALICIA Y ROBLES

Manuel Galicia R.
GALICIA Y ROBLES

Teresa Gómez Neri
GOODRICH, RIQUELME Y ASOCIADOS*

David Enríquez
GOODRICH, RIQUELME Y ASOCIADOS

David H. Brill
GOODRICH, RIQUELME Y ASOCIADOS

Eugenia Gonzalez
GOODRICH, RIQUELME Y ASOCIADOS

Bill Kryzda
GOODRICH, RIQUELME Y ASOCIADOS

Jorge León Orantes Vallejo
GOODRICH, RIQUELME Y ASOCIADOS

Jorge León
GOODRICH, RIQUELME Y ASOCIADOS

Tatiana Ortega
GOODRICH, RIQUELME Y ASOCIADOS

Cristina Sanchez-Urtiz
MIRANDA, ESTAVILLO, STAINES Y PIZARRO-SUAREZ

Gustavo Hernandez Gutierrez
PANALPINA

Carlos Montemayor
PRICEWATERHOUSECOOPERS

Patricia Schroeder
PRICEWATERHOUSECOOPERS

Salvador Esquivel Bernal
PRICEWATERHOUSECOOPERS

Carlos Frias
PRICEWATERHOUSECOOPERS

Fernando Rivadeneyra
RIVADENEYRA, TREVINO & DE CAMPO, S.C.

Yazbek Taja
RIVADENEYRA, TREVINO & DE CAMPO, S.C.

Carlos Sanchez-Mejorada
SANCHEZ-MEJORADA Y PASQUEL

Irela Robles Victory
SECRETARIA DE DESARROLLO ECONOMICO

MICRONESIA

Kenneth Barden
MINISTRY OF FINANCE

Seremea Arnold
TRANSCO LTD.

MOLDOVA

Lurie Lungu
ADVOCATE, LLP

Irina Moghiliova
BRODSKY USKOV LOOPER REED & PARTNERS

Nikolay Shadrin
BRODSKY USKOV LOOPER REED & PARTNERS

Celac Olga
BRODSKY USKOV LOOPER REED & PARTNERS

Glebb Morozov
BRODSKY USKOV LOOPER REED & PARTNERS

Alexi Ghertescu
BRODSKY USKOV LOOPER REED & PARTNERS

David A. Brodsky
BRODSKY USKOV LOOPER REED & PARTNERS

Irina Verhovetchi
BSMB LEGAL COUNSELLORS

Maximenco Serghei
BSMB LEGAL COUNSELLORS

Sirghi Viorel
BSMB LEGAL COUNSELLORS

Nicolae Vilcu
CUSTOMS SERVICE OF THE REPUBLIC OF MOLDOVA

Veacheslav Shokin
CONSOLIDATED AGRICULTURAL PROJECTS' MANAGEMENT UNIT

Liliana Sirbu
FIRST CADASTRE PROJECT

Alexander Turcan
LAW OFFICE OF ALEXANDER TURCAN

Carina Turcan
LAW OFFICE OF ALEXANDER TURCAN

Victor A. Levintsa
LEVINTSA & ASSOCIATES ADVOCATE

Rene Bijvoet
PRICEWATERHOUSECOOPERS

Nelea Moraru
PRICEWATERHOUSECOOPERS

Alexandra Placinta
PRICEWATERHOUSECOOPERS

Gabriela Cunev
PRICEWATERHOUSECOOPERS

Andrian Candu
PRICEWATERHOUSECOOPERS

Mihaela Mitroi
PRICEWATERHOUSECOOPERS

Svetlana Ceban
PRICEWATERHOUSECOOPERS

Pirnevu Ruslan
QUEHENBERGER-HELLMANN MOLDOVA SRL

Octavian Cazac
TURCAN & TURCAN

Veronica Bradautanu
TURCAN & TURCAN

MONGOLIA

Batzaya Bodikhuu
ANAND & ANAND ADVOCATES

David Buxbaum
ANDERSON & ANDERSON

Enkhtuya Nichibuu
ANDERSON & ANDERSON

Davaadorj Nomingerel
ANDERSON & ANDERSON

Batmunkh Javkhlant
ANDERSON & ANDERSON (BRAND FARRAR BUXBAUM)

Solongo Zulbaatar
ANDERSON & ANDERSON (BRAND FARRAR BUXBAUM)

Ulziideleg Taivan
CREDIT INFORMATION BUREAU

Daniel Mahoney
LYNCH & MAHONEY

Bayarmaa Badarch
LYNCH & MAHONEY

Elena Kaeva
PRICEWATERHOUSECOOPERS

Katherine Garkavets
PRICEWATERHOUSECOOPERS

Courtney Fowler
PRICEWATERHOUSECOOPERS

Matthew Tallarovic
PRICEWATERHOUSECOOPERS

Natalya Revenko
PRICEWATERHOUSECOOPERS

Telenged Baast
MTT MONGOLIAN TRANSPORT TEAM LLC BEIJING OFFICE

Batbold Amarsanaa
SCHOOL OF LAW, NATIONAL UNIVERSITY OF MONGOLIA

M. Odonhuu
TSETS LAW FIRM

N. Zorigt
TUUSHIN COMPANY LIMITED

Reginald Webb
PRICEWATERHOUSECOOPERS

MOROCCO

Youssef Berrada

Youssef El Fallah
ABA MOROCCO

Myriam Emmanuelle Bennani
AMIN HAJJI & ASSOCIÉS ASSOCIATION D'AVOCATS

Amin Hajji
AMIN HAJJI & ASSOCIÉS ASSOCIATION D'AVOCATS

Abdelmajid Khachai
BAKER & MCKENZIE, WONG & LEOW

Ahmed Lahrache
BANK AL-MAGHRIB

Maria Belafia
CABINET MAÎTRE BELAFIA

Richard Cantin
*CABINET NACIRI & ASSOCIÉS**

Hicham Naciri
CABINET NACIRI & ASSOCIÉS

Anis Mahfoud
CMS BUREAU FRANCIS LEFEBVRE

Frédéric Elbar
CMS BUREAU FRANCIS LEFEBVRE

Nadia Kettani
KETTANI LAW FIRM

Azzedine Kettani
KETTANI LAW FIRM

Mohamed Mehdi Ibn Abdeljalil
MOHAMED MEHDI IBN ABDELJALIL

Réda Oulamine
NACIRI & ASSOCIES / GIDE LOYRETTE NOUEL

Abdelwaret Kabbaj
PRICEWATERHOUSECOOPERS

Fatima Erradiom
PRICEWATERHOUSECOOPERS

Mark Badenhorst
PRICEWATERHOUSECOOPERS

Xavier Despin
SCAC MAROC - GROUP SDV

MOZAMBIQUE

Ali Eduardo Barrote
BARROTE CONSTRUCOES LDA

Anastacia Chamusse
CENTRAL DE REGISTROS DE CRÉDITO, BANK OF MOZAMBIQUE

Gabriel Machado
CONFEDERACAO DAS ASSOCIACOES ECONOMICAS DE MOCAMBIQUE

Rufino Lucas
CONSRUFIL

Christopher Tanner
FAO REPRESENTATION IN MOZAMBIQUE

Auxílio Eugénio Nhabanga
FERNANDA LOPES & ASSOCIADOS - ADVOGADOS

André Couto
H. GAMITO, COUTO, GONÇALVES PEREIRA E CASTELO BRANCO & ASSOCIADOS

Adrian Frey
JOSE CALDEIRA & ASSOCIATES

Orquídea Palmíra Massarongo
JOSE CALDEIRA & ASSOCIATES

Louise Alston
JOSE CALDEIRA & ASSOCIATES

José Caldeira
JOSE CALDEIRA & ASSOCIATES

Jennifer Garvey
KPMG AUDITORIA E CONSULTORIA, SARL

Manuel Eduardo Guta
MANI ARTE CONSTRUCOES LDA

Maria João Dionísio
MIRANDA, CORREIA, AMENDOEIRA & ASSOCIADOS

Rodrigo Ferreira Rocha
MIRANDA, CORREIA, AMENDOEIRA & ASSOCIADOS

Pedro Ernesto Chambe
MOCARGO SARL

Manuel Didier Malunga
NATIONAL DIRECTORATE OF REGISTRY AND NOTARIES

Paolo Pimenta
PIMENTA, DIONÍSIO E ASSOCIADOS - SOCIEDADE DE ADVOGADOS

Mark Badenhorst
PRICEWATERHOUSECOOPERS

Malaika Ribeiro
PRICEWATERHOUSECOOPERS

Maria Isabel Fernandes
PRICEWATERHOUSECOOPERS

Mariam Bibi Umarji
SA CONSULTORIA E INVESTIMENTOS LDA

Alexandra Carvalho
SOLE PRACTITIONER

Agostinho Zacarias Vuma
VUMA CONSTRUCOES LDA

Carlos de Sousa e Brito
CARLOS DE SOUSA E BRITO & ASSOCIADOS

NAMIBIA

Chris Brandt
CHRIS BRANDT & ASSOCIATES

Hans Gerdes
ENGLING, STRITTER & PARTNERS

Eckart Pfeifer
FISHER, QUARMBY & PFIFER

Herman Charl Kinghorn
KINGHORN ASSOCIATES

GF Kopplinger
LORENTZ & BONE

Hanno D. Bossau
LORENTZ & BONE

Paul A. E. Wolff
MANICA GROUP NAMIBIA (PTY) LTD.

Victor Mesquita
MANICA AFRICA

Renate Rossler
P.F. KOEP & CO.

Peter Koep
P.F. KOEP & CO.

Willem Carel Kotze
P.F. KOEP & CO.

Hennie Gous
PRICEWATERHOUSECOOPERS

NEPAL

Prem Shanker Shrestha
CREDIT INFORMATION BUREAU LTD.

Purna Chitra
CREDIT INFORMATION BUREAU LTD.

Madan Sharma
CSC & CO./ PRICEWATERHOUSECOOPERS

Bodhraj Niroula
CUSTOM OF NEPAL

Megh Raj Pokhrel
DHRUBA BAR SINGH THAPA & ASSOCIATES

Kusum Shrestha
KUSUM LAW FIRM

Sudheer Shrestha
KUSUM LAW FIRM

Shrawan Khanal
M.K. NIRMAN SEWA PVT. LTD.

Matrika Niraula
NIRAULA LAW CHAMBER

Bharat Rajupreti
PIONEER LAW ASSOCIATE

Devendra Pradhan
PRADHAN & ASSOCIATES

Purna Man Shakya
RELIANCE LAW FIRM

Ashok Man Kapali
SHANGRI-LA FREIGHT PVT. LTD.

NETHERLANDS

Marc Abraham
BRADA KUTTNER

Dunja Madunic
BRADA KUTTNER

Rolf S. Jelsma
BRADA KUTTNER

Hylda Wiarda
BRONSGEEST DEUR ADVOCATEN, MEMBER OF IUS LABORIS

Paul van der Molen
CADASTRE, LAND REGISTRY AGENCY AND MAPPING AGENCY

Barteline A. Cnossen
DE BRAUW BLACKSTONE WESTBROEK

Stefan Sagel
DE BRAUW BLACKSTONE WESTBROEK

Peter van Schilfgaarde
DE BRAUW BLACKSTONE WESTBROEK

Margriet H. de Boer
DE BRAUW BLACKSTONE WESTBROEK

Emilia L.C. van Egmond-de Wilde de Ligny
FACULTY OF TECHNOLOGY MANAGEMENT, EINDHOVEN UNIVERSITY OF TECHNOLOGY

Irene Vloerberg
FACULTY OF TECHNOLOGY MANAGEMENT, EINDHOVEN UNIVERSITY OF TECHNOLOGY

Glenn C. Haulussy
HAULUSSY ADVOKATEN BV

Rutger Schimmelpenninck
*HOUTHOFF BURUMA**

Henri Bentfort van Valkenburg
HOUTHOFF BURUMA

Jaap Koster
HOUTHOFF BURUMA

Natalia Lorenzo van Rooij
HOUTHOFF BURUMA

Els van der Riet
HOUTHOFF BURUMA

Jamila Tib
HOUTHOFF BURUMA

Marcel Willems
KENNEDY VAN DER LAAN

Taco de Lange
LEXENCE

A. van der Zwaan
MAERSK BENELUX B.V.

Michel Gadron
MAERSK BENELUX B.V.

Eugene Witjes
MINISTRY OF HOUSING, SPATIAL PLANNING AND THE ENVIRONMENT - GOVERNMENT BUILDINGS AGENCY

W.R. Bremer
MINISTRY OF HOUSING, SPATIAL PLANNING AND THE ENVIRONMENT - GOVERNMENT BUILDINGS AGENCY

Joost Cuijpers
MINISTRY OF SOCIAL AFFAIRS AND EMPLOYMENT

Paul Huijzendveld
MINISTRY OF SOCIAL AFFAIRS AND EMPLOYMENT

Jeroen Holland
NAUTA DUTILH ATTORNEYS

Jaap-Jan Trommel
NAUTA DUTILH ATTORNEYS

Richard W. Bakker
OCEAN-TRANS INTERNATIONAL BV

Frits Meijer
OTB RESEARCH INSTITUTE FOR HOUSING, URBAN AND MOBILITY STUDIES

Remco van der Linden
PRICEWATERHOUSECOOPERS BELASTINGADVISEURS NV

Jan Carel van Dorp
PRICEWATERHOUSECOOPERS BELASTINGADVISEURS NV

Karin Schreuder
STICHTING BUREAU KREDIET REGISTRATIE

Joop Lobstein
STICHTING BUREAU KREDIET REGISTRATIE

Hugo Reumkens
VAN DOORNE

NEW ZEALAND

Jane Wilson
BAYCORP ADVANTAGE

Chris Gordon
BELL GULLY

Niels Campbell
BELL GULLY

Alastair Charles Hercus
BUDDLE FINDLAY

Russell Lawn
BUILDLAW - KUMEU-HUAPAI LAW CENTRE

Geoff Bevan
CHAPMAN TRIPP

Lester Roy Dempster
CONVEYANCERS NZ LTD.

Michael McLean Toepfer
HESKETH HENRY

Richard Wilson
JACKSON RUSSELL

Don Grant
LAND INFORMATION NEW ZEALAND

John Spittal
LAND INFORMATION NEW ZEALAND

Kevin Kelly
LAND INFORMATION NEW ZEALAND

Robbie Muir
LAND INFORMATION NEW ZEALAND

Neill Sullivan
LAND INFORMATION NEW ZEALAND

Warwick Quinn
LAND INFORMATION NEW ZEALAND

Stuart Barnard
MINTER ELLISON RUDD WATTS

Jeffrey Lai
MINTER ELLISON RUDD WATTS

Kate Lane
MINTER ELLISON RUDD WATTS

Sean Gollin
MINTER ELLISON RUDD WATTS

Allen Bruford
NEW ZEALAND CUSTOMS SERVICE

Philip Coombe
PANALPINA WORLD TRANSPORT

Peter Boyce
PRICEWATERHOUSECOOPERS

Kevin Best
PRICEWATERHOUSECOOPERS

John Cuthbertson
PRICEWATERHOUSECOOPERS

Gregory Towers
*SIMPSON GRIERSON**

Rachel Menhennet
SIMPSON GRIERSON

Sarah Walsh
SIMPSON GRIERSON

Deepal Kumar
SIMPSON GRIERSON

Shelley Cave
SIMPSON GRIERSON

Keryn White
SIMPSON GRIERSON

Hershla Lfwersen
SIMPSON GRIERSON

Michael Cole
SIMPSON GRIERSON

NICARAGUA

Martin Garcia Raudez
ACZALAW

Minerva Bellorin
ACZALAW

José Aníbal Olivas Cajina
*ALVARADO Y ASOCIADOS**

Gloria Maria de Alvarado
ALVARADO Y ASOCIADOS

César Carlos Porras Rosses
ALVARADO Y ASOCIADOS

Maria Jose Bendaña
BENDAÑA & BENDAÑA

Jacinto Obregon Sanchez
BUFETE JURIDICO OBREGON Y ASOCIADOS

Humberto Carrión
CARRIÓN, SOMARRIBA & ASOCIADOS

Kenneth Gadea
ECODISE

Roberto Argüello Villavicencio
F.A. ARIAS & MUÑOZ

Gustavo Adolfo Vargas
F.A. ARIAS & MUÑOZ

Bertha Argüello de Rizo
F.A. ARIAS & MUÑOZ

Hernán Estrada
LEXINCORP

Ricardo Vega Jackson
NICARAGUAN CUSTOMS SERVICE

Ramon Ortega
PRICEWATERHOUSECOOPERS

Ludovino Colón Sánchez
PRICEWATERHOUSECOOPERS

Alejandro Fernandez
PRICEWATERHOUSECOOPERS

Mario Taylor
ROCEDES

James Voughn
ROCEDES

Carlos Bonilla
SUPERINTENDENCIA DE BANCOS Y DE OTRAS INSTITUCIONES FINANCIERAS

José Evenor Taboada
TABOADA & ASOCIADOS

Rodrigo Taboada
TABOADA & ASOCIADOS

NIGER

François Nare
CENTRALE DES RISQUES DE L'UNION MONÉTAIRE OUEST AFRICAINE

Jacques Chareyre
FIDAFRICA / PRICEWATERHOUSECOOPERS

Dominique Taty
FIDAFRICA / PRICEWATERHOUSECOOPERS

Edouard Messou
FIDAFRICA / PRICEWATERHOUSECOOPERS

Mounkaila Adama
Fati Kountche

Fati Kountche
CABINET FATI KOUNTCHE

Bernar-Oliver Kouaovi
CABINET KOUAOVI

Marc Lebihan
CABINET MARC LEBIHAN & COLLABORATEURS

Samna Daouda
SCPA MANDELA

Laurent Puerta
SDV - NIGER

NIGERIA

Ladi Taiwo
ABDULAI, TAIWO & CO.

Lawrence Fubara Anga
AELEX PARTNERS

Olu Funke Adekoya
AELEX PARTNERS

Nonyelum Okeke
AJUMOGOBIA & OKEKE

Oluseyi Abiodun Akinwunmi
AKINWUNMI & BUSARI

Olaleye Adebiyi
ALUKO & OYEBODE

Gbenga Oyebode
ALUKO & OYEBODE

Jobalo Oshikanlu
ALUKO & OYEBODE

S.Y. Salami
AVIOMARINE TRANSPORT AGENCIES LIMITED

Dozie Okwuosah
CENTRAL BANK OF NIGERIA

Uzoma Ogbonna
CHIEF LAW AGU EZETAH & CO.

Lawrence Ezetah
CHIEF LAW AGU EZETAH & CO.

Francisca Agbasi
CHIEF LAW AGU EZETAH & CO.

Taiwo Ayedun
CREDIT REGISTRY SERVICES LTD.

O.J. Ebohon
DE MONTFORT UNIVERSITY

Samuel Etuk
ETUK & URUA

F. O. Akrinrele
F.O. AKINRELE & CO.

Adamu M. Usman
F.O. AKINRELE & CO.

Olufemi Sunmonu
FEMI SUNMONU & ASSOCIATES

Ndubisi Chuks Nwasike
FIRSTCOUNSEL FIRM

Hauwa Evelyn Shekarau
H. E. SHEKARAU & CO.

Samuel O. Umah
HARRITEX GROUP

Tokunbo Agoro
JAIYE AGORO& CO.

NIGERIAN CUSTOMS AUTHORITY

Patrick Okonjo
OKONJO, ODIAWA & EBIE

Raphael E. Emezie
PANALPINA WORLD TRANSPORT (NIGERIA) LTD

Tolulope Olanrewaju
PRICEWATERHOUSECOOPERS

Steve Okello
PRICEWATERHOUSECOOPERS

Ken Aitken
PRICEWATERHOUSECOOPERS

Steve Kanyatte
PRICEWATERHOUSECOOPERS

Henrietta Onaga
PRICEWATERHOUSECOOPERS

Chike Obianwu
UDO UDOMA & BELO-OSAGIE

Daniel Agbor
UDO UDOMA & BELO-OSAGIE

Tunde Osasona
ZAFO GLOBAL LINKS LTD.

NORWAY

Johan Ratvik
ADVOKATFIRMA DLA NORDIC DA

Svein Sulland
ADVOKATFIRMAET SELMER DA

Bernt Olav Steinland
ADVOKATFIRMAET SELMER DA

Jorunn Eriksson
CREDITINFORM AS

Lars Carlsson
CREDITINFORM AS

Vegard Sivertsen
DELOITTE & TOUCHE TOHMATSU

Aase Aa. Lundgaard
DELOITTE & TOUCHE TOHMATSU

Nils-Petter Wedege
DIRECTORATE OF LABOUR INSPECTION

Amund Fougner
HJORT, MEMBER OF IUS LABORIS

Thomas S. Farhang
KVALE & CO. ANS

Robert Romansky
KVALE & CO. ANS

Anne Ulset Sande
KVALE & CO. ANS

Tore Ruud
OVERSEAS SHIPPING AS

Dag Halfdan Sem
PORT OF OSLO

Odd Hylland
PRICEWATERHOUSECOOPERS

Knut Ekern
PRICEWATERHOUSECOOPERS

Morten Beck
PRICEWATERHOUSECOOPERS

Tove Ihle-Hansen
PRICEWATERHOUSECOOPERS

Carl Christiansen
RAEDER ADVOKATFIRMA

Niels Kiaer
RIME & CO. ADVOKATFIRMA DAV

Finn Rime
RIME & CO. ADVOKATFIRMA DAV

Lillann Bugge
SCHJODT LAW FIRM

Claus R. Flinder
SIMONSEN FØYEN ADVOKATFIRMA DA

Helge Onsrud
STATENS KARTVERK (NORWEGIAN MAPPING AND CADASTRE AUTHORITY)

Finn Erik Engzelius
*THOMMESSEN KREFTING GREVE LUND AS**

Stein Fagerhaug
THOMMESSEN KREFTING GREVE LUND AS

Jorgen Lund
THOMMESSEN KREFTING GREVE LUND AS

Stig Berge
THOMMESSEN KREFTING GREVE LUND AS

Petter Bjerke
THOMMESSEN KREFTING GREVE LUND AS

Eirik Vikanes
THOMMESSEN KREFTING GREVE LUND AS

Bjørn H. Kise
VOGT & WIIG AS

Thomas Nordgard
VOGT & WIIG AS

Marit Håvemoen
WIKBORG, REIN & CO.

OMAN

Ala'a Eldin Mohammed
ABU-GHAZALEH INTELLECTUAL PROPERTY

Mansoor Jamal Malik
AL ALAWI, MANSOOR JAMAL & CO.

Sohaib Ishaque
AL ALAWI, MANSOOR JAMAL & CO.

Maqbool Khabori
AL KHABORI LEGAL CONSULTANTS

P.E. Lalachen
HASSAN AL ANSARI LEGAL CONSULTANCY

Mohammed Ahmed Ajham AlShahri
JANASHAL & SHAHRI

Pradhnesh Bhonsale
MAERSK SHIPPING SERVICES & CO. LLC

Rajan Karia
MIDDLE EAST SHIPPING CO.LTD.

Mohsin Al Haddad
MOHSIN AL-HADAD & AMUR AL-KIYUMI & PARTNERS

Pushpa Malani
PRICEWATERHOUSECOOPERS

Jeff Todd
PRICEWATERHOUSECOOPERS

Said Al Shahry
SAID AL SHAHRY LAW OFFICE

Deborah Hatfield
TROWERS & HAMLINS

Sarah Humpleby
TROWERS & HAMLINS

PAKISTAN

Salman Nasim
A. F. FERGUSON & CO.

Khalid Mahmood
A. F. FERGUSON & CO.

Rashid Ibrahim
A. F. FERGUSON & CO.

Jawad A. Sarwana
ABRAHAM & SARWANA

Farooq Abdullah
ABRAHAM & SARWANA

Masood Ahmed
ABRAHAM & SARWANA

Waheed Ahmad
AKHTAR SHABIR LAW ASSOCIATES

Mishael Ahmed
AZAM CHAUDHRY LAW ASSOCIATES

Farooq Akhtar
AZAM CHAUDHRY LAW ASSOCIATES

Nadia Chaudhry
Azam Chaudhry Law Associates

Mohammad Azam Chaudhry
Azam Chaudhry Law Associates

Rafiq. A. Nazir
Azam Chaudhry Law Associates

Tariq Bilal
Bilal Law Associates

Tariq Nasim Jan
Datacheck (Pvt) Limited

Omair Nasim
Empire Logistics

Ahmad Syed Akhter
Group 'O' Pyramid Logistics Group / Ms. Pyramid Pakistan

Haider Shamsi
Haider Shamsi and Co

Salman Talibuddin
Kabraji & Talibuddin Advocates & Legal Counsellors

Saleem uz Zaman
Kabraji & Talibuddin Advocates & Legal Counsellors

Khalid Daudpota
Khalid Daudpota & Co.

Anwar Mansoor Khan
Khan & Associates

Mansoor Khan
Khan & Associates

Said Khan
News-VIS Credit Information Services

Mahomed Jaffer
Orr Dignam & Co.

Mamoon Khan
Orr Dignam & Co.

Nadeem Ahmad
Orr Dignam & Co.

Rajesh Khanna
Port Services Corporation

Soli Parakh
PricewaterhouseCoopers

Rashid Ibrahim
PricewaterhouseCoopers

Ikram Fayaz
Qamar Abbas & Company

Abdul Rahman
Qamar Abbas & Company

Javed Khan
Raaziq International Pvt. Ltd.

Masood Khan Afridi
Rizvi, Isa, Afridi & Angell*

Ali Adnan Ibrahim
Rizvi, Isa, Afridi & Angell

Javed Iqbal Qureshi
Rizvi, Isa, Afridi & Angell

Faisal Fazli
Rizvi, Isa, Afridi & Angell

Muhammed Akhtar Javed
State Bank of Pakistan

Aftab Ahmed Khan
Surridge & Beecheno

Khurran Rashid
Surridge & Beecheno

Huma Shah
Surridge & Beecheno

Ilyas Zafar
Zafar & Associates LLP

PALAU

Kenneth Barden
Ministry of Finance (Republic of Palau)

John Ridgeway
Pacific Legal Network

PANAMA

Raúl Zuñiga Brid
Aleman, Cordero, Galindo & Lee

Alfredo Ramirez Jr.
Alfaro, Ferrer and Ramirez

Francisco Arias G.
Arias Fabrega & Fabrega

Jorge González
Arias, Aleman & Mora

José Miguel Navarrete
Arosemena, Noriega & Contreras*

Julio Cesar Contreras, III, Esq.
Arosemena, Noriega & Contreras

Shanina Jean Contreras J.
Arosemena, Noriega & Contreras

Luz María Salamina
Asociación Panameña de Crédito

Ricardo Eskildsen Morales
Eskildsen & Eskildsen

Jorge Garrido
Garrido & Garrido

Juan Tejada Mora
Icaza, Gonzalez-Ruiz & Aleman

Ramon Varela
Morgan & Morgan

Francisco Pérez
Patton Moreno & Asvat

Ebrahim Asvat
Patton Moreno & Asvat

Ivette Martínez S.
Patton Moreno & Asvat

Alejandro Fernandez
PricewaterhouseCoopers

Ramon Ortega
PricewaterhouseCoopers

Ludovino Colón Sánchez
PricewaterhouseCoopers

Alexandra Duque
Sucre, Arias & Reyes

Thais Chalmers
Sucre, Arias & Reyes

José Juan Márquez
Sucre, Arias & Reyes

Ernesto B. Arias
Sucre, Arias & Reyes

PAPUA NEW GUINEA

Anthony Smare
Allens Arthur Robinson

Vincent Bull
Allens Arthur Robinson

Lynette Baratai-Pokas
Celcor Inc.

Winifred T. Kamit
Gadens Lawyers

John Ridgway
Pacific Legal Network

Thomas Taberia
PricewaterhouseCoopers

John Leahy
PricewaterhouseCoopers

Rob Aarvold
Steamships Shipping & Transport

Gaudi Kidu
Structon Architects, Ltd.

PARAGUAY

Luis Breuer
Berkemeyer Attorneys and Counselors

Hugo Berkemeyer
Berkemeyer Attorneys and Counselors

Julio Gonzalez Caballero
Central de Riesgos Crediticios de BCP

Pablo Livieres Guggiari
Estudio Juridico Caniza-Livieres

Nestor Loizaga
Ferrere Abogados

Juan Bautista Fiorio Gimenez
Fiorio, Cardozo & Alvarado

Marcelo Alvarado
Fiorio, Cardozo & Alvarado

Armindo Riquelme
Fiorio, Cardozo & Alvarado

Ramón Antonio Castillo Saenz
Informconf S.A.

Roberto Moreno Rodriguez Alcala
Moreno Ruffinelli & Asociados

Esteban Burt
Peroni, Sosa, Tellechea, Burt & Narvaja*

Daniel Elicetche
PricewaterhouseCoopers

Nadia Gorostiaga
PricewaterhouseCoopers

Ana Laura Godin
PricewaterhouseCoopers

Karina Lozano
PricewaterhouseCoopers

Andrea Downes
Servimex SACI

Rodolfo Vouga
Vouga & Olmedo

María Sol Martínez
Vouga & Olmedo

Olga Dios
Vouga & Olmedo

Alejandro Piera
Zacarías y Fernández

Sebastian Lovera
Zacarías y Fernández

PERU

Ernesto Andrade Veloz
Andrade - Veloz and Associates

Luís Fuentes Villarán
Barrios Fuentes Urquiaga

José A. Delmar
Benites, De Las Casas, Forno & Ugaz

Rafael Lengua
Benites, De Las Casas, Forno & Ugaz

Manuel Ugarte
Benites, De Las Casas, Forno & Ugaz

Carlos Vegas
Camara Peruana de la Construccion

Sergio Valencoso
Certicom

Anabeli Gonzalez
Estudio Ferrero Abogados

Guillermo Ferrero
Estudio Ferrero Abogados

Marco Antonio Alarcón Piana
Estudio Luis Echecopar Garcia

Ricardo P. Silva
Estudio Muñiz, Forsyth, Ramirez, Perez-Taiman & Luna Victoria

Manuel P. Olaechea Du Bois
Estudio Olaechea*

José Antonio Olaechea
Estudio Olaechea

Jesús Matos
Estudio Olaechea

Manuel Villa-García
Estudio Olaechea

Guilhermo Alceu Auler
Forsyth & Arbe Abogados

Gianina Gotuzzo
Hernández & Rosselló Abogados

Juan Luis Hernández
Hernández & Rosselló Abogados

Jimy Francisco Atunga Rios
MAV Logistica y Transporte S.A.

Carlos Gamarra
Ministerio de Justicia del Peru

Juan Luis Avendaño C.
Miranda & Amado Abogados

Thomas Von Der Heyden
Panalpina Transportes Mundiales S.A.

Alonso Rey Bustamante
Payet, Rey, Cauvi Abogados

Mathias Reiser
Panalpina Transportes Mundiales S.A.

Raul Lozano-Merino
Peña, Lozano, Faura & Asociados

Humberto Allemant
PricewaterhouseCoopers

Pedro Grados Smith
Superintendencia de Banca y Seguros

PHILIPPINES

Tadeo F. Hilado
Abello Concepcion Regala & Cruz Law Firm

Teodore Regala
Angara Abello Concepcion Regala & Cruz

Emerico de Guzman
Angara Abello Concepcion Regala & Cruz

Gilberto Gallos
Angara Abello Concepcion Regala & Cruz

Manuel Batallones
BAP Credit Bureau

Ciriaco S. Calalang
Calalang Law Offices

Jesuito Morallos
Follosco Morallos & Herce

Ofelia Abueg-Sta.Maria
Land Registration Authority

Melva M. Evangelista-Valdez
Narciso Jimenez Gonzales Liwanag Bello Valdez & Caluya

Shirly E. Almazan
Panalpina World Transport (Philippines) Inc.

Victoria R. Tamayao
Picazo Buyco Tan Fider and Santos

Genevieve Limbo
PricewaterhouseCoopers

Tammy Lipana
PricewaterhouseCoopers

Zaber Protacio
PricewaterhouseCoopers

Redentor Zapata
Quasha Ancheta Peña & Nolasco

Janice Kae Ramirez
Quasha Ancheta Peña & Nolasco

Jazmin Banal
Romulo, Mabanta, Buenaventura, Sayoc & de los Angeles*

Olivia T. Olalia
Romulo, Mabanta, Buenaventura, Sayoc & de los Angeles

Ricardo J. Romulo
Romulo, Mabanta, Buenaventura, Sayoc & de los Angeles

Romeo M. Mendoza
Romulo, Mabanta, Buenaventura, Sayoc & de los Angeles

Connie Chu
Romulo, Mabanta, Buenaventura, Sayoc & de los Angeles

Nicanor N. Padilla
Siguion Reyna Montecillo & Ongsiako

Rolando Mario G. Villonco
Siguion Reyna Montecillo & Ongsiako

Romarie Villonco
Siguion Reyna Montecillo & Ongsiako

Cecile M.E. Caro
SyCip salazar Hernandez & Gatmaitan

Emmanuel C. Paras
SyCip Salazar Hernandez & Gatmaitan

Riza Faith Ybanez
SyCip Salazar Hernandez & Gatmaitan

Elena Melita Chica
The Law Firm of Coluso, Chica & Associates

Jazmin Banal
Romulo, Mabanta, Buenaventura, Sayoc & de los Angeles

POLAND

Andrzej Siemiatkowski
Allen & Overy

Tomasz Wojnarowicz
Allen & Overy

Arkadiusz Pedzich
Allen & Overy

Radomil Charzynski
Allen & Overy

Maciej Duszczyk
Biuro Informacji Kredytowej

Aleksander Borowicz
Biuro Informacji Kredytowej

Karina Kusz
Cargoforte Sp. z.o.o.

Tomasz Dys
Dyst Legal Law Office

Jaroslaw Wysocki
Geodesy and Cartography

Stanislas Dwernicki
Gide Loyrette Nouel Polska

Anna Ratajczyk
Gide Loyrette Nouel Polska

Magdalena Wolowska
Gide Loyrette Nouel Polska

Rafal Dziedzic
Gide Loyrette Nouel Polska

Robert Jędrzejczyk
Gide Loyrette Nouel Polska

Sergiusz Ciolkowski
Gide Loyrette Nouel Polska

Jean Rossi
Gide Loyrette Nouel Polska

Grzegorz Banasiuk
Gide Loyrette Nouel Polska

Dariusz Tokarczuk
Gide Loyrette Nouel Polska

Piotr Sadownik
Gide Loyrette Nouel Polska

Robert Windmill
Haarmann Hemmelrath & Partner

Ewelina Stobiecka
Haarmann Hemmelrath & Partner

Tomasz Brudkowski
Kochański Brudkowski & Partners

Janusz Zaleski
National Association of Building Employers

Marta Soltysik
Nörr Stiefenhofer Lutz Law Firm

Patryk Figiel
Nörr Stiefenhofer Lutz Law Firm

Katarzyna Domanska-Moldawa
Nörr Stiefenhofer Lutz Law Firm

Peter Urbanek
Nörr Stiefenhofer Lutz Law Firm

Piotr Kaim
PricewaterhouseCoopers

Piotr Kowalski
PricewaterhouseCoopers

Josef Banach
PricewaterhouseCoopers

Bartlomiej Raczkowski
Soltysinski Kawecki & Szlezak, member of Ius Laboris

Joanna Luzak
Soltysinski Kawecki & Szlezak, member of Ius Laboris

Krzysztof Pawlak
Soltysinski Kawecki & Szlezak, member of Ius Laboris

Tamasz Kanski
Soltysinski Kawecki & Szlezak, member of Ius Laboris

Steven Wood
TGC Polska Law Firm

Anna Dzieciatkowska
TGC Polska Law Firm

Dariusz Wasylkowski
Wardyński i Wspólnicy

Weronica Pelc
Wardyński i Wspólnicy

Krzysztof Wierzbowski
Wierzbowski i Wspólnicy

Bozena Ciosek
Wierzbowski i Wspólnicy

PORTUGAL

Marta Leitão
Abreu & Marques, Vinhas e Associados

Isabel Pires Marques
Abreu & Marques, Vinhas e Associados

Miguel de Avillez Pereira
Abreu, Cardigos & Associados

João Gonçalves Assunção
Abreu, Cardigos & Associados

Filipa Nevoa
Abreu, Cardigos & Associados

Pedro Sousa Uva
Abreu, Cardigos & Associados

Catarina Araújo
AICCOPN

Francisco Jose Maia Coelho
AICCOPN

Pedro Porto Dordio
António Frutuoso de Melo e Associados

José J. Tomaz Gomes
Associação de Empresas de Construção e Obras Públicas

Margarida Ramalho
Associação de Empresas de Construção e Obras Públicas

João Cadete de Matos
Banco de Portugal

Manuel P. Barrocas
Barrocas & Alves Pereira

Cristina Cabral Ribeiro
Barrocas & Alves Pereira

Jorge Neves
Barrocas & Alves Pereira

Francisco Lino Dias
Barros, Sobral, G. Gomes & Associados

Sonia Goncalves Anjo
Barros, Sobral, G. Gomes & Associados

Susana Braz
Barros, Sobral, G. Gomes & Associados

Inês Reis
Carlos Aguiar, P. Pinto & Associados, member of Ius Laboris

Carlos de Sousa e Brito
Carlos de Sousa e Brito & Associados

Antonio Souta
Centro de Formalidades de Empresa

Fernando Marta
Credinformacoes

Joao Moucheira
Directorate General of Registry and Notary Civil Service

António Luís Figueiredo
Directorate General of Registry and Notary Civil Service

Vitorino Oliveira
Directorate General of Registry and Notary Civil Service

Rita Gouveira
Goncalves Pereira, Castelo Branco & Associados

M. Bowman
IBICO

Cristina Dein
Jalles Advogados

Djamila Osman
Miranda, Correia, Amendoeira & Associados

Segismundo Pinto Basto
Morais Leitao, J. Galvao Teles & Associados*

Margarida Lima Rego
Morais Leitao, J. Galvao Teles & Associados

Filipa Pedroso
Morais Leitao, J. Galvao Teles & Associados

Vicky Rodriguez
Neville de Rougemont & Associados

Francisco Salgueiro
Neville de Rougemont & Associados

Ines Mendes Oliveira
Neville de Rougemont & Associados

Rosemary de Rougemont
Neville de Rougemont & Associados

Rui Amendoeira
Pereira de Miranda, Correia & Amendoeira

Ana Margarida Maia
Pereira de Miranda, Correia & Amendoeira

Jorge Lopes
Polytechnic Institute of Bragança

Rita Marques
PricewaterhouseCoopers

Carlos Bernardes
PricewaterhouseCoopers

Marta Elisa Machado
PricewaterhouseCoopers

Jorge Figueiredo
PricewaterhouseCoopers

Rita Granado Antunes
Vieira de Almeida & Associados

Fernando Resina da Silva
Vieira de Almeida & Associados

Patrícia Vinagre e Silva
Vieira de Almeida & Associados

PUERTO RICO

Rubén M. Medina-Lugo
Cancio, Nadal, Rivera & Díaz

Julio Vizcarrondo
Desarrollos Metropolitanos SE

Juan Carlos Pérez Otero
Fiddler, González & Rodríguez

Luis Mongil-Casasnovas
Martinez Odell & Calabria

Samuel Céspedes, Jr
McConnell Valdes

Harry Cook
McConnell Valdes

Jorge Ruiz Montilla
McConnell Valdes

Tomás Acevedo
McConnell Valdes

Victor Rodriguez
Multitransport & Marine Co.

Carmen Eva Garcias Cardenas
Nicholas Nogueras & Co.

Victor Rodriguez
PricewaterhouseCoopers

Fernando J. Bonilla Esq.
Puerto Rico Ports Authority

Ralph Vallone Jr.
Ralph Vallone Jr., Law Offices

Myriam Matos-Bermudez
Sosa Llorens Cruz Neris & Associates

James A. Arroyo
TransUnion de Puerto Rico

ROMANIA

Silviu Ginju
ADD Cargo

Veronica Grunzsnicki
Babiuc Sulica & Associates

Catalin Tripon
Babiuc Sulica & Associates

Serban Epure
Biroul de Credit

Potyesz Tiberu
Bitrans Ltd., Member of World Mediatrans Group

Daniel Bruma
Bostina & Associates

Ciprian Glodeanu
Bostina & Associates

Christina Spyridon
IKRP Rokas & Partners

Crenguta Leaua
Leaua & Cadar

Gelu-Titus Maravela
Musat & Asociatii

Ion Dragulin
National Bank of Romania

Manuela M. Nestor
Nestor Nestor Diculescu Kingston Petersen*

Cristina Virtopeanu
Nestor Nestor Diculescu Kingston Petersen

Laura Ardeleanu
Nestor Nestor Diculescu Kingston Petersen

Paraschiva Suica-Neagu
Nestor Nestor Diculescu Kingston Petersen

Laura Duca
Nestor Nestor Diculescu Kingston Petersen

Cristina Clujescu
PricewaterhouseCoopers

Oana Manuceanu
PricewaterhouseCoopers

Alina Manescu
PricewaterhouseCoopers

Roxana Teodorovici
PricewaterhouseCoopers

Romulus Badea
PricewaterhouseCoopers

Andreea Vatui
PricewaterhouseCoopers

Dan Badin
PricewaterhouseCoopers

Diana Coroaba
PricewaterhouseCoopers

Anca Sandru
Racoti, Predoiu & Partners

Daniel Lungu
Racoti, Predoiu & Partners

Neil McGregor
S.C.P.A. Popescu & Asociatii

Arina Dobrescu
S.C.P.A. Popescu & Asociatii

Anamaria Corbescu
Salans

Perry V. Zizzi
Salans

Obie L. Moore
Salans

Tiberiu Csaki
Salans

Mihaela Marin
Salans

Acsinte Constantin Cristian
SC Romtrans SA Bucharest

Razvan Dinca
Stoica & Asociatii Attorney at Law

Cristiana Stoica
Stoica & Asociatii Attorney at Law

Theodor Catalin Nicolescu
Theodor Nicolescu Law Office

RUSSIA

Irina Strizhakova
Andreas Neocleous & Co.

Aexey Tokovinin
ANDREAS NEOCLEOUS & CO.

Evgeny Reyzman
BAKER & MCKENZIE

Andrey Zhdanov
BAKER & MCKENZIE

Stepan Lubavsky
BAKER & MCKENZIE

Vladimir Dragunov
BAKER & MCKENZIE

Dmitry Besedin
BESEDIN AVAKOV TARASOV & PARTNERS

David Griston
CMS CAMERON MCKENNA

Victor Sneguirev
DLA PIPER RUDNICK GRAY CARY

Marc Solovei
*GIDE LOYRETTE NOUEL**

Olga Revzina
GIDE LOYRETTE NOUEL VOSTOK

Julia Koroleva
GIDE LOYRETTE NOUEL VOSTOK

Janna Mansourova
GIDE LOYRETTE NOUEL VOSTOK

David Lasfargue
GIDE LOYRETTE NOUEL VOSTOK

Dimitry Kafanov
INMAR LEGAL CO.

Darya Angelo
LAW FIRM ALRUD

Anna Zvereva
LAW FIRM ALRUD

Sergey Gerasimov
LAW FIRM ALRUD

Alexander Belov
LAW FIRM ALRUD

Fedor Bogatyrev
LAW FIRM ALRUD

Anatoly E. Andriash
MACLEOD DIXON

Jason Sande
MACLEOD DIXON

Albert Abdouline
MAERSK LOGISTICS RUSSIA

Alexandra Andreeva
PANALPINA WORLD TRANSPORT

Irina Im
PRICEWATERHOUSECOOPERS

Steven Snaith
PRICEWATERHOUSECOOPERS

Andrey Shpak
PRICEWATERHOUSECOOPERS

Evgeny Sheenko
PRICEWATERHOUSECOOPERS

Elena Subocheva
RUSSIN & VECCHI

Natalia Prisekina
RUSSIN & VECCHI

Sergei Lazarev
RUSSIN & VECCHI

RWANDA

André Verbruggen
AVA

François Bikolimana
CABINET AUGECO SARL

Jean Marie Vianney Mugemana
CABINET D'AVOCATS MUGEMANA & ASSOCIES

Emile Masumbuko
CABINET MAÎTRE EMILE MASUMBUKO NDE

Isaie Mpayimana
CABINET ME ISAIE MPAYIMANA

Jean Haguma
HAGUMA & ASSOCIÉS

Christian Ndondera
HAGUMA & ASSOCIÉS

Eugene Rurangwa
MINISTÈRE DES TERRES, ENVIRONNEMENT, FORÊTS, EAU ET RESSOURCES NATURELLES

Angelique Kantangwa
NATIONAL BANK OF RWANDA

Annie Kairaba-Kyambadde
RWANDA INITIATIVE FOR SUSTAINABLE DEVELOPMENT (RISD) / LANDNET

Eric Nsengimana
WORLD FREIGHT SARL

SAMOA

Sili M. Alapati Brown
ALCC BROWN ENT. CO. LTD.

Andrew Holford
ANZ BANK SAMOA LTD.

Umni Kesaan
ANZ BANK SAMOA LTD.

Lawrie Burich
L. BURICH-BUILDING CONTRACTORS

Shelley Burich
L. BURICH-BUILDING CONTRACTORS

Jerry James S. Brunt
BRUNT & KELI

Murray Drake
DRAKE & CO.

Ruby Drake
DRAKE & CO.

Patrick Fepulea'I
FEPULEA'I & SHUSTER

George Latu
LATUE LAW OFFICE

Fiona Ey
LATUEY LAW OFFICE

Robert Barlow
KRASE, ENARI & BARLOW

Maria Melei
SAMOA CHAMBER OF COMMERCE & INDUSTRY

Paparu John Ryan
SAMOA PORTS AUTHORITY

J. Saufoi Moors
MINISTRY OF WORKS, TRANSPORT & INFRASTRUCTURE

Chris Grant
LAND EQUITY INTERNATIONAL

Denis Bracy
LAND EQUITY INTERNATIONAL

Kevin Nettle
LAND EQUITY INTERNATIONAL PTY LTD.

Arthur R. Penn
LESA MA PENN

Semi Leung Wai
LEUNG WAI LAW FIRM

Maiava V. Peteru
MAIAVA V.R. PETERU LAW FIRM

John Ridgway
PACIFIC LEGAL NETWORK

Elon P. Betham
SAMOA SHIPPING SERVICES LTD.

Leulua'iali'i Tasi Malifa
SOGILAW

Ray Schuster
OFFICE OF THE ATTORNEY GENERAL

Amaramo Sialoa
KVA CONSULT

Grace Stowers
STEVENSONS LAWYERS

Keilani Soloi
SOLOI SURVEY SERVICES

Toleafoa Toailoa
TOAILOA R.S.

Steve Baker
WESTPAC

SAO TOME AND PRINCIPE

Flávio Miguel Viegas Pinto
CENTRAL BANK OF SAO TOMÉ E PRÍNCIPE

Julio Miguel Silva
CONSTROME

Kiluange Tiny
JURISTEP

Edmar Carvalho
MIRANDA, CORREIA, AMENDOEIRA & ASSOCIADOS

Alberto Galhardo Simões
MIRANDA, CORREIA, AMENDOEIRA & ASSOCIADOS

Fernando Barros
PRICEWATERHOUSECOOPERS

Julian Ince
PRICEWATERHOUSECOOPERS

Pedro Calixto
PRICEWATERHOUSECOOPERS

Maria Cristina Lourenço do Sacramento
ATS-AGÊNCIA DE TRANSITOS VIAGENS E LOGÍSTICA LDA

SAUDI ARABIA

Smaer Pharaon
ABU-GHAZALEH LEGAL

David K. Johnson
AL JURAID & COMPANY / PRICEWATERHOUSECOOPERS

Soudki Zawaydeh
AL JURAID & COMPANY / PRICEWATERHOUSECOOPERS

Taj Eldin M. Hassan
AL-GHAZZAWI PROFESSIONAL ASSOCIATION

Belal Talal Al Ghazzawi
AL-GHAZZAWI PROFESSIONAL ASSOCIATION

Talal Amin Al Ghazzawi
AL-GHAZZAWI PROFESSIONAL ASSOCIATION

Jochen Hundt
AL-SOAIB LAW FIRM

Abdulaziz Zaibag
ALZAIBAG CONSULTANTS

Majed Mohammed Garoub
LAW FIRM OF MAJED M. GAROUB

George Sayen
LEGAL ADVISORS IN ASSOCIATION WITH BAKER & MCKENZIE LTD.

Adel ElZein
MOHAMED BEN LADEN LAW FIRM

Adel Elsaid
PANALPINA / GHASSAN

Sami Al-Sarraj
PRICEWATERHOUSECOOPERS

Fahd Al-Mufarrij
SAUDI ARABIAN MONETARY AGENCY

Tariq Javed
SAUDI ARABIAN MONETARY AGENCY

Mohammad S. Aba Al-Khail
SAUDI ARABIAN MONETARY AGENCY

Nabil Abdullah Al-Mubarak
SAUDI CREDIT BUREAU-SIMAH

Ali Abedi
THE ALLIANCE OF ABBAS F. GHAZZAWI & CO. AND HAMMAD & AL-MEHDAR

Abdul Kareem
THE ALLIANCE OF ABBAS F. GHAZZAWI & CO. AND HAMMAD & AL-MEHDAR

Ceyda Okur
THE ALLIANCE OF ABBAS F. GHAZZAWI & CO. AND HAMMAD & AL-MEHDAR

Mohammed Al-Jaddan
THE LAW FIRM OF YOUSEF AND MOHAMMED AL-JADDAN

Abdullah Al-Hashim
THE LAW FIRM OF YOUSEF AND MOHAMMED AL-JADDAN

John Beaumont
THE LAW FIRM OF YOUSEF AND MOHAMMED AL-JADDAN

Sameh M. Toban
TOBAN LAW FIRM

SENEGAL

Moustapha N'Doye
PRIVATE ATTORNEY

Andrée Diop-Depret
ARCHITECTE

Pap Oumar Sakho
CABINET D'AVOCATS OUMAR SAKHO

Rita Fall
AGENCE CHARGÉE DE LA PROMOTION DE L'INVESTISSEMENT ET DES GRANDS TRAVAUX

Amadou C. Sall
AGENCE CHARGÉE DE LA PROMOTION DE L'INVESTISSEMENT ET DES GRANDS TRAVAUX

Ameth Ba
CABINET BA & TANDIAN

Khaled Houda
CABINET KANJO KOITA

Fatimatou Zahra Diop
CENTRALE DES RISQUES DE L'UNION MONÉTAIRE OUEST AFRICAINE

François Nare
CENTRALE DES RISQUES DE L'UNION MONÉTAIRE OUEST AFRICAINE

Mamadou Sereme
CENTRALE DES RISQUES DE L'UNION MONÉTAIRE OUEST AFRICAINE

Ibrahima Mbodj
ETUDE MAÎTRE IBRAHIMA MBODJ

Ndjaye Mbodj
ETUDE MAÎTRE IBRAHIMA MBODJ

Sidy Abdallah Kanoute
ETUDE MAITRE SIDY KANOUTÉ

Jacques Chareyre
FIDAFRICA / PRICEWATERHOUSECOOPERS

Saliou Niang
FIDAFRICA / PRICEWATERHOUSECOOPERS

Olivier Wybo
FIDAFRICA / PRICEWATERHOUSECOOPERS

François Sarr
*FRANCOIS SARR & ASSOCIÉS**

Edgar Julienne
MAERSK LOGISTICS

Steven Jansen
MAERSK SEALAND

Ramatoulaye Diagne
ORDRE DES ARCHITECTES

Mame Adama Gueye
SCP MAME ADAMA GUEYE & ASSOCIES

Mamadou Mbaye
SCP MAME ADAMA GUEYE & ASSOCIES

SERBIA - MONTENEGRO

Katarina Nedeljkovic

Jovana Ilic
PRICEWATERHOUSECOOPERS

Jelena Djokic
PRICEWATERHOUSECOOPERS

Mike Ahern
PRICEWATERHOUSECOOPERS

Robert Brugger
PANALPINA WELTTRANSPORT GMBH

Nenad Tisma
BN BOS SPED

Neli Markovic
CREDIT INFORMATION SYSTEM

Mila Kasalica
CREDIT INFORMATION SYSTEM

Todd Robinson
HAYHURST ROBINSON LAW OFFICES

Miodrag Markovic
HAYHURST ROBINSON LAW OFFICES

Manolis Ktistakis
IKRP ROKAS & PARTNERS

Petar Stojanovic
JOKSOVIC, STOJANOVIC & PARTNERS

Julijana Jevtic
LAW OFFICES JANKOVIC, POPOVIC & MITIC

Natasa Cveticanin
LAW OFFICES JANKOVIC, POPOVIC & MITIC

Ivan Petrovic
LAW OFFICES JANKOVIC, POPOVIC & MITIC

Srdja M. Popovic
LAW OFFICES POPOVIC, POPOVIC, SAMARDZIJA & POPOVIC

Lidija Tomasovic
LAW OFFICES POPOVIC, POPOVIC, SAMARDZIJA & POPOVIC

Zivka Djuric
MINISTRY OF LABOUR, EMPLOYMENT AND SOCIAL AFFAIRS

Relja Zdravkovic
SCHOENHERR RECHTSANWAELTE

Oliver Haussmann
SCHOENHERR RECHTSANWAELTE

Relja Zdravkovic
SCHOENHERR RECHTSANWAELTE

Oliver Haussmann
SCHOENHERR RECHTSANWAELTE

Dubravka Kosic
STUDIO LEGALE SUTTI

Bojana Bregovic
WOLF THEISS

Vidak Kovacevic
WOLF THEISS

Milos Zivkovic
ZIVKOVIC & SAMARDZIC LAW OFFICE

SIERRA LEONE

Denis Cordel
BOLLORÉ DTI - SDV

Jean Marcel Gariador
BOLLORÉ DTI - SDV

Darcy White
PRICEWATERHOUSECOOPERS

George Kwatia
PRICEWATERHOUSECOOPERS

Charles Egan
PRICEWATERHOUSECOOPERS

Shaira Adamali
PRICEWATERHOUSECOOPERS

Abdul Tejan-Cole
A. TEJAN-COLE AND ASSOCIATES

Sonkita Conteh
A. TEJAN-COLE AND ASSOCIATES

Oliver Onylander
ADELE CHAMBERS

Berthan Macaular
BASMA & MACAULAY

Mariama Dumbuya
LEGAL ACCESS THROUGH WOMEN YEARNING EQUALITY RIGHTS AND SOCIAL JUSTICE (L.A.W.Y.E.R.S.)

Farid Alghali
ROBERTS AND PARTNER

Ibrahim S. Yillah
ROBERTS AND PARTNER

Emmanuel Roberts
ROBERTS AND PARTNER

Centus Macauley
ROBERTS AND PARTNER

Corneleius Adeyemi Max-Williams I
SIERRA LEONE SHIPPING AGENCIES LTD.

Rowland S.V. Wright
WRIGHT & CO. BARRISTERS & SOLICITORS

SINGAPORE

Aloysius Leng
ABRAHAMLOW

Monica Neo
CHANTAN LLC

George Tan
CHANTAN LLC

Sam Bonifant
CLIFFORD CHANCE

Nandakumar Ponniya
CLIFFORD CHANCE

Ai-Chuin Serene Chee
DONALDSON & BURKINSHAW*

Sharon Tay
DONALDSON & BURKINSHAW

Chi Duan Gooi
DONALDSON & BURKINSHAW

David Teo
DONALDSON & BURKINSHAW

Chit Fai Kelry Loi
DONALDSON & BURKINSHAW

Bok Hoay Tan
DONALDSON & BURKINSHAW

Latiff Ibrahim
HARRY ELIAS PARTNERSHIP

Alvin Lingam
HARRY ELIAS PARTNERSHIP

Mun Wah Cheong
JTC CORPORATION

Benjamin Yap
KELVIN CHIA PARTNERSHIP

Tony Chua
MAERSK SINGAPORE PTE LTD.

Freddy Kuan
MULTIMODAL TRANSPORT GROUP NETWORK

Eric Swee
PANALPINA WORLD TRANSPORT (S) PTE LTD

See Tiat Quek
PRICEWATERHOUSECOOPERS

Deepak Kaul
PRICEWATERHOUSECOOPERS

Paula Eastwood
PRICEWATERHOUSECOOPERS

Kala Anandarajah
RAJAH & TANN

Lim Wee Teck
RAJAH & TANN

Ong Hway Cheng
RAJAH & TANN

Lee Lay See
RAJAH & TANN

Priya Selvam
RAJAH & TANN

Teng Siu Ing
SINGAPORE LAND AUTHORITY

Beng Hong Ong
WONG TAN & MOLLY LIM LLC

SLOVAKIA

Renatus Kollar
ALLEN & OVERY

Sonia Horváthová
ALLEN & OVERY BRATISLAVA, S.R.O.

Pavol Erben
BLAHA, ERBEN & PARTNERI

Jana Moravcikova
ČECNAHOVÁ RAKOVSKÝ*

Katarina Cechova
ČECNAHOVÁ RAKOVSKÝ

Tomáš Rybár
ČECNAHOVÁ RAKOVSKÝ

Michaela Jurková
ČECNAHOVÁ RAKOVSKÝ

Tomáš Zarecký
ČECNAHOVÁ RAKOVSKÝ

Zuzana Petrasova
ČECNAHOVÁ RAKOVSKÝ

Tomáš Maretta
ČECNAHOVÁ RAKOVSKÝ

Roman Bircak
ČECNAHOVÁ RAKOVSKÝ

Jana Štelbacká
ČECNAHOVÁ RAKOVSKÝ

Radoslav Saly
ČECNAHOVÁ RAKOVSKÝ

Martin Javorcek
CMS CARNOGURSKÝ

Juraj Elias
CMS CARNOGURSKÝ

Tomás Kamenec
DEDÁK & PARTNERS, S.R.O.

Jana Brezinova
DEDÁK & PARTNERS, S.R.O.

Peter Neštepný
DETVAI LUDIK MALÝ UDVAROS

Jozef Malý
DETVAI LUDIK MALÝ UDVAROS

Miloš Kachňák
DETVAI LUDIK MALÝ UDVAROS

Michaela Špetková
GEODESY, CARTOGRAPHY AND CADASTRE AUTHORITY OF THE SLOVAK REPUBLIC

Nadezda Niksova
GEODESY, CARTOGRAPHY AND CADASTRE AUTHORITY OF THE SLOVAK REPUBLIC

Martin Bednár
HMG & PARTNERS, S.R.O.

Monika Berecova
MINISTRY OF LABOUR, SOCIAL AFFAIRS AND FAMILY

Milan Šemelák
MINISTRY OF LABOUR, SOCIAL AFFAIRS AND FAMILY

Roman Turok-Hetes
NATIONAL BANK OF SLOVAKIA

Lenka Očkaiková
PETERKA & PARTNERS

Ondrej Dusek
PETERKA & PARTNERS

Robert Brugger
PANALPINA WELTTRANSPORT GMBH

Todd Bradshaw
PRICEWATERHOUSECOOPERS

Georgina Galova
PRICEWATERHOUSECOOPERS

Radmila Benkova
PRICEWATERHOUSECOOPERS

Clare Moger
PRICEWATERHOUSECOOPERS

Zuzana Valerova
PRICEWATERHOUSECOOPERS

Ján Budinský
SCB – SLOVAK CREDIT BUREAU, S.RO.

Dagmar Zukalova
SKLEGAL, LAW OFFICE

Michal Luknar
SQUIRE, SANDERS & DEMPSEY S.R.O.

Lenka Subenikova
WOLF THEISS

Erik Steger
WOLF THEISS

SLOVENIA

Tina Rozman Kasnik
BANK OF SLOVENIA

Simon Bračun
COLJA, ROJS & PARTNERJI

Barbara Kozaric
DELOITTE & TOUCHE TOHMATSU

Andraz Brodnjak
DELOITTE & TOUCHE TOHMATSU

Nada Drobnic
DELOITTE & TOUCHE TOHMATSU

Marina Ferfolja Howland
FERFOLJA, LJUBIC IN PARTNERJI

Renata Šterbenc
LAW OFFICE JADEK & PENSA

Aleksandra Jemc
LAW OFFICE JADEK & PENSA

Pavle Pensa
LAW OFFICE JADEK & PENSA

Sreco Jadek
LAW OFFICE JADEK & PENSA

Ursa Penca
LAW OFFICE JADEK & PENSA

Boris Ruzic
MINISTRY OF LABOUR, FAMILY AND SOCIAL AFFAIR

Borut Brezovar
MINISTRA OF LABOUR, FAMILY AND SOCIAL AFFAIR

Grega Peljhan
ODVETNIŠKA DRUŽBA COLJA, ROJS & PARTNERJI, O.P., D.N.O.

Robert Brugger
PANALPINA WELTTRANSPORT GMBH

Janja Ovsenik
PRICEWATERHOUSECOOPERS

Danilo Marinovic
PRICEWATERHOUSECOOPERS

Lucijan Klemencic
PRICEWATERHOUSECOOPERS

Crtomir Borec
PRICEWATERHOUSECOOPERS

Iain McGuire
PRICEWATERHOUSECOOPERS

Florian Kirchhof
SCHOENHERR RECHTSANWALTE

Simon Seibert
SEIBERT SEIBERT

Rudi Šelih
ŠELIH, ŠELIH, JANEZIC & JARKOVIC

Andrej Jarkovič
ŠELIH, ŠELIH, JANEZIC & JARKOVIC

Natasa Pipan Nahtigal
ŠELIH, ŠELIH, JANEZIC & JARKOVIC

Alojz Zupančič
SLOVENIAN CUSTOMS ADMINISTRATION

Borut Cvar
SURVEYING AND MAPPING AUTHORITY OF THE REPUBLIC OF SLOVENIA

Bozena Lipej
SURVEYING AND MAPPING AUTHORITY OF THE REPUBLIC OF SLOVENIA

SOLOMON ISLANDS

Don Whinfield
THE BLUFF CONSULTING AND AGRICULTURE

Bruce Saunders
BJS AGENCIES LIMITED

John Ridgway
PACIFIC LEGAL NETWORK

Wayne Morris
PRICEWATERHOUSECOOPERS

SOUTH AFRICA

Fatima Bhyat

Roelof Grové
ADAMS & ADAMS

Michael Adcock
BOWMAN GILFILLAN*

Claire Tucker
BOWMAN GILFILLAN

Fatima Laher
BOWMAN GILFILLAN

Tim Gordon-Grant
BOWMAN GILFILLAN

Michael Vorster
BOWMAN GILFILLAN

Heidi Bell
BOWMAN GILFILLAN

Kim Goss
BOWMAN GILFILLAN

Paul Coetser
BRINK COHEN LE ROUX

Randall van Voore
CLIFFE DEKKER

Osafo Gyimah
CONSTRUCTION INDUSTRY DEVELOPMENT BOARD

Llevellyn Van Wyk
CSIR

Ivan Tshimangwe
DELANGE INC

Eamonn Quinn
EAMONN DAVID QUINN ATTORNEY

Miranda Feinstein
EDWARD NATHAN

Gretchen De Smit
EDWARD NATHAN

Andrea Bezuidenhout
FINMARK TRUST

Jude Kearncy
LEBOEUF LAMB GREENE & MACRAE

Mary Chege-Mwangi
LEBOEUF LAMB GREENE & MACRAE

Rajen Ranchhoojee
LeBoeuf Lamb Greene & MacRae

Victor Mesquita
Manica Africa

Erle Koomets
PricewaterhouseCoopers

Jenny Murphy
Safcor Panalpina

Peter Sands
SDV Transami (Pty) Ltd

Ralph Zulman
Supreme Court of Appeal of South Africa

Lauren Flemming
TransUnion ITC

Ann Boulton
TransUnion ITC

Renee Kruger
Webber Wentzel Bowens

SPAIN

José Gómez Garrido
Altius S.A.

Cristina Calvo
Ashurst

Anselmo Diaz Fernández
Bank of Spain

Nicolas Nogueroles
Colegio de Resgitradores de la Propiedad y Mercantiles de España

Guillermo Frühbeck
Dr. Frühbeck Abogados y Economistas

Fermin Córdoba Gavín
Echecopar Abogados Law Firm

Miquel Palleres
ED Altaya

Nicolas Vedrenne
Experian Bureau de Credito

Ana Just
Luris Valls Abogados

Carlos Vall
Luris Valls Abogados

Calvin A. Hamilton
Monereo, Meyer & Marinel-Lo

Sönke Schlaich
Monereo, Meyer & Marinel-Lo

Andres Monereo Velasco
Monereo, Meyer & Marinel-Lo

Alfonso Pedrajas
Mullerat

Iván Delgado
Pérez-Llorca

Pedro Pérez-Llorca Zamora
Pérez-Llorca

Siro Arias
PricewaterhouseCoopers

Basilio Aguirre
Registro de la Propiedad de España

Roser Ràfols
Roca Junyent Advocats

Iñigo Sagardoy de Simón
Sagardoy & Abogados, member of Ius Laboris

Ricardo Rebate Labrandero
Sánchez Pintado, Núñez & Asociados

Pilar Salinas
Sánchez Pintado, Núñez & Asociados

Marco Zambrini
Uría & Menéndez*

Arancha Seva García
Uría & Menéndez

Charles Coward
Uría & Menéndez

Candido Paz-Ares
Uría & Menéndez

Alejandro Ferreres
Uría & Menéndez

Pablo González-Espejo
Uría & Menéndez

Rafael Sebastián
Uría & Menéndez

Eduardo Rodríguez-Rovira
Uría & Menéndez

SRI LANKA

Ajith Nivard Cabraal
Cabraal Consulting Group (Pvt) Ltd, Management Consultants

N.P.H. Amarasena
Credit Information Bureau of Sri Lanka

Avindra Rodrigo
F.J. & G De Saram*

Roshani Kobbekaduwa
F.J. & G De Saram

Ayomi Aluwihare-Gunawardene
F.J. & G De Saram

John Wilson, Jr.
John Wilson Partners

Rujaratnam Senathi Rajah
Julius & Creasy

Amila Fernando
Julius & Creasy

T.G. Gooneratne
Julius & Creasy

Madawan Amarasiri
Mega Trend International Pvt. Ltd.

Asiri Perera
MIT Cargo Ltd

Paul Ratnayeke
Paul Ratnayeke Associates

Daya Weeraratne
PricewaterhouseCoopers

Subashini Abraham
Sudath Perera Associates

Sudath Perera
Sudath Perera Associates

Ramani Muttettuwegama
Tichurelvam Associates

Asanka Abeysekera
Tichurelvam Associates

Sharmela de Silva
Tiruchelvam Associates

Niranjan Sinnethamby
Tiruchelvam Associates

Mayuri Kodikara
Tiruchelvam Associates

Mahinda Haradasa
Varners Lanka Office

SUDAN

Mohamed Osman
Darka for Trading and Services Co. Ltd.

Abdel Gadir Warsama Ghalib
Dr. Abdel Gadir Warsama Ghalib & Associates Legal Firm

Abdullah A. Abozaid
Law Office of Abdullah A. Abozaid

Tarig Mahmoud Elsheikh
Mahmoud Elsheikh Omer & Associates

SWEDEN

Carl Östring
Advokatfirman Fylgia KB

Lars Nylund
Advokatfirman Fylgia KB

Magnus Graner
Advokatfirman Lindahl

Olof Hallberg
Advokatfirman Lindahl

Pernilla Carring
Advokatfirman Lindahl

Martin Pagrotsky
Advokatfirman Vinge

Robert Wikholm
Advokatfirman Vinge

Lars Hartzell
Elmzell Advokatbyrå HB, member of Ius Laboris

Karl-Arne Olsson
Gärde Wesslau

Peder Hammarskiöld
Hammarskiöld & Co.

Eric Halvarsson
Hammarskiöld & Co.

Susanne Öhbom
Hökerberg & Söderqvist Advokatbyrå KB

Mattias Örnulf
Hökerberg & Söderqvist Advokatbyrå KB

Bengt Kjellson
Lantmäteriet

Camilla Levinsson
Magnusson Wahlin Qvist Stanbrook Advokat

Mats Berter
Magnusson Wahlin Qvist Stanbrook Advokat

Martin Wallin
MaÎtreLinklaters Advokatbyra

Henric Diefke
Mannheimer Swartling Advokatbyrå

Hans Andersson
Ministry of Industry, Employment and Communications

Lennart Palm
NNR (Board of Swedish Industry and Commerce for Better Regulation)

Tomas Lööv
NNR (Board of Swedish Industry and Commerce for Better Regulation)

Stefan Sjöblom
Panalpina Sweden AB

Christa Persson
Panalpina Sweden AB

Hedda Stiernstedt
PricewaterhouseCoopers

Roger Gavelin
PricewaterhouseCoopers

Ake Radberg
Swedish Construction Federation

Tommy Bisander
UC AB

Malin Ohlin-Akermark
Vinge KB, Advokatfirman*

SWITZERLAND

Robert Lüssi
Administration Fédérale des Douanes Suisses

Peter R. Altenburger
Altenburger & Partners

Frédéric Bétrisey
Baker & McKenzie

Philippe de Salis
Borel & Barbey

Andrea Molino
Brunoni Pedrazzini Molino Mottis

Barbara Stöckli-Klaus
Froriep Renggli

Beat M. Barthold
Froriep Renggli

Marc-André Tudisco
Interkantonaler Verband für Arbeitnehmerschutz

Wassilos Lytras
Maersk Logistics Switzerland Ltd.

Jacques Tissot
Office chargé du droit du registre foncier et du droit foncier

Urs Klöti
Pestalozzi Lachenal Patry*

Robert Furter
Pestalozzi Lachenal Patry

Eva Leuthold
Pestalozzi Lachenal Patry

Karl Arnold
Pestalozzi Lachenal Patry

Guy-Philippe Rubeli
Pestalozzi Lachenal Patry

Michael Kramer
Pestalozzi Lachenal Patry

Marcel Zehnder
PricewaterhouseCoopers

Katja Roppelt
PricewaterhouseCoopers

Andrin Waldburger
PricewaterhouseCoopers

Martina Schmid
PricewaterhouseCoopers

Beat Büchler
SBI Gruppe der Schweizerischen Bauindustrie

Daniel Steudler
Swiss Federal Directorate of Cadastral Surveying

Suzanne Eckert
Wenger Plattner

Marc Tütsch
Wenger Plattner

Hans R. Hintermeister
ZEK Switzerland

SYRIA

Movazza Al-Ashhab
Accounting Center

Kanaan Al_Ahmar
Al-Ahmar & Partners

Alissar Al-Ahmar
Al-Ahmar & Partners

Moussa Mitry
Damascus University / Louka & Mitry Law Office

Ousama Karawani
Karawani Law Office

Fady Kardous
Kardous Law Office

Mazen Khaddour
Law Office of M Khaddour

Housam Safadi
Safadi Bureau

Nabih Alhafez
SFS (Speed Forward Shipping)

Riad Daoudi
Syrian Arab Consultants Law Office

Hani Bitar
Syrian Arab Consultants Law Office

TAIWAN, CHINA

Andrew Yeh
Panalpina Taipei

Justin Liang
Baker & McKenzie

Bee Leay Teo
Baker & McKenzie

Cindy Chou
Chen, Shyuu& Pun

James Hong
Chen, Shyuu& Pun

Zue Min Hwang
Chinese National Association of General Contractors

C.F. Tsai
Deep & Far, Attorneys at Law

John Chen
Formosa Transnational, Attorneys at Law

Yuling Hsu
Formosa Transnational, Attorneys at Law

Chun-Yih Cheng
Formosa Transnational, Attorneys at Law

Fang-Ting Kuo
Joint Credit Information Center

Julie Chu
Jones Day

Serina Chung
Jones Day

Margaret Huang
LCS & Partners

Victor Chang
LCS & Partners

Jocelyn Liu
LCS & Partners

Rich Lin
LCS & Partners

Wen-Horng Kao
PRICEWATERHOUSECOOPERS

Joyce Cheng
PRICEWATERHOUSECOOPERS

Shing-Ping Liu
PRICEWATERHOUSECOOPERS

C.Y. Huang
TSAR & TSAI LAW FIRM*

Edgar Y. Chen
TSAR & TSAI LAW FIRM

James J.M. Hwang
TSAR & TSAI LAW FIRM

Chen Hui-ling
WINKLER PARTNERS

Rachel Chiao
WINKLER PARTNERS

Wayne Lee
YANGMING PARTNERS

Stephen Franck
YANGMING PARTNERS

Charles Hwang
YANGMING PARTNERS

TANZANIA

Manish Vyas

Pamela David
CREDIT REFERENCE BUREAU
AFRICA LTD.

Johnson Jasson
JOHNSON JASSON & CO.
ASSOCIATES

Leopold Thomas Kalunga
KALUNGA & CO. ADVOCATES

Naimi Dyer
KALUNGA & CO. ADVOCATES

Leopold Thomas Kalunga
KALUNGA & CO. ADVOCATES

Grace Shao
MAAJAR, RWECHUNGURA,
NGULUMA & MAKANI

Alex Nguluma
MAAJAR, RWECHUNGURA,
NGULUMA & MAKANI

Charles R. B. Rwechungura
MAAJAR, RWECHUNGURA,
NGULUMA & MAKANI

Mwanjala Njama
MAERSK LOGISTICS TANZANIA
LTD.

Siri A. Malai
MALAI FREIGHT

Nimrod Mkono
MKONO & CO. LAW FIRM

Wilbert Kapinga
MKONO & CO. LAW FIRM

Aisha Naiga
MKONO & CO. LAW FIRM

Rishit Shah
PRICEWATERHOUSECOOPERS

David Tarimo
PRICEWATERHOUSECOOPERS

Philippe de la Khetulle
SDV AMI TANZANIA

Mohamed Sumar
SUMAR VARMA ASSOCIATES

Santosh Gajjar
SUMAR VARMA ASSOCIATES

THAILAND

Stephen Ogunlana
ASIAN INSTITUTE OF
TECHNOLOGY

Narong Leungbootnak
ASIAN INSTITUTE OF
TECHNOLOGY

Suwat Kerdphon
BANGKOK METROPOLITAN LAND
OFFICE

Ratana Poonsombudlert
CHANDLER AND THONG-EK

Jessada Sawatdipong
CHANDLER AND THONG-EK

Peradach Patanachan
CLIFFORD CHANCE

Paul Gregory
CLIFFORD CHANCE

Rawee Wan Thongsrimadum
CLIFFORD CHANCE

Nipa Wongyeekul
DEJ-UDOM & ASSOCIATES

Kowit Somwaiya
LAWPLUS LTD.

Pornsaran Sangsatra
PANALPINA WORLD TRANSPORT
(THAILAND LTD.

Suttipong Srisaard
PRICEWATERHOUSECOOPERS

Thavorn Rujivanarom
PRICEWATERHOUSECOOPERS

Vira Kammee
SIAM CITY LAW OFFICES
LIMITED

Picham Sukparangsee
SIAM CITY LAW OFFICES
LIMITED

Sawat Sangkavisit
SIAM PREMIER INTERNATIONAL
LAW OFFICE LTD.

Veronica Siow
SIAM PREMIER INTERNATIONAL
LAW OFFICE LTD.

William Lehane
SIAM PREMIER INTERNATIONAL
LAW OFFICE LTD.

Erik Jalava
S-NET FREIGHT (HOLDINGS)
PTE. LTD.

Samma Kitsin
THAI CREDIT BUREAU

Wanna Rakyao
THAILAND LAND TITLING
PROJECT OFFICE

Cynthia Pornavalai
TILLEKE & GIBBINS
INTERNATIONAL LTD.

Pimvimol Vipamaneerut
TILLEKE & GIBBINS
INTERNATIONAL LTD.*

John Fotiadis
TILLEKE & GIBBINS
INTERNATIONAL LTD.

Piyanuj Ratprasatporn
TILLEKE & GIBBINS
INTERNATIONAL LTD.

Pascale Prud'homme
TILLEKE & GIBBINS
INTERNATIONAL LTD.

Dussadee Rattanopas
TILLEKE & GIBBINS
INTERNATIONAL LTD.

Noppramart Prasitmonthon
TILLEKE & GIBBINS
INTERNATIONAL LTD.

David Lyman
TILLEKE & GIBBINS
INTERNATIONAL LTD.

Harold K. Vickery Jr.
VICKERY & WORACHAI LTD

Chinnavat Chinsangaram
WHITE & CASE

Sakchai Limsiripothong
WHITE & CASE

TIMOR-LESTE

Kim Glenn
ARD INC.

Edwin Urresta
ARD INC.

Phoebe Kalazane
ARD INC.

Tiago Sarmento
JSMP–JUDICIAL SYSTEMS
MONITORING PROGRAMME

Eusebio Guterres
LAIFET CONSULTANT AND
ADVOCACY

Pedro Sousa
MINISTRY OF JUSTICE

Georgina de Mello
PIU-SEP

Amandino Benevides
PROVEDOR'S OFFICE

Silveiro Pinto
PROVEDOR'S OFFICE

Sebastiao Dias Ximenes
PROVEDOR'S OFFICE

Amandino Benevides
PROVEDOR'S OFFICE

Silveiro Pinto
PROVEDOR'S OFFICE

Alzira Lay
SDV LOGISTICS

Eric Mancini
SDV LOGISTICS

Rafael Ribeiro
SDV LOGISTICS

Jose Pedro Camoes
TIMOR LESTE LEGAL AID LBH-
TL

Vital dos Santos
VSP - VITAL DOS SANTOS &
PARTNERS

Gustavo Bussinger
BANK PAYMENT AUTHORITY

Hau Kium Foo
CHINESE BUSINESS ASSOCIATION

Pedro Aparicio
CONSULTORIA DE LEI

Martin Breen
CONSULTORIA DE LEI

Edio da Costa
MINISTRY OF DEVELOPMENT

Rui Castro
PRIVATE INVESTOR

Alzira Lay
SDV LOGISTICS

Eric Mancini
SDV LOGISTICS

Rafael Ribeiro
SDV LOGISTICS

Francisco Soares
SERVICO DO IMPOSTO DE TIMOR
LESTE

Benjamin Sanches
THE ASIA FOUNDATION

Dionisio Babo Soares
THE ASIA FOUNDATION

Americo Laia
TIMOR TELECOM, SA

Rui Gomes
UNDP–UNITED NATIONS
DEVELOPMENT PROGRAMME

Vorasakdi Arora
UNMISET

Stephen Vance
USAID - TIMOR LESTE

TOGO

François Nare
CENTRALE DES RISQUES DE
L'UNION MONÉTAIRE OUEST
AFRICAINE

Jean-Marie Adenka
CABINET ADENKA

Galolo Soedjede
CABINET D'AVOCATS

John Kokou
CABINET D'AVOCATS

Martial Akakpo
CABINET MARTIAL AKAKPO

Alexis Aquereburu
CABINET ME A.C. AQUEREBURU

Koffi Alinon
CRCD / LANDNET

Kofi Kumodzi
DRH–GLOBAL EXCEL
INTERNATIONAL

Jacques Chareyre
FIDAFRICA /
PRICEWATERHOUSECOOPERS

Dominique Taty
FIDAFRICA /
PRICEWATERHOUSECOOPERS

Edouard Messou
FIDAFRICA /
PRICEWATERHOUSECOOPERS

Richard Akpoto–Kougbleneou
L'ECOLE AFRICAINE DES MÉTIERS
DE L'ARCHITECTURE ET DE
L'URBANISME (EAMAU)
STUDIO ALPHA A.I.C.

Yves Maillot
SDV / SAGA - BOLLORE GROUP

Jean Marcel Gariador
SDV - BOLLORÉ DTI

Denis Cordel
SDV - BOLLORÉ DTI

TONGA

Sione Tuitavake Fonua
PRIVATE LAWYER

Penisimani L. Latu
INTELLECTUAL PROPERTY AND
COMPANY REGISTRATION

Hastings L. Faapoi
HASDRA

Teimumu Tapueluelu
WESTPAC

Laki M. Niu
LAKI NIU OFFICES

Salesi Mataele
OCEANTRANZ

Manu Mataele
OCEANTRANZ

William Clive Edwards
TONGASAT

Christine 'Uta'atu
'UTA'ATU AND ASSOCIATES

Elmer Sionasa
UTA'ATU AND ASSOCIATES

Paul Pelzer
ANZ

David Garrett
GARRETT & ASSOCIATES

Petunia Tupou
FUNGATEIKI LAW OFFICE

Teleisia M. Sifisa
KIWI (TONGA) LTD.

Arthur Budvietas
KRAMER TONGA LTD.

Bryan Welch
PACIFIC FINANCE & INVESTMENT
LTD

John Ridgway
PACIFIC LEGAL NETWORK

Tomasi Fakahua
SIONE TOMASI NAITE FAKAHUA
LAW OFFICE

Diana Warner
SKIP'S CUSTOM JOINERY LTD.

Tapu Penuve
TONGA CHAMBER OF COMMERCE

Aisea Petelo
TONGA DEVELOPMENT BANK

Simione Sefanaia
TONGA DEVELOPMENT BANK

Lee Miller
TONGA NEW ZEALAND BUSINESS
ASSOCIATION

Alvina Tu'inukuafe Manu
WESTPAC

TUNISIA

Ibed Tanazefti

Lamine Bellagha
ADLY BELLAGHA AND ASSOCIATES

Adly Bellagha
ADLY BELLAGHA AND ASSOCIATES

Mohamed Moncef Barouni
AVOCATS CONSEILS REUNIS

Faiza Feki
CENTRAL BANK OF TUNISIA

Radhi Meddeb
COMETE ENGINEERING

Noureddine Ferchiou
FERCHIOU & ASSOCIATES
MEZIOU KNANI

Lina bou Richa
FERCHIOU & ASSOCIATES
MEZIOU KNANI

Héla Ben Miled
FERCHIOU & ASSOCIATES
MEZIOU KNANI

Elyès Ben Mansour
GAIJI AND BEN MANSOUR

Amina Larbi
GIDE LOYRETTE NOUEL

Amel Ferchichi
GIDE LOYRETTE NOUEL

Kamel Ben Salah
GIDE LOYRETTE NOUEL

Sami Kallel
KALLEL & ASSOCIATES

Adel Saibi
MAERSK LOGISTICS

Mouelhi Lotfi
MAERSK TUNISIE

Faouzi Mili
MILI AND ASSOCIATES

Mabrouk Maalaoui
PRICEWATERHOUSECOOPERS

Marie Louise Gam
PRICEWATERHOUSECOOPERS

Abderrahmen Fendri
PRICEWATERHOUSECOOPERS

Salaheddine Caid Essebsi
THE SALAHEDDINE CAID ESSEBSI AND ASSOCIATES

TURKEY

Rüçhan Derici
3E DANISMANLIK LTD. STI.

Feyza Tukel
BIRCANOGLU LAW FIRM

Senem Gursoy
BIRCANOGLU LAW FIRM

Erol Bircanoglu Jr.
BIRCANOGLU LAW FIRM

Sebnem Onder
CAKMAK ORTAK AVUKAT BUROSU

Zeynep Cakmak
CAKMAK ORTAK AVUKAT BUROSU

I. Hakki Arslan
CENTRAL BANK OF THE REPUBLIC OF TURKEY

Devrim Çukur
ÇUKUR & YILMAZ

Dilara Duman
DTB DIS TICARET BILGI MERKEZI

Y. Selim Sariibrahimoglu
DTB DIS TICARET BILGI MERKEZI

Kazim Derman
KKB KREDIT KAYIT BUREAU

Selen Gures
LAW OFFICES OF M. FADLULLAH CERRAHOGLU

Aysegül Yalçinmani
LAW OFFICES OF M. FADLULLAH CERRAHOGLU

Melis Biskin
LAW OFFICES OF M. FADLULLAH CERRAHOGLU

Fadlullah Cerrahoglu
LAW OFFICES OF M. FADLULLAH CERRAHOGLU

Burcu Mutulu
LAW OFFICES OF M. FADLULLAH CERRAHOGLU

Yelda Dogan
LAW OFFICES OF M. FADLULLAH CERRAHOGLU

Sule Dilek Çelik
LAW OFFICES OF M. FADLULLAH CERRAHOGLU

Arcan Fayatorbay
MAERSK DENIZCILIK A.S.

Mehmet Gün
MEHMET GÜN & CO.

Nee Tasdemir
MEHMET GÜN & CO.

Ural Özbek
MEHMET GÜN & CO.

Baris Kalayci
MEHMET GÜN & CO.

Bilge Saltan
MEHMET GÜN & CO.

Ugur Aktekin
MEHMET GÜN & CO.

Selma Toplü Ünlü
MEHMET GÜN & CO.

Elvan Aziz
PAKSOY & CO.

Serdar Paksoy
PAKSOY & CO.

Peter M. Anetsberger
PANALPINA WORLD TRANSPORT NAKLIYAT LTD. TURKEY

Sefika Pekin
PEKIN & BAYAR LAW FIRM*

Elif Tezcan
PEKIN & BAYAR LAW FIRM

Selim Yavuz
PEKIN & PEKIN

Ahmed Pekin
PEKIN & PEKIN

Burcu Acarturk
PEKIN & PEKIN

Sezin Okkan
PEKIN & PEKIN

Hande Hamevi
PEKIN & PEKIN

Pinar Tanilkan
PEKIN & PEKIN

Lale Giray
PEKIN & PEKIN

Fuat Tuac
PEKIN & PEKIN

Faruk Sabuncu
PRICEWATERHOUSECOOPERS

Ekin Altintas
PRICEWATERHOUSECOOPERS

H. Barıc Yalçın
PRICEWATERHOUSECOOPERS

Mehmet Artemel
SERAP ZUVIN LAW OFFICES

Canan Ersen
SERAP ZUVIN LAW OFFICES

Serap Zuvin
SERAP ZUVIN LAW OFFICES

M. Selçuk Polat
TURKISH CONTRACTORS ASSOCIATION

Nihat Ozdemir
TURKISH CONTRACTORS ASSOCIATION

Kadriye Baysal
TURKISH CONTRACTORS ASSOCIATION

UGANDA

Stuart Forster
BRITISH HIGH COMMISSION

David F.K. Mpanga
A.F. MPANGA, ADVOCATES

Robert Kiggundu
ARCH FORUM LTD.

Rose Namarome
LEX UGANDA ADVOCATES & SOLICITORS

Pious Olaki
LEX UGANDA ADVOCATES & SOLICITORS

Charles Odere
LEX UGANDA ADVOCATES & SOLICITORS

Rachel Mwanje Musoke
MUGERWA & MASEMBE, ADVOCATES

Assumpta Kemigisha
NANGWALA, REZIDA & CO. ADVOCATES

Alex Rezida
NANGWALA, REZIDA & CO. ADVOCATES

Osborne Wanyoike
PRICEWATERHOUSECOOPERS

Russell Eastaugh
PRICEWATERHOUSECOOPERS

Paul Frobisher Mugamba
PRICEWATERHOUSECOOPERS

Fatuma Nabulime
SDV TRANSAMI - UGANDA

Stephen Batanda
SDV TRANSAMI - UGANDA

Ezekiel Tuma
SHONUBI, MUSOKE & CO.

Alan Shonubi
SHONUBI, MUSOKE & CO.

UKRAINE

Yevgeniy Karpov
ASTAPOV LAWYERS

Valeria Kazadorova
BAKER & MCKENZIE

Yaroslav Gregirchak
CHADBOURNE AND PARKE

Alexei Sirenko
DELTA EXPRESS INTERNATIONAL

Vadim Nemirovskiy
FORMAG

Ruslan Israpilov
GRISCHENKO & PARTNERS

Sergei Voitovich
GRISCHENKO & PARTNERS

Natalia Artemova
GRISCHENKO & PARTNERS

Viktor Andriyaka
GRISCHENKO & PARTNERS

Vira Potyekhina
GRISCHENKO & PARTNERS

Galina P. Zagorodnyuk
KONNOV & SOZANOVSKY

Ilona Melnichuk
KONNOV & SOZANOVSKY

Alexey Pokotylo
KONNOV & SOZANOVSKY

Sergei Konnov
KONNOV & SOZANOVSKY

Yuriy Brykaylo
KONNOV & SOZANOVSKY

Maksym Kopeychykov
LAW FIRM "ILYASHEV AND PARTNERS"

Ilya Onyschenko
LAW FIRM "IP&C CONSULT"

Markyeyev Sergiy
MAERSK UKRAINE

Oleg Zagnitko
MAGISTER & PARTNERS

Pavel Zakharov
PANALPINA WORLD TRANSPORT LTD

Maria Livinska
PRICEWATERHOUSECOOPERS

Jorge Intriago
PRICEWATERHOUSECOOPERS

Svetlana Bilyk
PRICEWATERHOUSECOOPERS

Oleg Shevchuk
PROXEN

Victor Kachurenko
SHEVCHENKO DIDKOVSKIY & PARTNERS

Oleksandr Padalka
SHEVCHENKO DIDKOVSKIY & PARTNERS

Igor A. Shevchenko
SHEVCHENKO DIDKOVSKIY & PARTNERS

Igor Svechkar
SHEVCHENKO DIDKOVSKIY & PARTNERS

Markian Silecky
SILECKY LAW FIRM

Maryana Yarmolenko
SILECKY LAW FIRM

Oleg Alyoshin
VASIL KISIL & PARTNERS

Valeriy Lukinov
VENISSA LTD.

UNITED ARAB EMIRATES

Nabil A. Issa
AFRIDI & ANGELL*

Hassen A. Ferris
AFRIDI & ANGELL

Vandana Rupani
AFRIDI & ANGELL

Hussan M.K. Hourani
AL TAMIMI & COMPANY

Sydene Helwick
AL TAMIMI & COMPANY

Ammar Al-Saleh
AL TAMIMI & COMPANY

Lisa Dale
AL TAMIMI & COMPANY

Precilla D'Souza
AL TAMIMI & COMPANY

Suneer Kumar
AL-SUWAIDI & COMPANY

Mahamed Suwaidi
AL-SUWAIDI & COMPANY

Theresa Abrefa
BERRYMANS LACE MAWER

Saeed Abdulla Al Hamiz
CENTRAL BANK OF THE UAE

Neil Taylor
DAVIS LANGDON

Satish Mehta
DUN & BRADSTREET SAME LTD.

Zahid I. Hameed
FISHTE & COMPANY LEGAL CONSULTANCY

Walid Karam
HABIB AL MULLA & CO.

Habib M. Al Mulla
HABIB AL MULLA & CO.

Salah El Dien Al Nahas
HADEL AL DHAHIRI & ASSOCIATES

Abdul Latif Essa
HILAL ASSOCIATES

Rashid Ahmed Hilal
HILAL ASSOCIATES

Henrik Petersen
MAERSK SEALAND

Desmond Balendra
PANALPINA GULF LLC

Dean Rolfe
PRICEWATERHOUSECOOPERS

Sanjay Manchanda
PRICEWATERHOUSECOOPERS

Khaled Amin
SHALAKANY LAW OFFICE

Ayman Hamdy
SHALAKANY LAW OFFICE

Jennifer Bibbings
TROWERS & HAMLINS

Natalie Seeff
TROWERS & HAMLINS

UNITED KINGDOM

Simon Cookson
ASHURST

Laura Cram
ASHURST

Paul Sillis
COLLYER-BRISTOW

David Crosthwaite
DAVIS LANGDON

Jim Meikle
DAVIS LANGDON

Sarah Lawson
DENTON WILDE SAPTE

Michael Steiner
DENTON WILDE SAPTE

Michael Brown
EVERSHEDS LAW FIRM

Gillian Key-Vice
EXPERIAN LTD

Paul Samuel Gilbert
FINERS STEPHENS INNOCENT

Daniel Joseph Gabay
REDWOOD (INTL) LTD.

Julia Yates
FRESHFIELDS BRUCKHAUS DERINGER

John Meadows
HM LAND REGISTRY

Steve Mallen
KNIGHT FRANK

Richard Lister
LEWIS SILKIN SOLICITORS, MEMBER OF IUS LABORIS

Sandro Knecht
PANALPINA

Nick Francis
PRICEWATERHOUSECOOPERS

Kerry Coston
PRICEWATERHOUSECOOPERS

Richard Collier-Keywood
PRICEWATERHOUSECOOPERS

Jeremy Ray
PRICEWATERHOUSECOOPERS

Phil Morrison
FREIGHTNET

Andrew D. Haywood
ROLLINGSONS SOLICITORS

Christopher Mallon
WEIL, GOTSHAL & MANGES

Katherine Stones
WEIL, GOTSHAL & MANGES

Sally Willcock
WEIL, GOTSHAL & MANGES

Emma Malkin
WEIL, GOTSHAL & MANGES

Simon Graham
WRAGGE & CO. LLP

Jane Bates
WRAGGE & CO. LLP

Andrew Glaze
WRAGGE & CO. LLP

UNITED STATES

Brian E. Clark
APM TERMINALS

Craig Foil
APM TERMINALS N.A.

Lillian E. Rice
CLEARY, GOTTLIEB, STEEN & HAMILTON

Ose Asemota
CLIFFORD CHANCE US, LLP

David Newberg
COLLIER, HALPERN, NEWBERG, NOLLETTI, & BOCK

Raymond McGuire
CONTRACTORS' ASSOCIATION OF GREATER NEW YORK

Pierre le Roux
INTERGRAPH MAPPING AND GEOSPATIAL SOLUTIONS

Charles L. Kerr
MORRISON AND FOERSTER

Matthew Meade
MORRISON AND FOERSTER

Deodat Ramsarran
NYC DEPARTMENT OF BUILDINGS

David Nelson
PANALPINA

Kurt Diener
PANALPINA

Robert Morris
PRICEWATERHOUSECOOPERS

Penny Vaughn
PRICEWATERHOUSECOOPERS

Gregory A. Lee
PRICEWATERHOUSECOOPERS

Kelly J. Murray
PRICEWATERHOUSECOOPERS

Samuel Nolen
*RICHARDS, LAYTON & FINGER, P.A.**

Bradford L. Livingston
SEYFARTH SHAW LLP, MEMBER OF IUS LABORIS

David Snyder
SNYDER & SNYDER

Frederick Turner
SNYDER & SNYDER

Mike Calder
THE FIRST AMERICAN CORPORATION, 1 FIRST AMERICAN WAY

John Ralls
THELEN REID & PRIEST LLP

Jason Vonderhaar
TRANSUNION

Jonel Jordan
TRANSUNION

Veronica Glanville
UNITED STATES BANKRUPTCY COURT

Stephen Raslavich
UNITED STATES BANKRUPTCY COURT

URUGUAY

César I. Aroztegui
AROZTEGUI & ASOCIADOS / BRONS & SALAS

Luis Baccino
AROZTEGUI & ASOCIADOS / BRONS & SALAS

Marcelo Femenías
BADO, KUSTER, ZERBINO & RACHETTI

Elbio L. Kuster
BADO, KUSTER, ZERBINO & RACHETTI

Ariel Imken
BANCO CENTRAL DEL URUGUAY

Matilde Milicevic Santana
CLEARING DE INFORMES

Maria Isabel Bonaffon
DIRECCIÓN GENERAL DE REGISTROS

Gabriel Ejgenberg
ESTUDIO BERGSTEIN

Nelly Kleckin
ESTUDIO BERGSTEIN

Ricardo Mezzera
ESTUDIO DR. MEZZERA

Agustín Etcheverry Reyes
ESTUDIO DR. MEZZERA

Federico Carrau
ESTUDIO DR. MEZZERA

Diego Galante
GALANTE & MARTINS

Carlos Brandes
*GUYER & REGULES**

Corina Bove
GUYER & REGULES

Alejandro Miller Artola
GUYER & REGULES

Alvaro Tarabal
GUYER & REGULES

María Durán
HUGHES & HUGHES

Noelia Eiras
HUGHES & HUGHES

Laura Arocena
HUGHES & HUGHES

Conrado Hughes Delgado
HUGHES & HUGHES

Juan Frederico Fischer
LVM ATTORNEYS AT LAW

Ricardo Olivera-García
OLIVERA & DELPIAZZO

Fabrizio Fava
PANALPINA

Alfredo Inciarte Blanco
PEREZ DEL CASTILLO - NAVARRO - INCIARTE - GARI

Maria Jose Santos
PRICEWATERHOUSECOOPERS

Sergio Franco
PRICEWATERHOUSECOOPERS

UZBEKISTAN

Sergio Purin
AHLERS

Ibrahim Mukhamedjanov
AZIZOV & PARTNERS

Ibrahim Mukhamedjanov
AZIZOV & PARTNERS

Jamol Askarov
CHADBOURNE AND PARKE

Sergey Shirov
DENTON WILDE SAPTE

Mouborak Kambarova
DENTON WILDE SAPTE

Sofiya Shakhrazieva
DENTON WILDE SAPTE

Umid A. Aripdjanov
GRATA LAW FIRM

Alexander Samborsky
MAIN ADMINISTRATION OF GEODESY, CARTOGRAPHY AND STATE CADASTRE

Abdulkhamid Muminov
PRICEWATERHOUSECOOPERS

Natalia V. Lopaeva
SUPREME ECONOMIC COURT OF THE REPUBLIC OF UZBEKISTAN

VANUATU

Mark Stafford
BDO BARRETT & PARTNERS

Christopher Dawson
DAWSON BUILDERS

Chris Kernot
FAMOUS PACIFIC SHIPPING VANUATU

John Malcolm
GEOFFREY GEE & PARTNERS BARRISTERS - SOLICITORS

David Hudson
HUDSON & SUGDEN

John Ridgway
PACIFIC LEGAL NETWORK

Garry Blake
RIDGEWAY BLAKE PARTNERS

Silas Charles Hakwa
SILAS CHARLES HAKWA & ASSOCIATES

VENEZUELA

Tamara Adrian
ADRIAN & ADRIAN

Rinaldo Mauricio Alcalá
PANALPINA C.A.

Carlos Velandia Sanchez
ASOCIACIÓN VENEZOLANA DE DERECHO REGISTRAL

Miguel Angel Pérez Lavaud
AVELEDO KLEMPRER RIVAS PEREZ TRUJILLO SANZ & ASOCIADOS

Carlos Plaza
BAKER & MCKENZIE

Rossanna D'Onza
BAKER & MCKENZIE

Mercedes Briceño
CONAPRI

Eduardo Porcarelli
CONAPRI

Patricia Milano Hernández
DE SOLA PATE & BROWN

Arturo de Sola Lander
DE SOLA PATE & BROWN

Alvaro Gonzalez-Ravelo
ESCRITORIO CALCANO-VETANCOURT

Ruben Gotberg
ESPIÑEIRA, SHELDON Y ASOCIADOS/PRICEWATERHOUSE COOPERS

Fernando Miranda
ESPIÑEIRA, SHELDON Y ASOCIADOS/PRICEWATERHOUSE COOPERS

María Corina Arocha
ESPIÑEIRA, SHELDON Y ASOCIADOS/PRICEWATERHOUSE COOPERS

Alejandro Giolito
ESPIÑEIRA, SHELDON Y ASOCIADOS/PRICEWATERHOUSE COOPERS

Jorge Acedo-Prato
*HOET PELAEZ CASTILLO & DUQUE**

Alfredo Basalo-Rodríguez
HOET PELAEZ CASTILLO & DUQUE

Carlos Dominguez
HOET PELAEZ CASTILLO & DUQUE

Fernando Pelaez-Pier
HOET PELAEZ CASTILLO & DUQUE

Luiz Ignacio Mendoza
RODRIGUEZ & MENDOZA

Servio T. Altuve Jr.
SERVIO T. ALTUVE R. & ASOCIADOS

Edison Carrero
SUPERINTENDENTE DE BANCOS

Francisco Aleman Planchart
TINOCO, TRAVIESO, PLANCHART & NUÑEZ

Gustavo Enrique Planchart Pocaterra
TINOCO, TRAVIESO, PLANCHART & NUÑEZ

Oscar Ignacio Torres
TRAVIESO EVANS ARRIA RENGEL & PAZ

VIETNAM

Yee Chung Seck
BAKER & MCKENZIE

Giles Thomas Cooper
BAKER & MCKENZIE

ThanhHa Tran
BAKER & MCKENZIE

Frederick Burke
BAKER & MCKENZIE

Nguyen Hoang Kim Oanh
BAKER & MCKENZIE

Tran Manh Hung
BAKER & MCKENZIE

Tran YenTrang Phan
BAKER & MCKENZIE

Dang Linh Chi
BAKER & MCKENZIE

Anna Ou
BAKER & MCKENZIE

Dao Thu Huong
BAKER & MCKENZIE

Brett Ashton
CHESTERTON PETTY

Nasir PKM Abdul
FLÉCHEUX, NGO & ASSOCIÉS

Pierre Anglès d'Auriac
FLÉCHEUX, NGO & ASSOCIÉS

Doan Chien
GIDE LOYRETTE NOUEL

Florent Fassier
GIDE LOYRETTE NOUEL

Julien Madon
GIDE LOYRETTE NOUEL

Nicholas Audier
GIDE LOYRETTE NOUEL

Phong-anh Hoang
GIDE LOYRETTE NOUEL

Le Quang Phong
INTECO. LTD. INTERNATIONAL FREIGHT FORWARDER

Nguyen Suong Dao
JOHNSON STOKES & MASTER

Thomas J. Treutler
JOHNSON STOKES & MASTER

Suong Dao Nguyen
JOHNSON STOKES & MASTER

John Hickin
JOHNSON STOKES & MASTER

V.N. Trinh
PANALPINA WORLD TRANSPORT

Ho Dang Thanh Huyen
PRICEWATERHOUSECOOPERS

Richard Irwin
PRICEWATERHOUSECOOPERS

Van Thi Quynh Dinh
PRICEWATERHOUSECOOPERS

Do Thi Thu Ha
PRICEWATERHOUSECOOPERS

Uan Pham Cong
STATE BANK OF VIETNAM

Nguyen Tuan Minh
TILLEKE & GIBBINS INTERNATIONAL LTD.

Viet D. Phan
TRAN H. N. & ASSOCIATES

Pham Nghiem XuanBac
VISION & ASSOCIATES INVESTMENT & MANAGEMENT CONSULTANTS

WEST BANK AND GAZA

Fadi Kattan
ARAB CLEARING AGENT

Hiba Husseini
HUSSEINI AND HUSSEINI

Rami Husseini
HUSSEINI AND HUSSEINI

Mohamed Khader
LAUSANNE TRADING CONSULTANTS

YEMEN

Moh'd Ali Lajam
MIDDLE EAST SHIPPING CO.LTD.

Ali Sheikh Alamakdi
YEMPAC CARGO

Abdalla Al-Meqbeli
ABDALLA AL-MEQBELI & ASSOCIATES

Noura Yahya H. Al-Adhhi
CENTRAL BANK OF YEMEN

Abdulla Al-Olofi
CENTRAL BANK OF YEMEN

Khaled Al Buraihi
KHALED AL BURAIHI FOR ADVOCACY & LEGAL SERVICES

Mohamed Taha Hamood
Al-Hashimi
*MOHAMED TAHA HAMOOD
& CO.*

Nageeb Alkadi
*NAGEEB ALKADI & ASSOCIATE
OFFICES*

Saeed Sohbi
SAEED HASSAN SOHBI

ZAMBIA

Victor Mesquita
MANICA AFRICA

Azizhusein Adam
AD ADAMS & CO.

Kanti Patel
*CHRISTOPHER, RUSSELL COOK
& CO.*

Rachel Ngala
*CHRISTOPHER, RUSSELL COOK
& CO.*

Robin Durairajah
CORPUS GLOBE ADVOCATES

Mwelwa Chibesakunda
CORPUS GLOBE ADVOCATES

Elias Chipimo
CORPUS GLOBE ADVOCATES

Harriet Kapampa Kapekele
CORPUS GLOBE ADVOCATES

John Sichinsambwe
*DEPARTMENT OF OCCUPATIONAL
HEALTH AND SAFETY*

Bonaventure Chibamba
Mutale
ELLIS & CO.

Henry Musonda
KIRAN & MUSONDA ASSOCIATES

David Doyle
MANICA ZAMBIA

Marjorie Grace Mwenda
MG JOHNSON-MWENDA & CO.

Noah Siasimuna
*MINISTRY OF LABOUR AND
SOCIAL SECURITY*

Pixie Kasonde-Yangailo
P.H. YANGAILO & COMPANY

Shaira Adamali
PRICEWATERHOUSECOOPERS

Jyoti Mistry
PRICEWATERHOUSECOOPERS

Danmore Nyanga
PRICEWATERHOUSECOOPERS

ZIMBABWE

Lindsay Cook
ATHERSTONE & COOK

Innocent Chagonda
ATHERSTONE & COOK

Jonathan Moyo
*CALDERWOOD, BRYCE, HENDRIE
& PARTNERS*

Thembiwe Mazingi
COGHLAN, WELSH & GUEST

Peter Lloyd
GILL GODLONTON & GERRANS

Hayley Thornicroft
GILL GODLONTON & GERRANS

Obert Chaurura Gutu
GUTU & CHIKOWERO

Archibald Munyoro Gijima
HARARE LAW

H.M. Kantor
KANTOR & IMMERMAN

Paul Fraser
*LOFTY & FRASER LEGAL
PRACTITIONERS*

Grant Davies
MANICA AFRICA

Victor Mesquita
MANICA AFRICA

Mark Badenhorst
PRICEWATERHOUSECOOPERS

Manuel Lopes
PRICEWATERHOUSECOOPERS

Stenford Moyo
SCANLEN & HOLDERNESS

John Meyburgh
STUMBLES AND ROWE

Richard H. S. Beattie
THE STONE BEATTIE STUDIO

Tshuma
WEBB, LOW & BARRY

Trust Salpisio Manjegwah
WINTERTONS LAW FIRM

Filonzi Bosha
ZIMBABWE REVENUE AUTHORITY

*Member of Lex Mundi

Additional PricewaterhouseCoopers contributors as *Doing Business* went to press:

Khalid Mehmood
Salman Nasim
AFGHANISTAN

Kledi Kodra
ALBANIA

Ludmila Kosarenko
ARMENIA

Jacqueline Hassarati
Irene Yeung
AUSTRALIA

Rudolf Krickl
AUSTRIA

Igor Dankov
BELARUS

Fousseni Traore
Jean Claude Wognin
BENIN

Suada Slijivo
BOSNIA AND HERZEGOVINA

L. Jayawickrama
BOTSWANA

Fousseni Traore
Jean Claude Wognin
BURKINA FASO

Roger Ouk
CAMBODIA

Anthony Nkinzo
CONGO, DEM. REP.

Benedicte Wiberg
DENMARK

Peep Kalamae
ESTONIA

Agatha Chan
HONG KONG, CHINA

Zsofia Domotor
HUNGARY

Aija Klavinska
LATVIA

Ami Ravelomanana
William Randrianarivelo
MADAGASCAR

Fousseni Traore
Jean Claude Wognin
MALI

Ram L. Roy
Ramesh Doma
MAURITIUS

Robert Walker
MOZAMBIQUE

Wanita Lala
NEW ZEALAND

Fousseni Traore
Jean Claude Wognin
NIGER

Bukkie Adewuyi
NIGERIA

Linda Levett
PAPUA NEW GUINEA

Gregory Joseph Sojnocki
SOLOMON ISLANDS

Jaume Cornudella
SPAIN